# SPRING AND AUTUMN ANNALS OF WU AND YUE

# SPRING AND AUTUMN ANNALS OF WU AND YUE

## An Annotated Translation of *Wu Yue Chunqiu*

JIANJUN HE

CORNELL EAST ASIA SERIES
AN IMPRINT OF
CORNELL UNIVERSITY PRESS
*Ithaca and London*

Number 206 in the Cornell East Asia Series

Copyright © 2021 by Cornell University

All rights reserved. Except for brief quotations in a review, this book, or parts thereof, must not be reproduced in any form without permission in writing from the publisher. For information, address Cornell University Press, Sage House, 512 East State Street, Ithaca, New York 14850. Visit our website at cornellpress.cornell.edu.

First published 2021 by Cornell University Press

Library of Congress Cataloging-in-Publication Data

Names: Zhao, Ye, active 40, author. | He, Jianjun (Researcher in Chinese literature and cultural history), translator, writer of supplementary textual content.
Title: Spring and autumn annals of Wu and Yue: an annotated translation of Wu Yue Chunqiu / Jianjun He.
Other titles: Wu Yue chun qiu. English.
Description: Ithaca: Cornell University Press, 2021. | Series: Cornell East Asia series; number 206 | Includes bibliographical references and index.
Identifiers: LCCN 2020050825 (print) | LCCN 2020050826 (ebook) | ISBN 9781501754340 (hardcover) | ISBN 9781501754357 (epub) | ISBN 9781501754364 (pdf)
Subjects: LCSH: Zhao, Ye, active 40. Wu Yue chun qiu. | China—History—Warring States, 403-221 B.C. | China—History—Spring and Autumn period, 722-481 B.C.
Classification: LCC DS747.2.Z44613 2021 (print) | LCC DS747.2 (ebook) | DDC 931/.03—dc23
LC record available at https://lccn.loc.gov/2020050825
LC ebook record available at https://lccn.loc.gov/2020050826

*To my family*

# Contents

# Acknowledgments

Many times over the years as I was working on this manuscript I imagined this moment: writing the acknowledgments before publication. When the moment finally came, I realized that my acknowledgments section would be short and personal, as there were no grants available for translating the *Wu Yue Chunqiu*, nor were there research institutions to accommodate me with a semester or so to focus on my writing. The completion of this book concluded a journey of self-cultivation supported by true care and friendship.

This project began with a translation exercise suggested by my academic advisor, Dr. Stephen Durrant, while I was his student at the University of Oregon. I owe special gratitude to Dr. Durrant for inspiring me to work on this fascinating work, *Wu Yue Chunqiu*. In the years that followed, while dealing with job relocations, new working environments, and increased teaching and administrative responsibilities, researching and translating *Wu Yue Chunqiu* became a comfort. The process of working on this book was more meaningful to me than the final manuscript, for it helped me to understand both my scholarly potential and the value of my colleagues and loved ones.

I am grateful to Dr. Paul Fischer and Dr. Michael Fishlen for their careful reading of my entire draft. The many insightful comments and meticulous corrections they offered certainly improved the readability and scholarly quality of my book. All remaining errors are purely mine. My gratitude also goes to Dr. Maram Epstein for her consistent support both as a mentor and as a friend. I thank my editor at Cornell University Press, Mai Shaikhanuar-Cota, for her patience and guidance in preparing for the publication of this book, which made the experience stress-free and enjoyable for me. I am also indebted to my copyeditor, Katherine Thompson, for proofreading the manuscript.

Finally, I would like to thank my family, my wife Qian and my sons Hanchen and Yuchen, for their love and support. This book is dedicated to them.

# SPRING AND AUTUMN ANNALS OF WU AND YUE

# Introduction

There are few texts from the Han era as intriguing and challenging as *Wu Yue Chunqiu* 吳越春秋 (*Spring and Autumn Annals of Wu and Yue*, hereafter abbreviated as *WYCQ*), a chronicle attributed to Zhao Ye 趙曄 (fl. 60–80). *WYCQ* is a text that recounts the rise and fall of Wu and Yue, two rival states located in southeastern China during the late Spring and Autumn period (771–475 BCE). The rich content of *WYCQ*, together with its skillful structure and sophisticated presentation of events and historical figures, have helped the text earn an enduring reputation among scholars and readers. *WYCQ* is often praised as one of the earliest regional histories, a work that foreshadows the popularity of later gazetteers. It is the most important source for studies of Wu-Yue history as well as the history of the Jiangsu 江蘇 and Zhejiang 浙江 regions. The text has also had a marked influence on Chinese literature, as many poems, vernacular stories, and dramas draw inspiration from it.

Despite being recognized as an important early text, basic questions about the authorship and appropriate genre classification of *WYCQ* have never been resolved. The controversies surrounding how to evaluate *WYCQ* make the text especially fascinating and valuable. *WYCQ* contains a mixture of historical accounts and fictional tales. The fictional tales focus on anomalies and supernatural events, topics that are subjects of criticism in the *Analects*. Their narratives often celebrate revenge and intrigues. All of these materials are unredacted reflections of the thoughts and intellectual interests of the Eastern Han (25–220), a dynamic period when *jinwen* 今文 (New Text), *guwen* 古文 (Old Text), *chenwei* 讖緯 (apocryphal) doctrines, and other religions and philosophies vied for dominance in the marketplace of ideas.[1]

## Section I. Authorship and Date

*WYCQ* is attributed to Zhao Ye, who lived in the early period of Eastern Han. According to his biography in *Hou Hanshu* 後漢書, Zhao Ye was a native of Shanyin 山陰 County in Kuaiji 會稽 Commandery, located in modern-day Shaoxing 紹興, Zhejiang Province. Zhao Ye's dates are not specified by *Hou Hanshu*. His brief biography mentions that he worked as a local clerk when he was young. Ashamed of his service for the superintendent, Zhao Ye resigned and traveled to Sichuan 四川, where he studied the Han Tradition of the *Odes* (韓詩) under Du Fu 杜撫.[2] For over twenty years Zhao Ye concentrated on his studies; meanwhile, his family in Kuaiji thought he had already died since there had been no news from him. Only after Du Fu died did Zhao Ye return home. By that time he had earned himself a reputation as a scholar, so the local government summoned him to return to service. Zhao Ye was not interested in serving again and chose to remain at home, where he eventually died as a commoner.[3]

The *Hou Hanshu* biography lists two books under Zhao Ye's name: one is *WYCQ* and the other is *Shi xi li shenyuan* 詩細歷神淵. Judging from its title, the second book is probably an exegesis to *Shijing* influenced by apocryphal texts (*weishu* 緯書); it reflects both Zhao Ye's scholarly background and the intellectual trend of his time, as the Eastern Han produced the largest

1. For the history of Wu and Yue, see Meng Wentong 蒙文通, *Yueshi congkao* 越史叢考 (Beijing: Renmin chubanshe, 1983); Dong Chuping 董楚平, *Wu Yue wenhua xintan* 吳越文化新探 (Hangzhou: Zhejiang renmin chubanshe, 1988); Mao Ying 毛穎 and Zhang Min 張敏, *Changjiang xiayou de Xu Shu yu Wu Yue* 長江下游的徐舒與吳越 (Wuhan: Hubei jiaoyu chubanshe, 2005); Feng Puren 馮普仁, *Wu Yue wenhua* 吳越文化 (Beijing: Wenwu chubanshe, 2007); Xie Chen 謝忱, *Gou Wu shi xinkao* 勾吳史新考 (Beijing: Zhongguo wenlian chubanshe, 2000); Chen Qiaoyi 陳橋驛, *Wu Yue wenhua luncong* 吳越文化論叢 (Beijing: Zhonghua shuju, 1999); see also Olivia Milburn, *The Glory of Yue: An Annotated Translation of the Yuejue shu* (Brill: Sinica Leidensia, 2010) and *Cherishing Antiquity: The Cultural Construction of an Ancient Chinese Kingdom* (Cambridge: Harvard University Press, 2013); Erica Fox Brindley, *Ancient China and the Yue: Perceptions and Identities on the Southern Frontier, c.400 BCE–50 CE* (Cambridge: Cambridge University Press, 2015).

2. Du Fu's biography in the *Hou Hanshu* reports that Du Fu had studied the Han Tradition of *Shijing* 詩經 under the famous scholar Xue Han 薛漢. During the Jianchu 建初 period (76–84), he was appointed as *Gongche ling* 公車令, Director of Official Carriages, but died at the post several months later. See Fan Ye 范曄, *Hou Hanshu* (Beijing: Zhonghua shuju, 1962), 79:2573.

3. *Hou Hanshu*, 79:2575.

number of apocryphal books.[4] At first, it seems that both works were only circulated in Zhao Ye's local area. Almost a hundred years later when the famous scholar Cai Yong 蔡邕 (133–192) visited Kuaiji, he read and was impressed by Zhao Ye's *Shi xi li shenyuan*. Cai Yong introduced it to scholars in the capital, and the text was then broadly studied.[5]

Zhao Ye spent twenty years studying under Du Fu, who died sometime between 76 and 84 CE. From this we extrapolate that Zhao Ye probably lived through the reigns of Emperor Guangwu 光武帝 (r. 25–57 CE), Emperor Ming 明帝 (r. 58–75 CE), Emperor Zhang 章帝 (r. 75–88 CE), perhaps even Emperor He 和帝 (r. 88–105 CE). The *Hou Hanshu* biography also lists *WYCQ* before *Shi xi li shenyuan*, which might suggest that *WYCQ* predates the *Shi xi li shenyuan*. We might presume that *WYCQ* was composed during Zhao Ye's years in Kuaiji, which was once the center of Yue in the Spring and Autumn period.[6]

The reception of *WYCQ* is not mentioned in Zhao Ye's biography, and although *Hou Hanshu* provides no information on the circulation of *WYCQ*, there is evidence to suggest that Zhao Ye's book was well received. Books inspired by *WYCQ* began to appear starting in late Eastern Han. These books either had the same title or were composed as commentaries to Zhao Ye's work. Two other works titled *Wu Yue Chunqiu* were written soon after Zhao Ye's death: one by Zhao Qi 趙岐 (108–201), the renowned scholar and author of the *Commentary on Mengzi* 孟子章句 and the other written by an unknown scholar in late Eastern Han. Both works have been lost.[7] In addition to rewriting Zhao Ye's original text, other texts are clearly based on *WYCQ*. Zhang Xia 張遐, a contemporary to Chen Fan 陳璠 (d. 168), compiled *Wu Yue Chunqiu waiji* 吳越春秋外紀 (*The Outer Records of Spring and Autumn Annals of Wu and Yue*) as an addition to Zhao Ye's work. The Western Jin 西晉 (265–316) historian Guo Ban's 郭頒 (?–?) *Wu Yu Chunqiu ji* 吳越春秋記 (*Records from Spring and Autumn Annals of Wu and Yue*) is probably a selection of important events reported in *WYCQ*.[8]

---

4. Zhao Ye's teacher Du Fu studied under Xue Han, who was a master of *chenwei* and omenology. See Xue Han's biography in *Hou Hanshu*, 79:2573.

5. *Hou Hanshu*, 79:2575.

6. Huang Rensheng 黃仁生, for example, believes *WYCQ* was written before Zhao Ye's period of study in Sichuan. See Huang Rensheng, *Xinyi Wu Yue Chunqiu* 新譯吳越春秋 (Taipei: Sanmin shuju, 1996), 3.

7. Zhou Shengchun 周生春, *Wu Yue Chunqiu jijiao huikao* 吳越春秋輯校匯考 (Shanghai: Shanghai gujichubanshe, 1997), preface, 1.

8. Cf. Cang Xiuliang 倉修良, "*Wu Yue Chunqiu jijiao huikao* xu" 吳越春秋輯校匯考序, in *Wu Yue Chunqiu jijiao huikao* 吳越春秋輯校匯考, 1.

Most of the other *WYCQ* versions and additions were lost before the seventh century. When Tang (618–906) historians added the "Jingji zhi" 經籍志 (Treatise on Classics) chapter to *Suishu* 隋書, there were only three *WYCQ* related texts included in their catalog of extant early classics.[9] The first of these is Zhao Ye's *WYCQ* in twelve chapters. The other two are Yang Fang's 楊方 (ca. late third century to early fourth century CE) *Wu Yue Chunqiu xiaofan* 吳越春秋削繁 (*Abbreviated Spring and Autumn Annals of Wu and Yue*) in five chapters and Sui scholar Huangfu Zun's 皇甫遵 (?–?) *Wu Yue Chunqiu zhuan* 吳越春秋傳 (*Tradition of Spring and Autumn Annals of Wu and Yue*) in ten chapters.[10]

The title of Yang Fang's book suggests that it is an edited, shorter version of Zhao Ye's book. Huangfu Zun's *zhuan* should be an interpretation and commentary on Zhao Ye's work. However, the Song dynasty (960–1279) catalog *Chongwen zongmu* 崇文總目 that was completed in 1041 did not include Yang Fang's book. Instead, it listed an anonymous ten-chapter *WYCQ* as well as Huangfu Zun's *Wu Yue Chunqiu zhuan*. Thus began the long history of controversy over the authorship of the current *WYCQ*. Because, according to *Suishu*, Zhao Ye's book comprised twelve chapters but the Song catalog records a ten-chapter version. From the Song period on down, there have been scholars arguing that the current *WYCQ* is in fact Huangfu Zun's commentarial edition. Important proponents of this theory include Ma Duanlin 馬端臨 (1245–1322) and Yu Jiaxi 余嘉錫 (1884–1955). Other scholars such as Wang Qisun 王芑孫 (1755–1817) and Huang Yunmei 黃云眉 (1898–1977) believe that the current *WYCQ* is Yang Fang's book and that the five original chapters were divided into ten chapters by later editors. The Ming scholar Yang Shen 楊慎 (1488–1559) complained that it was impossible to discern whether the author is Zhao Ye or Yang Fang. Meanwhile, Xu Tianhu 徐天祜 (who passed the civil examination in 1262), Zhang Xincheng 張心澂 (1887–1973), and editors of the "Siku quanshu zongmu tiyao" 四庫全書總目提要 defended Zhao Ye's authorship.[11]

---

9. The "Jingji zhi" is a bibliography of some 3,217 books stored in the palace libraries. It was compiled on an imperial order between 641–656 and is based upon Ruan Xiaoxu's 阮孝緒 *Qilu* 七錄 from the Liang 梁 (502–557). For a study of "Jingji zhi," see Yao Zhenzong 姚振宗, *Suishu Jingji zhi kaozheng* 隋書經籍志考證 (Shanghai: Shanghai guji chubanshe, 1995). See also Du Yunhong 杜雲虹, *Suishu Jingji zhi yanjiu* 隋書經籍志研究 (Beijing: Wenwu chubanshe, 2016).

10. Wei Zheng 魏征, *Suishu* (Beijing: Zhonghua shuju, 1973), 33:960.

11. For detailed discussions, please see Cao Lindi 曹林娣, "Guanyu *Wu Yue Chunqiu* de zuozhe ji chengshu niandai" 關於吳越春秋的作者及成書年代, *Xibei daxue xuebao* 西北大學學報, no. 4 (1982): 68–73, 89; Liang Zonghua 梁宗華, "Xianxing shijuanben *Wu Yue Chunqiu* kaozhi" 現行十卷本吳越春秋考識, *Dongyue luncong* 東岳論叢 1 (1988): 54–57; Lin Xiaoyun 林小雲, "*Wu Yue Chunqiu* juanzhi kaobian" 吳越春秋卷帙考辨, *Minjiang xueyuan xuebao* 閩江學院學報 30, no. 4 (2009):

The theory that treats Yang Fang as the author is based upon pure speculation. Believing that the language style of *WYCQ* is different from that of other Han writings, Wang Qisun suspects that the extant *WYCQ* is probably a Jin (265–420) work compiled by Yang Fang. Wang Qisun's argument is supported by Huang Yunmei who cites Yang Fang's biography in *Jinshu* 晉書, which states that Yang Fang "compiled" *WYCQ*.[12] Huang Yunmei further proposes that Yang's five chapters were split into ten chapters that replaced Zhao Ye's original book. The problem with this theory is that it completely ignores the *Suishu* record that states that Yang's book is titled *Xiaofan*, which literarily means to "delete the trivial" and is therefore clearly an abridgement of Zhao Ye's *WYCQ*.

The same mistake is found in the theory attributing the current *WYCQ* to Huangfu Zun. The original title of Huangfu Zun's book is *Wu Yue Chunqiu zhuan*. In the Chinese commentary tradition, *zhuan* suggests an interpretation or an annotation to a classic. Huangfu Zun's book is therefore a commentary and might simply be an annotation in ten chapters of Zhao Ye's earlier work. This is probably one reason for the discrepancy in chapter numbers. Another possibility is that two of Zhao Ye's original chapters have been lost. This latter possibility is supported by the fact that there are *WYCQ* quotations in seventh- and tenth-century texts that are not found in the current *WYCQ*.[13] In the absence of new evidence, there is no convincing reason to doubt Zhao Ye's authorship. Even though the current *WYCQ* may not be complete, it is still best viewed as a first-century chronicle that reflects the thought and intellectual trends of the time.

There have been many printings of *WYCQ* in the past. The earliest extant edition was published with commentary by Xu Tianhu in the late thirteenth century, soon after the Yuan dynasty (1271–1368) was founded. The project was initiated by a Yuan governor of the Wu-Yue region who requested that Xu Tianhu edit Zhao Ye's book as a way to honor the local history and culture. Xu's editorial work included correcting mistakes found in earlier editions, providing annotations, and comparing records with those in *Zuozhuan* 左傳, *Shiji* 史記, and *Guoyu* 國語. Although Xu Tianhu did not create a thorough collection of all available editions and relied entirely upon a ten-chapter

27–29, 33. See also Wang Peng 王鵬, "Dangdai *Wu Yue Chunqiu* yanjiu jianshu" 當代吳越春秋研究簡述, *Huangshan xueyuan xuebao* 7, no. 5 (2005): 64–66.

12. Fang Xuanling 房玄齡, *Jinshu* 晉書 (Beijing: Zhonghua shuju, 1974), 68:1832.

13. For example, there are *WYCQ* quotes in *Shiji* commentaries as well as in Li Shan's 李善 (630–689) commentary to *Zhaoming wenxuan* 昭明文選. The Tang encyclopedia *Yiwen leiju* 藝文類聚 (completed in 624) and the Song *Taiping yulan* 太平禦覽 (completed in 984) also contain *WYCQ* passages not seen in the current version. See Zhou Shengchun, 260–272.

Song text, his work on *WYCQ* became the most popular edition and contributed to the transmission and preservation of the text.[14]

## Section II. The Genre of *WYCQ*

In addition to the controversy surrounding its authorship, scholars have also long been debating the proper genre classification of *WYCQ*—that is, whether *WYCQ* is a reliable history or a fictional work with little historical value. The word *Chunqiu* in the title of the book is inherited from the classical annals of Lu 魯 in the Spring and Autumn period. By the early Warring States (475–221 BCE) *Chunqiu* was already part of the Confucian canon and a model for chronicles to come as it was believed that the Lu *Chunqiu* was edited by Confucius and therefore conveyed the master's subtle political criticism. Because of this, a book titled *Chunqiu* is expected to be a serious account of historical facts, just like the *Spring and Autumn Annals* and later histories such as *Shiji* and *Hanshu* 漢書. However, in examining the *chunqiu* books compiled from the late Warring States to the Eastern Han, it was found that this is not always an accurate assumption. For example, *Lüshi Chunqiu* 呂氏春秋 (*Spring and Autumn Annals of Master Lü*, compiled around 239 BCE) is a collection of political and philosophical essays. The *Yanzi Chunqiu* 晏子春秋 (*Spring and Autumn Annals of Master Yan*, finalized in the first century CE) contains random stories, speeches, and remonstrations attributed to Yanzi. Even the early Western Han chronicle *Chu Han Chunqiu* 楚漢春秋 (*Spring and Autumn Annals of Chu and Han*) compiled by Lu Jia 陸賈 (ca. 228–140 BCE), accounts of historical events are also mixed with extraordinary records.[15] The flexibility of *Chunqiu* texts can be further attested by the "Yiwen zhi" 藝文志 classification found in *Hanshu*, where *Lüshi Chunqiu* is regarded as a work of the *zajia* 雜家, Miscellaneous School, and *Yanzi Chunqiu* is listed as a work of a Confucian master (*Rujia* 儒家).[16] Though some excerpts from *Chun Han Chunqiu* are considered historical in nature, neither the *Lüshi Chunqiu* nor the *Yanzi Chunqiu* is regarded as a work of history. This suggests that in pre-Qin and early Han, *Chunqiu* indicates not only chronicles

---

14. See, for example, Jin Yongping 金永平, "*Wu Yue Chunqiu* Xu Tianhu zhu qianyi" 吳越春秋徐天祜註淺議, *Hangzhou shifan daxue xuebao* 杭州師範大學學報, no. 4 (1991): 101–105; Wang Meizhi汪梅枝, "*Wu Yue Chunqiu* Xu Tianhu yinzhu tanxi" 吳越春秋徐天祜音註探析, *Jiangxi jiaoyu xueyuan xuebao* 江西教育學院學報 25, no. 4 (2005): 43–46.

15. *Chu Han chunqiu* recounts the battles between Liu Bang 劉邦 (256–195 BCE) and Xiang Yu 項羽 (232–202 BCE) after the fall of Qin 秦 (221–206 BCE). The original text was lost; the current version contains fragments collected from early sources, especially Sima Qian's *Shiji*.

16. See Ban Gu 班固, *Hanshu* (Beijing: Zhonghua shuju, 1962), 30:1741, 1724.

but also books compiled for political reading. Thus, later *Chunqiu* texts are in line with the Lu classic that conveys criticisms made by Confucius. In other words, in early times, "historical texts" were conceptualized differently.

This different concept of history is further attested by the categorization of *Chu Han Chunqiu* in *Suishu*. There is no history category in *Hanshu*; the "Yiwen zhi" chapter groups historical texts under the *Chunqiu* category and treats the works of Lu Jia and Sima Qian equally as chronicles. However, by the seventh century when the "Jingji zhi" was compiled, the classification of *jing* 經 (Confucian classics), *shi* 史 (historical texts), *zi* 子 (work of masters), and *ji* 集 (individual works) was already a guiding principle for scholars. Moreover, in the *shi* category, historical texts were further divided into subcategories such as standard history (*zhengshi* 正史), ancient chronicles (*gushi* 古史), and miscellaneous history (*zashi* 雜史). While Sima Qian's work is honored as a standard history under this system, *Chu Han Chunqiu* is considered a miscellaneous history, a category of nonstandard history that also includes Zhao Ye's *Wu Yue Chunqiu*.

The concept of miscellaneous histories begins from *Suishu*. Miscellaneous histories are generally considered inferior to standard history because of their violations of Confucian historiographic principles. The "Jingji zhi" chapter explains the categorization of miscellaneous histories, citing a number of criticisms. First, the wording and selection of events in these works are different from those of standard histories such as the *Chunqiu*, *Shiji*, and *Hanshu*; they are products without due scholarship (率爾而作). Second, these chronicles are compiled by scholars without historiographic knowledge; their writings are colored by their individual historical viewpoints and the structures of their texts are problematic. Finally, the presentations of the past in these texts are marred by strange and exaggerated stories such that it is impossible to distinguish reality from fiction.[17]

While acknowledging that miscellaneous histories are records of the past written by scholars during periods of political turmoil when official historiography was out of commission, the "Jingji zhi" criticism of miscellaneous history hones in on the lack of serious scholarship, random structure, and most problematically, the combination of facts and improbable stories in these texts. Therefore, despite the fact that these chronicles report certain historical moments experienced by the authors and contain materials from early records, they are disqualified from the selection of "real history" because they clearly bear their individual author's mark and lack a sanctioned, unified tone.

---

17. *Suishu*, 33:962.

Miscellaneous history has thus never been taken seriously by historians; this remains true today. These works are not considered good sources from which to learn about the past and they are read more for entertainment purposes. To modern scholars, works of miscellaneous history are valuable for literary and folk cultural studies rather than for understanding a certain historical moment or society in the past. However, I argue that miscellaneous history is, in fact, valuable for its preservation of diverse cultural elements of the past and its presentation of many philosophical thoughts that are distinctively non-Confucian. These are the contributions of *WYCQ* that I will discuss later.

When the *Suishu* "Jingji zhi" chapter evaluates historical texts, the *WYCQ* is the example on which criticisms of miscellaneous history are centered. Some of the criticisms are certainly warranted if *WYCQ* is judged only by its historical accuracy. There are errors in the book's presentation of the past, including problems with dating historical events, issues with adopting inaccurate sources, and distortion of facts recorded in early and reliable materials. However, we must be aware that these standards for evaluating history texts were adopted by Tang Confucian scholars during the time when a civil service examination system was officially adopted by the state. The concept of historiography was quite complicated and different before the Tang dynasty, especially when the writing of dynastic history had not yet become a government project.

From its beginning, Chinese historiography was never an independent discipline. It has always been deeply intertwined with politics and religion and therefore has always been invested in recording events of both the human and supernatural worlds. Although court scribes are mentioned in early sources, writing history of the past was never a state enterprise. Instead, histories were privately written and were products of individual endeavors, although some of the authors were state historians. In other words, before Sui and Tang, there were historical texts but no unified, systemized historiography. The fundamental rules of historiography that we apply to the classics are in fact medieval Chinese concepts that arose when Confucian ideology became dominant.

Indeed, early Chinese historical texts are very diverse in terms of their forms, styles, structures, and titles. Although we cannot peruse records from other states, such as those composed by scribes in Jin and Chu, it is hard to believe that they would follow the format and narrative style of the *Chunqiu* from Lu. It is equally impossible to imagine that there were shared principles or interests in selecting historical materials and presenting them in writing during the "Hundred Schools" era. In the Warring States period, the difference between *jing* and *shi* was obscure and the boundary between *shi* and *wen* was similarly flexible. Even in Han times, during which *Shiji* and *Hanshu* were produced, there were still many chronicles created that were labeled as miscellaneous by later scholars. The Later Han interests in Five Phases and *chenwei* 讖緯 undoubtedly had profound influence in many cultural areas, including historiography, which foreshadowed the rich *zashi* tradition in the following generations. If we merely judge by the number of texts produced from Warring States to Wei-Jin 魏晉 (third to fifth centuries), it becomes clear that miscellaneous history was indeed an important category.

As in *WYCQ*, the dominant characteristic of miscellaneous history is its inclusiveness. Miscellaneous history texts are often criticized for their "impetuous" and careless adoption of questionable sources. Many materials presented in miscellaneous history texts are perceived by later historians as exaggerated and unreliable. The seemingly random structure of the texts casts further doubt on their quality. However, these flaws are also what make miscellaneous history texts valuable, because they preserve original, authentic, and raw materials that survived the editorial tendencies of Confucian historians. Compared to records pertaining to Wu and Yue local tradition found in the *Zuozhuan*, *Guoyu*, and *Shiji*, texts like the *WYCQ* present much richer and more detailed materials. In fact, the famous three commentaries to *Shiji* (*Shiji jijie* 史記集解, *Shiji zhengyi* 史記正義, *Shiji suoyin* 史記索隱) all use *WYCQ* to correct and supplement Sima Qian's reports.

Besides their inclusive selection of materials, miscellaneous history texts are also valuable for the diverse cultural perspectives they present. Standard histories from imperial China focus on the power center and are interested in describing important persons and critical moments while excluding anything peripheral, trivial, or strange; their view of the past is narrowed down to the upper spectrum of society. As a result, standard histories are excellent for their historical accuracy but offer little in terms of cultural diversity. Miscellaneous history, on the other hand, is valuable in preserving and presenting more diverse insights into the culture of historical periods, which allows us a more comprehensive view of the past.

This diverse, unscreened overview of culture as shown in miscellaneous history texts is a vivid reminder that the past has always been a world in which many active intellectual positions competed with each other for influence. These competing voices were not simply restricted to a particular social stratum; they penetrated every level of society and became part of people's daily lives. The world of thought in miscellaneous history is not filtered through Confucian censorship, and therefore it permits us access to other versions of the past. For example, *WYCQ* contains many details distinctively related to *yinyang* and *shushu* 數術 (computational techniques) theories. These details have often been criticized by later scholars as strange fictional notions that thus lower the historiographic quality of the text. However, they are truthful reflections of their own time if we consider the historical fact that these theories, together with *chenwei*, were dominant modes of thought in Eastern Han when *WYCQ* was written. *WYCQ* is, in fact, one of the few texts in which these important Eastern Han modes of thought are preserved in detail.

In addition to its presentism in judging early chronicles by medieval Confucian standards, another mistake that *Suishu* made when evaluating *WYCQ* in particular and miscellaneous history in general is tied to its misunderstanding of Han historiography and the way in which it wrongly conceptualizes *Shiji* and *Hanshu* as the only forms of historical writing. In fact, the Han interest in writing history produced many historical texts. These texts were sponsored by the central court, regional governments, and local communities as well as sometimes being independent projects. These diverse forms of patronage and authorship directly resulted in the large number of miscellaneous histories produced in the Han period. Of over two hundred Eastern Han historical texts recorded in early sources, at least fifty-eight are regarded as miscellaneous histories.[18]

While the Han elite clearly took an interest in writing history, common people also shared the desire to "leave a name" 留名 for themselves. In comparison to earlier times, the subjects of historical writing in Eastern Han were extended from those at the center of the power or involved in critical historical moments to any individual who had the desire and means to hire a personal historian. Many of these individual histories are in the form of stele inscriptions that commemorate the life of a deceased individual and praise his virtue and achievements. In fact, stele inscriptions constitute a large portion of the historical texts produced in Eastern Han. Essentially, historical writings of this period became personal projects rendered in different styles and media.

## Section III. The content and value of *WYCQ*

*WYCQ* is an individual project influenced by the intellectual trends and textual traditions of its time. Students of *WYCQ* must not forget its connection to the nature and function of history as conceptualized in early times when

18. See Yao Zhenzong 姚振宗, *Hou Han yiwenzhi* 後漢藝文志, in *Shiyuan congshu* 適園叢書, edited by Zhang Junheng 張鈞衡 (1872–1927) (Shanghai: guoxue fulunshe, 1911), 2:178.

reading the text, but they should, at the same time, recognize the influences of the dominating Eastern Han *jingzhuan* 經傳 (classics and commentaries) tradition on the compilation of *WYCQ*.

From its beginning, Chinese history was meant to record important events and individuals. The function of history is to provide examples from which people in later times can draw lessons. In other words, history texts teach people how to behave and function in patterned situations and environments. They provide guidance in the political world, judged virtually by practicability and usefulness. If the *jing* (classic) text provides philosophical principles, then the *shi* (history) text offers real cases to examine and examples to prove these principles. In this sense, *shi* explains and confirms the wisdom in *jing*. Thus, by its nature, the Chinese history text is an exegesis and commentary, as a *zhuan* (commentary) to a *jing*.

The *zhuan* tradition dates back to at least the Warring States period. The most famous *zhuan* works are the three commentaries to *Chunqiu*: *Zuozhuan* 左傳, *Gongyang zhuan* 公羊傳, and *Guliang zhuan* 谷梁傳. However, if we examine these three commentaries carefully, we notice that their contents, formats, and interests are different. *Gongyang* and *Guliang* focus on explaining the subtle meaning of the *Chunqiu* text, paying particular attention to word choice; *Zuozhuan*, however, supplements the dry *Chunqiu* records with rich and vivid accounts of events and speeches. In other words, *Zuozhuan* selects history to explain *Chunqiu*. In addition to these commentaries, *Guoyu* which was called *Chunqiu waizhuan* 春秋外傳 in Han times, is regarded as an exegesis to *Chunqiu* with selected recordings of intellectual debates. Despite their different preferences in terms of style and content, all these texts collect materials from early sources in order to interpret the *Chunqiu*.

*Zhuan* literature became an important scholarly tradition in the Han period. Because of their preservation of early sources and their close relationship to the classics, *zhuan* were sometimes given equal status as the classics. Han texts such as *Huainanzi* 淮南子, *Shiji*, and *Hanshu* often cite *zhuanshu* 傳書 (commentary books) as authoritative sources.[19] Unlike later commentaries that focus on word definitions and pronunciation, *zhuan* collect stories and record speeches in order to illustrate the teachings of classics. In addition to citing precedents from the past, they also present these precedents through narrative. Thus we have *neizhuan* 內傳 (Inner Tradition) works such as *Gongyang* and *Guliang* that focus on explaining the subtle meanings of the classics. *Waizhuan* 外傳 (Outer Tradition) takes a step away from the original text: instead of word-by-word interpretation, *waizhuan* cite stories to prove the

19. See, for example, the "Wuxing zhi" 五行志 chapter in *Hanshu*, 27:1476.

wisdom of the classics. The best example of *waizhuan* is the *Hanshi waizhuan* 韓詩外傳 (*Outer Tradition of the Han School of the Songs*), which contains three hundred anecdotes and stories that illustrate the *Shijing*.

Many of the Han *zhuanshu* are *waizhuan*; compiling these books required great knowledge of anecdotes and stories. Because of the political agendas and didactic tones of the classics, *zhuanshu* cite and summarize the past to provide political allegory for the present. In other words, *zhuanshu* use history to offer political commentary on the present. Thus the Han anecdotic texts such as *Lienü zhuan* 列女傳 (*Traditions of Exemplary Women*) and *Shuoyuan* 說苑 (*Garden of Talks*), as well as the so-called miscellaneous histories such as *Yandanzi* 燕丹子 (*Master Yandan*), *Yue jue shu* 越絕書 (*The Glory of Yue*), and *WYCQ*, were all regarded as *zhuanshu* in the Han dynasty. As Xu Fuguan 徐復觀 (1902–1982) explains, there were two methods through which pre-Qin and Western Han thinkers expressed their thoughts. One involves directly voicing one's ideas. The other resembles the way of *Chunqiu*, that is, using ancient people's deeds and words to convey one's own thoughts.[20]

The opening chapter in the *Yue jue shu* provides evidence to support Xu Fuguan's theory. In discussing the difference between *jing* and *zhuan*, the *Yue jue shu* chapter argues that *jing* discuss an issue while *zhuan* explain/extend its meaning (經者，論其事，傳者，道其意). It further argues that *zhuan* are not reflections of a single mind, as they copy and cite various sources. Even though these sources are not immediately related to the original teaching, they are adopted as analogies in order to illustrate that teaching (引類以托意).[21]

Like its sister book *Yue jue shu*, *WYCQ* recounts history in order to provide political commentary on the present. It is both *zhuan* and *shi*, reflecting the thought and intellectual interests of Eastern Han.

The rise and fall of Wu and Yue are at the center of the *WYCQ* narrative. Focusing primarily on the political, military and diplomatic relationship and conflicts between these two states, the book draws political lessons from historical precedents. These historical precedents are presented through sophisticated narrative structure, vivid descriptions of events, and rich records of speeches. As commentator Xu Tianhu concludes:

20. Xu Fuguan 徐復觀, *Liang Han sixiang shi* 兩漢思想史 (Shanghai: Huadong shifan daxue chubanshe, 2002), 3:1.

21. See Li Bujia 李步嘉, *Yue jue shu jiaoshi* 越絕書校釋 (Beijing: Zhonghua shuju, 2016), 3. Olivia Milburn translates this as: "The canonical sections are records of historical fact, the traditions talk about their significance. The outer sections are the work of more than one hand, or they are somewhat contradictory, or there are errors of fact, or they reduplicate the same information." See Milburn, *The Glory of Yue*, 75.

其言上稽天時，下測物變，明微推遠，燎若蓍蔡。至於盛衰成敗之跡，則彼己君臣，反覆上下。其議論，種、蠡諸大夫之謀，迭用則霸；子胥之諫，一不聽則亡；皆鑿鑿然，可以勸誡萬世，豈獨為是邦二千年故實哉！

Its words investigate heavenly order above and examine changes of matters down in the world. In illustrating the subtle and inferring from the ancient, it demonstrates principles as clear and bright as the yarrow and oracle bone divinations. As for the trajectory of prosperity and decline, success and demise, Wu and Yue in turn become ruler and subject, above and below each other. As for its discussions, the planning of ministers such as Wen Zhong 文種 and Fan Li 范蠡 can make any ruler a hegemon if they are alternatively adopted. A state will fall if any of the remonstrations of Wu Zixu 伍子胥 are not heard. These are irrefutable. They can provide advice and admonishment to ten thousand generations, and they are indeed not only the two thousand year old matters of this region![22]

The retelling of the past is thus aimed to serve the present. The inclusive and encyclopedic presentations of history that we see in *WYCQ* therefore acquire a contemporary political significance. This practically oriented knowledge of the past is a distinctive *Gongyang* tradition, in which making use of learning in order to govern the world is the ultimate goal (經世致用).

We see strong *Gongyang* influences in *WYCQ*. The text intends to demonstrate "the way of becoming a hegemon" 王霸之道 and pays great attention to discussing how to enrich a state and strengthen its military power in order to defeat its enemies. The Confucian emphasis on ritual is largely ignored in *WYCQ*. Instead, the text is rich in discussions and theories that concern improving the prosperity of the state. Many of these resonate with Mencius's emphasis on cherishing and benefiting the people but rarely with Mencius's preaching on humaneness (*ren* 仁).[23]

In addition to governance, strengthening the wealth of the state and defeating the enemy in a hostile environment are other related major themes in *WYCQ*. The second half of the book, especially chapters eight, nine, and ten, consists of conversations between Goujian and his advisors on empowering

22. Cf. Zhang Jue 張覺, *Wu Yue Chunqiu jiaozheng zhushu* 吳越春秋校證注疏 (Beijing: Zhishi chanquan chubanshe, 2014), 3.

23. For example, in responding to Goujian's inquiry on governance, Wen Zhong indicates the key is "loving the people" (愛民而已). He further explains that the ruler should bring the people benefits instead of harming them, make them successful instead of failing them, allow them to survive instead of killing them and provide for them instead of robbing them. See Zhang Jue, 247.

Yue and conquering Wu. The most famous strategy elaborated in these conversations is Wenzhong's Nine Schemes (*jiushu* 九術) that highlight corrupting the enemy from inside, a policy that was repeatedly recommended and applied throughout Chinese history.

This interest in practical strategies is also evident in many accounts related to military tactics. Military experts such as Wu Zixu and Sun Wu 孫武 are among the dominant figures in *WYCQ*. Discussions on the arts of war are richly presented in the text, and they probably come from pre-Qin Military School (*bingjia* 兵家) sources. Moreover, in *WYCQ* such military school thought coordinates with other doctrines in order to create the most efficient policy for winning in a competitive world. The best example of this appears in chapter ten, which consists of elaborate counsel, given by Goujian's advisors on preparing for war against Wu, that equally highlights military advice, the legalist approach in mobilizing the entire state, and the Confucian observation of the Mandate of Heaven.

The *Gongyang* differentiation of *nei* (inside/us) and *wai* (outside/other) is another important theme in *WYCQ*. The text consists of ten chapters evenly divided into two parts. Part one relates the history of Wu in five chapters while the other half is devoted to Yue. The opening chapters in each part introduce the genealogy of the states. These are then followed by chapters narrating the Wu and Yue histories, respectively. While the Wu history follows a loosely chronological order and describes the trajectory of Wu's rise and fall, the Yue chapters are organized around Goujian's revenge. Chapter titles also reflect this different treatment. The three core chapters in the Wu section are titled *neizhuan* (Inner Tradition), while all the Yue chapters are called *waizhuan* (Outer Tradition). Considering the fact that Zhao Ye was a native of Kuaiji, the former heartland of Yue, this positioning of Wu as legitimate and Yue as the outsider is quite perplexing. Qian Fu 錢福 (1461–1504), the Ming editor of *WYCQ*, laments that the reason behind this distinction is "impossible to understand" (不可曉矣).[24]

This seemingly surprising arrangement is easy to understand if examined by the *Gongyang* standard. The fundamental idea in the *Gongyang* tradition is *dayitong* 大一統 (valuing unification); all *Gongyang* thought is built upon this notion. Clearly stated in the opening line in the *Gongyang Commentary*, this political view is repeatedly addressed throughout the text and is confirmed by all *Gongyang* scholarship. Dong Zhongshu 董仲舒 (179–104 BCE) is probably the most important advocate of the *Gongyang* and its *dayitong* notion. In his memorial to Emperor Wu 武帝 (r. 141–87 BCE), Dong Zhongshu praises

24. Zhang Jue, 354.

*Chunqiu* for valuing unification as the principle of heaven and earth, the universal rule of the past and present (天地之常經，古今之通義).[25] Because this unification takes place under the sole ruler selected by the Mandate of Heaven, the Zhou kings in the past and the Han emperors in Dong's time, it confirms the legitimate succession of power and prescribes a hierarchical order to all "others" in terms of their relationship to the central authority. In this sense, differentiating between "us" and the "other" is important in maintaining that hierarchy.

The notions of *nei* and *wai* are ubiquitous in *Gongyang*'s treatment of each state. Because the founder of Wu was a descendant of the Zhou royal clan and Yue was generally viewed as uncivilized in the Spring and Autumn period, Wu had a higher status in the eyes of the central states. In *Chunqiu*, only the rulers of the central states are called *zi* 子, an honorable title enjoyed by key figures of the Zhou household. However, there are two places in the classic where Wu kings are addressed as *zi*, and the *Gongyang Commentary* argues that this demonstrates that Wu was valued by Confucius and was treated as a member of the *zhu Xia* 諸夏, the "us".[26] Yue, on the other hand, had already been marked as an *yi* 夷, an uncivilized tribe, in *Chunqiu*.

Dong Zhongshu and *jinwen* scholars agree with this *Gongyang* distinction. As a student of the *Gongyang* school, Zhao Ye follows this *Gongyang* view and identifies his chapters concerning Helü and Fuchai as *neizhuan*, because these two Wu kings are addressed as *zi* in *Chunqiu*. All chapters on Yue, however, continue the *Chunqiu* classification and are named *waizhuan*.

Readers of *WYCQ* can hardly miss another popular *Gongyang* notion in the chapters, that is, the *Gongyang* justification for and encouragement of revenge. Clan vengeance was an ancient practice and pre-Qin Confucians were never shy about advocating for its necessity. In the "Tangong" 檀弓 chapters in *Liji* 禮記 (*Book of Rites*), seeking revenge for one's family members is strongly encouraged by Confucius.[27] *Gongyang* pushes this notion further by glorifying the idea of nine generations of revenge (*jiushi fuchou* 九世復仇). In discussing Qi's vengeance against Marquis Ji recorded in *Chunqiu*, *Gongyang* praises the act of revenge that Lord Xiang of Qi 齊襄公 performed for his ancestor who lived nine generations prior, and confirms that the call

---

25. *Hanshu*, 56: 2523.

26. Lord Ding 4 and Lord Ai 12. See *Chunqiu Gongyang zhuan*, in Ruan Yuan 阮元 (1764–1849), *Shisanjing zhushu* 十三經註疏 (Beijing: Zhonghua shuju, 1982), 2337, 2351.

27. For example, in answering Zixia's 子夏 questions on how to deal with the foe of one's parents and brothers, Confucius says that one would not wish to live under the same sky with the foe of one's parents, and will not serve in the same court with the foe of one's brothers. See Sun Xidan 孫希旦, *Liji jijie* 禮記集解 (Beijing: Zhonghua shuju, 1989), 200.

for vengeance for family does not expire, even if a hundred generations have passed (九世猶可以復仇乎？ 雖百世可也).[28]

Influenced by *Gongyang*, revenge was regarded in Han times as a son's filial duty, a friend's faithful deed, and a natural choice for a loyal subject. It was a heroic deed that deserved recognition, celebration, and praise, and it was considered worthy of commemoration in history. *Hanshu* and *Hou Hanshu* contain many revenge stories, involving not only common people but also scholars and officials. Seeking revenge even became an honorable action that could win one a good reputation during the Eastern Han period. Because of this, it is not surprising that revenge is also a major theme in the *WYCQ*. The chapters on Yue are basically the tale of Goujian's revenge against Wu. In addition to this, chapters three, four, and five are structured around Wu Zixu's retaliation against Chu, whose king wrongly executed his father and older brother. Driven by his anger, Wu Zixu eventually defeats Chu, conquers its capital, and mutilates the body of King Ping of Chu. This detail regarding the mutilation of King Ping's body is a Han addition. Warring States texts do not mention Wu Zixu mutilating the corpse. Qin and early Han texts only give accounts in which King Ping's tomb was flogged by Wu troops. *Shiji* is the first text describing how King Ping's body was whipped by Wu Zixu. *WYCQ* added more details to this drama, explaining that while Wu Zixu lashed the corpse three hundred times, he also stomped on the body, dug out its eyes, and scolded the deceased.[29] *Shiji*'s account changes Wu-Yue enmity into a story of personal vengeance. The *WYCQ* further glorifies Wu Zixu's extreme actions of revenge, which are warranted according to *Gongyang* thought.

The *Gongyang*'s theory of correspondence between heaven and man (*tianren ganying* 天人感應) finds plentiful expression in *WYCQ* narratives. Developed from the notion of the Mandate of Heaven, the theory of correspondence between man and heaven became an important political philosophy in the Warring States period that both acknowledged the authority of the ruler and granted the *shi* 士 class the power to judge and admonish the ruler. That is, although the ruler was chosen by heaven, the right of interpreting the will of heaven was held by the *shi*. In Western Han, Dong Zhongshu argued for the divine power of the emperor, but he further read unusual natural phenomena as demonstrations of the correspondence between heaven and the affairs of man and used omens to monitor and restrain the power of the emperor. During Eastern Han, when *jinwen* scholarship became more and

28. See Ruan Yuan, *Shisanjing zhushu*, 2226.

29. See *WYCQ*, 4.23.

more apotheosized, this notion of correspondence between heaven and man dominated the minds of *jinwen* scholars. Zhao Ye was also strongly influenced by this political cosmology.

There are many accounts concerning auspicious and ominous signs in *WYCQ*. For example, chapter eight records a hill that suddenly appeared after Fan Li constructed a small city for Goujian. Fan Li read this supernatural phenomenon as a sign suggesting Yue's future prosperity, believing that the hill moved to Yue because of the virtue of King Goujian. This linking of unusual phenomena with political events also figures in many tales concerning omens. The most famous story of this kind describes the flight of the Zhanlu 湛盧 sword. In this tale, after the detested King Helü's killing of innocent people, the sword that was previously in his possession magically leaves Wu by itself and travels along the river to Chu.[30]

In the eyes of Tang historians, these strange tales in *WYCQ* seriously undermine the historical accuracy of the text and lower it to its classification as a miscellaneous chronicle. This criticism, nevertheless, fails to acknowledge the *chenwei* culture reflected in *WYCQ*. In fact, in Eastern Han, for studies of classics, the *chenwei* school was as popular as *guwen* and *jinwen* scholarship. There were probably just as many *weishu* (apocryphal texts) produced as *guwen* and *jinwen* exegeses. Developed from the *jinwen* interest in omenology, the *chenwei* mode of thought combined not only *guwen* and *jinwen* learnings but also other important schools of thought in order to broaden its ability to carry more political messages and form stronger ties with the power center. Eastern Han was the heyday for *chenwei* scholarship and many apocryphal books were produced during this time. The founder of Eastern Han, Emperor Guangwu 光武 (r. 25–57), was an early patron of *chenwei*, and many officials and commoners in Eastern Han were believers as well. The popularity of apocryphal books can also be attested by frequent citations of *weishu* in Eastern Han stele inscriptions in which *weishu* are quoted as classics.[31]

A major theme in *weishu* is establishing prophecies. One can hardly miss this Eastern Han intellectual fascination with divination and prognostications while reading *WYCQ*. There are many *shushu* and *fangji* 方技 (methods) found in the narratives. These include the arts of physiognomy, dream interpretation, and prognostication on adversities as well as divinations. These seemingly strange records allow us access to the minds and beliefs of the

30. See *WYCQ*, 4.15.

31. See Pi Xirui 皮錫瑞, "Hanbei yin wei kao" 漢碑引緯考, in *Hanbei yin jing kao* 漢碑引經考, (Changsha: *Shifutang congshu* 師伏堂叢書, 1904), 1–45b.

Han people, to whom divination and interpretation of signs were important parts of their daily lives. Moreover, these records teach us about early divination techniques that disappeared after the Han period. For example, two lost divination texts, *Yumen* 玉門 (*Jade Gate*) and *Jinkui* 金匱 (*Golden Basket*), are frequently mentioned in *WYCQ*, and the methods cited from them allow us to reconstruct the ancient *liuren* 六壬 divination system that was unknown to people after the Han dynasty.[32]

## Section IV: The literary legacy of *WYCQ*

From a literary perspective, *WYCQ* is an important text that is admired for its complicated narratives and skillful presentation of characters. The main sources of *WYCQ* are *Zuozhuan*, *Guoyu*, *Shiji*, and *Yue jue shu*, but the source material was revised and developed considerably. For example, Wu Zixu's flight from Chu is only mentioned in one sentence in *Zuozhuan*, which reports Wu Zixu went to Wu and persuaded Zhouxu 州吁 of the benefits of attacking Chu. *Shiji* presents more details about his journey, describing how Wu Zixu sought refuge in Song 宋 and Zheng 鄭, made a narrow escape at the Shao Pass 韶關, received help from a fisherman, and begged for food on the road. *WYCQ* extends the *Shiji* story into a six-hundred-word-long epic, in songs and narratives, and highlights the dramatic and sometimes extreme deeds of the characters. In *WYCQ*, the fisherman who helped Wu Zixu escape commits suicide in order to keep Wu's secret. The same sacrifice is made by a new character who was not found in earlier sources, a woman washing silk by the river who chooses to drown herself in order to protect Wu Zixu. The suicides of two strangers highlight the themes of courage and justice in Wu Zixu stories.[33]

Similar developments can also be seen in stories concerning Goujian. Although the basic outline of the tale of Goujian's slavery in Wu and his final revenge is found in Sima Qian's *Shiji*, *WYCQ* devotes almost the entirety of the chapters on Yue to presenting Goujian's legend in detail. Chapters seven to ten focus on Goujian's life as a captive, the humiliation he suffered, and his determination, as well as the darkness in his personality, to successfully

32. For more discussion on divination records in *WYCQ*, see Liu Xiaozhen 劉曉臻, "*Wu Yue Chunqiu* zhong de zhanpu fangshi ji tedian" 吳越春秋中的占卜方式及特點, *Wenzhou daxue xuebao* (social science edition) 22, no. 1 (2009): 48–53.

33. For more discussion on the Wu Zixu tale, see David Johnson, "Epic and History in Early China: The Matter of Wu Tzu-hsu," *Journal of Asian Studies* 40, no. 2 (1981): 255–271. See also David Johnson, "The Wu Tzu-hsu *pien-wen* and Its Sources," pts. 1 and 2, *Harvard Journal of Asiatic Studies* 40, no. 1 (1980): 93–156; 40, no. 2 (1980): 465–505.

create a character with flesh and bones. The *WYCQ* retelling of Goujian is also rich in poetry, essays, expanded conversations, and polished speeches.

It is certainly not an overstatement that *WYCQ* contributes tremendously to the Chinese literary tradition. For students of Chinese literature, *WYCQ* is a treasure that preserves many early sources, records, and narratives, as well as songs and poems. For example, the fisherman's song and the farewell songs performed by Goujian and his ministers are valuable in studying folk literature and the *Chuci* 楚辭 poems of Eastern Han. The insertion of songs and poems in the middle of the narrative also foreshadows the popular late imperial vernacular narrative technique in which poems were used to begin and comment on certain episodes of a story. In addition to this, *WYCQ* provides sources and inspiration to later literature. In Tang and Song encyclopedias such as *Beitang shuchao* 北堂書鈔, *Yiwen leiju* 藝文類聚, *Chuxue ji* 初學記, and *Taiping yulan* 太平禦覽, many quotations from *WYCQ* are selected for literary uses; they are allusions any good writer must know. Scholars specializing in Wei-Jin literature cannot ignore the *WYCQ* influences on the *zhiguai* 志怪 (Recording Anomalies) tales popular in the third and fourth centuries. One example is the legend of the swordmakers Ganjiang 干將 and Moye, which is one of the most famous *zhiguai* stories. In early texts, Ganjiang and Moye are said to be master and disciple; *WYCQ* is the first text that refers to them as a couple. This change leads to the Wei-Jin tales recounting the murder of the couple by King Fuchai and the revenge exacted by Ganjiang and Moye's son. These stories found in texts like *Lieyi zhuan* 列異傳, *Soushen ji* 搜神記, and *Shiyi ji* 拾遺記 are clearly adopted from *WYCQ* accounts.

From medieval to late imperial periods, *WYCQ* continued to serve as a source for storytelling and theatrical performances. This is best seen in the adoption and development of *WYCQ*'s Wu Zixu stories. Admired for his loyalty and worthy of sympathy because of his tragic death, Wu Zixu had already been mentioned in pre-Qin texts. However, a more complicated narrative featuring Wu Zixu is presented in *Shiji* where Sima Qian follows Wu Zixu's journey to Wu and reports on his military success and his final death. *Shiji* builds the structure of the Wu Zixu legend, but the *WYCQ* accounts transform Wu Zixu into a true hero. The Dunhuang 敦煌 folk story *Wu Zixu bianwen* 伍子胥變文 adopts the *WYCQ* accounts.[34] The Ming editor Feng

34. The Dunhuang texts were found in the Mogao Caves 莫高窟 in Dunhuang in the early twentieth century. The texts are both religious and secular manuscripts dating from the late fourth to the early eleventh centuries. The manuscripts include a variety of topics such as history, folk songs, dance, and mathematics. Many Buddhist, Daoist, Nestorian, and Christian documents written in Chinese, Khotanese, Sanskrit, Sogdian, Hebrew, and Tibetan were also discovered in the caves.

Menglong's 馮夢龍 (1574–1646) revision of the historical fiction *Lieguo zhi* 列國志 is also based upon *WYCQ*. In fact, chapters seventy-one to eighty-three in Feng Menglong's revision retell *WYCQ* stories. Feng Zhi's 馮至 novel *Wu Zixu* written in the 1940s was inspired by *WYCQ*. In 1980, the famous writer Xiao Jun 蕭軍 (1907–1988) published *Wu Yue Chunqiu shihua* 吳越春秋史話, a rewriting of *WYCQ* in modern Chinese.

In addition to Wu Zixu, the *WYCQ* stories of Goujian, Fan Li, and the legendary beauty Xishi 西施 have also been popular topics for Chinese drama in the past and present. From Song and Yuan to Ming and Qing, there were many dramas developed from *WYCQ* retellings of the stories of these historical figures. These *WYCQ* legends are also currently performed on stage in a variety forms by local opera companies. Indeed, the vitality and long-lasting influence of *WYCQ* come precisely from its encyclopedic and uncensored presentation of the thought and intellectual interests of its time; its preservation of valuable early sources, many of which are lost today; and its sophisticated and inspiring narratives.

Over the past three decades, *WYCQ* has drawn tremendous scholarly attention in China. Since the 1980s, numerous articles discussing the cultural, historical, and literary value of *WYCQ* have been published in Chinese academic journals. Several modern Chinese translations of *WYCQ* are also available to Chinese readers. In addition to this, Chinese graduate students are producing new MA theses and PhD dissertations on this text every year. In comparison to this rich body of Chinese language scholarship, studies on *WYCQ* in Western languages are still inadequate. Werner Eichhorn produced a German translation in 1969 and John Lagerwey's very well-written but unpublished 1975 dissertation contains a translation of the first five chapters of the book, which is the only English translation available to readers. In recent years, the history of Wu and Yue has begun to draw more scholarly attention. Several books on this subject have been published in recent years, including Olivia Milburn's 2010 translation and annotation of *Yue jue shu*, as well as her 2013 study of the cultural construction of Wu entitled *Cherishing Antiquity*. Erica Brindley's *Ancient China and the Yue* is another important book to consult for the studies of this particular region. This new, complete translation and more thorough English-language analysis of *WYCQ* serves as a complement to the rising scholarly interest in Wu and Yue history.

My translation and annotation take full advantage of both Chinese and English scholarship. I frequently consult several modern Chinese translations

---

For studies of Dunhuang literature, see, for example, Victor H. Mair, *Tun-Huang Popular Narratives* (Cambridge: Cambridge University Press, 1983).

of *WYCQ*, especially Zhang Jue's *Wu Yue Chunqiu jiaozheng zhushu*, Huang Rensheng's *Xinyi Wu Yue Chunqiu*, and Xue Yaotian's 薛耀天 *Wu Yue Chunqiu yizhu* 吳越春秋譯註.[35] Miao Lu's 苗麓 *Wu Yue Chunqiu jiaozhu* 吳越春秋校註；and Zhou Shengchun's *Wu Yue Chunqiu jijiao huikao* are also valuable sources for my annotation.[36] At the same time, Lagerwey's dissertation and Milburn's work on *Yue jue shu* are important references that I consult and compare. Because of the intertextual connections, the translation of *Zuozhuan* by Stephen Durrant, Li Wai-yee, and David Schaberg, and the *Shiji* translation edited by William Nienhauser are equally important to my translation and annotation.[37]

---

35. Xue Yaotian 薛耀天, *Wu Yue Chunqiu yizhu* 吳越春秋譯註 (Tianjin: Tianjin guji chubanshe, 1992).

36. Miao Lu 苗麓, *Wu Yue Chunqiu jiaozhu* 吳越春秋校註 (Nanjing: Jiangsu guji chubanshe, 1999).

37. Stephen Durrant, Li Wai-yee, and David Schaberg, trans., *Zuo Tradition/Zuozhuan: Commentary on the "Spring and Autumn Annals"* (Seattle: University of Washington Press, 2016); William Nienhauser, ed., *The Grand Scribe's Records*, 9 vols. (Bloomington: Indiana University Press, 1994–).

# 吳越春秋吳太伯傳第一

## Chapter 1

# The Tradition of the Great Earl of Wu[1]

## Introduction

This opening chapter of *WYCQ* accounts for the origin and lineage of the Wu royal family. Because the founders of Wu were descendants of the Zhou, the description of the Wu family lineages therefore begins with the legendary Houji, the Zhou ancestor and cultural hero who, according to Chinese mythology, started agriculture. Two other heroes in early Zhou history, Gongliu and Gugong Danfu, are introduced in the narrative with emphasis on their kind deeds and their noble characters. Both Gongliu and Gugong Danfu are praised for being able to transform people with their virtue, which caused the people to render homage to them despite the fact that the time and environment in which they lived were difficult and even hostile. This theme of the true ruler, who yields power yet people come to serve him precisely due to his noble nature, is continued in the story of Taibo and Zhongyong, the legitimate successors of the Zhou

1. The Chinese text of *WYCQ* is based upon a 1306 edition, the so-called Dade ben 大德本, which is the earliest extant *WYCQ* edition. The errors of the Dade edition are indicated and corrected in footnotes of the chapters. Punctuation is based upon Zhang Jue's *Wu Yue Chunqiu jiaozheng zhushu*.

state. They yielded the position to their youngest brother after realizing that their father's intention was to eventually hand down the throne to the younger brother's son, Chang, the future King Wen of Zhou. Like their father Gugong Danfu, who cared for the people over land and power, Taibo and Zhongyong also valued filial duties over their political careers and fled to the land of the uncivilized in order to make sure their father's wish would be realized. Just as Gugong Danfu's noble deeds attracted people to render homage to him, Taibo and Zhongyong's yielding of power encouraged the locals to serve them as their rulers. Virtue instead of schemes, yielding rather than competition define rulership in the stories of the Wu family origin and lineage. This is different from the dominant theme in the second half of the text, in which schemes becomes the prevailing focus in the narratives of Yue.

The sources of this chapter's contents are chiefly the "Basic Annals of Zhou" (Zhou benji 周本紀) in *Shiji*, though the chapter highlights only the stories of Houji, Gongliu, and Gugong Danfu and ignores the list of minor successors in the Zhou lineage. It also adopts narratives from the "Hereditary Household of Taibo of Wu" (Wu Taibo shijia 吳太伯世家) but adds details, such as how Taibo and Zhongyong returned to Zhou to attend their father's funeral and Taibo's explanation of the title of the state of Wu. The purpose of such revision is, again, to highlight Taibo's noble nature. This theme of yielding the throne to the virtuous is continued in the succeeding chapter in which King Shoumeng wants to establish his youngest son Jizha as his successor.

## Translation

1.1. 吳之前君太伯者，后稷之苗裔也。后稷其母台氏之女姜嫄，為帝嚳元妃。年少未孕，出游於野，見大人跡而觀之，中心歡然，喜其形像，因履而踐之。身動，意若為人所感。後妊娠。恐被淫泆之禍，遂祭祀以求，謂「無子」。履上帝之跡，天猶令有之。姜嫄怪而棄于阨狹之巷，牛馬過者折易而避之。復棄于林中，適會伐木之人多。復置于澤中冰上，眾鳥以羽覆之。后稷遂得不死。姜嫄以為神，收而養之長，因名「棄」。為兒時，好種樹禾黍、桑麻、五穀。相五土之宜，青赤黃黑，陵水高下，粢稷、黍禾、蕖麥、豆稻，各得其理。堯遭洪水，人民泛濫，遂高而居。堯聘棄，使教民山居，隨地造區，研營種之術。三年餘，行人無飢乏之色。乃拜棄為農師，封之台，號為后稷，姓姬氏。后稷就國為諸侯。卒，子不窋立。遭夏氏世衰，失官，奔戎狄之間。其孫公劉。

1.1. Taibo,[2] the former ruler of Wu, was a descendant of Houji.[3] Houji's mother was Jiang Yuan,[4] a daughter of the Tai lineage,[5] who had become the primary wife of Lord Ku.[6] When she was young and had not yet become pregnant, she went out strolling in the wild. She saw the footprint of a giant and inspected it. Feeling delighted in her heart, she enjoyed the shape of the footprint and then moved forward and stepped on it. Her body shook and her mind felt as if it were touched by someone. Soon she was pregnant.[7] Fearing accusations of lewdness, she made a sacrifice and prayed, asking

---

2. Taibo means the "Great Eldest Brother." In early China the oldest son was called Bo 伯, the second Zhong 仲, the third Shu 叔, and the youngest Ji 季. In the following stories, Taibo and Zhongyong, the second son, left Zhou in order to realize their father's will of handing down the state to the son of their youngest brother, Jili. Bo is also potentially a station title, an earl.

3. Early Chinese names can be challenging to render in English. In early China, people's names included a *xing* 姓, which was the title of the lineage, a group of people descended from the same ancestor; at the same time, within a large lineage there were small family branches who used their land or posts to identify themselves, this is called a *shi* 氏. A person's *xing* does not change; however, his *shi* might be subject to change due to many reasons such as relocation or a change of job. *Ming* 名 was the given name of a person. Sometime a person was addressed by *xing* and *ming*, in other cases by *shi* and *ming*. However, since in addition to given names, men in early times could also have a style name (*zi* 字) when they reached adulthood, they could be mentioned by their style name. To make the situation more complicated, their rank among their brothers, their official posts, and even honorific prefixes could be used to address men in early China. For example, in *Zuozhuan*, Confucius's father is called Shuliang He 叔梁紇. The family is descended from Yin and the family name, *xing*, is Zi 子, and their *shi* is Kong 孔. Shuliang is his style name and He is his given name. Another example is Wu Zixu 伍子胥, the hero in *WYCQ*. Wu is probably the *shi* of the Ji 姬 lineage who resettled in Wulu 伍鹿 and took the name of the location as their *shi*. Zixu is his style name; his given name is Yun 員. In *WYCQ* Wu Zixu is called Wu Zixu, Zixu, or Wu Xu. Other figures in *WYCQ* also show similar inconsistency in terms of the way they are mentioned. In order to not confuse the readers, I will choose the most common name for the characters and keep all their names consistent throughout my translation. If the surname and the given name of a person are clear, I will follow the common practice and keep the surname before the given name and separate them: for example, Fan Li 范蠡, the Yue minister. However, if a person's name is not mentioned in the surname-plus-given-name pattern, or if it is impossible to discern the difference, I will not leave space between the characters of the names: thus Taibo is translated as Taibo, not Tai Bo, since Tai is a honorific prefix and Bo indicates his rank among his brothers. As for Houji, Hou was the title of a tribal leader in early Chinese, Ji literally means millet. Therefore Houji means "Lord of Millet," which is not his real name. However, since he was famously known as Houji, not by his given name Qi, I will translate his name as Houji, instead of Hou Ji.

4. Jiang is her *xing*, her family name; Yuan is her style. See *Shiji*, 4:111.

5. Tai is also from the Jiang lineage and the family resides at Tai, thus Tai is the *shi*. The state of Tai is located in modern-day Wugong 武功 County, Shaanxi Province.

6. Di Ku, Lord Ku, is also called Gaoxinshi 高辛氏, a legendary ruler who was said to be the great grandson of the Yellow Emperor. Chinese mythology says that Lord Ku had four wives and each of the wives gave birth to a son who later became the ancestor of Yao, Lord Zhi, and the ancestors of the ruling families of Shang and Zhou. See *Shiji*, 1:14.

7. This story of Jiang Yuan impregnated by stepping on the footprint of a giant and the following tales concerning her son Qi appeared first in poem #236 ("Sheng min" 生民) in the *Book of Songs* (*Shijing* 詩經). The story is also reported in Sima Qian's chapter on the Zhou lineage.

to not give birth to a child. However, because she had stepped on the footprint of the High God,[8] heaven still commanded that she give birth to a son. Jiang Yuan thought this an ill sign and abandoned the baby in a narrow lane. Horses and cows passing in the lane changed their paths and avoided stepping on the child. She then left him in the woods, but it happened that there were many woodcutters. Again she put the baby on the ice in a marsh, but a flock of birds covered the child with their feathers. Houji therefore was able to survive. Jiang Yuan then considered this child divine; she picked him up and raised him. When he grew up, he was consequently called "Qi" (abandoned). When he was a child he was fond of planting common millet, glutinous millet, mulberry, hemp, and all the five grains.[9] He examined what is appropriate to plant in each of the five types of land,[10] as well as in the dark brown, red, yellow, and black earth,[11] in the hills, the wetlands, the high land, and the low land; thus each of the common millet, panicled millet, glutinous millet, spiked millet, tarrow, wheat, beans, and rice obtained the most reasonable way to grow. Yao's era suffered from flooding, people were submerged in water, so they moved to and dwelled on high ground.[12] Yao invited Qi to teach the people how to live in the mountains, how to construct residences in accordance with the terrain, and how to study and manage the methods of planting grains. After more than three years, there was no expression of hunger on the faces of the people traveling on the roads. Yao therefore appointed Qi as the Master of Agriculture, and enfeoffed him in Tai.[13] Qi was called Houji and his surname was Ji. Houji went to his state and became a lord. After he died, his son Buzhu was established. Buzhu

---

See *Shiji*, 4:111. See James Legge, *The Chinese Classics: The She King* (Hong Kong: Hong Kong University Press, 1960), 2:465–72.

8. High God, Di 帝 or Shang Di 上帝, was the dominant god worshipped by the Shang people. Reference to him is still found in some of the early Zhou poems but was later replaced by the anthropomorphic Heaven.

9. There are different explanations concerning what the five grains are. According to *Zhouli* 周禮, the five grains include glutinous millet, panicled millet, beans, wheat, and rice. See Zhang Jue, 9n13; Huang Rensheng, 3n19.

10. 五土 refers to five types of land: forest, marsh, hills, level land near a river, and low land.

11. These different colors of earth are associated with different regions. The text "Yugong" 禹貢, which was attributed to the Great Yu 大禹 who managed flooding and toured the world, states that in each region the color of the soil and the qualities of the land vary. This description of the geographical differences is adopted in both "Basic Annals of Xi, 夏本紀" in *Shiji*, and the "Wuxing zhi" 五行志 chapter in *Hanshu*. See *Shiji*, 2:52–75 and *Hanshu*, 28:1524–34.

12. Yao is a son of Lord Ku and supposedly ruled China in approximately the twenty-fourth century BCE. According to Chinese myth, there was a large flood during Yao's time; Yao appointed Yu to control the flood. The story of Yu managing the flood is also reported in chapter 6 of *WYCQ*.

13. This is the same Tai from which Houji's mother is derived.

encountered the decline of the Xia rule and lost his title. He ran away to the land of the Rong and Di.[14] His grandson was Gongliu.

1.2. 公劉慈仁，行不履生草，運車以避葭葦。公劉避夏桀於戎狄，變易風俗，民化其政。公劉卒，子慶節立。

1.2. Gongliu was kind and humane.[15] When he walked he never stepped on living grass, and when he drove his chariot he avoided running over newly grown weeds. Gongliu avoided King Jie of Xia and lived in the regions of Rong and Di.[16] He changed their customs and practices, and the people were transformed by his rule. When Gongliu died, his son Qingjie succeeded him.

1.3. 其後八世而得古公亶甫。脩公劉、后稷之業，積德行義，為狄人所慕。薰鬻、戎姤而伐之，古公事之以犬馬牛羊，其伐不止；事以皮幣、金玉、重寶，而亦伐之不止。古公問：「何所欲？」曰：「欲其土地。」古公曰：「君子不以養害害所養。國所以亡也而為身害，吾所不居也。」古公乃杖策去邠，踰梁山而處岐周曰：「彼君與我何異？」邠人父子兄弟相帥，負老攜幼，揭釜甑而歸古公。居三月，成城郭，一年成邑，二年成都，而民五倍其初。

1.3. Eight generations after Qingjie there was Gugong Danfu,[17] who continued the accomplishments of Gongliu and Houji. Gugong Danfu accumulated his virtue and practiced righteousness and was admired by the Di people. Fearing Gugong Danfu's capability, Xunyu and Rong attacked him.[18] Gugong Danfu presented them with dogs, horses, cattle, and goats but their attacks did not stop. He presented them with skins, silks, gold, jade, and valuable treasures, yet the attacks did not abate. Gugong Danfu asked them, "What do you want?" The answer was, "We want this land of yours." Gugong Danfu said, "A gentleman will not cause harm to what he uses to nourish himself,[19] because this is the root of the demise of a state and causes

---

14. This is also found in "Basic Annals of Zhou," in *Shiji*; see *Shiji* 4:112. As Zhang Jue points out, there is a chronological problem in this account: Qi's son Buzhu lived six to seven hundred years before the decline of Xia. See Zhang Jue, 10n21. Rong and Di were tribes that lived west and north of Zhou; there were often wars and conflicts between Zhou and the Rong and Di.

15. The poem #250, titled "Gongliu" in the *Book of Songs*, praises Gongliu's deeds. See James Legge, *The She King*, 2:483–89.

16. King Jie was the last king of Xia and an infamous tyrant. See *Shiji*, 2:88.

17. A list of succession from Qingjie to Gugong Danfu is found in Sima Qian's "Hereditary Household of Zhou." See *Shiji*, 4:113.

18. These are the tribes living in northern China in early times. The reason they attacked Gugong Danfu was probably because they felt threated by the Di's admiration of Gugong Danfu.

19. The sentence here is a bit corrupted. It is nevertheless a famous quotation found in several early texts including *Mengzi* 孟子, *Zhuangzi* 莊子, *Liezi* 列子, *Lüshi chunqiu*, and *Huainanzi*.

harm to the gentleman himself. I will not reside in this land." Holding his driving whip, Gugong Danfu left Bin, crossed Mount Liang, and settled on the Zhou Plain near Mount Qi.[20] Addressing the people of Bin, he asked, "What is the difference between their rulers and me?"[21] The people of Bin, fathers, sons, and brothers led each other; carrying their elders and holding their children in their arms, with pots and steamers on their shoulders, they rendered homage to Gugong Danfu. Within three months of living there, he finished the inner wall and the outer rampart. After one year, he walled the settlement. Two years later it was made into a capital city and the population was five times larger than when he had just arrived.[22]

1.4. 古公三子，長曰太伯，次曰仲雍，雍一名吳仲，少曰季歷。季歷娶妻太任氏，生子昌。昌有聖瑞。古公知昌聖，欲傳國以及昌，曰：「興王業者，其在昌乎？」因更名曰季歷。太伯、仲雍望風知指，曰：「歷者，適也。」知古公欲以國及昌。古公病，二人託名採藥於衡山，遂之荊蠻。斷髮文身，為夷狄之服，示不可用。

1.4. Gugong Danfu fathered three sons. The oldest one was called Taibo, the second was Zhongyong, who was also called Wuzhong.[23] The youngest was called Jili. Jili took Lady Tairen as his wife, and she gave birth to a son named Chang. Chang was born with a sagely mark.[24] Gugong Danfu knew that Chang was sagely and wanted to eventually hand down the state

---

According to the quotations in these texts, the sentence should be: "A gentleman will not cause harm to those he nourishes with what he uses to nourish." 君子不以所養害其所養. *Shiji* presents a much clearer statement from Gugong Danfu on his decision: "Gugong Danfu said, 'When people establish a ruler it is to benefit them. Now the reason the Rong and Di do battle with us is because of my lands and peoples. What is the difference whether the people are with me or with them? Now, the people want to go to war on my account. But if you kill people's fathers and sons in war and then rule over them, this is something I could not bear to do." See *Shiji*, 4:113–14. See also Mencius, *Mencius*, trans. D. C. Lau (London: Penguin Books, 2004), 27; Guo Qingfan 郭慶藩, *Zhuangzi jishi* 莊子集釋 (Beijing: Zhonghua shuju, 2015), 956; Yang Bojun 楊伯峻, *Liezi jishi* 列子集釋 (Beijing: Zhonghua shuju, 2014), 275; He Ning 何寧, *Huainanzi jishi* 淮南子集釋 (Beijing: Zhonghua shuju, 2015), 848, 1287–88.

20. There are several mountains named Liang. This Mount Liang is located in modern-day Qian 乾 County in Shaanxi Province. Mount Qi is in modern-day Qishan County, Shaanxi Province, where the Zhou Plain 周原 is also located.

21. Gugong Danfu is trying to persuade the people to stay in their land and accept the new rulers.

22. Poem #237, which is titled "Mian" 緜 in the *Book of Songs*, describes Gugong Danfu's resettlement near Mount Qi. See James Legge, *The She King*, 2:437–41.

23. Wuzhong was called Yuzhong in *Shiji*. See *Shiji*, 4:115.

24. Chang is the future King Wen of Zhou 文王 (twelfth century BCE), one of the founders of the Zhou Dynasty. The sagely mark referred to here is described in an apocryphal text as a "cinnabar-red document" that was delivered to Chang's residence by a bird. See the commentary to Sima Qian's "Basic Annals of Zhou," in *Shiji*, 4:115.

to Chang. He said, "The one who will establish the achievements of a king is perhaps Chang!" He then renamed his youngest son Jili.[25] Taibo and Zhongyong observed the situation and understood what this meant.[26] They said, "Li means Di."[27] They realized that Gugong Danfu wanted to eventually hand down the state to Chang. When Gugong Danfu was ill, taking the excuse that they would pick medical herbs on Mount Heng, the two brothers then went to the Man tribes of Jing.[28] They cut off their hair and tattooed their bodies,[29] they put on the garments of the Yi and Di, in order to demonstrate that they could not be utilized in governing.

1.5. 古公卒，太伯、仲雍歸，赴喪畢，還荊蠻。國民君而事之，自號為勾吳。吳人或問何像而為勾吳，太伯曰：「吾以伯長居國，絕嗣者也，其當有封者，吳仲也。故自號勾吳，非其方乎？」荊蠻義之，從而歸之者千有餘家，共立以為勾吳。數年之間，民人殷富。遭殷之末世衰，中國侯王數用兵，恐及於荊蠻，故太伯起城，周三里二百步，外郭三百餘里。在西北隅，名曰故吳，人民皆耕田其中。

1.5. When Gugong Danfu died, Taibo and Zhongyong returned. After the funeral was over, they went back to the Man tribes of Jing.[30] People of the state looked to them as rulers and served them; they called their region Gouwu.[31] When some of the Wu people asked him for what reason their

25. Presumably, Jili previously had a now-unknown name that was changed to Jili.

26. 望風 (*wangfeng*) literally means "to observe the wind." In an early period, this might have had a relationship with the method of observing vapors to make predictions. In *Shiji* and *Hanshu* it is often used to describe ministers predicting the emperor's intention by observing signs or small details from court.

27. The characters 歷 (*li*) and 適 (*shi*) both mean "to go to," "to encounter" and "to surpass." However, 適 is also a homonym of another character 嫡 (*di*) that refers to the eldest son of the primary wife, that is, to the legitimate successor. Thus, there is a subtle hint in Jili's name that he should be the successor.

28. This detail is not found in *Shiji* but in, for example, *Lunheng*. See Huang Hui, ed., 黃暉, *Lunheng jiaoshi* 論衡校釋 (Beijing: Zhonghua shuju, 2015), 972.

29. This is a custom belonging to southern tribes in early China; people in the states in the central plain did not cut their hair or tattoo their bodies.

30. The brothers returning to Zhou in order to attend their father's funeral is not found in *Shiji*.

31. The presence of "gou" as a part of the name of Wu presents something of a mystery. It is interesting that Yue 越 is also sometimes written with the initial character 於 (*yu*), which might also have begun with an initial guttural sound in old Chinese. Yan Shigu suggested that these initial syllables might be remnants of non-Han languages of this area. But Yan's conclusion is contested, see Zhang Jue, 16n1. However, in bronze inscription, 勾吳 is written as 工敔 (*gongyu*), 攻吾 (*gongwu*), or 句敔 (*gouyu*). (See Gu Jianxiang 谷建祥 and Wei Yihui 魏宜輝, "Pizhou Jiunüdun suochu bianbo mingwen kaobian" 邳州九女墩所出編鎛銘文考辨, *Kaogu* 考古, no. 11 (1999): 71–73.) Based on his study of the discovered Wu bronze vessels, Dong Shan observes that the makers of the bronze vessels have different ways of inscribing their names in Chinese characters. Often characters are added to

land was called Gouwu, Taibo said, "I am the one who should succeed the throne in my native state yet I have no heir to succeed me. He who should possess the land is Wuzhong. For this reason I called this region Gouwu, is this not appropriate?"[32] The Man tribes of Jing considered this to be a correct principle. Those who came and rendered homage to the two brothers numbered more than a thousand households, together they established Taibo and formed the state of Gouwu. Within several years, the people became prosperous. During that time when the last generations of Yin had fallen into decline, the lords and kings in the central states repeatedly engaged in military conflicts. Afraid that these conflicts would reach the Man tribesmen of Jing, Taibo constructed a city with an inner wall that was three *li* and two hundred paces in perimeter, and an outer rampart that was more than three hundred *li*.[33] The city was constructed in the northwestern part of the land and its name was "Old Wu." The people all plowed their fields within the outer ramparts.

1.6. 古公病將卒，令季歷讓國於太伯，而三讓不受，故云太伯三以天下讓。於是季歷蒞政，脩先王之業，守仁義之道。季歷卒，子昌立，號曰西伯。遵公劉、古公之術業於養老，天下歸之。西伯致太平，伯夷自海濱而往。西伯卒，太子發立，任周召而伐殷，天下已安，乃稱王。追謚古公為大王，追封太伯於吳。

1.6. Gugong Danfu fell ill and was about to die. He ordered Jili to yield the state to Taibo. Jili yielded three times yet Taibo did not accept, therefore there was the saying that "three times Taibo yielded the world."[34] Jili then ruled and governed. He continued the accomplishments of the former kings and followed the Ways of humaneness and righteousness. After Jili died, his son Chang was instated and was called the Earl of the West. The Earl of the West followed the methods of Gongliu and Gugong Danfu and strove to

---

the names as prefixes or infixes with no specific meaning. He argues that Chinese characters were in fact used as symbols of pronunciation for the local names. A similar phenomenon is found in the names of the Yue kings, as Dong Shan points out, and these all suggest that in the late Spring and Autumn period Chinese characters were learned by the Wu and Yue people who used the characters to record local names. See Dong Shan 董珊, *Wu Yue timing yanjiu* 吳越題名研究 (Beijing: Kexue chubanshe, 2014), 95–100.

32. If we follow Dong Shan's theory above, the characters 勾吳 (*gouwu*) were simply adopted to indicate the local pronunciation.

33. One *li* is approximately one-third of a mile.

34. This is a quotation from the *Analects* where Confucius praises Taibo: "Surely we can say that Taibo possessed ultimate Virtue! He declined rulership of the world three times, and yet remained unpraised because the common people never learned of his actions." Translation adapted from Confucius, *Analects*, trans. Edward Slingerland (Indianapolis, IN: Hackett Publishing Company, 2003), 78.

nourish the elderly. The world rendered homage to him.[35] The Earl of the West brought peace to the kingdom, so Boyi left the seacoast and went to him.[36] When the Earl of the West died, his heir-apparent Fa was established; he entrusted Lord Zhou and Lord Shao to attack Yin.[37] After the world was pacified, he then changed his title to king. He gave Gugong Danfu the posthumous title of the "Great King" and granted Taibo the land of Wu.

1.7. 太伯祖卒，葬於梅里平墟。仲雍立，是為吳仲雍。仲雍卒，子季簡、簡子叔達、達子周章、章子熊、熊子遂、遂子柯相、相子彊鳩夷、夷子餘喬疑吾、吾子柯廬、廬子周繇、繇子屈羽、羽子夷吾、吾子禽處，處子專、專子頗高、高子句畢立。是時，晉獻公滅周北虞虞公，以開晉之伐虢氏。畢子去齊、齊子壽夢立，而吳益彊，稱王。凡從太伯至壽夢之世，與中國時通朝會，而國斯霸焉。

1.7. After Taibo died he was buried in Meili pingxu.[38] Zhongyong was established and he was Zhongyong of Wu.[39] When Zhongyong died, his son Jijian succeeded him. Jijian's son was Shuda, Shuda's son was Zhouzhang, Zhouzhang's son was Xiong, Xiong's son was Sui, Sui's son was Kexiang, Kexiang's son was Qiangjiuyi, Qiangjiuyi's son was Yuqiao yiwu, Yuqiao yiwu's son was Kelu, Kelu's son was Zhouyao, Zhouyao's son was Quyu, Quyu's son was Yiwu, Yiwu's son was Qinchu, Qinchu's son was Zhuan, Zhuan's son was Pogao, Pogao's son was Goubili.[40] At that time, Lord Xian

35. This is also found in "Basic Annals of Zhou," see *Shiji*, 4:116.

36. Boyi 伯夷 and Shuqi 叔齊 are sons of Lord Guzhu. Their father wanted to make the younger brother, Shuqi, his successor. After their father died, Shuqi yielded the position to Boyi; but the latter, following their father's will, rejected it. Consequently both of them gave up the throne and rendered homage to the Earl of the West. When King Wu, son of the Earl, decided to attack the last Shang king, the brothers considered this disloyal. After the Zhou was established, they refused to eat and starved to death. See Sima Qian's biography of Boyi and Shuqi, *Shiji*, 61:2123.

37. Lord Zhou was the younger brother of King Wu. When King Wu died, his son King Ping was still young and Lord Zhou acted as regent. Lord Shao was enfeoffed in the land of Yan after the demise of Shang. He was the founder of the state of Yan.

38. Zhang Jue believes pingxu is a small hill in Meili district, located in Wu County, Jiangsu Province. See Zhang Jue, 19n2.

39. Zhongyong was also called Yuzhong in *Zuozhuan* and *Shiji*. However, because his great-grandson was enfeoffed in Yu by King Wu of Zhou and was thus called Yuzhong as well, here the narrator addresses the Wu ruler as Zhongyong of Wu to distinguish him from his descendant. See Durrant, Li, and Schaberg, 277; Yang Bojun 楊伯峻, *Chunqiu Zuozhuan zhu* 春秋左傳註 (Beijing: Zhonghua shuju, 1995), 307; *Shiji*, 4:115, 31:1446.

40. This list of Wu succession basically adheres to the *Shiji* record; however, *Shiji* reports that after King Wu conquered Shang he sought the descendants of Taibo and Zhongyong. King Wu found Zhouzhang but Zhouzhang was already a ruler in Wu. King Wu then instated Zhouzhang's younger brother in Xiaxu 夏墟 and made him the ruler of the state of Yu. He was thus called Yuzhong. Also, in *Shiji*, Zhouzhang's son was named Xiongsui. *WYCQ* mistakenly refers to two persons, Xiong and Xiong's son Sui. See *Shiji*, 31:1446–47.

of Jin had destroyed the state of Yu to the north of the Zhou[41] because the Lord of Yu had opened its state to Jin's attack of the Guo clan.[42] Goubili's son was Quqi, and when Quqi's son Shoumeng was instated, Wu increased in strength, and he assumed the title of king.[43] Altogether, from Taibo down to Shoumeng's era,[44] Wu and the central states frequently came to one another's courts and held meetings, and the state of Wu even acted as overlord.

---

41. This is the state of Yu that King Wu granted to Zhouzhang's brother.

42. Jin was a powerful state in the north during the Spring and Autumn period. Lord Xian of Jin wanted to attack a small state called Guo, but in doing so he had to pass through Yu. The ruler of Yu foolishly believed Lord Xian's promise that Jin would share the land of Guo with Yu and permitted Jin access to travel through Yu. After Guo was destroyed, on their way back to Jin through Yu, the Jin troops conquered Yu as well. See *Zuozhuan*, Lord Xi 5; Yang Bojun, 307–12; Durrant, Li, and Schaberg, 277–79.

43. In the Spring and Autumn period, only the ruler of the Zhou court was called king while the rulers of the individual states were given titles such as Lord, Marquise, or Prince. However, the rulers of some southern states such as Chu, Wu, Yue, and Xu 徐 also called themselves kings.

44. As Zhang Jue points out, the sentence here is corrupt. According to *Shiji*, it should read: "Altogether from Taibo to Shoumeng there were nineteen generations. When it came to Shoumeng's era, Wu and the central state began to frequently come to one another's courts and hold meetings." See Zhang Jue, 21n11.

# 吳越春秋吳王壽夢傳第二

## CHAPTER 2

# The Tradition of King Shoumeng of Wu

### Introduction

"The Tradition of King Shoumeng of Wu" covers the time during the reign of King Shoumeng and the reigns of his three sons. The main foci of this chapter include King Shoumeng's admiration of Zhou ritual, the succession among King Shoumeng's sons, and the rivalry between Wu and Chu.

There are some important discrepancies between this *WYCQ* chapter and the accounts in Sima Qian's *Shiji* concerning this period of history. The *WYCQ* chapter starts with discussion of King Shoumeng's admiration of Zhou ritual and music. This is not recorded in other extant pre-Qin and Han texts. Interestingly, what is probably the most famous encounter between the Wu and Zhou culture, the story of Jizha commenting on the performances of the *Odes* and the ritual dances, is not mentioned in the *WYCQ* chapter. In contrast, both *Zuozhuan* and *Shiji* record Jizha's observation of the Zhou culture in considerable detail as well as with great enthusiasm.[1]

1. The *Zuozhuan* reports that when Jizha visited the state of Lu he made a request to observe performances of the Zhou *Odes* and ritual dances. Jizha demonstrated such great knowledge of Zhou culture that not only was he able to offer brilliant comments on the songs and dances, but he was also able to distinguish their origins, whether they were folk songs from a certain state or dance performances for particular events. See *Zuozhuan*, Lord Xiang 29; Yang Bojun, 1161–66; Durrant, Li, and Schaberg, 1243–44. See also *Shiji*, 31:1452.

The decision behind such selections and deletions is probably meant to emphasize the difference between Wu culture and the culture of the central states, represented by Zhou ritual. Although King Shoumeng applauds Zhou ritual, his words indeed point out that Wu has its own customs. However, in the *Zuozhuan* and *Shiji* accounts, Jizha was portrayed simply as a master of Zhou culture and an example of the idea that "the son of heaven has failed his duties and scholarship is preserved by the Yi people at the corners of the world" (*tianzi shiguan, xuezai siyi* 天子失官，學在四夷) and did not present any unique culture of his own region.[2]

Another important event in this *WYCQ* chapter is the succession among King Shoumeng's sons. In comparison to *Shiji*, the *WYCQ* chapter has elaborate accounts of King Shoumeng's will in passing down the throne to Jizha, Zhufan's attempt to yield the position to his brother, and his suicidal behaviors that were intended to shorten his rule and hasten the process of Jizha's accession. Details concerning the rivalry between Wu and Chu are also added in the *WYCQ* narratives.

## Translation

2.1. 壽夢元年，朝周，適楚，觀諸侯禮樂。魯成公會於鍾離，深問周公禮樂，成公悉為陳前王之禮樂，因為詠歌三代之風。壽夢曰：「孤在夷蠻，徒以椎髻為俗，豈有斯之服哉！」因歎而去，曰：「於乎哉，禮也！」

2.1. In the first year of King Shoumeng (585 BCE), the king was received in audience by the king of Zhou.[3] He then visited Chu and observed the rites and music of the many lords there.[4] He met Lord Cheng of Lu in Zhongli and intensively asked in depth about the rites and music of the Duke of Zhou.[5] Lord Cheng fully introduced the rites and music of the kings previous to him; he further chanted and sang the ballads of the three dynasties for

2. See *Zuozhuan*, Lord Zhao 17; Yang Bojun, 1389; Durrant, Li, and Schaberg, 1545.

3. This is during the late Eastern Zhou. Eastern Zhou (770–255 BCE) is divided into two periods: the Spring and Autumn period (771–476 BCE) and the Warring States period (475–221 BCE). Although power was in the hands of the rulers in each of the states, the Zhou king was still the nominal ruler of the empire.

4. Chu was a state located in southern China, including most of modern-day Hubei, Anhui, and Hunan provinces.

5. According to the *Chunqiu* and the *Zuozhuan*, the meeting occurred in the fifteenth year of Lord Cheng of Lu (576 BCE). In the *Shiji*, "nian biao" 年表, Sima Qian recorded this event in the tenth year of King Shoumeng, which is different from the *WYCQ* account above. Zhongli was a small state located on the border between Chu and Wu, and it was later probably conquered by its two powerful neighbors. Zhongli was near the modern-day location of Fengyang County in Anhui Province.

the king.[6] Shoumeng said, "I, the orphan, live in the land of southern tribes. I only comply with the local customs by tying my hair in a mallet-shaped knot,[7] how can I have clothing such as this!"[8] He then sighed and departed, saying, "Alas! The rites of Zhou!"

2.2. 二年，楚之亡大夫申公巫臣適吳，以為行人。教吳射御，導之伐楚。楚莊王怒，使子反將，敗吳師。二國從斯結讎。於是吳始通中國，而與諸侯為敵。

2.2. In the second year of King Shoumeng (584 BCE), Shen lord Wuchen,[9] the fugitive grand minister of Chu, came to Wu and was appointed as a foreign envoy.[10] He taught the people of Wu the skills of archery and chariot driving and led them to attack Chu.[11] King Zhuang of Chu was angry.[12] He sent Zifan to command the troops and defeated the Wu army. Because of this, the two states became enemies. From this time Wu began to have contact with the central states and became a rival of the many lords.

2.3. 五年，伐楚，敗子反。

2.3. In the fifth year of King Shoumeng (581 BCE), Wu attacked Chu and defeated Zifan.

2.4. 十六年，楚恭王怨吳為巫臣伐之也，乃舉兵伐吳，至衡山而還。

2.4. In the sixteenth year of King Shoumeng (570 BCE), King Gong of Chu resented that Wu had attacked them for Wuchen. He raised troops to attack Wu. The troops reached Hengshan and returned.[13]

---

6. The three dynasties refer to Xia (c. 2700–c.1600 BCE), Shang (c. 1600–1046 BCE), and Zhou (1046–226 BCE).

7. The mallet-shaped knot was a hairstyle popular among the tribes that lived in eastern and southern China in early periods.

8. This refers to the cloth and dressings used in ritual performance.

9. Wuchen was the magistrate of Shen County of Chu; therefore he was called Wuchen, the Lord of Shen.

10. Both the *Zuozhuan* and the *Shiji* state that Wuchen did not serve as the official in charge of foreign relations in Wu but his son did. See *Shiji*, 31:1448.

11. According to the *Zuozhuan*, Zifan wanted to take Xiaji as his wife, and Wuchen dissuaded him from doing so. However, later on, Wuchen married Xiaji and fled to Jin with her. Zifan therefore resented Wuchen. He killed Wuchen's clansmen and took their properties. Wuchen swore to avenge his clansmen. He came to Wu from Jin and persuaded Wu to attack Chu. See *Zuozhuan*, Lord Cheng 2 and Lord Cheng 7; Yang Bojun, 803–05, 834–35; Durrant, Li, and Schaberg, 727–29, 767. See also Xu Yuangao 徐元誥, *Guoyu jijie* 國語集解 (Beijing: Zhonghua shuju, 2002), 492.

12. King Zhuang of Chu was one of the five hegemons in the Spring and Autumn period, but he had already died by that time. It should be King Gong's 恭王 reign.

13. See also *Zuozhuan*, Lord Xiang 3; Yang Bojun, 926; Durrant, Li, and Schaberg, 901. *Shiji*, 31:1448. Hengshan is located south of modern-day Wuxing County in Zhejiang Province.

2.5. 十七年，壽夢以巫臣子狐庸為相，任以國政。

2.5. In the seventeenth year of King Shoumeng (569 BCE), Shoumeng appointed Wuchen's son Huyong as the prime minister, entrusting him with state affairs.

2.6. 二十五年，壽夢病將卒。有子四人：長曰諸樊，次曰餘祭，次曰餘昧，次曰季札。季札賢，壽夢欲立之，季札讓，曰：「禮有舊制，奈何廢前王之禮，而行父子之私乎？」

壽夢乃命諸樊曰：「我欲傳國季札，爾無忘寡人之言。」諸樊曰：「周之太王知西伯之聖，廢長立少，王之道興。今欲授國於札，臣誠耕於野。」王曰：「昔周行之德，加於四海，今汝於區區之國，荊蠻之鄉，奚能成天子之業乎？且今子不忘前人之言，必授國以次及于季札。」諸樊曰：「敢不如命？」

壽夢卒，諸樊以適長攝行事，當國政。

2.6. In the twenty-fifth year of King Shoumeng (561 BCE), Shoumeng was ill and was about to die. He had four sons: the first son was called Zhufan, the second was Yuzhai, the third was Yumo, and the fourth was Jizha. Jizha was excellent and Shoumeng wanted to establish him. Jizha declined, saying, "Ritual has its old regulations. How can we abandon the rites of former kings to satisfy the personal preferences of a father and a son?" Shoumeng therefore commanded Zhufan, saying, "I want to hand down the state to Jizha, and you should not forget my words." Zhufan replied, "When King Tai of Zhou recognized the sageliness of Xibo,[14] he deposed his oldest son and established the youngest Xibo, and the kingly way flourished. Now you desire to pass the state on to Jizha; I, your servant, sincerely request to plow in the wilds."[15] The king said, "In the past the virtue of Zhou spread through the world. Now how can you, living in a small state that is located in the land of the Jing tribe, accomplish the work of the son of heaven? Now you should not forget the word of your father and be sure to hand down the state to Jizha in succession." Zhufan said, "I dare not but obey your command!" Shoumeng died. Zhufan, the oldest legitimate son of Shoumeng, served as regent and held the reins of government.[16]

---

14. Taiwang 太王, the Grand King, is Gugong Danfu 古公亶父, see *WYCQ*, 1.4, 1.6. Xibo refers to King Wen of Zhou.

15. Suggesting that he would resign from his candidacy.

16. See also *Shiji*, 31:1449. Several recently unearthed Wu swords have Zhufan's name (written as "Fufa" 姑發) inscribed on the bodies of the swords. See Cao Jinyan 曹錦炎, "Wu jizi jianming kaoshi" 吳季子劍銘考釋, *Dongnan wenhua*, no. 4 (1990): 109–110. Wang Hui 王輝, "Guanyu 'Wuwang Gufa jian' shiwen de jige wenti" 關於吳王姑發劍釋文的幾個問題, *Wenwu*, no. 10 (1991): 89–90.

2.7. 吳王諸樊元年，已除喪，讓季札，曰：「昔前王未薨之時，嘗晨昧不安，吾望其色也，意在於季札。又復三朝悲吟而命我曰：『吾知公子札之賢，欲廢長立少。』重發言於口。雖然我心已許之，然前王不忍行其私計，以國付我，我敢不從命乎？今國者，子之國也，吾願達前王之義。」

季札謝曰：「夫適長當國，非前王之私，乃宗廟社稷之制，豈可變乎？」

諸樊曰：「苟可施於國，何先王之命有！太王改為季歷，二伯來入荊蠻，遂城為國，周道就成，前人誦之不絕於口，而子之所習也。」

札復謝曰：「昔曹公卒，廢存適亡，諸侯與曹人不義而立於國。子臧聞之，行吟而歸。曹君懼，將立子臧，子臧去之，以成曹之道。札雖不才，願附子臧之義。吾誠避之。」

吳人固立季札，季札不受而耕於野，吳人舍之。諸樊驕恣，輕慢鬼神，仰天求死。將死，命弟餘祭曰：「必以國及季札。」乃封季札於延陵，號曰延陵季子。

2.7. In the first year of King Zhufan of Wu (560 BCE),[17] after the mourning period had ended, the king abdicated his position to Jizha, saying, "Previously, before the former king passed away, he once was restless both morning and night. I observed from his expression that his thoughts were fixed upon Jizha. Moreover, he repeatedly sighed with grief in court and commanded me, saying, 'I know Gongzi Jizha is worthy.'[18] He wanted to dismiss his oldest son and establish the youngest; however, he hesitated to say this out loud. Although this was the case, in my heart I had already accepted his decision. However, the former king could not bear to carry out his personal plan, so he entrusted me with the state. How dare I not follow his command? Now the state is your state. I want to fulfill the intention of the former king." Jizha declined, saying, "The oldest legitimate son rules the state—this is not the former king's personal wish but is according to the regulations established in ancestral temples and at state altars; how can we change it?" Zhufan said, "If doing so will benefit our state, why must we adhere to the former kings' commands? King Tai of Zhou changed his successor to Jili,[19] and the two brothers came to this land of the Jing tribe.[20] They then built a city and founded the state, and the Way of Zhou was thus accomplished. That the people of the past praised them ceaselessly is a story you know well." Again

17. According to *Shiji*, the first year of King Zhufan was 560 BCE.

18. Gongzi literally means "son of a lord."

19. Jili was the father of King Wen of Zhou.

20. The two brothers were Taibo and Zhongyong. Taibo was the founder of Wu.

Jizha declined: "In the past when Lord Xuan of Cao died,[21] the son of his concubine lived on, while the son of his main wife perished. The many lords and people of Cao did not consider it right that he was established in the state.[22] When Zizang heard of this he sighed and returned to Cao. The lord of Cao was afraid. The many lords wanted to establish Zizang, but Zizang fled from Cao in order to maintain the proper way of governance in Cao. Although I, Jizha, am a man without capacity, I wish to be in accord with Zizang's integrity. I sincerely would avoid accepting the position." The people of Wu insisted on establishing Jizha. But Jizha did not accept this and ploughed in the outlying fields. Therefore the people of Wu gave up on him. Zhufan purposely acted proud and unruly. He was irreverent to spirits and gods. Looking up to heaven, he prayed for death. When he was about to die, he commanded his younger brother Yuzhai, saying, "You must eventually hand down the state to Jizha." Yuzhai therefore presented Jizha land in Yanling, and they called him "Master Ji of Yanling."[23]

2.8. 餘祭十二年，楚靈王會諸侯伐吳，圍朱方，誅慶封。慶封數為吳伺祭，故晉楚伐之也。吳王餘祭怒曰：「慶封窮來奔吳，封之朱方，以效不恨士也。」即舉兵伐楚，取二邑而去。

2.8. In the twelfth year of King Yuzhai (536 BCE),[24] King Ling of Chu assembled troops of the many lords to attack Wu.[25] They besieged Zhufang and killed Qingfeng.[26] Qingfeng often spied upon Chu for Wu, and that is the reason Jin and Chu attacked him.[27] King Yuzhai of Wu was furious and said,

---

21. In the thirteenth year of Lord Cheng of Lu (578 BCE), Jin allied with Qi, Lu, Song, Wei, Zheng, and Cao to attack Qin. Lord Xuan of Cao died amongst the troops.

22. The son of the concubine refers to Gongzi Fuchu. After the death of Lord Xuan of Cao, people of Cao entrusted Fuchu with the state and sent Zizang to bring the Lord's body back. However, Fuchu killed the crown prince and established himself as the new ruler of Cao. See the *Zuozhuan*, Lord Cheng 13; Yang Bojun, 866–67; Durrant, Li, and Schaberg, 811.

23. See also *Shiji*, 31:1452.

24. There are discrepancies between *Zuozhuan* and *Shiji* concerning the dates when Yuzhai was serving as the Wu king. Yang Bojun believes that Yuzhai only ruled four years (547–544 BCE). His brother Yumo ruled for seventeen years (543–527 BCE). However, the "Wu shijia" 吳世家 (Hereditary Household of Wu) chapter in *Shiji* reports that Yuzhai served as the king for seventeen years (547–531 BCE). See *Zuozhuan*, Lord Xiang 31; Yang Bojun, 1190; Durrant, Li, and Schaberg, 1283. See also *Shiji*, 31:1460.

25. Also recorded in *Zuozhuan*, Lord Zhao 4; Yang Bojun, 1253; Durrant, Li, and Schaberg, 1373.

26. Zhufang is located south of modern-day Zhenjiang city in Zhejiang Province. Qingfeng was an official of Qi. After Qi minister Cui Zhu assassinated Lord Zhuang of Qi and established Lord Jing, Qingfeng and Cui Zhu were the prime ministers. One year later Qingfeng killed Cui Zhu. The next year he was attacked by other powerful families of Qi and fled to Lu and Wu. See *Zuozhuan*, Lord Xiang 25; Yang Bojun, 1095–7; Durrant, Li, and Schaberg, 1139–40; *Zuozhuan*, Lord Xiang 28; Yang Bojun, 1145–9; Durrant, Li, and Schaberg, 1219–29. See also *Shiji*, 32:1502–3.

27. According to *Zuozhuan* and *Shiji*, Jin did not join the attack.

"When Qingfeng was in desperate straits he sought refuge here in Wu, and I granted him the land of Zhufang. This was to show that Wu is not hostile toward talented men." He immediately mobilized troops and attacked Chu. The Wu army conquered two cities of Chu and returned.[28]

2.9. 十三年，楚怨吳為慶封故伐之，心恨不解，伐吳，至乾谿，吳擊之，楚師敗走。

2.9. In the thirteenth year of King Yuzhai (535 BCE), the king of Chu resented that Wu had attacked them because of Qingfeng. Unable to quench his hatred, he launched a military expedition against Wu. When the Chu troops arrived at Qianxi,[29] they were attacked by Wu troops. The Chu army was defeated and retreated.[30]

2.10. 十七年，餘祭卒，餘昧立。四年卒，欲授位季札，季札讓，逃去。曰：「吾不受位明矣。昔前君有命，已附子臧之義。潔身清行，仰高履尚，惟仁是處，富貴之於我，如秋風之過耳。」遂逃歸延陵。吳人立餘昧子州于，號為吳王僚也。

2.10. In the seventeenth year of King Yuzhai (531 BCE), Yuzhai died and Yumo was established.[31] In the fourth year of King Yumo (527 BCE), Yumo died. Before his death, Yumo wanted to hand over the throne to Jizha. Jizha declined. He fled from Wu, saying, "I have already made it clear that I will not accept the throne. In the past, when the former king issued this command, I had already brought myself into accord with Zizang's integrity. My person and behavior are pure, I admire great moral fortitude and practice my nobility, and act only in accordance with the principles of humaneness. Wealth and rank have as much to do with me as autumn wind blowing by my ears." Therefore he fled back to Yanling. The people of Wu established Yumo's son Zhouyu as the new king, and he was called "King Liao of Wu."

---

28. See *Zuozhuan*, Lord Zhao 4; Yang Bojun, 1255; Durrant, Li, and Schaberg, 1379.

29. Qianxi was located southeast of modern-day Bo County in Anhui Province.

30. See *Zuozhuan*, Lord Zhao 6; Yang Bojun, 1280; Durrant, Li, and Schaberg, 1411.

31. *Zuozhuan*, Lord Xiang 29 records that King Yuzhai was assassinated by a Yue captive who was appointed by Yuzhai as a guard of the king's boat. When Yuzhai boarded the boat, the guard stabbed him with a knife. See Yang Bojun, 1157; Durrant, Li, and Schaberg, 1237.

# 吳越春秋王僚使公子光傳第三

## CHAPTER 3

# The Tradition of King Liao Commanded Gongzi Guang

## Introduction

The title of the chapter comes from its opening sentence, which is different from the other annalistic chapter titles of the text. It was actually not an unusual practice among early texts for the first sentence or words of the chapter to be adopted as the chapter title. For example, all chapters in the *Analects* are named after the first two words of the chapter, and those titles, similar to this current work, do not reflect the content of the chapters.[1] In fact, chapter three of the *WYCQ* focuses on two loosely connected stories: Wu Zixu's flight from Chu to Wu and Gongzi Guang's assassination of King Liao of Wu. Although these events occur during the time when King Liao is ruling Wu, the king is indeed not the center of the narrative, and this is probably the reason why the chapter is marked by its first sentence instead of being called "The Tradition of King Liao."[2]

1. Pre-Qin texts usually do not have a title for the text or a chapter title. Titles of the texts are often given by later editors who also usually choose the first two or three characters of the opening sentence of each chapter as the chapter title.

2. Two dagger-axes found in Shanxi 山西 in 1961 contain the inscription 王子于之用戈 (*wangzi Yu zhi yong ge*) "Prince Yu's dagger-axe." Zhang Han 張頷 argues that this Prince Yu is the Wu Prince Zhouyu 州于, the future King Liao of Wu. See Zhang Han 張頷, "Shanxi Wanrong chutu cuojin niaochongshu ge mingwen kaoshi" 山西万榮出土錯金鳥蟲書戈銘文考釋, in *Zhang Han xueshu wenji* 張頷學術文集 (Beijing: Zhonghua shuju, 1995), 34–37.

The hero of this chapter is Wu Zixu. A pivotal figure in the rival history between Wu and Yue, Wu Zixu's story begins to unfold in this chapter. In fact, the narratives of the chapter can be divided into three sections: the injustice of the deaths of Wu Zixu's father and brother, Wu Zixu's journey to Wu, and Gongzi Guang's assassination of King Liao. As we can see, more than two-thirds of the chapter's narrative focuses on Wu Zixu: his fleeing from Chu; the dangers he encounters on his journey to Wu; and his recommendation of Zhuanzhu to Gongzi Guang, which leads to the assassination of King Liao. There is little doubt that Wu Zixu's story in this chapter comes from early sources, especially those that are recorded in Sima Qian's biography of Wu Zixu in the *Shiji*.[3] However, it is the *WYCQ* story that transforms Wu Zixu from a historical to a literary figure. Similar to all legends of heroes in world literature, Wu Zixu has to overcome many difficulties and survive dangers on his journey to Wu. Using his own wit and relying upon help from extraordinary people, Wu Zixu escapes the Shao Pass, is rescued by a fisherman and a woman washing silk by the river, and finally arrives in Wu. Compared to the brief accounts in the *Shiji*, these three climactic episodes on his journey are developed into complicated stories and are dramatized by dialogue, tension, and detail in this *WYCQ* chapter.

The three sections of this chapter are dominated by the themes of loyalty and appreciation. Loyalty is presented in the first section about the death of Wu Zixu's father and brother, highlighted by Wu She's remonstration of the Chu kings and Wu Shang's filial piety. Wu Zixu's journey to Wu, as discussed above, is a typical hero's story in which danger and rescue create considerable tension in the narrative. The theme shifts to the idea of appreciation, after Wu Zixu arrives in Wu, beginning with the Wu market clerk's recognition of Wu Zixu as an extraordinary man, Wu Zixu's appreciation of Zhuanzhu, and the comparison between King Liao's false and Gongzi Guang's true appreciation of Wu Zixu.

3. In a 2006 excavation in Shuihudi 睡虎地, Yunmeng County 云夢, Hubei Province, over 2000 pieces of bamboo strips and wooden blocks containing stories, almanacs, computation texts, and legal documents were found in tomb #77, a Western Han tomb that belongs to the Emperor Wen (r. 180–157 BCE) and Emperor Jing (r. 157–141 BCE) periods. The 205 story strips found so far include the earliest version of the Wu Zixu story that contains the basic plots found in *Shiji*, *Yue jue shu*, and *WYCQ*. *Shiji*'s story is developed from this Shuihudi text. See Zhu Xiangrong 朱湘蓉, "Wenxueshi zhong Wu Zixu fuchou gushi qingjie de xingcheng—yi Hubei Yunmeng Shuihudi 77 hao Hanmu Wu Zixu gushi jian wei yiju" 文學史中伍子胥復仇故事情節的形成—以湖北云夢睡虎地 77 號漢墓伍子胥故事簡為依據, *Zhongyuan wenhua yanjiu* 中原文化研究, no. 2 (2015): 44–51.

## Translation

3.1. 二年，王僚使公子光伐楚，以報前來誅慶封也。吳師敗而亡舟。光懼，因捨，復得王舟而還。光欲謀殺王僚，未有所與合議，陰求賢，乃命善相者為吳市吏。

3.1. In the second year of King Liao of Wu (525 BCE), the king sent Gongzi Guang to launch a military expedition against Chu.[4] This was in retaliation for the previous invasion of Chu and the killing of Qingfeng.[5] The Wu troops were defeated and lost the boat of the former Wu king.[6] Gongzi Guang was afraid of this, so he attacked Chu by surprise, regained the boat, and then returned to Wu.[7] Gongzi Guang wanted to assassinate King Liao but did not yet have someone to conspire with. He secretly sought a worthy man and then appointed a man, who was good at physiognomy as the clerk of Wu market, in order to help him find one.

3.2. 五年，楚之亡臣伍子胥來奔吳。伍子胥者，楚人也，名員。員父奢，兄尚。其前名曰伍舉。以直諫事楚莊王。

王即位三年，不聽國政，沉湎於酒，淫於聲色。左手擁秦姬，右手抱越女，身坐鐘鼓之間而令曰：「有敢諫者，死！」於是伍舉進諫曰：「有一大鳥，集楚國之庭，三年不飛，亦不鳴。此何鳥也？」於是莊王曰：「此鳥不飛，飛則沖天；不鳴，鳴則驚人。」伍舉曰：「不飛不鳴，將為射者所圖，絃矢卒發，豈得沖天而驚人乎？」於是莊王棄其秦姬越女，罷鐘鼓之樂；用孫叔敖，任以國政。遂霸天下，威伏諸侯。

---

4. According to *Shiji*, Gongzi Guang is the son of the previous King Zhufan of Wu. However, in the *Shiben*, Gongzi Guang was said to be the son of King Yimei of Wu. In *Zuozhuan*, Lord Zhao 27, Guang claims that he is the descendant of the former king of Wu but does not specify the name of the king. Du Yu's commentary says that the king refers to King Zhufan. However, Fu Qian's commentary to *Shiben* argues that Guang is the son of King Yimei and King Liao is the younger brother of King Yimei. In either case, Gongzi Guang has the right to claim the kingship of Wu.

5. The event is reported in *WYCQ*, 2.8. Chu's killing of Qingfeng is reported in the "Hereditary Household of Wu" in *Shiji*, 31:1460. Chu's attack seems to be an effort to legitimize the authority of King Ling of Chu. The king's succession had been established through the assassination of the previous king and was thus not acknowledged by other lords. He therefore needed a military victory to win recognition. Qingfeng helped Cui Zhu and murder Lord Zhuang of Qi; he was the perfect target for King Ling. However, King Ling was humiliated by Qingfeng before the latter was executed. See *Shiji*, 40:1704–05.

6. We don't have much information about the boat. The earliest record of the loss of the boat is found in *Zuozhuan*, Lord Zhao 17, in which the boat is called Yuhuang 餘皇. Probably Yuhuang was Wu king's boat, it was then the flagship of the Wu fleet.

7. *Zuozhuan* has a much more elaborate story of Wu's dramatic regaining of the boat: Wu ambushed the Chu guards of the boat and attacked them by surprise. See Lord Zhao 17; Yang Bojun, 1392; Durrant, Li, and Schaberg, 1549–51. Xu Tianhu reads the character 捨 (*she*) as 掩 (*yan*), attacking by surprise.

莊王卒，靈王立。建章華之臺。與登焉。王曰：「臺美。」伍舉曰：「臣聞國君服寵以為美，安民以為樂，克聽以為聰，致遠以為明。不聞以土木之崇高，蟲鏤之刻畫，金石之清音，絲竹之淒唳以之為美。前莊王為抱居之臺，高不過望國氛，大不過容宴豆，木不妨守備，用不煩官府，民不敗時務，官不易朝常。今君為此臺七年，國人怨焉，財用盡焉，年穀敗焉，百姓煩焉，諸侯忿怨，卿士訕謗：豈前王之所盛，人君之美者耶？臣誠愚不知所謂也。」靈王即除工去飾，不遊於臺。由是伍氏三世為楚忠臣。

3.2. In the fifth year of King Liao (522 BCE), Wu Zixu, a Chu official who had fled from that state, came to Wu seeking refuge. Wu Zixu was a native of Chu; his name was Yun.[8] Yun's father was She; his older brother was Shang. His ancestor, who was called Wu Ju, had served King Zhuang of Chu by remonstrating straightforwardly.[9]

In the three years since King Zhuang had taken his place as king, he had never paid attention to state affairs. Instead, he gave himself over to wine and indulged in the pleasures of music and women. With his left hand embracing a lady from Qin and his right hand holding a girl from Yue, the king sat among bells and drums and issued a command, saying, "Anyone who dares to remonstrate shall be executed." At this point Wu Ju submitted his admonition, saying, "There was a big bird perched in the court of Chu; for three years it did not fly, nor did it sing, what kind of bird is it?" King Zhuang replied, "This bird may not have flown yet, once it does it will soar up to the heavens; it may not have cried out yet, once it does it will startle everyone." Wu Ju said, "If it does not fly nor cry, it will be targeted by hunters. If stringed arrows are suddenly let loose, how will the bird be able to soar to the heavens and startle everyone?" King Zhuang therefore dismissed his lady from Qin and the girl from Yue and canceled the performances of bell

---

8. Wu Zixu's given name is Yun, Zixu is probably his style name by which he is best known. Wu Zixu is also called Shenxu 申胥 in *Yue jue shu*, which is his name in the Zhangjiashan 張家山 Han text "Gailu" 蓋廬 as well. See Zhangjiashan ersiqi hao hanmu zhujian zhengli xiaozu 張家山二四七號漢墓竹簡整理小組, *Zhangjiashan hanmu zhujian [247 hao mu]* 張家山漢墓竹簡 [二四七號墓] (Beijing: Wenwu chubanshe, 2001). See also Cao Jinyan 曹錦炎, "Lun Zhangjiashan Hanjian Gailu" 論張家山漢簡蓋廬, *Dongnan wenhua* 東南文化, no. 9 (2002): 62–69. In *WYCQ* he is called Wu Zixu, Zixu, or sometimes Wu Yun. In order to keep the translation consistent, I will use Wu Zixu as his name throughout of the text. The *WYCQ* stories of Wu Zixu are elaborated accounts of his biography in Sima Qian's *Shiji* as well as brief records of him in *Zuozhuan*, Lord Zhao 20. See Yang Bojun, 1407–08; Durrant, Li, and Schaberg, 1569–71.

9. *Qian* 前, "front," should be read here as *xian* 先, meaning "former" and "previous." *WYCQ* uses *qian* instead of *xian* to refer to ancestors or former kings. *Zuozhuan*, Lord Xiang 26.10 records that Wu Ju was slandered in Chu and fled to Zheng. He was finally able to return to Chu because of his friend Shengzi's 聲子 help. See Lord Xiang 26; Yang Bojun, 1119–23; Durrant, Li, and Schaberg, 1175–83.

and drum. He employed Sunshu Ao and entrusted him with state affairs.[10] Chu therefore became the hegemon of the world and its power subdued the many lords.[11]

After King Zhuang died, King Ling was established as king.[12] He built the Zhanghua Terrace and ascended it with Wu Ju.[13] The king said, "The terrace is beautiful." Wu Ju replied, "I, your subject, have heard that a ruler considers keeping his favorite subjects in his control as beautiful,[14] giving peace to the people as a joy, hearing admonishments as melodious, and being able to cause people to come from far as enlightening. I have not heard that a ruler regards the majesty and loftiness of architecture, the engraving and decoration of animal shapes and patterns on buildings,[15] the clear sounds of bells and drums, and the plaintive music of string and bamboo instruments as beautiful. Previously King Zhuang built the Baoju Terrace. It was only tall enough to observe the vapors above the state,[16] spacious enough to accommodate banquets. The wood that was used did not detract from the preparation of city defenses and the cost did not trouble the government. The people did not have to abandon their seasonal field work and the officials did not have to alter their daily court services. Now my lord has spent seven years building this terrace. The people in the capital are upset about it,[17] our resources are exhausted by it, harvests are undermined because of it, all the officials are troubled by it,[18] the many

---

10. Sunshu Ao served as the prime minister to King Zhuang of Chu. He is mentioned in *Zuozhuan*, Lord Xuan 12 and in the *Shiji*, 119:3099.

11. The above admonition of Wu Ju and King Zhuang's response are also reported in *Shiji*, 40:1700, and in *Hanfeizi*. See Chen Qiyou 陳奇猷, *Hanfeizi jishi* 韓非子集釋 (Shanghai: Shanghai renmin chubanshe, 1974), "Yulao" 喻老 chapter, 412–13. An almost identical Warring States conversation between King Wei of Qi 齊威王 and Chunyu Kun 淳于髡 is found in *Shiji*, 126:3197.

12. According to *Shiji*, King Gong succeeded King Zhuang after the latter died. The position was then passed down to King Kang and his son Jiaao. Wei assassinated Jiaao and became King Ling. King Ling relied upon Wu Ju to legitimize his succession. See *Shiji*, 40:1703–04.

13. According to *Shuijing zhu* (*Annotation to the Classic of River* 水經注), the terrace was located in modern-day Jianli County, Hubei Province.

14. This conversation is also found in *Guoyu*, see Xu Yuangao, 493. An alternative reading of the word *fu chong* 服寵 is "the many lords receive favor from the king of Zhou because of their virtue." See Wei Zhao's 韋昭 commentary in *Guoyu*, in Xu Yuangao, 493.

15. The Chinese word *chong*, "worms," here refers to animal, meaning the animal shapes on the beams and pillars of a building.

16. See *Guoyu* "Chu yu" chapter, Xu Yuangao, 493. The vapor of the state refers to the vapor and clouds of certain shapes that are regarded as ominous signs. This metaphor is frequently mentioned in early texts.

17. In pre-Qin texts 國 (*guo*) often refers to the capital city.

18. 百姓 (*baixing*) here refers to many officials. From early times until the Spring and Autumn period only the nobles possessed a surname, so in pre-Qin texts *baixing* usually refers to the officials or aristocrats. For example, in the "Yaodian" and "Pangeng" chapters in *Shangshu*, both Yao and

lords are angry and complain about it,[19] and the nobles and senior officials denounce and slander it. Are such things something that previous kings praised and rulers considered spectacular? I, your subject, am truly unwise, and I do not understand what you have just said." King Ling then immediately dismissed the artisans and effaced the decorations; he did not visit the terrace anymore. Since then the Wu clan for three generations have been loyal ministers of Chu.[20]

3.3. 楚平王有太子名建，平王以伍奢為太子太傅，費無忌為少傅。平王使無忌為太子娶於秦，秦女美容，無忌報平王，曰：「秦女天下無雙，王可自取。」王遂納秦女為夫人而幸愛之，生子珍；而更為太子娶齊女。無忌因去太子而事平王，深念平王一旦卒而太子立，當害己也，乃復讒太子建。建母蔡氏無寵，乃使太子守城父，備邊兵。

3.3. King Ping of Chu had a prince named Jian.[21] King Ping appointed Wu She the chief tutor of the prince and Bi Wuji the assistant tutor. King Ping sent Bi Wuji to Qin to receive a bride for the prince. The Qin girl was beautiful. Bi Wuji reported to King Ping, saying, "The beauty of the Qin girl is peerless. Your Majesty should take her for yourself."[22] The king then took the Qin girl as a consort and favored her. She gave birth to a son named Zhen. The king then arranged for the prince to marry a girl from Qi instead. Because of this, Bi Wuji left the prince to serve King Ping. He was deeply concerned that once King Ping had died and the prince was established, the new king would certainly harm him. He therefore further slandered Prince Jian. Jian's mother Lady Cai was not favored by the king.

---

Pangeng address the nobles and officials as *baixing*. The *Guoyu* passage directly states: 百官煩焉 (*baiguan fanyan*) "the many officials were troubled by it."

19. *Guoyu* says that King Ling invited the many lords to visit the terrace but no one came. See Xu Yuangao, 494.

20. *Guoyu* has a much more elaborate remonstration of Wu Ju and does not recount King Ling's retreat from the terrace. See Xu Yuangao, 493–97.

21. King Ping of Chu was named Qiji 棄疾. According to *Zuozhuan*, before Qiji became the king of Chu he once served as a Chu diplomat to the state of Cai. The daughter of a Cai border official eloped with him and gave birth to prince Jian. See Lord Zhao 19; Yang Bojun, 1401; Durrant, Li, and Schaberg, 1561. *Shiji* reports that King Ling lost his throne due to a coup led by Chu nobles and died soon after that. Qiji forced his two brothers to commit suicide and established himself as the new king. See *Shiji*, 40:1708.

22. This is also recorded in *Shiji*, 40:1712; and in *Zuozhuan*, Lord Zhao 19.2; Yang Bojun, 1401; Durrant, Li, and Schaberg, 1561. Besides King Ping of Chu, *Zuozhuan* reports three other rulers who took their sons' brides as their own wives: Lord Hui of Lu, Lord Xian of Jin, and Lord Xuan of Wei. All of the states suffered succession crises due to these illicit marriages.

The king then sent the prince to guard Chengfu, preparing for military conflict along the border.[23]

3.4. 頃之，無忌日夜言太子之短，曰：「太子以秦女之故，不能無怨望之心，願王自備。太子居城父將兵，外交諸侯，將入為亂。」平王乃召伍奢而按問之。奢知無忌之讒，因諫之，曰：「王獨奈何以讒賊小臣而疏骨肉乎？」無忌承宴，復言曰：「王今不制，其事成矣，王且見擒。」平王大怒，因囚伍奢，而使城父司馬奮揚往殺太子。奮揚使人前告太子急去，不然將誅。三月，太子奔宋。

3.4. Shortly after this, Bi Wuji spoke to the king day and night about the faults of the prince, saying, "The prince, because of the girl from Qin, must have a resentful heart. I wish Your Majesty would prepare yourself for this. The prince stays in Chengfu and leads troops. Outside of the state he befriends many lords. He is going to enter the capital and rebel." King Ping then summoned Wu She and closely questioned him about this. Wu She knew of Bi Wuji's slander; he thereupon took the opportunity to admonish the king, saying, "Why exactly would Your Majesty alienate your own flesh and blood because of a slanderous petty minister?" When the king was at leisure, Bi Wuji took the opportunity to further say, "If now Your Majesty does not control it, his plan will succeed, and Your Majesty will be imprisoned." King Ping became furious. He therefore put Wu She in jail and ordered Fenyang, Supervisor of the Military at Chengfu, to go and kill the prince. Fenyang sent a person ahead to tell the prince to leave immediately, otherwise he would be executed. In the third month, the prince fled to the state of Song.[24]

3.5. 無忌復言平王曰：「伍奢有二子，皆賢，不誅且為楚憂。可以其父為質而召之。」

王使使謂奢曰：「能致二子則生，不然，則死。」

伍奢曰：「臣有二子，長曰尚，少曰胥。尚為人慈溫仁信，若聞臣召輒來。胥為人少好於文，長習於武，文治邦國，武定天下，

23. See also *Shiji*, 40:1713 and *Zuozhuan*, Lord Zhao 19.6; Yang Bojun, 1402; Durrant, Li, and Schaberg, 1563. The same strategy was seen in Shensheng's story. Shensheng's father Lord Xian of Jin favored his concubine's son and sent Shensheng to guard Quwo. Shensheng was later slandered and forced to commit suicide. See *Zuozhuan* Lord Min 1, Lord Xi 4; Yang Bojun, 258, 295–99; Durrant, Li, and Schaberg, 233, 269.

24. This narrative is almost identical to the account in Wu Zixu's biography in *Shiji*. *WYCQ* adopts this story from *Shiji*. See *Shiji*, 66:2172. See also *Zuozhuan*, Lord Zhao 20; Yang Bojun, 1407; Durrant, Li, and Schaberg, 1569.

執綱守戾，蒙垢受恥，雖冤不爭，能成大事。此前知之士，安可致耶？」

平王謂伍奢之譽二子，即遣使者駕駟馬，封函印綬往許召子尚、子胥。令曰：「賀二子，父奢以忠信慈仁，去難就免。平王內慚囚繫忠臣，外愧諸侯之恥，反遇奢為國相，封二子為侯，尚賜鴻都侯，胥賜蓋侯，相去不遠三百餘里。奢久囚繫，憂思二子，故遣臣來奉進印綬。」

尚曰：「父繫三年，中心切怛，食不甘味，嘗苦飢渴，晝夜感思，憂父不活，惟父獲免，何敢貪印綬哉？」

使者曰：「父囚三年，王今幸赦，無以賞賜，封二子為侯。一言當至，何所陳哉？」

尚乃入報子胥，曰：「父幸免死，二子為侯，使者在門，兼封印綬，汝可見使。」

子胥曰：「尚且安坐，為兄卦之。今日甲子，時加於巳，支傷日下，氣不相受。君欺其臣，父欺其子。今往方死，何侯之有？」

尚曰：「豈貪於侯，思見父耳。一面而別，雖死而生。」

子胥曰：「尚且無往。父當我活，楚畏我勇，勢不敢殺；兄若誤往，必死不脫。」

尚曰：「父子之愛，恩從中出，徼倖相見，以自濟達。」

於是子胥歎曰：「與父俱誅，何明於世，冤讎不除，恥辱日大。尚從是往，我從是決。」

尚泣曰：「吾之生也，為世所笑，終老地上，而亦何之？不能報仇，畢為廢物。汝懷文武，勇於策謀，父兄之讎，汝可復也。吾如得返，是天祐之，其遂沉埋，亦吾所喜。」

胥曰：「尚且行矣，吾去不顧，勿使臨難，雖悔何追！」

旋泣辭行，與使俱往。楚得子尚，執而囚之，復遣追捕子胥，胥乃貫弓執矢去楚。楚追之，見其妻。曰：「胥亡矣，去三百里。」使者追及無人之野，胥乃張弓布矢，欲害使者，使者俯伏而走。胥曰：「報汝平王，欲國不滅，釋吾父兄；若不爾者，楚為墟矣。」使返報平王。王聞之，即發大軍追子胥至江，失其所在，不獲而返。

子胥行至大江，仰天行哭林澤之中，言：「楚王無道，殺吾父兄，願吾因於諸侯以報讎矣。」聞太子建在宋，胥欲往之。

伍奢初聞子胥之亡，曰：「楚之君臣，且苦兵矣。」

尚至楚就父，俱戮於市。

3.5. Bi Wuji furthermore made a suggestion to King Ping, saying, “Wu She has two sons and both of them are worthy. If we do not kill them, they will become a worry for Chu. We could use their father as our hostage and thereby summon them.” The king sent an envoy and informed Wu She, saying, “If you could call your two sons to come, you will survive; otherwise, you will die." Wu She said, "I, your subject, have two sons. The elder is named Wu Shang and the younger Wu Zixu. Wu Shang, as a person, is kind, gentle, humane, and trustworthy. If he heard my call, he would come immediately. Wu Zixu, as a person, was fond of civil service when he was young and practiced military arts when he grew up. Civil service governs the state and military arts stabilize the realm. Wu Zixu holds fast to his principles and restrains his anger. He would tolerate slander and endure humiliation. Even if he were wronged, he would not dispute it. He will thus be able to achieve great things. This is a man of foresight; how would you make him come?"[25]

King Ping figured that Wu She was bragging about his two sons.[26] He then sent an emissary driving a four-horse carriage and carrying official seals and ribbons in sealed boxes to deceptively summon Wu Shang and Wu Zixu,[27] and to declare to them,[28] "Congratulations to the two of you! Your father Wu She, because of his loyalty, trustworthiness, kindness, and humaneness, has avoided calamity and received a pardon. In his heart, King Ping was ashamed for imprisoning a loyal minister, and outside of the state, he feared humiliation before the many lords. Therefore, reversing himself, he has appointed Wu She as the prime minister and installed you two as marquises.[29] Wu Shang is to be given the title of Marquis of Hongdo,[30] Wu Zixu Marquis of Gai.[31] They are not far from each other, only three hundred *li*. Wu She has been imprisoned for a long time and worriedly misses his two sons. For these reasons the king sent me to come and present to you these seals and ribbons."

---

25. Bi Wuji's suggestion and Wu She's comments on his two sons are also found in *Shuihudi*, strips #96–98. It is developed in Wu Zixu's biography in *Shiji*. See *Shiji*, 66:2172. The *Yue jue shu* narrative shows a much closer connection to the *Shuihudi* text. For *Yue jue shu* accounts, see Li Bujia, 17–18; Milburn, 83–84.

26. An alternative reading of this sentence is: King Ping told Wu She, "Indeed you are praising your sons!" It does not appear that he is addressing Wu She here because in the previous paragraph it says that the king sent an envoy to Wu She and asked him to call his sons.

27. 駟馬 (*sima*) refers to the carriage pulled by four horses; it is faster than a carriage pulled by two horses. In the past, official seals were usually tied with silk ribbons of different colors to indicate the post and rank.

28. 令 (*ling*) should be rendered here as 告 (*gao*), "to declare," "to announce."

29. This is a much more elaborate narrative in comparison to that in *Shiji*, 66:2172. The envoy is saying that the king has changed his mind from punishing Wu She to rewarding his loyalty. The *Sibu beiyao* 四部備要 edition has 反進 (*fanjin*) instead of 反遇 (*fanyu*). 遇 (*yu*) means to "treat," to "entertain." For example, in *Shiji*, Scholar Hou 侯生 said to Prince Wuji 無忌 of Wei that the prince has treated him well (*gongzi yu chen hou* 公子遇臣厚). See *Shiji*, 77:2380.

30. In Eastern Han, Hongdu was a library in the capital city Luoyang where the imperial books were stored. It was also the name of a gate at the palace and an academy was established near it. This is probably not a real county or district named Hongdu in the Spring and Autumn period.

31. Gai was actually a place in Qi, not Chu, and the king of Chu had no control over it. Like the name of Hongdu, Gai is probably a Chu land made up by the narrator.

Wu Shang said, "My father was detained for three years.[32] My heart was saddened by this.[33] When I ate, I could not enjoy the flavor of the food. Everything I tasted was bitter and I suffered from hunger and thirst. Day and night I thought deeply of him and worried that father would not survive. I want only that my father be released, how dare I covet the seal and ribbon?"[34]

The emissary said, "Your father was in jail for three years. Fortunately, now the king has pardoned him. Because the king had nothing else to bestow upon him, he is installing the two of you as marquises. This news should cause you to go to your father. What else is there to be said?"

Wu Shang then entered the room and reported this to Wu Zixu, saying, "Our father was fortunate enough to avoid death. The two of us are being made marquises. The emissary is at the door, ready to present the seals and ribbons to us. You should meet the emissary."

Wu Zixu said, "Shang, please sit down and I will make a divination about this for you, my brother. Today is the *jiazi* day (seventh day) and the hour now is the division of *si* (9–11 a.m.).[35] The Earthly Branch that indicates the hour is harmed by the Heavenly Stem that indicates the date from below;[36] their *qi* cannot accommodate each other. This suggests that either the ruler is deceiving his ministers or a father is deceiving his son.[37] Thus we will certainly meet death if we go now, what kind of marquisship would that be?"[38]

---

32. According to *Zuozhuan*, the events of Wu She being arrested, Wu Shang and Wu Zixu being summoned by the king, Wu Shang's later execution with his father, and Wu Zixu's flight all occurred in the seventh year of King Ping of Chu (522 BCE). See Lord Zhao 20; Yang Bojun, 1407–09; Durrant, Li, and Schaberg, 1569–71. This also contradicts *WYCQ*, 3.4.

33. 忉 (*ren*) means "grieved" and 怛 (*tan*) means "sorrow and sadness."

34. Wu Shang's response to the emissary is not found in *Zuozhuan*, *Shuihudi*, *Shiji*, and *Yue jue shu*. This is a *WYCQ* addition.

35. From the Shang Dynasty (ca. 1250 BCE), people used ten heavenly stems and twelve earthly branches to reckon the date. The ten heavenly stems include: *jia* 甲, *yi* 乙, *bing* 丙, *ding* 丁, *wu* 戊, *ji* 己, *geng* 庚, *xin* 辛, *ren* 壬, and *gui* 癸; the twelve earthly branches are: *zi* 子, *chou* 丑, *yin* 寅, *mao* 卯, *chen* 辰, *si* 巳, *wu* 午, *wei* 未, *shen* 申, *you* 酉, *xu* 戌, and *hai* 亥. The combinations of the stems and branches form a cycle of sixty terms. The first term *jiazi* combines the first stem with the first branch, the second term combines the second stem with the second branch. In total, this generates sixty terms to record day and year. Because this event occurred after the third month of the fifth year of King Liao of Wu (see *WYCQ*, 3.4.), it was the next *jiazi* day, which was the seventh day in the fourth month of the year. In addition to this, the twelve earthly branches were also used to mark the time of the day, which was divided into twelve periods, each period being registered by one earthly branch. The period of *si* corresponds to nine to eleven o'clock in the morning.

36. According to the Five Phases principle, the hourly division *si* corresponds to fire while *zi* in the date *jiazi* is associated with water. One Five Phases theory suggests that the five phases overcome each other, and water extinguishes fire, thus the day brings harm to the hours.

37. The earthly branches reckoning hours also symbolize ministers while the heavenly stems are the ruler. When the branch is harmed by the stem, it suggests that the minister will be harmed by the ruler. Therefore Wu Zixu believes that they will be killed by King Ping together with their father if they follow the king's command.

38. Wu Zixu's divination is not found in *Shiji* or *Yue jue shu*.

Wu Shang said, "It is not that I am longing for the marquisship; I simply want to see our father. If I could see him once and bid farewell to him, I would be content whether I live or die."

Wu Zixu said, "Shang, please do not go. I shall secure father's life. Chu is afraid of my bravery and because of this situation dares not kill him. If you, my brother, make the wrong decision and go, you definitely will not escape death."

Wu Shang said, "The love between father and son is where affection comes from. If by any chance I could see him, I would take the chance to extend my affection to him."

Upon hearing this, Wu Zixu sighed and answered, "If you and father were both killed, how could you show your innocence to the world? If injustice and enmity are not avenged, humiliation will grow every day. Shang, if you depart from here, this is where I will bid you farewell."[39]

Wu Shang shed tears and said, "If I survive, I will be laughed at by the world, and if I end up an old man on this earth, to which state should I go?[40] All in all, I am useless if I cannot revenge father's death. You have steeped yourself in the civil and military arts, are brave in strategizing, and are capable of responding to the injustices done to your father and older brother. If I can return, it will be a blessing from heaven. But if I thereby die for this, it is also what I am happy to do."

Wu Zixu said, "Please go, Shang. I will leave without looking back. I hope you will not encounter difficulty; for even if you become remorseful how will you pursue another course of action?"[41]

Wu Shang then shed tears, bid farewell to Wu Zixu, and departed together with the emissary. Once Chu captured Wu Shang, they detained and jailed him. Furthermore, the Chu king sent men to chase after and catch Wu Zixu. Wu Zixu thereupon left Chu with a stretched bow and nocked arrow.[42] When

---

39. In *Shiji*, Wu Shang is portrayed as a filial son and dominates the speech. He understands the danger and is willing to sacrifice his life in order to follow his father's summons. At the same time, he asks Wu Zixu to flee in order to avenge their father. In *WYCQ*, however, Wu Zixu is the dominant one and Wu Shang is no longer a character with a strong personality.

40. This refers to the story of Jizi 急子 in *Zuozhuan*, Lord Huan 16. Lord Xuan of Wei sent his son Jizi to Qi and arranged bandits to kill the son at the border. When Jizi's half-brother told him their father's plan and urged him to run away, Jizi refused, saying that a son must obey his father and only if there is a state where there is not a father can a son disregard his father's command. Jizi then prepared to be assassinated on his journey. Wu Shang is using this story to demonstrate his filial piety. For Jizi's story, see Yang Bojun, 146; Durrant, Li, and Schaberg, 127–29.

41. Wu Zixu is saying that if Wu Shang is to be killed by the king it is too late for him to feel regret.

42. Sima Zhen's 司馬貞 commentary to Wu Zixu's biography in *Shiji* reads 貫 (*guan*) as 彎 (*wan*), "stretching." See *Shiji*, 66:2172.

the Chu army was chasing him, they met his wife, who told them, "Wu Zixu is gone. He has already escaped three hundred *li*."[43] When an emissary caught up with Wu Zixu in the wild fields, Wu Zixu stretched his bow and notched an arrow, attempting to kill the emissary, but the emissary ducked and ran away. Wu Zixu said, "Report this to your King Ping: if he wants to keep his state from being destroyed, he must release my father and brother. If he refuses to do so, Chu will be ruined."[44] The emissary returned and reported this to King Ping. Hearing this, the king immediately sent a large number of troops to apprehend Wu Zixu. They arrived at the river but lost his trail, so they returned without having captured him.

Wu Zixu arrived at a large river. Looking up at the sky, he wandered and cried among groves and marshes, saying, "The king of Chu is unjust; he killed my father and older brother. I wish I could rely upon the lords and seek my revenge." He heard that Jian, the prince of Chu, was in Song. Wu Zixu wanted to go there.

When Wu She heard that Wu Zixu had fled, he said, "The ruler and ministers of Chu will soon suffer warfare."

Wu Shang arrived at the Chu capital and joined his father. They were executed at the market together.

3.6. 伍員奔宋，道遇申包胥，謂曰：「楚王殺吾兄父，為之奈何？」申包胥曰：「於乎！吾欲教子報楚，則為不忠；教子不報，則為無親友也。子其行矣，吾不容言。」子胥曰：「吾聞父母之讎，不與戴天履地；兄弟之讎，不與同域接壤；朋友之讎，不與鄰鄉共里。今吾將復楚，辜以雪父兄之恥。」申包胥曰：「子能亡之，吾能存之；子能危之，吾能安之。」胥遂奔宋。

3.6. Wu Zixu hurried to Song. On the road he ran into Shen Baoxu and told him, "The king of Chu killed my older brother and my father. What should I do about this?"[45] Shen Baoxu said, "Alas! Were I to council you to

---

43. This is not found in *Shuihudi*, *Shiji*, and *Yue jue shu*. In comparison to these three earlier sources, *WYCQ* has added several female characters with speeches and actions. These new characters include Wu Zixu's wife, Goujian's wife singing, and the Yue girl skillful in fighting with a sword. *WYCQ* also changes Moye into a female sword master and makes her and Ganjiang a couple.

44. *Shuihudi* strips #38, 37, 36, and 35 contain fragments of Wu Zixu's words to the emissary. This is adopted by *Yue jue shu*. *Shiji* does not have any conversation between Wu Zixu and the emissary.

45. Shen Baoxu was a Chu minister. When Wu Zixu conquered the Chu capital Ying, Shen Baoxu went to Qin begging for help. He cried at the Qin court for seven days and seven nights. Eventually the ruler of Qin was moved by his loyalty to Chu and sent troops to save Chu. Accounts of Shen Baoxu are found in *Zuozhuan*, Lord Ding 4; *Zhanguo ce*; and *Shiji*. See Yang Bojun, 1548; Durrant, Li, and Schaberg, 1761; Liu Xiang 劉向 *Zhangguo ce* (Shanghai: Shanghai guji chubanshe, 1985), 517; and *Shiji*, 40:1716.

seek revenge against Chu, then I would be disloyal; but were I to council you not to seek vengeance, then I would be abandoning a friend. Perhaps you should go; I cannot say anything." Wu Zixu said, "I have heard that 'one cannot live under the same sky and stand on the same ground with the enemy of one's parents, cannot reside in the same land or adjacent neighborhood with the enemy of one's brother, cannot live in the nearby village or in the same alley with the enemy of one's friend.'[46] Now I am going to avenge Chu's crime in order to wipe out my father's and brother's shame."[47] Shen Baoxu said, "Although you can destroy Chu, I can save it; although you can endanger it, I can rescue it."[48] Wu Zixu then hurried to Song.[49]

3.7. 宋元公無信於國，國人惡之。大夫華氏謀殺元公，國人與華氏，因作大亂。子胥乃與太子建俱奔鄭，鄭人甚禮之。太子建又適晉，晉頃公曰：「太子既在鄭，鄭信太子矣。太子能為內應而滅鄭，即以鄭封太子。」太子還鄭，事未成，會欲私其從者，從者知其謀，乃告之於鄭。鄭定公與子產誅殺太子建。

3.7. Lord Yuan of Song was not trusted in his state and the people hated him. The Hua clan, serving as grand ministers, plotted to kill Lord Yuan. People in the capital were on the Hua clan's side, thereby causing great disorder.[50] Wu Zixu fled to Zheng with Prince Jian. Zheng accorded them great respect. Prince Jian furthermore went to Jin. Lord Qing of Jin said, "Since you, Prince, have already been to Zheng and Zheng trusts you, if you will be our insider and help us destroy Zheng, we will accordingly enfeoff Zheng to you." The prince returned to Zheng. His plan was not yet complete when it happened that he secretly wanted to kill his

---

46. The "Quli" 曲禮 chapter in *Liji* says that one cannot live under the same sky with the enemy of one's father; when running into the foe of one's brother, one attacks immediately without going home to retrieve a weapon; one should also not reside in the same state with the enemy of a friend. See Sun Xidan, 87.

47. The word 辜 (*gu*) means 罪 (*zui*), "crime."

48. This encounter is not found in *Shuihudi*, *Shiji*, or *Yue jue shu*.

49. *Lüshi chunqiu* has a story of Wu Zixu ascending Mount Taihang and observing the state of Zheng. He realized that Zheng was not the state that could help him avenge his father; he thereupon traveled south and arrived at Xu. *Shuihudi* strip #100 also has fragment sentences that describe Wu Zixu ascending Mount Taihang and deciding to leave the state (not specified due to the loss of the pieces). See Xu Weiyu 許維遹, *Lüshi chunqiu jishi* 呂氏春秋集釋 (Beijing: Zhonghua shuju, 2015), 231.

50. *Zuozhuan*, Lord Zhao 20.3 reports that Lord Yuan hated the Hua and Xiang clans. The Hua and Xiang clans then plotted to kill the lord. They killed some supporters of the lord and detained him. Eventually the lord was forced to make a covenant with Hua and Xiang. See Yang Bojun, 1409–10; Durrant, Li, and Schaberg, 1573.

attendant.[51] The attendant knew his plan and reported this to Zheng. Lord Ding of Zheng and Zichan executed Jian.[52]

3.8. 建有子名勝，伍員與勝奔吳。到昭關，關吏欲執之，伍員因詐曰：「上所以索我者，美珠也。今我已亡矣，將去取之。」關吏因舍之。

與勝行去，追者在後，幾不得脫。至江，江中有漁父乘船從下方泝水而上。子胥呼之，謂曰：「漁父，渡我！」如是者再。漁父欲渡之，適會旁有人窺之，因而歌曰：「日月昭昭乎侵已馳，與子期乎蘆之漪。」

子胥即止蘆之漪。漁父又歌曰：「日已夕兮，予心憂悲；月已馳兮，何不渡為？事寖急兮，當奈何？」子胥入船。漁父知其意也，乃渡之千潯之津。

子胥既渡，漁父乃視之，有其飢色。乃謂曰：「子俟我此樹下，為子取餉。」漁父去後，子胥疑之，乃潛身於深葦之中。有頃，父來，持麥飯、鮑魚羹、盎漿，求之樹下，不見，因歌而呼之，曰：「蘆中人，蘆中人，豈非窮士乎？」如是至再，子胥乃出蘆中而應。漁父曰：「吾見子有飢色，為子取餉，子何嫌哉？」子胥曰：「性命屬天，今屬丈人，豈敢有嫌哉？」

二人飲食畢，欲去，胥乃解百金之劍以與漁者：「此吾前君之劍，中有七星，價直百金，以此相答。」漁父曰：「吾聞楚之法令：得伍胥者，賜粟五萬石，爵執圭，豈圖取百金之劍乎？」遂辭不受。謂子胥曰：「子急去，勿留，且為楚所得？」子胥曰：「請丈人姓字。」漁父曰：「今日凶凶，兩賊相逢，吾所謂渡楚賊也。兩賊相得，得形於默，何用姓字為？子為蘆中人，吾為漁丈人，富貴莫相忘也。」子胥曰：「諾。」既去，誡漁父曰：「掩子之盎漿，無令其露。」漁父諾。子胥行數步，顧視漁者，已覆船自沉於江水之中矣。

3.8. Jian had a son named Sheng; Wu Zixu escaped to Wu with Sheng. When they arrived at the Shao Pass,[53] the official at the pass wanted to arrest them. Wu Zixu thereupon lied to him, saying, "The reason the king searches for me is because I have a beautiful pearl. Now I have lost it. If you arrest me,

51. The character 殺 (*sha*), "to kill," is missing here.

52. See also Wu Zixu's biography in *Shiji*, 66:2173.

53. The Shao Pass is at the border between Chu and Wu. It is located in modern-day Hanshan County in Anhui Province.

I will tell the king that you have taken and swallowed it."[54] The official at the pass then released them.[55]

Wu Zixu escaped on foot with Sheng. Their pursuers followed them and they were close to being caught. When they arrived at the river,[56] there was an old fisherman rowing a boat against the stream. Wu Zixu called the fisherman, saying, "Fisherman, take us across the river!" He shouted this twice. When the fisherman was about to take them across the river, it happened there was someone nearby spying on them; therefore the fisherman sang:

The bright sun and moon are slowly receding,[57]
I will meet you at the reedy bank.

Wu Zixu then waited at the bank of reeds. The fisherman again chanted:

Now the sun has already set,
And my heart is filled with sorrow.
The moon is already gone,
So why not cross the river?
The situation is urgent,
What should we do about it?

Wu Zixu jumped into the boat. The fisherman understood his intention and took him to a crossing point that was far away.[58]

After Wu Zixu had already crossed the river, the fisherman looked at him and saw that he looked hungry. He then told Wu Zixu, "Wait for me under this tree, sir; I will fetch some food for you." After the fisherman had gone, Wu Zixu was suspicious of him and hid himself deep in the reeds. Soon the

---

54. This line in the *Sibu congkan* 四部叢刊 edition is 將去取之 (*jiang qu qu zhi*). However, in the "Shuolin shang" 說林上 chapter in *Hanfeizi*, Wu Zixu tells the pass official that he has lost the pearl and that he will tell the king of Chu that the official has swallowed the pearl if the official arrests Wu Zixu and sends him to the court. Wu Zixu thus is suggesting to the official that the king might believe Wu Zixu and cut the official's belly open to retrieve the pearl if the official arrests him. See Chen Qiyou, 421.

55. This episode is not found in *Shiji*.

56. There is a controversy as to which river this is. Some believe it is the Li River 溧水 while others think it is the Yangzi River. Because of the fictional nature of Wu Zixu's story, I will simply leave the river unidentified.

57. The line in *Yue jue shu* reads: "日昭昭，侵已施 (*ri zhaozhao, jin yi shi*)." 侵 (*qin*) is the alternative of 浸 (*jin*), "slowly, gradually." 施 (*shi*) and 馳 (*chi*) are interchangeable here, meaning "the sun is slanting." See Li Bujia, 18; Milburn, 85.

58. According to Xu Tianhu, 潯 (*xun*) should be read as 尋 (*xun*), which is a measure of length that is eight *chi* 尺. Cf. Zhang Jue, 49n8. A thousand *xun* is meant just to suggest the distance is very far.

fisherman returned with wheat meal, salted fish stew, and a bottle of water.[59] He looked for Wu Zixu under the tree but could not find him, so he called him, singing, "Man in the reeds, man in the reeds, aren't you worthy but in dire straits?" He called out like this twice; Wu Zixu then emerged from the reeds and answered him. The fisherman said, "I saw you, sir, looking hungry and went to fetch food for you. Why do you doubt my intentions?" Wu Zixu said, "My life once belonged to heaven but now it is in your hands, old sir.[60] How could I dare have any doubt about you?"[61]

When the two of them had finished eating and drinking and were about to part, Wu Zixu took off his sword, which was worth a hundred pieces of gold, and presented it to the fisherman, saying, "This sword belonged to my deceased father. It has the Seven Stars of the Northern Dipper carved on it and is valued at one hundred pieces of gold.[62] I repay your kindness with this." The fisherman replied, "I have heard the command of the Chu King: whoever catches Wu Zixu will be awarded fifty thousand piculs of grain and the honorific rank of Jade Tablet Holder.[63] Why then would I want to take a sword worth a hundred pieces of gold?" He thus declined and did not accept it. He told Wu Zixu, "Please leave quickly, sir. Do not stay, or you will be caught by Chu." Wu Zixu said, "May I have your name, old sir?" The fisherman said, "It is an ominous day today; two outlaws met.[64] I am the so-called one who rowed the Chu outlaw across the river. Two outlaws got along with each other and their rapport demonstrates itself through tacit agreement. What is the use of asking for names? You, sir, are the man in the reeds and I am an old fisherman. Don't forget me if you become rich and noble." Wu Zixu said, "I promise." When he was about to leave, he cautioned the fisherman, "Hide your water bottle, do not let it be found." The fisherman agreed. After walking several paces, Wu Zixu looked back at the fisherman. The fisherman had already overturned his boat and drowned himself in the river.

---

59. 鮑魚 (*baoyu*) here refers to salted fish. 盎 (*ang*) is a container with a big bottom and narrow top.

60. 丈人 (*zhangren*) is an honorific way to address elders.

61. The fisherman feeding Wu Zixu is not found in other texts. This detail is added by the author of *WYCQ*.

62. The Seven Stars of the Northern Dipper is the constellation of Ursa Major.

63. This is an honorific rank Chu established in the Spring and Autumn period. It is the highest honorific rank in Chu. The jade tablet, *gui*, is often used in ritual ceremonies and is held by a king, lord, or prince.

64. Referring to Wu Zixu and the fisherman himself.

3.9. 子胥默然，遂行至吳。疾於中道，乞食溧陽。適會女子擊綿於瀨水之上，筥中有飯。子胥遇之，謂曰：「夫人，可得一餐乎？」女子曰：「妾獨與母居，三十未嫁，飯不可得。」子胥曰：「夫人賑窮途少飯，亦何嫌哉？」女子知非恆人，遂許之，發其簞筥，飯其盎漿，長跪而與之。子胥再餐而止。女子曰：「君有遠逝之行，何不飽而餐之？」子胥已餐而去，又謂女子曰：「掩夫人之壺漿，無令其露。」女子歎曰：「嗟乎！妾獨與母居三十年，自守貞明，不願從適，何宜饋飯而與丈夫？越虧禮儀，妾不忍也。子行矣。」子胥行五步，反顧，女子已自投於瀨水矣。於乎！貞明執操，其丈夫女哉！

3.9. Wu Zixu was dumbstruck and then traveled to Wu. He was struck by illness on his way. As he was begging for food at Liyang, it happened there was a woman pounding silk padding at the bank of the Lai River.[65] She had a basket with food in it.[66] Wu Zixu approached her and asked, "Lady, may I have a meal?" The woman said, "I live alone with my mother; at the age of thirty I have not yet married.[67] I cannot offer you any meal." Wu Zixu said, "Lady, please relieve a desperate man on the road. Even if the food is only a little, what complaint would I have?" The woman knew that he was not an ordinary man and thereupon agreed to his request.[68] She opened her basket and gave him her water.[69] Kneeling uprightly,[70] she presented the food to him. Wu Zixu took two bites and stopped. The woman said, "You, noble sir, have a long trip, why don't you eat to your heart's content?" After finishing his meal, Wu Zixu was about to leave. He told the woman, "Please hide your water bottle; do not let it be found." The woman sighed, "Alas, I have lived alone with my mother for thirty years. I have kept my chastity and did not want to get married. How is it appropriate for me to present food and give it to a man?[71] Trespassing, and violating ritual and etiquette are what I cannot bear. Please go, sir." Wu Zixu walked five steps. When he looked back, the woman had already thrown herself

65. Liyang is located in modern-day Jiangsu Province, Liyang County. Lai River is also found in Liyang County.

66. 筥 (*ju*) is a round-shaped basket made of bamboo strips.

67. Women at that time were usually married around the age of fifteen. Thirty is considered very late.

68. 恆 (*heng*) is the same as 常 (*chang*), "common, ordinary."

69. 簞 (*dan*) is also a round-shaped food container made of bamboo.

70. Straightening one's back while kneeling is a posture that shows respect.

71. 丈夫 (*zhangfu*) here refers to an adult man. It was considered inappropriate for a woman to present food to a strange man, as serving food is a wife's duty to her husband.

into the Lai River. Alas! Being chaste, wise, and able to maintain her virtue, she was indeed a woman with a man's merits![72]

3.10. 子胥之吳，乃被髮佯狂，跣足塗面，行乞於市，市人觀，罔有識者。翌日，吳市吏善相者見之，曰：「吾之相人多矣，未嘗見斯人也，非異國之亡臣乎？」乃白吳王僚，具陳其狀：「王宜召之。」王僚曰：「與之俱入。」

公子光聞之，私喜曰：「吾聞楚殺忠臣伍奢，其子子胥勇而且智，彼必復父之讎來入於吳。」陰欲養之。

市吏於是與子胥俱入見王，王僚怪其狀偉：身長一丈，腰十圍，眉間一尺。王僚與語三日，辭無復者。王曰：「賢人也！」子胥知王好之，每入語，語遂有勇壯之氣，稍道其讎，而有切切之色。王僚知之，欲為興師復讎。

公子謀殺王僚，恐子胥前親於王而害其謀，因讒：「伍胥之諫伐楚者，非為吳也，但欲自復私讎耳。王無用之。」

子胥知公子光欲害王僚，乃曰：「彼光有內志，未可說以外事。」入見王僚，曰：「臣聞諸侯不為匹夫興師用兵於比國。」王僚曰：「何以言之？」子胥曰：「諸侯專為政，非以意救急後興師。今大王踐國制威，為匹夫興兵，其義非也。臣固不敢如王之命。」吳王乃止。

3.10. After he arrived at Wu, Wu Zixu untied his hair and pretended to be crazy.[73] He bared his feet, smeared mud on his face, and begged in the market. People in the market stared at him but none of them could recognize him. The next day, the clerk of Wu market, who was good at physiognomy,[74] saw him and said, "I have inspected many people, yet I have not seen a man like him. Isn't he a fugitive minister from another state?" He then reported this to King Liao of Wu, described Wu Zixu in detail, and suggested, "Your Majesty should summon him."[75] King Liao said, "Bring him in with you."

Upon hearing this, Gongzi Guang was secretly delighted, saying, "I have heard that Chu has murdered the loyal minister Wu She. Wu She's son Wu

72. Occasionally we have the narrator speaking to us in the story, which is not unusual in Chinese storytelling. Here the narrator is praising the woman. This is not found in *Yue jue shu*, see Li Bujia, 18; Milburn, 86.

73. In the past, men usually tied their hair in a knot on the top of their head. Untied hair was either a non-Chinese custom or an indicator of the mentally ill.

74. This refers to *WYCQ*, 3.1 in which Gongzi Guang secretly sought worthy men and appointed one who, as the clerk of the market, was good at physiognomy.

75. The narrative is a little bit conflicting here. The clerk was hired by Gongzi Guang who wanted to find a worthy man to assist in his plan of assassinating King Liao. The story here, however, says that Wu Zixu was recommended to the king instead.

Zixu is brave and wise. He must have come to Wu in order to avenge his father." He secretly wanted to support him.

The market clerk then went to court with Wu Zixu to receive an audience from the king. King Liao marveled at Wu Zixu's huge build: he was one *zhang* tall, his waist was ten *wei* around and the gap between his eyebrows was one *chi* wide.[76] King Liao conversed with Wu Zixu for three days and found that Wu Zixu never repeated any words.[77] The king said, "This is a worthy man." Wu Zixu knew that the king liked him. Every time he entered the palace to talk with the king, he showed an air of bravery and heroism. Over time, he mentioned his foe with a display of intense hatred. King Liao thereupon knew that Wu Zixu wanted the Wu state to mobilize its troops and seek revenge for him.

Gongzi Guang plotted to assassinate King Liao and was afraid that Wu Zixu's being favored by the king would undermine his plan; he thereupon slandered Wu Zixu, saying, "Wu Zixu's plan to attack Chu is not for the benefit of Wu. He simply wants it for his own personal revenge. Your Majesty should not adopt his plan."

Wu Zixu knew that Gongzi Guang intended to kill King Liao and therefore said to himself, "This Gongzi Guang has ambitions within this state; he cannot be persuaded about matters that concern other states." He entered the court to see King Liao and told him, "I, your subject, have heard that the many lords do not, for the sake of commoners, mobilize troops and dispatch soldiers to neighboring states."[78] King Liao asked, "Why do you say this?" Wu Zixu answered, "Many lords handle state affairs by themselves and do not act from willfulness. They only mobilize their troops to rescue those in great danger. Now Your Majesty rules this state and holds the power; if you send the troops for a commoner, then the cause is not just. I, your subject, resolutely dare not follow Your Majesty's command." The King of Wu then abandoned his plan.

---

76. These are all measurements of length. One *zhang* equals roughly 2.31 meters. Ten *wei* equals roughly 1.55 meters and one *chi* is approximately 0.231 meters. In ancient texts, a large and impressive physical body often indicates that a person possesses great virtue. This is clearly influenced by Mencius's belief that there is invariably a physical demonstration of one's inner moral quality. For discussion on this, see Mark Csikszentmihalyi, *Material Virtue: Ethics and the Body in Early China* (Leiden: Brill, 2004).

77. This is to suggest that Wu Zixu is an eloquent speaker and has many ideas to give as advice to the king.

78. 比國 (*biguo*) means 鄰國 (*linguo*), "neighboring state." Here Wu Zixu refers to Chu.

3.11. 子胥退耕於野，求勇士薦之公子光，欲以自媚。乃得勇士專諸。

專諸者，堂邑人也。伍胥之亡楚如吳時，遇之於途。專諸方與人鬥，將就敵，其怒有萬人之氣，甚不可當。其妻一呼即還。子胥怪而問其狀：「何夫子之怒盛也，聞一女子之聲而折道，寧有說乎？」專諸曰：「子視吾之儀，寧類愚者也？何言之鄙也？夫屈一人之下，必伸萬人之上。」子胥因相其貌：碓顙而深目，虎膺而熊背，戾於從難。知其勇士，陰而結之，欲以為用。遭公子光之有謀也，而進之公子光。

光既得專諸而禮待之。公子光曰：「天以夫子輔孤之失根也。」專諸曰：「前王餘昧卒，僚立，自其分也。公子何因而欲害之乎？」光曰：「前君壽夢有子四人：長曰諸樊，則光之父也；次曰餘祭；次曰餘昧；次曰季札。札之賢也，將卒，傳付適長，以及季札。念季札為使，亡在諸侯未還，餘昧卒，國空，有立者，適長也，適長之後，即光之身也。今僚何以當代立乎？吾力弱，無助於掌事之間，非用有力徒，能安吾志。吾雖代立，季子東還，不吾廢也。」專諸曰：「何不使近臣從容言於王側，陳前王之命，以諷其意，令知國之所歸。何須私備劍士，以捐先王之德？」光曰：「僚素貪而恃力，知進之利，不睹退讓。吾故求同憂之士，欲與之并力。惟夫子詮斯義也。」專諸曰：「君言甚露乎，於公子何意也？」光曰：「不也，此社稷之言也，小人不能奉行，惟委命矣。」專諸曰：「願公子命之。」公子光曰：「時未可也。」專諸曰：「凡欲殺人君，必前求其所好。吳王何好？」光曰：「好味。」專諸曰：「何味所甘？」光曰：「好嗜魚之炙也。」專諸乃去，從太湖學炙魚，三月得其味，安坐待公子命之。

3.11. Wu Zixu retreated from the court and plowed in the fields. He looked for a brave man whom he would introduce to Gongzi Guang, hoping this would earn him Guang's favor. He eventually found a brave man named Zhuanzhu.[79]

Zhuanzhu was a native of Tangyi. When Wu Zixu was running away from Chu and going to Wu, he encountered Zhuangzhu along his way. At that time Zhuanzhu was fighting with a man. When he was about to approach his rival, his rage was so formidable that it had an air of being able to overwhelm ten thousand men. However, once his wife called him, he returned immediately. Perplexed by this, Wu Zixu asked Zhuanzhu the reason, "How furious was your anger; yet you turned away once you heard

79. Zhuanzhu is also mentioned in *Zuozhuan*, Zhao 27. Sima Qian wrote a biography of Zhuanzhu, see *Shiji*, 26:2516–18. The *WYCQ* story of Zhuanzhu is much more elaborate than Sima Qian's account. The following *WYCQ* stories of Zhuanzhu's fighting with people, Wu Zixu's recommendation of Zhuanzhu to Gongzi Guang, and the conversation between Zhuanzhu and Gongzi Guang on whether King Liao should be assassinated are not reported in Sima Qian's *Shiji*.

a woman's voice. Is there an explanation for this?" Zhuanzhu said, "Look at my demeanor, sir. Do I look like a foolish man? Why are your words so mean? Those able to bend under one man will certainly be able to rise above ten thousand men." Wu Zixu then examined Zhuanzhu's features. He had bulging eyebrow ridges but deep eyes. His chest resembled that of a tiger and his back that of a bear. He engaged problems with fury. Wu Zixu knew that Zhuanzhu was a brave man and secretly befriended him, planning to use him. It happened that Gongzi Guang had some plans for usurpation, so Wu Zixu recommended Zhuanzhu to him.

After Gongzi Guang had obtained allegiance from Zhuanzhu, he treated Zhuanzhu with respect. Gongzi Guang said, "Heaven uses you, sir, to make up for my loss of the position of legitimate successor." Zhuanzhu asked, "After the former king Yumo had died, Liao was established, due to his legitimate status. You, Gongzi, for what reason want to kill him?" Gongzi Guang explained, "The former king had four sons.[80] The oldest was called Zhufan, who was my father. The second was Yuzhai, the third was Yumo, and the youngest was Jizha. Because Jizha was worthy, when the former king was about to die, he passed the throne to his first son, but hoped it would eventually reach Jizha. When Yumo died, Jizha was serving as a diplomat to the states of other lords' and was unable to return. Thus the throne lacked a candidate. If anyone was to be established, it had to be the oldest living son. The descendant of the oldest son is me, Guang. Now, for what reason is it proper for Liao to replace me and be established?[81] My power is weak and I received no assistance from those who have control of state affairs. Without relying upon a man of strength, how can I achieve my ambition? If I were to replace Liao as king, then when Jizha returned from the East he would not depose me." Zhuanzhu said, "In order to insinuate his thoughts on the matter, why don't you have the king's favored ministers talk to him at their leisure to explain the former king's unheeded command and thus inform the king to whom the state rightly belongs? Why is it necessary to secretly retain a swordsman, thereby neglecting the virtue of the former king?" Gongzi Guang answered, "King Liao is always greedy and relies upon his power. He knows the benefits of advancing yet pays no attention to yielding. I therefore seek a man who can share my worries and I wish to strive together with him. I hope that you, sir, are able to interpret the meaning of

---

80. This is King Shoumeng.

81. King Shoumeng had four sons: Guang was the son of the eldest son, Zhufan; and Liao the son of the third son, Yumo. The first three sons had died, and the throne should have been handed down to the youngest son Jizha, but he refused. So, instead of it passing to Guang, the son of Zhufan, Yumo instead gave it to his own son Liao before he died.

my words."[82] Zhuanzhu said, "Your words are too explicit. What, after all, is your intention?" Gongzi Guang replied, "It is not that my words are too explicit: they are about the fate of the state. But I, a humble man, am not able to carry it out. I simply entrust my life to you." Zhuanzhu said, "I wish you, Gongzi, would issue your command." Gongzi Guang said, "The time is not yet proper." Zhuanzhu asked, "In general, if one plots to kill a ruler, one must find what the ruler favors before carrying out the action. What does the king of Wu like?" Gongzi Guang said, "The king is fond of food." Zhuanzhu asked, "What dish is his favorite?" Gongzi Guang said, "He likes grilled fish." Zhuanzhu then left and went to Taihu Lake to learn how to grill fish. After three months, he mastered the art and waited calmly for the command from Gongzi Guang.

3.12. 八年，僚遣公子伐楚，大敗楚師。因迎故太子建母於鄭，鄭君送建母珠玉簪珥，欲以解殺建之過。

3.12. In the eighth year (519 BCE), King Liao sent Gongzi Guang to attack Chu and he inflicted massive losses upon Chu.[83] He then received the deceased prince Jian's mother from Zheng. The lord of Zheng gave Jian's mother pearls, jade, hairpins, and jade earrings, wishing to ameliorate his wrongdoing in executing Jian.[84]

3.13. 九年，吳使光伐楚，拔居巢、鍾離。吳所以相攻者，初，楚之邊邑胛梁之女與吳邊邑處女蠶，爭界上之桑，二家相攻，吳國不勝，遂更相伐，滅吳之邊邑。吳怒，故伐楚，取二邑而去。

3.13. In the ninth year (518 BCE), Wu sent Gongzi Guang to attack Chu. Gongzi Guang conquered Juchao and Zhongli. The reason for Wu's attack was because, previously, a girl from Biliang, a city on the border of Chu, and a young girl from a city on the border of Wu, both raised silkworms and competed for mulberry leaves along the border. The two families fought against each other and the family in Wu lost. Then the two states mutually

---

82. Gongzi Guang is saying that he wishes Zhuanzhu could understand his intention and help him to assassinate King Liao.

83. *Zuozhuan*, Zhao 23 has a more detailed account on this event. It is also recorded in *Shiji*, "Hereditary Household of Chu," with much elaborated stories. See Yang Bojun, 1445–46; Durrant, Li, and Schaberg, 1621–23; *Shiji*, 40:1714.

84. Jian plotted with the state of Jin to destroy the state of Zheng and was executed by Zheng. See *WYCQ*, 3.7.

attacked one another. Wu's city near the border was destroyed. Wu was angry about this and thereupon attacked Chu, took two cities, and left.[85]

3.14. 十二年，冬，楚平王卒。伍子胥謂白公勝曰：「平王卒，吾志不悉矣！然楚國存，吾何憂矣？」白公默然不對。伍子胥坐泣於室。

3.14. In the twelfth year (515 BCE), in winter, King Ping of Chu died. Wu Zixu told Sheng, Lord Bai,[86] that "King Ping has already died. Our plan cannot be completed. However, the state of Chu still exists, so why should we be concerned about not having a target for our revenge?" Lord Bai kept silent and did not respond. Wu Zixu sat in the room and cried.

3.15. 十三年，春，吳欲因楚葬而伐之，使公子蓋餘、燭傭以兵圍楚，使季札於晉，以觀諸侯之變。楚發兵絕吳後，吳兵不得還。於是公子光心動。伍胥知光之見機也，乃說光曰：「今吳王伐楚，二弟將兵，未知吉凶，專諸之事於斯急矣。時不再來，不可失也。」於是公子見專諸曰：「今二弟伐楚，季子未還，當此之時，不求何獲？時不可失。且光，真王嗣也。」專諸曰：「僚可殺也，母老子弱，弟伐楚，楚絕其後。方今吳外困於楚，內無骨鯁之臣，是無如我何也。」

四月，公子光伏甲士於窋室中，具酒而請王僚。僚白其母，曰：「公子光為我具酒，來請期，無變悉乎？」母曰：「光心氣怏怏，常有愧恨之色，不可不慎。」王僚乃被棠銕之甲三重，使兵衛陳於道，自宮門至於光家之門，階席左右皆王僚之親戚，使坐立侍，皆操長戟交軹。酒酣，公子光佯為足疾，入窋室裹足，使專諸置魚腸劍炙魚中進之。既至王僚前，專諸乃擘炙魚，因推匕首，立戟交軹倚專諸胸，胸斷臆開，匕首如故，以刺王僚，貫甲達背，王僚既死，左右共殺專諸，衆士擾動，公子光伏其甲士以攻僚衆，盡滅之。遂自立，是為吳王闔閭也。乃封專諸之子，拜為客卿。

---

85. *Shiji* has more details on this. It reports that the two families attacked each other, and the Wu family from Biliang was killed. The minister of Biliang was angry about this and attacked the Chu city Zhongli with his troops. Hearing this, the king of Chu was furious and dispatched the Chu army and destroyed Biliang. This caused the anger of the king of Wu, who sent Gongzi Guang to attack Chu with assistance from Chu prince Jian's mother's family. Gongzi Guang destroyed the Chu towns Zhongli and Jucao. See *Shiji*, 40:1714.

86. Lord Bai is Chu prince Jian's son. After Jian was killed by the Zheng people, Sheng fled to Wu with Wu Zixu. Years later he was summoned by the prime minister of Chu, who let Sheng reside in Bai town. Sheng was thus called Lord Bai. He soon rebelled, killing the Chu prime minister and other officials and holding King Hui of Chu as a hostage. He eventually failed and committed suicide. See *Zuozhuan*, Lord Ai 16; Yang Bojun, 1700–04; Durrant, Li, and Schaberg, 1947–53.

季札使還至吳，闔閭以位讓，季札曰：「苟前君無廢，社稷以奉，君也。吾誰怨乎？哀死待生，以俟天命。非我所亂，立者從之，是前人之道。」命哭僚墓，復位而待。

公子蓋餘、燭傭二人將兵遇圍於楚者，聞公子光殺王僚自立，乃以兵降楚，楚封之於舒。

3.15. In the thirteenth year (514 BCE), in spring, Wu wanted to take advantage of the Chu king's funeral to attack Chu. Gongzi Gaiyu and Gongzi Zhuyong were dispatched to lead the troops to besiege Chu.[87] Jizha was sent to Jin in order to observe the lords' response. Chu sent troops and cut off Wu's retreat; the Wu army was unable to return. At that time, Gongzi Guang's thoughts were stirred up.[88] Wu Zixu knew that Gongzi Guang had seen the opportunity, so he persuaded Gongzi Guang, saying, "Now the king of Wu is attacking Chu. His two brothers are commanding the troops, but their fate cannot yet be predicted. The matter entrusted to Zhuanzhu becomes urgent now. This opportunity will not come a second time; do not fail to seize it." Gongzi Guang then went to Zhuanzhu, saying, "Now the two brothers of the king are attacking Chu and Jizha has not yet returned. At a moment like this, what will we gain if we fail to pursue it? Opportunity knocks but once. Moreover, I, Guang, am the true successor of the throne." Zhuanzhu said, "Liao can be killed. His mother is old and his son is young. Moreover, his brothers are attacking Chu and their retreat was cut off by Chu. Now Wu is troubled outside by Chu and inside the state there are no loyal and upright ministers; in this situation he can do nothing to prevent us."

In the fourth month, Gongzi Guang hid armored men in the basement. He then prepared wine and invited King Liao. King Liao told his mother, saying, "Gongzi Guang prepared wine for me and requested a meeting. Perhaps there is nothing to be concerned about." His mother said, "Gongzi Guang is discontented and often has the appearance of humiliation and resentment. You cannot be careless." King Liao then put on three layers of the Tangyi armor and positioned soldiers and guards on the road from the palace gate to the door of Guang's house.[89] On the left and right stairs were all relatives of King Liao. He made both his sitting and standing attendants hold long halberds and cross their weapons with each other. After they were intoxicated by wine, Gongzi Guang pretended to have a pain in his foot and entered the basement to wrap it. He sent Zhuanzhu to hide a "fish-intestine style"

87. This is also recorded in *Zuozhuan*, Lord Zhao 27; see Yang Bojun, 1482; Durrant, Li, and Schaberg, 1673.

88. Referring to Gongzi Guang's plan to assassinate King Liao.

89. Tangyi was a Chu town famous for its iron works, especially weapon-making.

dagger inside a grilled fish and present it to the king.[90] When he arrived in front of King Liao, Zhuanzhu opened the grilled fish and then thrust the dagger forward. The crossed halberds stabbed Zhuanzhu's chest: his chest was broken and his belly cut, but his dagger still thrust toward King Liao, penetrating the latter's armor, and reaching all the way to his back. King Liao died immediately. The king's guards killed Zhuanzhu but the king's men were startled. Gongzi Guang had hidden his armored soldiers and now they attacked King Liao's men and killed them all. He then established himself and was titled King Helü of Wu. The king enfeoffed Zhuanzhu's son and appointed him to a ministerial office.[91]

When Jizha returned to Wu from his diplomatic mission, Helü yielded the throne to him. Jizha said, "If sacrifices to former kings are not neglected and the spirits of land and harvest are offered sacrifices, then you are my king. Who am I to complain? I only lament the deceased and serve the living, following my fate as bestowed by heaven. That I cause no upheaval and obey the one enthroned—this is the principle of those who came before us."[92] He tearfully reported his mission at the tomb of King Liao and then returned to his post and waited upon Helü.

Upon hearing that Gongzi Guang had assassinated King Liao and enthroned himself, the two, Gongzi Gaiyu and Gongzi Zhuyong, who commanded the troops and were surrounded by Chu, led their army to surrender to Chu. Chu gave them land in Shu.

---

90. The sword is so named because of the pattern on its edge that resembled fish intestines.

91. The *WYCQ* story of the assassination of King Liao by Gongzi Guang and Zhuanzhu is developed from the *Zuozhuan* and Sima Qian's *Shiji*. However, details such as Wu Zixu suggesting that Gongzi Guang seize the opportunity of the king's two brothers being out of the capital to attack Chu and King Liao's mother warning the king of the danger of Gongzi Guang's banquet are added by the *WYCQ* account.

92. Jizha's words are also recorded in *Shiji* and *Zuozhuan*, Lord Zhao 27. See *Shiji*, 3:1465; Yang Bojun, 1484; Durrant, Li, and Schaberg, 1675.

# 吳越春秋闔閭內傳第四

## Chapter 4

# The Inner Tradition of Helü

## Introduction

The title of this chapter raises some interesting questions. First, it does not follow the precedent of the previous chapter in which the chapter's first sentence was adopted as its title. This might suggest that Helü was considered a legitimate ruler in the Wu royal linage who inherited the authority passed down from the founder Taibo and King Shoumeng; the reign of King Liao, on the other hand, was treated as a transitional period much like the short-lived Qin dynasty. Even more interesting is that the traditions of the Wu king Helü and his successor Fuchai are titled as the "inner tradition," while at the same time, the chapters of the two kings from Yue, Wuyu, and Goujian, are identified as "outer tradition." Considering the fact that in traditional Chinese thought "inner" 内 (*nei*) is associated with the orthodox, superior "us," and "outer" 外 (*wai*) with the inferior, heterodox "other," the decision to treat the state of Wu as the legitimate one and Yue as its subordinate is perplexing. Yue conquered Wu and become the new hegemon among the states and the attributed author of *WYCQ*, Zhao Ye, was from the Yue region.

The content of the chapter loosely follows the chronology of King Helü's rule. The structure of the chapter apparently continues the *Shiji* tradition, especially as seen in the Basic Annals, in which the goal of providing a comprehensive picture of the time is still the top priority. However, the *WYCQ*'s interest in storytelling often ignores the concise and clear principles of historical writing, indulging instead in introducing anecdotes and occasionally even lengthy tales. The result of this is that the presentation of the characters is more successful than the development of historical threads. In addition to this, many of the accounts in the chapter contradict historical texts such as the *Zuozhuan* and *Shiji* and might be simply adapted from folklore. For example, Yaoli's assassination of Qingji in this chapter is different from the *Zuozhuan* account; it is probably developed from legends circulating during the Warring States period.

Moreover, a considerable number of the stories in this chapter are of a supernatural nature or reflect strong *yinyang* and *chenwei* influences that were typical during the Eastern Han time. These include the stories of Ganjiang casting swords, a father killing his sons in order to make hooks, and the Zhanlu sword fleeing from Wu. In addition to this, the story of Wu Zixu imitating the patterns of heaven and the earth and building the Wu city portrays Wu Zixu as more of a Han magician (*shushu zhishi* 術數之士) than a minister. Even the events in this chapter that are consistent with historical records are more elaborate and pay special attention to details in the historical narratives. For example, this *WYCQ* chapter includes added descriptions of Sun Wu's anger when training the palace ladies, and Lord Huan of Qin chanting the Odes in responding to Shen Baoxu. The readers' overall impression of the chapter is that it is more fictional than historical, probably initiating the so-called historical fiction (*yanyi xiaoshuo* 演義小說) popular in late imperial times.

## Translation

4.1. 闔閭元年，始任賢使能，施恩行惠，以仁義聞於諸侯。

4.1. In the first year of King Helü (514 BCE), the king started to use the worthy, employ the capable, bestow favor, and give benefits to the people. He was famous among the many lords for his humaneness and dutifulness.

4.2. 仁未施，恩未行，恐國人不就，諸侯不信，乃舉伍子胥為行人，以客禮事之，而與謀國政。闔閭謂子胥曰：「寡人欲彊國霸王，何由而可？」伍子胥膝進，垂淚頓首曰：「臣，楚國之亡虜也。父兄棄捐，骸骨不葬，魂不血食。蒙罪受辱，來歸命於大王，幸不加戮，何敢與政事焉？」闔閭曰：「非夫子，寡人不免於縶禦之使；今幸奉一言之教，乃至於斯。何為中道生進退耶？」子胥曰：「臣聞謀議之臣，何足處於危亡之地，然憂除事定，必不為君主所親。」闔閭曰：「不然。寡人非子無所盡議，何得讓乎？吾國僻遠，顧在東南之地，險阻潤濕，又有江海之害；君無守禦，民無所依；倉庫不設，田疇不墾。為之奈何？」子胥良久對曰：「臣聞治國之道，安君理民，是其上者。」闔閭曰：「安君治民，其術奈何？」子胥曰：「凡欲安君治民，興霸成王，從近制遠者，必先立城郭，設守備，實倉廩，治兵庫。斯則其術也。」闔閭曰：「善。夫築城郭，立倉庫，因地制宜，豈有天氣之數以威鄰國者乎？」子胥曰：「有。」闔閭曰：「寡人委計於子。」

子胥乃使相土嘗水，象天法地，造築大城。周迴四十七里，陸門八，以象天八風，水門八，以法地八聰。築小城，周十里，陵門三，不開東面者，欲以絕越明也。立閶門者，以象天門，通閶闔風也。立蛇門者，以象地戶也。闔閭欲西破楚，楚在西北，故立閶門以通天氣，因復名之破楚門。欲東并大越，越在東南，故立蛇門以制敵國。吳在辰，其位龍也，故小城南門上反羽為兩鯢鱙以象龍角。越在巳地，其位蛇也，故南大門上有木蛇，北向首內，示越屬於吳也。

4.2. Before his humaneness spread and his kindness was put into practice, he was concerned that the people would not draw near to him and the many lords would not trust him, therefore he promoted Wu Zixu as his diplomatic envoy.[1] He treated Wu Zixu with the rites for foreign guests and discussed with him the affairs of state.[2] Helü asked Wu Zixu, "I, a man of little virtue, want to strengthen the state and become the hegemon of the allied lords. How should I proceed to achieve this?" Moving forward on his knees,[3] Wu Zixu shed tears and kowtowed, saying, "I, your subject, am a fugitive slave of Chu. I have abandoned my father and older brother, thus their bodies and bones are unburied and their souls receive no blood sacrifices.[4] Wronged and humiliated, I render my life to you, the great king. I would be fortunate to avoid execution. How dare I participate in government affairs." Helü said, "If not for you sir, I, a man of little virtue, would

1. *Xingren* 行人 was the official who took charge of foreign relations. Another famous *xingren* was Wuchen 巫臣, former magistrate of Chu county Shen. The Chu minister Zifan 子反 wanted to marry Lady Xiaji 夏姬. Wuchen dissuaded him from marrying Xiaji and took her as his own wife instead, fleeing with her to Jin. He then came to Wu and served as a *xingren*, teaching Wu troops the arts of archery and chariot driving and leading them to attack Chu. See *Zuozhuan*, Lord Cheng 2; Yang Bojun, 803–05; Durrant, Li, and Schaberg, 727–29. See also *WYCQ*, 2.2.

2. It became more common starting in the late Spring and Autumn period for people to travel to other states to serve as officials there. During the Warring States period, in the state of Qin this type of official was called a "guest minister" 客卿 (*keqing*).

3. People usually sat on their knees in early China. Chairs were probably introduced into China during the Tang dynasty (618–905) but did not become popular until much later.

4. Animal blood was offered to the ancestors as a sacrifice.

not have escaped the jailer.[5] Now, fortunately, I have received your instruction and so have been able to reach this stage.[6] Why do you want to retreat midway to our goal?" Wu Zixu said, "I have heard that when an advisor makes plans for a ruler, he does more than place himself in danger for his ruler. But after trouble is resolved and the situation settled, he is certainly not favored by the ruler."[7] Helü said, "It is not like that. Without you, there would be no one with whom I could thoroughly discuss governmental affairs. Why are you being so modest?[8] My state is in a remote area, situated in the Southeast. Its terrain is difficult and its weather humid; and it also has disastrous floods caused by rivers and the sea. The ruler has no means to defend his state and the people have nothing to rely on. Granaries and storehouses have not yet been built and the fields have not yet been ploughed. What should I do about all this?" After a long while, Wu Zixu replied, "I have heard that the way of governing a state takes stabilizing the ruler and administrating the people as the best plan." Helü asked, "What are the strategies for stabilizing the ruler and governing the people?" Wu Zixu answered, "Those who want to stabilize the ruler; govern the people; rise up to become hegemon, or king; and cause the neighboring states to follow and the distant states to be controlled must first build walled cities, establish defenses and stockpiles, fill the barns and granaries, and make ready the arsenals—this then is the plan."[9] Helü said, "Excellent! As for constructing walled cities, and setting up barns and storehouses, appropriate measures can be implemented in accordance with local conditions. Are there any means of utilizing the configuration of heavenly *qi* to cause the submission of the neighboring states?" Wu Zixu answered, "There are." Helü said, "I, a man of little virtue, entrust the plan to you, sir."

Wu Zixu therefore dispatched men to observe the land and inspect the rivers.[10] Imitating the pattern of heaven and modeled after the earth, he constructed a large city with a surrounding wall forty-seven *li* long. The wall

---

5. Both 縶 (*zhi*) and 槷 (*yu*), which is an alternative to 圉 (*yu*), mean "to arrest, to jail."

6. Referring to Wu Zixu's recommendation of Zhuanzhu in the assassination of King Liao.

7. The meaning of this sentence is that the minister devotes himself to solving problems for the ruler but is usually not favored by the ruler after the crisis is averted.

8. An alternative reading for this sentence is: "How is it possible that I blame you?" Here the word 讓 (*rang*) is read as to blame, to criticize.

9. This seems to be a common theme found not only in military school discussions but also in legalist texts such as the "Ten Mistakes" (Shiguo 十過) chapter in *Hanfeizi*, where Zhang Mengtan 張孟談 gave Zhao Xiangzi 趙襄子 similar advice. See Chen Qiyou, 178–79.

10. 嘗 is read as 試 here, meaning "to test," "to investigate," and "to inspect." The "Yiwen zhi" chapter in *Hanshu* records texts concerning the techniques of investigating the shape of land and choosing an auspicious location for settlement. These texts are categorized as characteristic of the *xingfa* 形法 school. Interestingly, *Shanhai jing* 山海經 is considered a "xingfa" text. See *Hanshu*, 30:1774–75.

had eight ground gates, which symbolized the eight winds in the sky.[11] It also had eight water gates, which symbolized the eight outlets at the edges of the earth.[12] He also constructed a small city, with a city wall ten *li* in circumference.[13] This city had three tall gates. The reason it did not have a gate facing east was to cut off Yue's culture.[14] The city had a Chang Gate to imitate the Heavenly Gate, allowing the west wind to go through.[15] The erecting of Snake Gate was to imitate the Earthly Gate.[16] Helü wanted to destroy Chu to the west. Because Chu was located northwest of Wu, Chang Gate was thus erected in order to channel in heavenly *qi*. For this reason it was also named the Gate of Destroying Chu. Helü also wanted to annex Yue. Yue was located southeast of Wu, and for this reason Snake Gate was erected in order to suppress the rival state.[17] Wu corresponded to the *chen* constellation and its animal was the dragon, and because of this, on the roof of the southern gate of the small city, two small spiraling dragons were carved, symbolizing

---

11. The eight winds refer to the winds from the eight directions: northeast, east, southeast, south, southwest, west, northwest, and north. They were given specific names in *Huainanzi*. See Liu An, *The Huainanzi: A Guide to the Theory and Practice of Government in Early Han China*, trans. and ed. John S. Major, Sarah A. Queen, Andrew Seth Meyer, and Harold D. Roth (New York: Columbia University Press, 2010), 155. The eight winds system is probably developed from the Shang four winds system. In oracle bone inscriptions there were already records of four winds: the eastern wind is called *xie* 协, the southern wind is *kai* 凱, the western wind is *yi* 夷, and the northern wind is *di* 狄. See Hu Houxuan 胡厚宣 ed., *Jiaguwen heji* 甲骨文合集 (Beijing: Zhongguo shehui kexue chubanshe, 1999), 14294. *Shiji* also records Wei Xian's 魏鮮 theory of using the eight winds for divination. See the "Tianguan shu" 天官書 chapter in *Shiji*, 27:1340. For a summary of the techniques of wind divination, see Li Ling 李零, *Zhongguo fangshu kao* 中國方術考 (Beijing: Dongfang chubanshe, 2001), 52–7.

12. According to *Huainanzi*, there are eight gates located at the eight ultimate regions: the Azure Gate to the northeast, the Opening Brightness Gate to the east, the Yang Gate to the Southeast, the Summer Heat Gate to the south, the White Gate to the southwest, the Changhe Gate to the west, the Gate of Darkness to the northwest and the Winter Cold Gate to the north. See Roth, Major, Queen and Meyer trans., *Huainanzi*, 158. In the Illuminate Hall (*mingtang* 明堂) theory, it also features eight windows, and each window symbolizes one of the eight winds. See Chen Li 陳立, *Baihutong shuzheng* 白虎通疏證 (Beijing: Zhonghua shuju, 2015), 265–6.

13. This is also recorded in *Yue jue shu*, "Wu di zhuan" 吳地傳 chapter. See Li Bujia, 31; Milburn, 96.

14. This is a form of cosmological thought common in the Han. Because Yue is located southeast of Wu, the belief then is that by blocking the east gate of the city, the air of culture will not be able to be transmitted to Yue cosmologically.

15. According to the "Lüshu" 律書 chapter in *Shiji*, 閶闔風 (*helüfeng*) is the west wind. See *Shiji*, 25:1248. In modern-day Suzhou, there is still a location called Chang Gate.

16. In Chinese correlative thinking, the snake corresponds to the earthly branch 巳, which resembles a door.

17. In the same manner of thinking, the twelve earthly branches / constellations correspond to the twelve regions, as well as the twelve zodiac animals, rat, ox, tiger, rabbit, dragon, snake, horse, ram, monkey, dog and boar. Wu's location corresponds to the earthly branch *chen* and the dragon. Yue is southeast of Wu, corresponding to the earthly branch *si* and the snake, therefore the gate is named Snake Gate.

the horns of a dragon.[18] Yue's location corresponded to the constellation of *si* and its animal was the snake. Because of this, on the south gate there was a wooden snake. The body of the snake faced north and its head faced into the inner quarters of the city, which showed that Yue belonged to Wu.

4.3. 城郭以成，倉庫以具，闔閭復使子胥、屈蓋餘、燭傭，習術戰騎射御之巧，未有所用，請干將鑄作名劍二枚。干將者，吳人也，與歐冶子同師，俱能為劍。越前來獻三枚，闔閭得而寶之，以故使劍匠作為二枚：一曰干將，二曰莫耶。莫耶，干將之妻也。

干將作劍，采五山之鐵精，六合之金英。候天伺地，陰陽同光，百神臨觀，天氣下降，而金鐵之精不銷淪流，於是干將不知其由。莫耶曰：「子以善為劍聞於王，使子作劍，三月不成，其有意乎？」干將曰：「吾不知其理也。」莫耶曰：「夫神物之化，須人而成，今夫子作劍，得無得其人而後成乎？」干將曰：「昔吾師作冶，金鐵之類不銷，夫妻俱入冶爐中，然後成物。至今後世，即山作冶，麻絰蒸服，然後敢鑄金於山。今吾作劍，不變化者，其若斯耶？」莫耶曰：「先師親爍身以成物，吾何難哉！」於是干將妻乃斷髮剪爪，投於爐中，使童女童男三百人鼓橐裝炭，金鐵乃濡。遂以成劍，陽曰干將，陰曰莫耶，陽作龜文，陰作漫理。

干將匿其陽，出其陰而獻之。闔閭甚重。既得寶劍，適會魯使季孫聘於吳，闔閭使掌劍大夫以莫耶獻之。季孫拔視，劍之鍔中缺者大如黍米。歎曰：「美哉，劍也！雖上國之師，何能加之！夫劍之成也，吳霸；有缺，則亡矣。我雖好之，其可受乎？」不受而去。

4.3. Once the walled cities were built and granaries and storehouses were provisioned, Helü then sent Wu Zixu to subdue Gaiyu and Zhuyong.[19] When they were practicing the skills of fighting, horse riding, archery, and chariot driving, there were no appropriate weapons to use. The king then requested that Ganjiang make two excellent swords. Ganjiang was a man of Wu who studied under the same master as Master Ouye.[20] Both of them were good at making swords. Previously, Yue had come and presented three swords as tribute. After obtaining these swords, Helü treasured them. Because of this, he asked the sword master to make two more. One sword was called Ganjiang and the other Moye. Moye was the wife of Ganjiang.

---

18. 反羽 (*fanyu*) is 反宇 (*fanyu*), meaning that "the edges of the roof spiral upward."

19. In the thirteenth year of King Liao of Wu, Gaiyu and Zhuyong surrendered to Chu and were enfeoffed in Shu by Chu, see *WYCQ*, 3.15.

20. Master Ouye was probably the most famous sword maker in early China. *Yue jue shu* records him making swords for King Goujian and the Chu king. See Li Bujia, 302; Milburn, 281–82.

In order to make the swords, Ganjiang collected the finest iron from the five mountains and the best metals of the world.[21] He chose the proper time and the ideal location to cast the weapons. The sun and the moon were equally visible,[22] all the spirits came to observe and the *qi* of the heavens descended, but the essence of the iron and metals still did not melt and flow. At that moment, Ganjiang did not know the reason. Moye said, "Because of your reputation for making good swords, you are known to the king and were asked by him to make these swords. After three months, they are still incomplete. Is there an explanation for this?" Ganjiang said, "I do not know the reason for my failure." Moye said, "In general, the transformation of a marvelous object must have a human element to be completed. Now for your making of these swords, perhaps you need to receive assistance from the proper person and then you will be successful?" Ganjiang said, "In the past, when my master was making a sword and the metals and irons did not melt, only after he and his wife both jumped into the furnace was the sword made. Even now, when going to the mountains to smelt metal, later generations wear hemp mourning belts and put on grass robes,[23] after which they then dare to forge metal in the mountains. Now in making my swords, is this perhaps the reason that the metals did not melt?" Moye said, "Our deceased master melted his body in order to make the sword, how could we consider this impossible?" Thereupon Moye cut off her hair and nails and threw them into the furnace.[24] They further commanded three hundred young boys and girls to work the furnace bellows and add charcoal. Then the metals and iron finally melted and the swords were made. The male sword was named Ganjiang and the female, Moye. On the male sword the pattern of a tortoise shell was engraved; on the female sword the pattern represented flowing water.[25]

---

21. The names of the five mountains vary in texts, but here probably refers to the famous mountains. The term *liuhe* 六合, translated somewhat loosely here, refers to heaven, earth, and the four directions, suggesting the world.

22. *Yinyang* here refer to the sun and the moon. That the sun and the moon are equally visible suggests the time of either early morning or early evening.

23. 麻絰菽服 are dresses for funeral or sacrifice. When the term is used as a verb in a sentence it implies that the craftsmen from later generations wore funeral dress and offered sacrifices to legendary sword masters before forging metal.

24. This is an action of symbolic self-mutilation; stories of this type are often found in early texts. For example, when there was a drought, Tang 湯, the founder of the Shang dynasty cut off his hair and fingernail to make a prayer for rain.

25. For further reading on Ganjiang and Moye, see Anne Birrell, *Chinese Mythology: An Introduction* (Baltimore: The Johns Hopkins University Press, 1993), 221–224. Scholarship on magic swords can be found in Milburn, *The Glory of Yue*, 273–293.

Ganjiang concealed the male sword but brought out the female one and presented it to the king. Helü treasured it very much. After he had obtained this precious sword, it happened that Lu sent Jisun to Wu for an official visit.[26] Helü ordered the grand minister in charge of swords to present the Moye sword to Jisun as a gift. Jisun pulled out the sword and inspected it. On the edge of the sword there was a chip as big as a grain of millet. He sighed, "How wonderful is this sword! Even the masters from the superior states could not surpass this![27] That this sword was made indicates that Wu will become a hegemon. That it has a chip means Wu will fall. Although I like it, how could I accept it?" He left without accepting it.

4.4. 闔閭既寶莫耶，復命於國中作金鉤。令曰：「能為善鉤者，賞之百金。」吳作鉤者甚眾。而有人貪王之重賞也，殺其二子，以血亹金，遂成二鉤，獻於闔閭，詣宮門而求賞。王曰：「為鉤者眾，而子獨求賞，何以異於眾夫子之鉤乎？」作鉤者曰：「吾之作鉤也，貪王之賞而殺二子，亹成二鉤。」王乃舉眾鉤以示之：「何者是也？」王鉤甚多，形體相類，不知其所在。於是鉤師向鉤而呼二子之名：「吳鴻，扈稽，我在於此，王不知汝之神也。」聲絕於口，兩鉤俱飛，著父之胸。吳王大驚，曰：「嗟乎！寡人誠負於子。」乃賞百金。遂服而不離身。

4.4. Since the king had already treasured the Moye sword, he further commanded the people in the state to make golden hooks.[28] The order read, "The one who makes the best hook will be rewarded with a hundred gold pieces." There were many who made hooks in Wu. Among them was one who longed for the huge reward. He killed his two sons and smeared their blood on the gold.[29] In this way he made two hooks, presented them to Helü,

---

26. Jisun was from one of the three eminent families in Lu who actually seized power within the state. The three families are all descendants of Lord Huan of Lu.

27. During the Spring and Autumn period, states such as Wu and Chu called the states in the Central Plain the upper states, because they were located in the upper region of the Yellow River while Wu and Chu belonged to the lower region of the Yangzi River. For the same reason, Yue called Wu the upper state, as the Yangzi River flows through Wu before reaching Yue.

28. Huang Rensheng believes that this is a weapon shaped like a sword but with a curved blade. However, *gou* 鉤 commonly refers to belt hooks in ancient times. Moreover, there are several belt hooks discovered have the name of King Helü inscribed on the hooks. Cao Jinyan argues these are the hooks worn by the Wu king. See Huang Rensheng, 70n28. See also Cao Jinyan 曹錦炎, "Wuwang Guang tongdaigou xiaokao" 吳王光銅帶鉤小考, *Dongnan wenhua* 東南文化, no. 2 (2013): 90–93.

29. 亹 is an alternative to 釁, which means to consecrate a drum or bell by rubbing on it the blood of a slaughtered animal. In ancient times, drums, bells, and other metal vessels were often anointed with animal blood as a sacrifice for good fortune. A famous story of this sort is found in *Mencius* where King Hui of Liang 梁惠王 spared a cow that was about be slaughtered for its blood to consecrate a new bell. See *Mencius*, 9.

and went to the palace gate to ask for the reward. The king said, "There are many hooks that have been made but only you request the reward. How are your hooks different from the many others?" The hook maker replied, "When I was making the hooks, I longed for the king's reward, so I killed my two sons and used their blood when making the two hooks." The king then showed him all the hooks, saying, "Which ones are yours?" The king had many hooks and their shapes were similar. No one knew where the two hooks were. The hook maker then called out his two sons' names to the hooks, "Wuhong, Huji, I am here. The king does not know your spirits." Once this cry came out of his mouth, two hooks flew together and attached themselves to the father's chest. The king of Wu was greatly surprised, saying, "Alas! Indeed I slighted you." He then rewarded the man with the hundred gold pieces and never removed the hooks.

4.5. 六月，欲用兵，會楚之白喜來奔。吳王問子胥曰：「白喜何如人也？」子胥曰：「白喜者，楚白州犁之孫。平王誅州犁，喜因出奔，聞臣在吳而來也。」闔閭曰：「州犁何罪？」子胥曰：「白州犁，楚之左尹，號曰郤宛，事平王，平王幸之，常與盡日而語，襲朝而食。費無忌望而妒之，因謂平王曰：『王愛幸宛，一國所知，何不為酒一至宛家，以示群臣於宛之厚？』平王曰：『善。』乃具酒於郤宛之舍。無忌教宛曰：『平王甚毅猛而好兵，子必前陳兵堂下、門庭。』宛信其言，因而為之。及平王往，而大驚，曰：『宛何等也？』無忌曰：『殆且有篡殺之憂，王急去之！事未可知。』平王大怒，遂誅郤宛。諸侯聞之，莫不歎息。喜聞臣在吳，故來。請見之。」

闔閭見白喜而問曰：「寡人國僻遠，東濱海。側聞子前人為楚荊之暴怒，費無忌之讒口，不遠吾國而來於斯，將何以教寡人？」喜曰：「楚國之失虜，前人無罪，橫被暴誅。臣聞大王收伍子胥之窮厄，不遠千里故來歸命。惟大王賜其死。」闔閭傷之，以為大夫，與謀國事。

4.5. In the sixth month, the king desired to launch a military expedition against Chu. It happened at that time Bo Pi from Chu came to seek refuge.[30] The king of Wu asked Wu Zixu, "What kind of man is Bo Pi?" Wu Zixu said, "Bo Pi is the grandson of Bo Zhouli. King Ping of Chu executed Zhouli;[31] Pi

---

30. He is also called Bo Pi 伯嚭 or Bo Pi 帛喜. He is also referred to as Chief Chancellor Pi 太宰喜 (*Taizai Pi*).

31. See *WYCQ*, 3.3. According to *Zuozhuan*, Bo Zhouli was executed by Gongzi Yu, the future King Ling of Chu, not by King Ping of Chu, see *Zuozhuan*, Lord Zhao 1; Yang Bojun, 1223; Durrant, Li, and Schaberg, 1333.

then fled Chu. He came to Wu because he heard that I, your subject, am in Wu." Helü said, "What offense did Zhouli commit?" Wu Zixu replied, "Bo Zhouli was the Administrator on the Left of Chu and was styled Xi Yuan.[32] He served King Ping and was favored by King Ping.[33] The king often talked with him all day long and had executive breakfasts with him. Bi Wuji saw this and was jealous.[34] He then said to King Ping, 'That Your Majesty loves and favors Xi Yuan is known by the whole state. Why not prepare wine and visit Yuan's house in order to show to the various ministers your appreciation of Yuan?' King Ping said, 'Excellent!' He then prepared wine at Xi Yuan's house. Bi Wuji instructed Xi Yuan, saying, 'King Ping is resolute, brave, and is fond of weapons. You, sir, must display weapons in advance at the yard in front of the door.'[35] Xi Yuan trusted his words and prepared accordingly. When King Ping arrived he was greatly surprised, asking, 'What does Xi Yuan intend to do?' Bi Wuji said, 'I am afraid that you are going to have to worry about usurpation. Your Majesty should leave hurriedly; it is impossible to be certain about the matter.' King Ping was furious and consequently killed Xi Yuan.[36] When the many lords heard this, not one of them did not lament. Bo Pi has heard that I, your subject, am in Wu, for this reason he came and requested an audience from you."

Helü granted Bo Pi an audience and asked him, saying, "I, a man of little virtue, have a state that is remotely located to the east near the ocean. I have heard from others that your ancestors fell victim to the king of Chu's furious temper and Bi Wuji's slander. You did not consider that my state is far away and came here. What will you teach me, a man of little virtue?" Bo Pi said, "I am a runaway prisoner from Chu. My predecessor innocently and unjustly suffered a violent execution. I, your subject, have heard that Your Majesty accommodated Wu Zixu when he was in dire straits; therefore I did not regard a thousand *li* as far away to put myself

---

32. Xu Guang's 徐廣 commentary to *Shiji* suggests that Bo Zhouli's son was Xi Yuan, who fathered Bo Pi. See *Shiji*, 31:1465.

33. We know from the above note that Bo Zhouli and Xi Yuan were father and son. Bo Zhouli died in the first year of Lord Zhao of Lu (541 BCE). According to *Zuozhuan*, Xi Yuan died twenty-seven years later, in the twenty-seventh year of Lord Zhao of Lu. King Ping of Chu died in the twenty-sixth year of Lord Zhao of Lu, so it was impossible that Xi Yuan was executed by King Ping of Chu. The *WYCQ* passage here confuses Bo Zhouli with Xi Yuan.

34. Bi Wuji is the one who slandered Wu Zixu's father. See *WYCQ*, 3.3.

35. 前 (*qian*) should be read as 先 (*xian*), "in advance," here.

36. *Zuozhuan*, Lord Zhao 27, records a similar story but replaces King Ping of Chu with the Chu prime minister Zichang who killed the entire Xi clan. See Yang Bojun, 1485; Durrant, Li, and Schaberg, 1677.

under your command. I only wish Your Majesty will grant me a proper death."[37] Helü felt sorry for him. He made Bo Pi a high official and consulted with him on state affairs.

4.6. 吳大夫被離承宴問子胥曰：「何見而信喜？」子胥曰：「吾之怨與喜同。子不聞河上歌乎？『同病相憐，同憂相救。驚翔之鳥，相隨而集；瀨下之水，回復俱流。』胡馬望北風而立，越鷰向日而熙。誰不愛其所近，悲其所思者乎？」被離曰：「君之言外也，豈有內意以決疑乎？」子胥曰：「吾不見也。」被離曰：「吾觀喜之為人，鷹視虎步，專功擅殺之性，不可親也。」子胥不然其言，與之俱事吳王。

4.6. Beili, a high official of Wu, took the opportunity during some leisure time to ask Wu Zixu, "Why did you present Bo Pi to the king and trust him?" Wu Zixu said, "My grudge is similar to that of Bo Pi. Have you not heard 'Song of the River?': 'Fellow sufferers have shared empathy; fellow worriers offer mutual assistance. Startled birds follow each other and gather together; waters flowing passed a boulder are brought together by an eddy.' Horses from Hu stand toward the north wind;[38] swallows from Yue face the sun and play.[39] Who does not love those close to him and feel longing for the absent one in his heart?" Beili said, "What you have said is all extraneous. Might you have an inclination in your heart to settle this equivocation?" Wu Zixu said, "I don't know of any." Beili said, "According to my observation, Bo Pi is the kind of person who stares like a hawk and walks like a tiger, which suggests that his nature is to pursue only profit, and that he kills only to suit himself. You should not be close to him." Wu Zixu did not agree with Beili's words. He served the king of Wu with Bo Pi.

4.7. 二年，吳王前既殺王僚，又憂慶忌之在鄰國，恐合諸侯來伐。問子胥曰：「昔專諸之事，於寡人厚矣。今聞公子慶忌有計於諸侯，吾食不甘味，臥不安席，以付於子。」

子胥曰：「臣不忠無行，而與大王圖王僚於私室之中，今復欲討其子，恐非皇天之意。」

37. This is an expression that indicates that Bo Pi now entrusts the king of Wu with his life and fate.

38. 胡 (*hu*) is the general name for the nomadic people who dwelt along the northwestern border of China during early times. It often refers to the Xiongnu people during the Qin and Han dynasties.

39. This seems to have been a famous saying in Eastern Han. It appears in one of the nineteen ancient songs (*gushi shijiu shou* 古詩十九首) composed during Eastern Han.

闔閭曰：「昔武王討紂而後殺武庚，周人無怨色。今若斯議，何乃天乎？」

子胥曰：「臣事君王，將遂吳統，又何懼焉？臣之所厚其人者，細人也。願從於謀。」

吳王曰：「吾之憂也，其敵有萬人之力，豈細人之所能謀乎？」

子胥曰：「其細人之謀事，而有萬人之力也。」

王曰：「其為何誰？子以言之。」

子胥曰：「姓要名離。臣昔嘗見曾折辱壯士椒丘訢也。」

王曰：「辱之奈何？」

子胥曰：「椒丘訢者，東海上人也。為齊王使於吳，過淮津，欲飲馬於津。津吏曰：『水中有神，見馬即出，以害其馬。君勿飲也。』訢曰：『壯士所當，何神敢干？』乃使從者飲馬於津，水神果取其馬，馬沒。椒丘訢大怒，袒裼持劍入水，求神決戰。連日乃出，眇其一目。遂之吳，會於友人之喪。訢恃其與水戰之勇也，於友人之喪席而輕傲於士大夫，言辭不遜，有陵人之氣。要離與之對坐。合坐不忍其溢於力也，時要離乃挫訢曰：『吾聞勇士之鬥也，與日戰不移表，與神鬼戰者不旋踵，與人戰者不達聲。生往死還，不受其辱。今子與神鬥於水，亡馬失御，又受眇目之病，形殘名勇，勇士所恥。不即喪命於敵而戀其生，猶傲色於我哉！』於是椒丘訢卒於詰責，恨怒並發，暝即往攻要離。於是要離席闌至舍，誡其妻曰：『我辱勇士椒丘訢於大家之喪，餘恨蔚恚，暝必來也，慎無閉吾門。』至夜，椒丘訢果往。見其門不閉，登其堂不關，入其室不守，放髮僵臥，無所懼。訢乃手劍而捽要離，曰：『子有當死之過者三，子知之乎？』離曰：『不知。』訢曰：『子辱我於大家之眾，一死也；歸不關閉，二死也；臥不守御，三死也。子有三死之過，欲無得怨。』要離曰：『吾無三死之過，子有三不肖之愧，子知之乎？』訢曰：『不知。』要離曰：『吾辱子於千人之眾，子無敢報，一不肖也；入門不咳，登堂無聲，二不肖也；前拔子劍，手挫捽吾頭，乃敢大言，三不肖也。子有三不肖而威於我，豈不鄙哉？』於是椒丘訢投劍而嘆曰：『吾之勇也，人莫敢眥占者，離乃加吾之上，此天下壯士也。』臣聞要離若斯，誠以聞矣。」

吳王曰：「願承宴而待焉。」

4.7. In the second year (513 BCE), the king of Wu had already assassinated King Liao. However, he was still worried that Qingji was in the neighboring states and he feared that Qingji would ally the many lords to attack Wu.[40] The king told Wu Zixu, "Previously, your recommendation

40. Qingji was the son of King Liao. *Zuozhuan* has a different report of Qingji's death; the report states that in the twenty-first year of the reign of King Fuchai (475 BCE) Qingji remonstrated against Fuchai and then fled to Chu out of fear. In the winter of that year, upon hearing that Yue was about

of Zhuanzhu showed your deep affection for me, a man of little virtue. Now I have heard that Gongzi Qingji has conceived a plan with the many lords. I thus cannot enjoy delicacies when I eat, and cannot feel comfortable when I lay down on my mat. I entrust this matter to you, sir."

Wu Zixu replied, "I, your subject, am not loyal and possess no virtuous deeds. However, I planned the killing of King Liao with Your Majesty in a private room. Now you want further to chastise his son; this, perhaps, does not accord with the intention of August Heaven."

Helü said, "In the past King Wu chastised Zhou and killed Wugeng, yet later on the people of Zhou did not appear to be resentful.[41] Now when we discuss this matter, how would this disobey heaven's will?"[42]

Wu Zixu said, "I, your subject, serve Your Majesty and will definitely defend the legitimacy of the state. What fear then do I have? The one I esteem is a man of small physique. I wish you could make plans with him."

The king of Wu said, "What worries me is that our enemy has the strength of ten thousand people. How is this possible for a man of such small stature?"

Wu Zixu answered, "In planning things this man of small physique has the power of ten thousand men."

The king asked, "Who is he? Please tell me."

Wu Zixu replied, "His surname is Yao and his given name is Li. I have seen him insult the strong man Jiaoqiu Xi."

The king said, "How did he insult this man?"

Wu Zixu said, "Jiaoqiu Xi is a man who lived by the eastern sea. He came to Wu as an envoy for the king of Qi. When he was passing a ford at the Huai River, he wanted to water his horse at the ford. The clerk at the ford told him, 'There is a spirit in the river. When he sees the horse he will come out and do harm to it. Please do not water your horse, sir.' Jiaoqiu Xi said, 'The horse belongs to a brave man, which spirit dares to offend me?' He therefore asked his attendants to water the horse at the ford. As he was told, the river spirit

---

to attack Wu, he made a request to return to Wu in order to defeat Yue. After his return, he planned to execute some disloyal ministers and make peace with Yue, and he was killed by the people of Wu. See *Zuozhuan*, Lord Ai 20; Yang Bojun, 1715–16; Durrant, Li, and Schaberg, 1967.

41. King Wu refers to King Wu of Zhou, who conquered Shang. Zhou, the last king of Shang killed himself after he was defeated by King Wu. Wugeng was Zhou's son. After Shang was conquered, King Wu enfeoffed him as the lord of Shang. When the young King Cheng inherited the throne after King Wu passed away, Duke Zhou served as the regent. Wugeng conspired with Duke Zhou's brothers, Lord Guan and Lord Cai, and rebelled. He was eventually killed by Duke Zhou. The *WYCQ* mistakenly states that King Wu executed Wugeng. See *Shiji*, 4:126, 132.

42. Sun Yirang 孫詒讓 (1848–1908) reads 乃 as 反, to turn against. The sentence then serves as a response to Wu Zixu's doubt that killing King Liao's son Qingji might not be in accordance with the will of heaven. See Zhang Jue, 77n4.

took his horse. The horse disappeared into the river. Jiaoqiu Xi was greatly angered. Taking off his upper clothing and holding a sword, he jumped into the river and sought a battle with the spirit. After several days he finally emerged from the river having lost one eye. After this he went to Wu. During a gathering at a friend's funeral, Jiaoqiu Xi, presuming upon his courage battling in the river, slighted men of service and officers at the friend's funeral banquet. His words were arrogant and his attitude was insulting. Yao Li and Jiaoqiu Xi sat face to face. Everyone sitting there could not bear his bragging about his strength.[43]

"Yao Li then humiliated Jiaoqiu Xi, saying, 'I have heard about the fighting of a brave man. He defeated the sun before the shadow of the sundial moved, defeated spirits and ghosts in fewer moments than one needs to turn on one's heels, defeated people before his voice reached their ears. He went to fight as a living person and returned as a corpse, but never would he accept any humiliation. Now you, sir, fought with the spirit in the river. Your horse has vanished, your driver is gone, and you suffered the damage of losing an eye. Gaining a brave reputation at the price of mutilating one's body is what a brave man feels shame about. You failed to die in the hands of the enemy but cared only about saving your life. How could you still display an arrogant demeanor in front of me?' At this moment Jiaoqiu Xi had been summarily rebuked, causing his hatred and anger to ignite. He would assault Yao Li as soon as it turned dark.

"When Yao Li arrived at home after the banquet ended, he warned his wife,[44] saying, 'I have insulted the brave man Jiaoqiu Xi at a funeral banquet of a rich clan. He was left full of hate, frustration, and anger. When it turns dark he will certainly come to our house. Make sure you do not close our gate.' When night came, Jiaoqiu Xi indeed arrived and saw the gate was not closed. He found the door was not bolted when he ascended the hall, and there was no guard when he entered the room. Yao Li untied his hair, lay still on his bed, and feared nothing.[45] Holding a sword in one hand, Jiaoqiu Xi grabbed Yao Li and said, 'You insulted me in front of the crowd at a noble man's house, this is the first reason you should die. After you returned, you did not lock your gate, this is the second reason you should die. Lying here without guard, this is the third reason. You have three errors that deserve death, there is nothing you can be resentful about.' Yao Li said, 'I do not have

43. 溢 (*yi*) originally means water overflows, here is used to describe Jiaoqiu Xi's bragging of his courage.

44. 闌 (*lan*) means "end."

45. 僵臥 (*jiangwo*) refers to lying supine.

three errors that deserve death. You, however, have three shames of being virtueless. Do you know this?' Jiaoqiu Xi said, 'I do not know.' Yao Li said, 'I insulted you in front of a crowd of a thousand people yet you were not courageous enough to take revenge there, this is your first failure of virtue. Failing to cough and ascending to the hall silently, this is your second unworthiness.[46] Moving forward, drawing out your sword, and grasping my head, you then dare to speak aloud, this is your third unworthiness. You have these three failures of virtue yet you want to impose your power on me, isn't this despicable?' Jiaoqiu Xi then threw down his sword and sighed, 'My bravery makes no one dare to look at me askance. Yao Li, however, has bested me. He is one of the bravest men in the world.' I, your subject, have heard that Yao Li is like this, and sincerely report it to you."

The king of Wu said, "I wish to receive him when I have time."

4.8. 子胥乃見要離曰：「吳王聞子高義，惟一臨之。」乃與子胥見吳王。

王曰：「子何為者？」要離曰：「臣，國東千里之人，臣細小無力，迎風則僵，負風則伏。大王有命，臣敢不盡力！」吳王心非子胥進此人，良久默然不言。要離即進曰：「大王患慶忌乎？臣能殺之。」王曰：「慶忌之勇，世所聞也。筋骨果勁，萬人莫當。走追奔獸，手接飛鳥，骨騰肉飛，拊膝數百里。吾嘗追之於江，駟馬馳不及，射之闇接，矢不可中。今子之力不如也。」要離曰：「王有意焉，臣能殺之。」王曰：「慶忌明智之人，歸窮於諸侯，不下諸侯之士。」要離曰：「臣聞：『安其妻子之樂，不盡事君之義，非忠也；懷家室之愛，而不除君之患者，非義也。』臣詐以負罪出奔，願王戮臣妻子，斷臣右手，慶忌必信臣矣。」王曰：「諾。」

要離乃詐得罪出奔，吳王乃取其妻子，焚棄於市。

4.8. Wu Zixu then went to see Yao Li and told him, "The king of Wu has heard of your great virtue; he wishes you to visit him." Yao Li therefore came to see the king of Wu with Wu Zixu.

The king asked, "What are you capable of?" Yao Li said, "I, your subject, am a man living a thousand *li* away, east of the capital. I am thin, short, and

46. The *Liji* prescribes that when visiting another's house, one must raise his voice and ask the host for permission before entering the room. Coughing before entering the gate is also a way of alerting the host of the arrival of the guest. *Hanshi waizhuan* 韓詩外傳 reports an anecdote that Mencius accidentally saw his wife sitting alone in a room with her legs stretched out. Feeling the wife's behavior was not in accord with ritual, Mencius wanted to divorce her. However, Mencius's mother pointed out that Mencius failed to raise his voice before entering the room, a ritual prescribed in the *Liji*, and as a result he was not in a position to judge his wife. See Sun Xidan, 26. See also Xu Weiyu 許維遹, *Hanshi waizhuan jishi* 韓詩外傳集釋 (Beijing: Zhonghua shuju, 1980), 322.

lack physical strength. Facing toward the wind, I would fall on my back; putting my back against the wind, I would fall on my belly. However, if you, great king, have a command to issue, how dare I, your subject, not do my utmost?"

The king of Wu in his heart thought Wu Zixu did not recommend the right man. He was silent for quite a while before responding. Yao Li then moved forward and said, "Is Your Majesty worrying about Qingji? I, your subject, can kill him." The king said, "The bravery of Qingji is well known throughout the world. His bones and muscles are strong and ten thousand men are no match for him. He can catch fleeing beasts on foot, grab flying birds with his hand. Leaping and jumping, he can easily run several hundred *li* after he warms up by tapping his knees.[47] I have chased him to the river. My four-horse chariot could not catch up with him. Shooting at him, he could catch the arrow without looking at it and the arrow could not hit its mark. Now, your strength does not match his." Yao Li said, "If Your Majesty has any intentions regarding him, I can kill him." The king said, "Qingji is an intelligent man. Although he turned himself over to one of the lords because of his desperate situation, he never considered himself inferior to the men of the many lords." Yao Li said, "I, your subject, have heard that 'seeking comfort from wife and son yet refusing to devote oneself to the principle of serving one's ruler is considered disloyal; and cherishing the love from one's wife instead of getting rid of the worries of the ruler is not righteous.' I, your subject, will pretend to flee on account of committing a crime. I request Your Majesty kill my wife and son and cut off my, your subject's, right hand. Qingji will certainly trust me."[48] The king said, "Agreed."

Yao Li then pretended to commit an offense and ran away from Wu. The king of Wu then arrested his wife and son. He burned them and disposed of their bodies at the market.

4.9. 要離乃奔諸侯而行怨言，以無罪聞於天下。遂如衛，求見慶忌。見曰：「闔閭無道，王子所知。今戮吾妻子，焚之於市，無罪見誅。吳國之事，吾知其情，願因王子之勇，闔閭可得也。何不與我東之於吳？」慶忌信其謀。

---

47. 骨 (*gu*) and 肉 (*rou*) refer to Qingji's body. 騰 (*teng*) and 飛 (*fei*) describe his strength. Tapping at the knees is an action to warm up the body.

48. The *Taiping yulan* passage has different details: Yao Li suggests the Wu king should not only kill his wife and son but also burn their bodies at the market of Wu, then the king should throw their ashes in the air, put out an award of a thousand pieces of gold, and set a search perimeter of one hundred *li* for Yao Li's apprehension. *Lüshi chunqiu* also mentions the burning of bodies and throwing of ashes. See Zhang Jue, 80.

後三月，揀練士卒，遂之吳。將渡江於中流，要離力微，坐與上風，因風勢以矛鉤其冠，順風而刺慶忌，慶忌顧而揮之，三捽其頭於水中，乃加於膝上，「嘻嘻哉！天下之勇士也！乃敢加兵刃於我。」左右欲殺之，慶忌止之，曰：「此是天下勇士。豈可一日而殺天下勇士二人哉？」乃誡左右曰：「可令還吳，以旌其忠。」於是慶忌死。

要離渡至江陵，愍然不行。從者曰：「君何不行？」要離曰：「殺吾妻子，以事吾君，非仁也；為新君而殺故君之子，非義也。重其死，不貴無義。今吾貪生棄行，非義也。夫人有三惡以立於世，吾何面目以視天下之士？」言訖遂投身於江，未絕，從者出之。要離曰：「吾寧能不死乎？」從者曰：「君且勿死，以俟爵祿。」要離乃自斷手足，伏劍而死。

4.9. Yao Li then fled to the many lords and spread his complaint, and the world reckoned that he was innocent. He then went to Wei and requested to see Qingji. At their meeting, he said, "That Helü is tyrannical is what you, son of a king, know. Now he murdered my wife and son and burned their bodies in the market. They committed no crime but were executed. As for the matters of the state of Wu, I know the real situation. I wish, relying upon your power as the son of a king, to apprehend Helü. Won't you go east to Wu with me?" Qingji trusted his plan.

Three months later, Qingji selected soldiers and trained them. He then headed toward Wu. When they were about to cross the middle of a river, Yao Li, because of his weakness, sat on the windward side. Relying upon the force of the wind, he used his spear to hook off Qingji's cap, and, taking advantage of the wind's flow, he stabbed Qingji. Qingji looked back at him and shook off the spear. He pressed Yao Li's head into the water three times. Then he sat him on his knee, saying, "Alas, you are one of the bravest men in the world. You dare to use a weapon and injure me!" Qingji's attendants on the left and right wanted to kill Yao Li but were stopped by Qingji, who said, "This is one of the bravest men in the world. How can two brave men be killed in the same day?" He then instructed his attendants on the left and right, saying, "You should let him return to Wu in order to honor his loyalty." Qingji then died.

When Yao Li crossed the river and arrived at Jiangling,[49] he stopped with sorrow. His followers asked, "Why do you not advance?" Yao Li said, "Killing my wife and son in order to serve my ruler, this is inhumane; killing the

49. Jiangling was the capital city of Chu and was located in modern-day Jiangling County in Hubei Province. Yaoli would not be passing through Jiangling if he was returning to Wu from Wei.

son of the previous ruler for the sake of the new ruler, this is not righteous. People emphasize dying for a proper cause but do not value unrighteous deeds. Now I have coveted life and abandoned virtuous conduct, this is not worthy. As a man who has these three vices but yet lives in the world, I am ashamed to face the worthy men of the world." After finishing his words, he threw himself into the river. Before he died, his followers rescued him from the river. Yao Li said, "How can I not die?" The followers said, "Please do not die now, wait for your rank and salary." Yao Li then cut off his hands and feet and killed himself with a sword.[50]

4.10. 三年，吳將欲伐楚，未行。伍子胥、白喜相謂曰：「吾等為王養士，畫其策謀，有利於國，而王故伐楚，出其令，託而無興師之意，奈何？」有頃，吳王問子胥、白喜曰：「寡人欲出兵，於二子何如？」子胥、白喜對曰：「臣願用命。」吳王內計二子皆怨楚，深恐以兵往破滅而已。登臺向南風而嘯，有頃而嘆，群臣莫有曉王意者。子胥深知王之不定，乃薦孫子於王。

4.10. In the third year (512 BCE), the king of Wu wanted to launch a military expedition against Chu but the troops were not dispatched. Wu Zixu and Bo Pi had a conversation, saying, "We recruit men of talent for the king. We plan strategies and tactics for him; these bring benefits to the state. Yet the king now launches a military expedition against Chu.[51] He issued the command but is making excuses and shows no intention of mobilizing the troops. What should we do about this?" After a while, the king of Wu asked Wu Zixu and Bo Pi: "I, a man of little virtue, want to send the troops. What do you two think of this?" Wu Zixu and Bo Pi replied, "I, your subject, wish to follow your command." The king of Wu thought in his heart that both of them resented Chu. He was deeply worried that if they led the troops to Chu they would not stop until they destroyed Chu. He then ascended the terrace, faced the southern wind and whistled, sighing a short while later.[52] None of the ministers understood the intention of the king. But Wu Zixu accurately understood the king's hesitancy, he thereupon recommended Master Sun to the king.

---

50. This *WYCQ* account of Yao Li assassinating Qingji is adopted and developed from the account in the "Zhonglian" 忠廉 chapter in *Lüshi chunqiu*. See John Knoblock and Jeffrey Riegel, *The Annals of Lü Buwei* (Stanford: Stanford University Press, 2001), 248–9. See also Xu Weiyu, *Lüshi chunqiu jishi*, 247–48.

51. According to Zhang Jue, 故 (*gu*) should be rendered as 今 (*jin*), meaning "now." See Zhang Jue, 83.

52. The Wu king was worried that Wu Zixu and Bo Pi would completely destroy Chu in order to avenge their families' deaths.

4.11. 孫子者，名武，吳人也，善為兵法。辟隱深居，世人莫知其能。胥乃明知鑒辯，知孫子可以折衝銷敵，乃一旦與吳王論兵，七薦孫子。吳王曰：「子胥託言進士，欲以自納。」

而召孫子，問以兵法，每陳一篇，王不知口之稱善。其意大悅。問曰：「兵法寧可以小試耶？」孫子曰：「可，可以小試於後宮之女。」王曰：「諾。」孫子曰：「得大王寵姬二人，以為軍隊長，各將一隊。」令三百人皆被甲兜鍪，操劍盾而立，告以軍法，隨鼓進退，左右迴旋，使知其禁。乃令曰：「一鼓皆振，二鼓操進，三鼓為戰形。」於是宮女皆掩口而笑。孫子乃親自操枹擊鼓，三令五申，其笑如故。孫子顧視，諸女連笑不止。孫子大怒，兩目忽張，聲如駭虎，髮上衝冠，項旁絕纓。顧謂執法曰：「取鈇鑕。」孫子曰：「約束不明，申令不信，將之罪也。既以約束，三令五申，卒不卻行，士之過也。軍法如何？」執法曰：「斬！」武乃令斬隊長二人，即吳王之寵姬也。吳王登臺觀望，正見斬二愛姬，馳使下之令曰：「寡人已知將軍用兵矣。寡人非此二姬食不甘味，宜勿斬之。」孫子曰：「臣既已受命為將，將法在軍，君雖有令，臣不受之。」孫子復撝，鼓之，當左右進退，迴旋規矩，不敢瞬目，二隊寂然，無敢顧者。於是乃報吳王，曰：「兵已整齊，願王觀之，惟所欲用，使赴水火猶無難矣，而可以定天下。」吳王忽然不悅，曰：「寡人知子善用兵，雖可以霸，然而無所施也。將軍罷兵就舍，寡人不願。」孫子曰：「王徒好其言，而不用其實。」

4.11. Master Sun, whose name was Wu, was a man from Wu and was good at military strategy.[53] He resided in a remote place and lived in solitude; people of the world failed to know of his talent. Wu Zixu, by his nature, was perspicacious and discerning.[54] He knew that Master Sun could defeat the enemy and destroy them;[55] therefore, one day when he was discussing military affairs with the king of Wu, he recommended Master Sun seven times. The king of Wu thought: "Wu Zixu is using the excuse of introducing a talented man but really wants to advance himself."

The king then summoned Master Sun and asked him about military strategies. Each time he offered a response, the king said it was excellent, without even realizing words of praise were coming out of his mouth. The king was extremely delighted. He asked, "Can you put your military strategies

53. According to Sima Qian, Master Sun (Sunzi), or Sun Wu, was a man from Qi and a famous military strategist. *Shiji* has a short biography of Sun Wu, see *Shiji*, 65:2161. The book *Sunzi bingfa* 孫子兵法 (*The Art of War*) is attributed to Sunzi.

54. Zhang Jue reads 乃 (*nai*) as 固 (*gu*), inherently. See Zhang Jue, 84.

55. 衝 (*chong*) is a battle cart used to attack the city wall. Here 折衝 (*zhechong*) means to destroy the enemy's carts and cause the enemy to retreat.

to a little test?" Master Sun answered, "Yes. We can test them a little bit with the ladies in the palace." The king of Wu said, "As you wish." Master Sun said, "I would have your two favorite concubines be the commanding officers of military units, with each of them leading a unit." He ordered three hundred ladies to put on armor, wear helmets, and stand with sword and shield in their hands. He instructed them concerning the military rules and told them to follow the drum to advance and retreat, to turn left, right, and circle, and military prohibitions were all announced to them. He then issued a command, saying, "Rise up at the first beat of the drum; shout and move forward at the second beat;[56] line up in battle formation at the third beat." Hearing this, all the palace ladies covered their mouths and laughed. Master Sun then personally held the drumsticks and beat the drum. Repeatedly he issued commands and warnings, yet the ladies laughed as usual. Master Sun looked around, but the ladies kept laughing and could not stop. Master Sun was greatly angered. He suddenly opened his eyes wide and roared like a frightened tiger. His hair stood up and knocked off his hat and snapped the hat strings at his neck. Looking back, he told the law executor, "Bring the axe and hatchet."[57] Master Sun announced, "If orders are not clear and rules are not reliable—these are the faults of the generals; orders have already been issued and have been repeatedly enunciated, yet the soldiers do not move backward and forward—these are the faults of the officers. What does the military law prescribe for this?" The law executor answered, "They should be beheaded." Sun Wu then ordered the beheading of the two commanding officers, the favorite concubines of the king of Wu. The king of Wu was observing from the terrace and seeing Sun Wu was about to execute these two concubines, he sent an emissary on horseback to issue a command, "I, a man of little virtue, already know that you, general, are good at military arts. Without these two ladies, I, a man of little virtue, will not taste the flavor of my food. Please do not execute them." Master Sun replied, "I, your subject, have already received your command and serve as a general. Among the troops the general has the authority. Even though you, my ruler, have given an order, I, your subject, refuse to follow it." Master Sun returned to his command. He beat the drum; the other ladies, no matter if they should turn left or right, advance or retreat, or turn around, did so in accordance with the rules and dared not blink their eyes. The two units were quiet and no soldiers dared to turn their heads. Master

---

56. Sun Yirang interprets 操 (*cao*) as 譟 (*zao*), "to shout" and "to make noises." See Zhang Jue, 84.

57. These are weapons for execution.

Sun thereupon reported to the king of Wu, saying, "The soldiers have been trained well. I wish Your Majesty to inspect them. You can use them just as you wish. Even if you ordered them to throw themselves into a river or a fire, they would have no difficulty with it. Furthermore, you can use them to pacify the world." The king of Wu felt upset and unhappy, saying, "I, a man of little virtue, know you are good at military arts. Although with your assistance I could become the hegemon, there is no place I can use you. Please, general, dismiss the troops and return to your lodging. I do not want to inspect them." Master Sun commented, "The king is only fond of my words but fails to employ my actual talents."

4.12. 子胥諫曰：「臣聞，『兵者凶事，不可空試。』故為兵者，誅伐不行，兵道不明。今大王虔心思士，欲興兵戈以誅暴楚，以霸天下而威諸侯，非孫武之將，而誰能涉淮踰泗，越千里而戰者乎？」於是吳王大悅，因鳴鼓會軍，集而攻楚。孫子為將，拔舒，殺吳亡將二公子蓋餘、燭傭。謀欲入郢，孫武曰：「民勞，未可，恃也。」

4.12. Wu Zixu admonished the king, saying, "I, your subject, have heard: 'Military affairs are cruel matters and should not be carried out pointlessly.'[58] Therefore, those who command troops should not reveal their strategies if attacks are not intended to be carried out. Now Your Majesty sincerely wants to recruit talented men, and wishes to mobilize the troops and weapons to punish tyrannical Chu, thereby becoming hegemon of the world and overawing the lords. Without Sun Wu serving as the general, who else could ford the Huai River and cross the Si River, advance thousands of *li*, and then fight?" The king of Wu was then greatly delighted. He thereby ordered the drum to be beaten and troops to be summoned. Once the troops were assembled they attacked Chu. Master Sun served as the general. He conquered Shu and killed the fleeing generals of Wu, the two Gongzis Gaiyu and Zhuyong. When planning to enter Ying, Sun Wu said, "The people are exhausted. It cannot be done now. We must wait."[59]

4.13. 楚聞吳使孫子、伍子胥、白喜為將，楚國苦之，群臣皆怨，咸言費無忌讒殺伍奢、白州犁，而吳侵境，不絕於寇，楚國群臣有一朝之患。於是司馬成乃謂子常曰：「太傅伍奢，左尹白州犁，邦人莫知其罪，君與王謀誅之，流謗於國，至于今日，其言不絕，誠

58. The text *Laozi* states that military affairs are inauspicious matters (兵者, 不祥之器也). See John Wu, trans., *Tao Te Ching* (Boston: Shambhala, 2005), 63.

59. This is also reported in *Shiji*, 31:1466 and 66:2175.

惑之。蓋聞仁者殺人以掩謗者，猶弗為也。今子殺人以興謗於國，不亦異乎？夫費無忌，楚之讒口，民莫知其過。今無辜殺三賢士，以結怨於吳，內傷忠臣之心，外為鄰國所笑。且郤伍之家，出奔於吳，吳新有伍員、白喜，秉威銳志，結讎於楚。故彊敵之兵，日駭楚國，有事，子即危矣。夫智者除讒以自安，愚者受佞以自亡。今子受讒，國以危矣。」子常曰：「是曩之罪也，敢不圖之。」九月，子常與昭王共誅費無忌，遂滅其族，國人乃謗止。

4.13. When Chu heard that Wu had appointed Master Sun, Wu Zixu, and Bo Pi as generals, all thought that this was disastrous. All the ministers were aggrieved; they all said it was because Bi Wuji slandered and killed Wu She and Bo Zhouli that Wu was invading the borderlands and was constantly attacking Chu, becoming a sudden threat to the ministers of Chu.[60] Sima Cheng then said to Zichang,[61] "People in the state do not know what crimes the Grand Tutor Wu She and the Prime Minister on the Left Bo Zhouli have committed. You and the king together schemed and killed them. Thus, reproach spreads in the state. Even today talk about this continues. I truly feel puzzled about this. I have heard that killing people in order to stop criticism is something a man of humanity will not do. Now you kill people in order to foment slander in the state, isn't this different from what a man of humanity would do? As for Bi Wuji, he is a slander-monger in Chu; everyone knows his vice. Killing three worthy men who had committed no crime has now caused hatred from Wu.[62] Inside our state it pains the hearts of loyal officials; outside the state it causes us to be humiliated before our neighbors. Furthermore, the Xi and Wu clans fled and turned to Wu. Wu recently received Wu Zixu and Bo Pi, and, relying upon their power, are determined to rival Chu. For these reasons the troops of the powerful enemy intimidate Chu day after day. If Chu falls into disaster, then you, sir, will be in danger. It is said, 'a wise man gets rid of slanderers in order to ensure his own safety; a fool accommodates fawners and causes his own demise.' Now you receive slanderers, and the state is in danger because of this." Zichang said, "This is my, Nang's, fault.[63] How dare I not make plans for this?" In the ninth month,

---

60. It was Xi Yuan rather than Bo Zhouli who died after being slandered by Bi Wuji. See *WYCQ*, 4.5.

61. According to *Zuozhuan*, this should be the Minister of Shen 沈, going by the name of Shu 戌, who suggested to prime minister Zichang that he should kill Bi Wuji. See *Zuozhuan*, Lord Zhao 27; Yang Bojun, 1488; Durrant, Li, and Schaberg, 1681.

62. The three men probably refer to Wu She; Bo Zhouli; and Wu Shang, son of Wu She and brother to Wu Zixu. *Zuozhuan* contains a similar speech by Shu. See Lord Zhao 27; Yang Bojun, 1488; Durrant, Li, and Schaberg, 1681.

63. Zichang's name is Nangwa 囊瓦, Zichang is his style, *zi* 字.

Zichang and King Zhao together killed Bi Wuji. They then exterminated his entire clan.[64] As a result, people in the state ended their criticism.

4.14. 吳王有女滕玉，因謀伐楚，與夫人及女會蒸魚，王前嘗半而與女，女怒曰：「王食我殘魚辱我，不忘久生。」乃自殺。闔閭痛之甚，葬於國西閶門。外鑿池積土，文石為槨，題湊為中，金鼎玉杯、銀樽珠襦之寶，皆以送女。乃舞白鶴於吳市中，令萬民隨而觀之，遂使男女與鶴俱入羨門，因發機以掩之。殺生以送死，國人非之。

4.14. The king of Wu had a daughter named Tengyu. Because he was planning a military expedition against Chu, the king met with his wife and daughter for a meal. While they were eating a steamed fish,[65] the king ate half and then gave the rest to his daughter. His daughter was angry, saying, "The king insults me by feeding me a leftover fish. I cannot bear to live anymore."[66] She then committed suicide. Helü was deeply grieved. He buried her outside of the west gate of the capital, called the Chang Gate. Around the tomb a pond was dug, and earth was piled on the tomb. The outer coffin was made of stones with patterns;[67] inside the chamber, large logs were arranged centripetally.[68] Gold cauldrons, jade cups, silver wine vessels, and short top-garments decorated with pearls were all buried with her. The king furthermore arranged the performance of the white crane dance at the market in the capital and allowed thousands of people to follow and observe it. He then had all the men, women, and cranes enter into the tomb doors and triggered a trap to bury them. The people of the state all found fault with such killing of the living as sacrifices for the dead.[69]

4.15. 湛盧之劍，惡闔閭之無道也，乃去而出，水行如楚。

楚昭王臥而寤，得吳王湛盧之劍於床。昭王不知其故，乃召風湖子而問曰：「寡人臥覺而得寶劍，不知其名，是何劍也？」風湖子曰：「此謂湛盧之劍。」昭王曰：「何以言之？」風湖子曰：「臣聞吳王得越所獻寶劍三枚：一曰魚腸，二曰磐郢，三曰湛盧。魚腸之劍，已用殺吳王僚也；磐郢以送其死女；今湛盧入楚也。」昭王曰：「湛盧所以去者何也？」風湖子曰：「臣聞越王元常使歐冶子造劍五

64. See also *Zuozhuan*, Lord Zhao 27; Yang Bojun, 1488; Durrant, Li, and Schaberg, 1682.

65. There should be a character 食 (*shi*), to "eat," before 蒸魚 (*zhengyü*), "steamed fish." See Zhang Jue, 89n1.

66. 忘 (*wang*) should be 忍 (*ren*) here. See Zhang Jue, 89.

67. In ancient times coffins usually contained two layers. The outer layer was called 椁 (*guo*).

68. The chamber of a tomb belonging to a noble was often constructed with a large pile of logs, with the heads of the logs arranged centripetally. This is called 題湊 (*ticou*).

69. This story is cited by Tang scholar Li Shan (630–689) in his commentary to Bao Zhao's 鮑照 (414–466) "Wuhe fu" 舞鶴賦.

枚以示薛燭，燭對曰：『魚腸劍逆理不順，不可服也，臣以殺君，子以殺父。』故闔閭以殺王僚。一名磐郢，亦曰豪曹，不法之物，無益於人。故以送死。一名湛盧，五金之英，太陽之精，寄氣託靈，出之有神，服之有威，可以折衝拒敵。然人君有逆理之謀，其劍即出，故去無道以就有道。今吳王無道，殺君謀楚，故湛盧入楚。」昭王曰：「其直幾何？」風湖子曰：「臣聞此劍在越之時，客有酬其直者：有市之鄉三十，駿馬千匹，萬戶之都二。是其一也。薛燭對曰：『赤堇之山已令無雲，若耶之溪深而莫測，群臣上天，歐冶死矣。雖傾城量金，珠玉盈河，猶不能得此寶，而況有市之鄉，駿馬千匹，萬戶之都，何足言也？』」昭王大悅，遂以為寶。

4.15. The sword named Zhanlu, hating that Helü acted without regard for the Way, left Helü and departed Wu. Traveling by river it arrived in Chu.[70]

King Zhao of Chu arose from sleep and found the King of Wu's Zhanlu sword in his bed.[71] King Zhao did not understand the reason for this, so he summoned Master Fenghu and asked him, "I, a man of little virtue, woke up and found this valuable sword. I do not know the name of it. What sword is it?" Master Fenghu answered, "This is the sword Zhanlu." King Zhao asked, "What leads you to this judgment?" Master Fenghu replied, "I, your subject, have heard that the king of Wu obtained three valuable swords presented by Yue. One was called Yuchang, the second was Panying, and the third was Zhanlu. The Yuchang sword was used to kill King Liao of Wu and the Panying sword was buried with his deceased daughter. Now the Zhanlu sword has come to Chu."

King Zhao asked, "What is the reason for the Zhanlu sword leaving Wu?" Master Fenghu said, "I, your subject, have heard that Yuanchang, king of Yue, ordered Master Ouye to make five swords which he then showed to Xue Zhu.[72] Xue Zhu said, 'The Yuchang sword has a contrary pattern that is not submissive, it should not be carried by anyone. A minister might use it to assassinate his ruler; a son might use it to kill his father.' Subsequently

70. This story is also found in *Yue jue shu*, "Waizhuan ji baojian" 外傳記寶劍 chapter. See Li Bujia, 302; Milburn, 284–85. Interestingly, there are quite a number of stories about swords coming from the southern regions such as Wu, Yue, and Chu in early China. Even during the Jin 晉 dynasty (265–429), a legend of two famous ancient swords buried underground emitting purple vapors into the sky was recorded in the dynastic history. See the biography of Zhang Hua 張華 (232–300) in Fang Xuanling, *Jinshu*, 36:1075–76.

71. King Zhao of Chu was the son of King Ping of Chu, and his mother was a lady from Qin who was originally arranged to marry the heir apparent Jian, but King Ping took her as his own wife after Bi Wuji told him how beautiful she was. This led to the execution of Wu She, and the flight of Wu Zixu and the heir apparent Jian. See *WYCQ*, 3.3.

72. According to *Yue jue shu*, Xue Zhu was a master who specialized in sword connoisseurship. See Li Bujia, 301; Milburn, 279.

Helü used it to kill King Liao. Another one was named Panying, which was also called Haocao. It was an object made without following the proper rules and thus brought no benefit to people. For this reason it was buried with the dead. The third one was Zhanlu. It is made of the best of the five metals and contains the essence of the ultimate *yang* force.[73] *Qi* is contained in it and supernatural power resides in it. Pulling it out, it emits a divine light;[74] carrying it adds an awe-inspiring air to a man, enabling him to fight and defeat any enemy. However, if a ruler plots in a way that goes against principle, the sword will immediately depart, thus leaving the ruler without the Way and rendering itself to a ruler with the Way. Now the king of Wu acts with no regard to the Way. He killed the former ruler and harbored schemes against Chu. For these reasons the Zhanlu sword came to Chu."

King Zhao said, "What is the value of the sword?" Master Fenghu answered, "I, your subject, have heard that when this sword was still in Yue, there was one who offered a price that included thirty districts with markets, a thousand fine horses, and two large cities with ten thousand households each. This was just one price offered for it. At that time Xue Zhu responded, 'The Chijin Mountain is already closed in, thus no cloudy mist is available and the Ruoye Stream is now too deep to be measured.[75] All the spirits have already ascended to the heavens and Master Ouye has died.[76] Although using gold that can fill a city, pearls and jades that can fill a river, one still could not obtain this treasure. How could districts with markets, a thousand fine horses, and large cities with ten thousand households be worth mentioning?'" King Zhao was greatly delighted. He thereupon treasured the sword.

4.17. 闔閭聞楚得湛盧之劍，因斯發怒，遂使孫武、伍胥、白喜伐楚。子胥陰令宣言於楚曰：「楚用子期為將，吾即得而殺之；子常用兵，吾即去之。楚聞之，因用子常，退子期。吳拔六與潛二邑。

4.17. Upon hearing that Chu had obtained the Zhanlu sword, Helü was furious. He then commanded Sun Wu, Wu Zixu, and Bo Pi to launch a military expedition against Chu. Wu Zixu secretly sent people to spread a rumor

73. The five metals usually refer to gold, silver, bronze, lead, and iron. *Taiyang* 太陽 means the ultimate *yang*.

74. Zhang Jue argues that the word *shen* 神 actually means *guang* 光, "light." See Zhang Jue, 91.

75. The character 令 (*ling*) here is a mistake for 合 (*he*), meaning "to close." See Zhang Jue, 91. The Ruoye Stream, according to legends, was where Master Ouye made swords.

76. Both *Taiping yulan* and *Yue jue shu* write 臣 (*chen*) as 神 (*shen*), "spirits." The sentence is saying that all the spirits who helped Master Ouye have left and the master himself has died, so it is impossible to make fine swords again. See Li Bujia, 302.

in Chu, saying, "If Chu appoints Ziqi as its general, we will capture and kill him.[77] If Zichang commands the troops, we will then leave immediately." Hearing this, Chu then appointed Zichang and demoted Ziqi. Wu conquered the two cities of Lu and Qian.[78]

4.17. 五年，吳王以越不從伐楚，南伐越。越王元常曰：「吳不信前日之盟，棄貢賜之國，而滅其交親。」闔閭不然其言，遂伐，破檇里。

4.17. In the fifth year (510 BCE), the king of Wu launched a military expedition south to Yue with the excuse that Yue failed to follow Wu in attacking Chu. Yuanchang, king of Yue, said, "Wu betrayed our previous covenant,[79] abandoned its tributary state, and destroyed our friendship." Helü took these words lightly. He then attacked Yue and broke into Zuili.[80]

4.18. 六年，楚昭王使公子囊瓦伐吳，報潛、六之役。吳使伍胥、孫武擊之，圍於豫章。吳王曰：「吾欲乘危入楚都而破其郢。不得入郢，二子何功？」於是圍楚師於豫章，大破之。遂圍巢，克之，獲楚公子繁以歸，為質。

4.18. In the sixth year (509 BCE), king Zhao of Chu sent Gongzi Nangwa to attack Wu as revenge for Wu's expeditions in Qian and Lu.[81] Wu sent Wu Zixu and Sun Wu to attack and besiege them at Yuzhang. The king of Wu said, "I want to take advantage of this difficult time for Chu to enter its capital and destroy the city of Ying. If we cannot enter Ying, what achievement will the two of you have?" Wu therefore besieged the Chu troops in Yuzhang and soundly defeated them. Then Wu besieged Chao and conquered it. They captured Gongzi Fan,[82] and returned with him as a hostage.

4.19. 九年，吳王謂子胥、孫武曰：「始子言郢不可入，今果何如？」二將曰：「夫戰，借勝以成其威，非常勝之道。」吳王曰：「何謂也？」二將曰：「楚之為兵，天下彊敵也。今臣與之爭鋒，十亡一存，而王入郢者，天也，臣不敢必。」吳王曰：「吾欲復擊楚，奈何而有功？」伍胥、孫武曰：「囊瓦者，貪而多過於諸侯，而

77. Ziqi was the son of King Ping and served as the minister of war at that time.

78. Both cities are in modern-day Anhui Province.

79. This probably refers to the event during which Yuanchang presented three swords to Wu. See *WYCQ*, 4.15.

80. Located in modern-day Jiaxing 嘉興 County in Zhejiang Province.

81. Nangwa's style is Zichang, prime minister of Chu at that time.

82. The Chu minister defending Chao.

唐、蔡怨之。王必伐，得唐、蔡。」「何怨？」二將曰：「昔蔡昭公朝於楚，有美裘二枚，善珮二枚，各以一枚獻之昭王。王服之以臨朝。昭公自服一枚。子常欲之，昭公不與，子常三年留之，不使歸國。唐成公朝楚，有二文馬，子常欲之，公不與，亦三年止之。唐人相與謀，從成公從者，請馬以贖成公，飲從者酒，醉之，竊馬而獻子常，常乃遣成公歸國。群臣誹謗曰：『君以一馬之故，三年自囚，願賞竊馬之功。』於是成公常思報楚，君臣未嘗絕口。蔡人聞之，固請獻裘珮於子常，蔡侯得歸。如晉告訴，以子元與太子質而請伐楚。故曰『得唐、蔡而可伐楚。』」

4.19. In the ninth year, the king of Wu told Wu Zixu and Sun Wu, "At the beginning you have said that Ying was impossible to conquer. How is it so now?" The two generals replied, "As for war, relying upon one triumph to secure one's dominance is not a permanent way to victory." The king of Wu asked, "What do you mean by that?" The two generals answered, "The troops of Chu are a formidable force in the world. If we, your subjects, were to engage them on the battlefield now, our chance of survival versus death is one in ten. Whether Your Majesty's entering Ying is sanctioned by heaven, we, your subjects, cannot be certain." The king of Wu continued, "I want to attack Chu again. How can I achieve success?" Wu Zixu and Sun Wu responded, "Nangwa is greedy and has offended the lords many times. Tang and Cai bear grudges against him.[83] If Your Majesty definitely wants to attack Chu, you must form alliances with Tang and Cai." The king asked, "What grudges do Tang and Cai hold against Nangwa?" The two generals answered, "Previously Lord Zhao of Cai rendered homage to Chu. The lord brought two fine furs and two delicate jade pendants. He presented one of each to King Zhao of Chu. The king wore them at court. Lord Zhao wore the other set himself. Zichang desired them but Lord Zhao refused to give them up. Zichang detained him for three years and did not allow him to return to his state. When Lord Cheng of Tang paid homage to Chu, he brought two horses with patterns on their bodies. Zichang wanted them but the lord did not give them to him. He was also detained for three years. People of Tang conspired together and planned to obtain the horses from the attendants (of the lord) in order to use them for the release of Lord Cheng. They drank wine with the attendants and made them drunk, then stole the horses and presented them to Zichang. Zichang then allowed Lord

83. Tang was annexed by Chu in 505 BCE; Cai was forced to relocate its capital several times because of the Chu invasion. It was eventually conquered by Chu in 447 BCE.

Cheng to return to his state.[84] Ministers of Tang complained, 'You, our lord, for the matter of a single horse caused yourself three years imprisonment. We wish you to reward the merit earned by those stealing the horse.' Lord Cheng thereupon often desired to seek vengeance against Chu; and the ruler and the ministers of Tang never ceased talking about this. The people of Cai, upon hearing this, insistently urged Lord Zhao to present the fur and pendant to Zichang. The lord of Cai finally was able to return. He went to Jin and reported this. Using his own son Yuan and a minister's son as hostages, he pleaded for Jin to conduct a military expedition against Chu.[85] For these reasons we say, 'Obtain alliances with Tang and Cai and then we can launch a military expedition against Chu.'"

4.20. 吳王於是使使謂唐、蔡曰：「楚為無道，虐殺忠良，侵食諸侯，困辱二君，寡人欲舉兵伐楚，願二君有謀。」唐侯使其子乾為質於吳，三國合謀伐楚。舍兵於淮汭，自豫章與楚夾漢水為陣。子常遂濟漢而陣，自小別山至於大別山。三不利，自知不可進，欲奔亡。史皇曰：「今子常無故與王共殺忠臣三人，天禍來下，王之所致。」子常不應。

4.20. The king of Wu thereupon sent an emissary to deliver a message to Tang and Cai, saying, "Chu has acted without regard for the Way. It has brutally murdered loyal and good ministers, invaded many lords and devoured their land, and detained and insulted you, the two lords. I, a man of little virtue, want to raise the troops and launch a military expedition against Chu. I wish you, the two lords, would join me in making this plan." The marquis of Tang sent his son, Qian, to Wu as a hostage.[86] Then the three states conspired to launch a military expedition against Chu. They stationed troops at the northern bank of the Huai River and then in Yuzhang, wedging on both sides of the Han River, they and Chu formed battle lines. Zichang then crossed the Han River and formed a battle line. From the Small Bie Mountains to the Big Bie Mountains, he suffered three defeats. He knew himself that he could not move forward and wanted to run away. Scribe Huang told him, "Now you, Zichang, together with the king, killed three

84. These stories are also reported in *Zuozhuan*, Lord Ding 3; Yang Bojun, 1531; Durrant, Li, and Schaberg, 1743.

85. *Zuozhuan* records that the two hostages are the lord's son Yuan and a minister's son. There must be some mistake in the *WYCQ* sentence. See *Zuozhuan*, Lord Ding 3; Yang Bojun, 1531; Durrant, Li, and Schaberg, 1743.

86. According to *Zuozhuan*, this should be the lord of Cai. See *Zuozhuan*, Lord Ding 4; Yang Bojun, 1542; Durrant, Li, and Schaberg, 1753.

loyal ministers for no reason. The disaster sent down by heaven is caused by the king." Zichang did not reply.

4.21. 十月，楚二師陣於柏舉。闔閭之弟夫概晨起請於闔閭曰：「子常不仁，貪而少恩，其臣下莫有死志，追之，必破矣。」闔閭不許。夫概曰：「所謂『臣行其志不待命』者，其謂此也。」遂以其部五千人擊子常。大敗，走奔鄭，楚師大亂，吳師乘之，遂破楚眾。楚人未濟漢，會楚人食，吳因奔而擊，破之雍滯。五戰，徑至於郢。

4.21. In the tenth month, troops of both armies were deployed at Baiju.[87] After getting up in the morning, Fugai, the younger brother of Helü, entreated Helü, saying, "Zichang is not humane. He is greedy and lacks generosity; none of his subordinates has the will to die for him. If we pursue them, we will certainly defeat them." Helü did not permit this. Fugai said, "The saying that 'ministers may act in accordance with their own judgment without waiting for a command' refers to the current situation." He then led his own men, numbering five thousand, to attack Zichang. Zichang was thoroughly defeated and escaped to Zheng. The Chu army fell into great chaos; the Wu troops took advantage of this and thereupon destroyed the Chu forces. At the time the Chu army had yet to cross the Han River, it happened that the Chu soldiers were eating; then the Wu troops followed the fleeing Chu army and destroyed them at Yongzhi. After five battles, the Wu troops arrived at Ying.[88]

4.22. 王追於吳寇，出，固將亡，與妹季芉出河濉之間。楚大夫尹固與王同舟而去。

吳師遂入郢，求昭王。

王涉濉，濟江，入于雲中。暮宿，群盜攻之，以戈擊王頭，大夫尹固隱王，以背受之，中肩。王懼，奔鄖。大夫鍾建負季芉以從。

鄖公辛得昭王，大喜，欲還之，其弟懷怒曰：「昭王是我讎也！」欲殺之。謂其兄辛曰：「昔平王殺我父，吾殺其子，不亦可乎？」辛曰：「君討其臣，敢讎之者？夫乘人之禍，非仁也；滅宗廢祀，非孝也；動無令名，非智也。」懷怒不解。辛陰與其季弟巢以王奔隨。

吳兵逐之，謂隨君曰：「周之子孫在漢水上者，楚滅之。謂天報其禍，加罰於楚，君何寶之？周室何罪，而隱其賊？能出昭王，

87. The parallel *Zuozhuan* sentence does not have the character 楚 (*chu*). See *Zuozhuan*, Lord Ding 4; Yang Bojun, 1544; Durrant, Li, and Schaberg, 1755. Here I follow *Zuozhuan*.

88. This is also recorded in *Shiji*, 66:2176.

即重惠也。」隨君卜昭王與吳王，不吉，乃辭吳王曰：「今隨之僻小，密近於楚，楚實存我，有盟，至今未改。若今有難而棄之？今且安靜楚，敢不聽命？」吳師多其辭，乃退。

是時，大夫子期雖與昭王俱亡，陰與吳師為市，欲出昭王。王聞之，得免，即割子期心，以與隨君盟而去。

4.22. King Zhao of Chu was chased by the invading army of Wu, he ran out of the capital and planned to flee.[89] Together with his younger sister Jimi,[90] he fled to the area between the Yellow and the Ju Rivers. Yinggu, a high officer of Chu, left the capital in the same boat with the king.[91]

The Wu troops then entered Ying and searched for King Zhao.

King Zhao forded the Ju River, crossed over the Yangzi River, and hid in the Yun Marsh.[92] While asleep at night, the entourage was attacked by a group of outlaws who were about to strike the king's head with a halberd.[93] The high officer Yinggu shielded the king, using his back to block the weapon, and was hit on the shoulder.[94] The king was frightened and escaped to Yun. High officer Zhongjian carried Jimi on his back and followed the king.

Xin, lord of Yun, was greatly delighted when receiving King Zhao.[95] He wanted to help the king return. His younger brother Huai was angry about this, saying, "King Zhao is our foe." He wanted to kill the king and told his older brother Xin, saying, "In the past King Ping murdered our father. Now if we kill his son, isn't this fair?" Xin said, "Is there anyone who dares to act as a foe to a ruler because he punished his own subject? Taking advantage of someone in dire straits is not humane, causing the extermination of our clan

89. Zhang Jue renders 固 (*gu*) as 姑 (*gu*), "temporarily, for the time being." Lu Wenchao 卢文弨, however, argues it is a mistake for 國. See Zhang Jue, 99. Here I follow Lu Wenchao's reading.

90. Her last name is 芈 Mi. Ji indicates that she is the youngest among her siblings. According to *Zuozhuan*, her name is Biwo 畀我. See *Zuozhuan*, Lord Ding 4; Yang Bojun, 1545; Durrant, Li, and Schaberg, 1757.

91. According to *Zuozhuan*, the officer's name was Yin and he served as a "zhenyin" 箴尹, a censor, to the Chu king. See *Zuozhuan*, Lord Ding 4; Yang Bojun, 1545; Durrant, Li, and Schaberg, 1757.

92. Chu has two large marshes; one is called Yun Marsh, the other is Meng Marsh. They appear often in Han literature, especially in the *fu* 賦.

93. *Shiji* has different narratives describing this. In the "Chu shijia" 楚世家 (Hereditary household of Chu) it says that the locals at the marsh did not know that they had encountered the Chu king and shot him by accident. However, in Wu Zixu's biography, Sima Qian wrote that the king was attacked by bandits. See *Shiji*, 40:1715; *Shiji*, 66:2176.

94. *Zuozhuan* records that this was done by Wangsun Youyu 王孫由于, see Yang Bojun, 1546; Durrant, Li, and Schaberg, 1757.

95. Lord Xin of Yun was the son of Dou Chengran, then prime minister of Chu. King Ping, the father of King Zhao, killed Dou Chengran and ordered Lord Xin to live in Yun. He was therefore called Lord Xin of Yun. See *Zuozhuan*, Lord Zhao 14; Yang Bojun, 1366; Durrant, Li, and Schaberg, 1517.

and the discontinuation of our ancestral sacrifices is unfilial,[96] such actions of ill repute cannot be called wise." However, Huai could not allay his anger, and Xin and his youngest brother Chao secretly accompanied King Zhao as he raced on to Sui.[97]

The Wu troops pursued them, telling the lord of Sui, "We have heard that Zhou's descendants dwelling in the Han River area were all destroyed by Chu.[98] It is said that heaven is punishing Chu as retribution for the disasters Chu has caused. For what reason do you value him? What crime has the Zhou ruling clan committed? Yet you are giving shelter to their foe. If you would hand over King Zhao, this would be bestowing double kindnesses."[99] The lord of Sui divined on the matter of surrendering King Zhao to the king of Wu, and the prediction was not auspicious. He thus rejected the king of Wu, saying, "Now, considering the remote place and the small size of Sui and the fact that it is very close to Chu, our existence is in fact ensured by Chu. We have made a covenant with Chu and it has remained unchanged up to the present. If we abandon Chu now because it is in a dire situation, how would we serve you? If now, you could for a moment allow Chu to settle down, how could Chu dare to fail to listen to your command?" The Wu troops approved of his logic and thereafter retreated.

At that time, although the high officer Ziqi fled with King Zhao, he secretly made a deal with the Wu army and planned to hand over King Zhao to Wu. The king heard about this and was able to avoid this disaster. He cut Ziqi's chest and used the blood in a covenant with the lord of Sui and left.[100]

4.23. 吳王入郢，止留。伍胥以不得昭王，乃掘平王之墓，出其屍，鞭之三百，左足踐其腹，右手抉其目，誚之曰：「誰使汝用讒諛之

96. The punishment for regicide was extermination of the entire clan.

97. The ruling family of Sui was related to the Zhou kings. Sui was established in early Western Zhou but was annexed by Chu in the late Spring and Autumn period. This story is also recorded in *Shiji*, 66:2176. See also *Zuozhuan*, Lord Ding 4; Yang Bojun, 1546; Durrant, Li, and Schaberg, 1759.

98. *Zuozhuan*, Lord Xi 28, Luan Zhi said that along the Han River all the states ruled by the surname of Ji 姬, the surname of the Zhou royal house, have been destroyed by Chu. Sui and Wu were both descendants of the Zhou. See Yang Bojun, 459, 1547; Durrant, Li, and Schaberg, 417, 1759. See also *Shiji*, 66:2176.

99. Meaning it serves both heaven's will and the Zhou house.

100. This is not found in *Shiji*. *Shiji*, however, reports that the Sui people wanted to kill the king. Prince Qi (王子綦) saved the king by hiding him and pretending himself to be the king. See *Shiji*, 66:2176. Prince Qi is probably Major Qi (*Sima Qi* 司馬子綦) who was mentioned as a loyal minister who admonished King Zhao in both *Zhuangzi* and *Shuoyuan*. See Wang Xianqian 王先謙, *Zhuangzi jijie* 莊子集解 (Beijing: Zhonghua shuju, 2012), 306. See also Xiang Zonglu 向宗魯, *Shuoyuan jiaozheng* 說苑校證 (Beijing: Zhonghua shuju, 1987), 220.

口，殺我父兄，豈不冤哉？」即令闔閭妻昭王夫人，伍胥、孫武、白喜亦妻子常、司馬成之妻，以辱楚之君臣也。

4.23. The king of Wu entered Ying and stayed there. Wu Zixu, due to the fact that he could not capture King Zhao, excavated King Ping's tomb. He dug out the king's corpse and whipped it three hundred times. Stepping on the king's abdomen with his left foot and gouging out the king's eyes with his right hand,[101] Wu Zixu castigated the king, saying, "What led you to follow slanderous words and kill my father and older brother? Weren't they wronged?" He then suggested Helü take King Zhao's wife as his consort. Wu Zixu, Sun Wu, and Bo Pi also took Zichang's and Sima Cheng's wives in order to humiliate the ruler and ministers of Chu.

4.24. 遂引軍擊鄭，鄭定公前殺太子建而困迫子胥，故怨鄭。兵將入境，鄭定公大懼，乃令國中曰：「有能還吳軍者，吾與分國而治。」漁者之子應募，曰：「臣能還之。不用尺兵斗糧，得一橈而行歌道中，即還矣。」公乃與漁者之子一橈。子胥軍將至，當道扣橈而歌曰：「蘆中人。」如是再。子胥聞之，愕然大驚，曰：「何等人者？」即請與語：「公為何誰矣？」曰：「漁父者子。吾國君懼怖，令於國：『有能還吳軍者，與之分國而治。』臣念前人與君相逢於途，今從君乞鄭之國。」子胥歎曰：「悲哉！吾蒙子前人之恩，自致於此。上天蒼蒼，豈敢忘也？」於是乃釋鄭國，還軍守楚，求昭王所在日急。

4.24. Wu Zixu then led the troops to attack Zheng. Because previously Lord Ding of Zheng killed the Heir-Apparent Jian and forced Wu Zixu into a difficult situation, Wu Zixu thereupon bore a grudge against Zheng.[102] When the Wu troops were about to cross the border, Lord Ding of Zheng was greatly frightened.[103] He issued an order in the state, saying, "If there is anyone who can cause the Wu troops to retreat, I will share the state and govern it together with him." The fisherman's son answered the call,[104] saying, "I, your subject, can make the Wu troops return. I do not need any weapons or supplies. If I could have a small oar, I will sing and walk on the road, and the Wu troops will immediately retreat." The lord then gave the fisherman's son a small oar. When Wu Zixu's troops were about to arrive, the fisherman's son stood in the road, struck the oar and sang, "The Man in

---

101. *Shiji* writes that Wu Zixu whipped the king's corpse three hundred times. This additional mutilation of the body is not found in *Shiji*. See *Shiji*, 66:2176.

102. See *WYCQ*, 3.7.

103. Lord Ding of Zheng killed the Heir Apparent. However, it was in fact during the reign of Lord Xian of Zheng 鄭獻公 that the Wu troops were about to attack Zheng.

104. This is the fisherman who helped Wu Zixu across the river.

the Weeds." Thus he sang twice. Wu Zixu was greatly shocked upon hearing this, asking, "Who is this man?" He quickly invited him for a conversation and asked, "Who are you, sir?" The answer was, "I am the fisherman's son. My lord is terrified by your army. He issued an order in the state, saying, 'If there is anyone who can cause the Wu troops to retreat, I will share the land and govern the state with him.' I, your servant, thought of the fact that my deceased father had met you on the road; I now beg from you the survival of the state of Zheng." Wu Zixu lamented, "How tragic! I am indebted for the kindness granted by your deceased father and, because of this, have come to the present situation. Under the majesty of heaven, how dare I forget this?" He thereupon gave up his attack on the state of Zheng and returned the troops to guard Chu while he urgently sought the location of King Zhao every day.

4.25. 申包胥亡在山中，聞之，乃使人謂子胥曰：「子之報讎，其以甚乎？子，故平王之臣，北面事之。今於僇屍之辱，豈道之極乎？」子胥曰：「為我謝申包胥，曰：『日暮路遠，倒行而逆施之於道也。』」

申包胥知不可，乃之於秦，求救楚。晝馳夜趨，足踵蹠劈，裂裳裹膝，鶴倚哭於秦庭，七日七夜，口不絕聲。秦桓公素沉湎，不恤國事。申包胥哭已，歌曰：「吳為無道，封豕長蛇，以食上國，欲有天下，政從楚起。寡君出，在草澤，使來告急。」如此七日。桓公大驚：「楚有賢臣如是。吳猶欲滅之。寡人無臣若斯者，其亡無日矣。」為賦《無衣》之詩，曰：「豈曰無衣，與子同袍。王于興師，與子同仇。」

包胥曰：「臣聞戻德無厭，王不憂鄰國，疆埸之患。逮吳之未定，王其取分焉。若楚遂亡，於秦何利？則亦亡君之土也。願王以神靈存之，世以事王。」秦伯使辭焉，曰：「寡人聞命矣。子且就館，將圖而告。」包胥曰：「寡君今在草野，未獲所伏，臣何敢即安？」復立於庭，倚牆而哭，日夜不絕聲，水不入口。秦伯為之垂涕，即出師而送之。

4.25. Shen Baoxu was hiding in the mountains. When he heard what had happened, Shen Baoxu sent someone to Wu Zixu, saying, "Perhaps your revenge is too harsh. In the past you were a subject of King Ping and, facing north, you served him.[105] Now don't you consider this humiliation of mutilating the body too extreme for the proper Way?" Wu Zixu replied, "Please forward my gratitude to Shen Baoxu by delivering the following: 'The sun is

105. In ancient times, the ruler sat facing south and the ministers bowed to him facing north. Therefore, facing north indicates the position of a minister.

setting and my road is still far. I will arrive at the Way by walking backwards and going against common rules.'"[106]

Shen Baoxu knew that Wu Zixu could not be persuaded. He then went to Qin to beseech Qin to rescue Chu. Day and night he traveled hurriedly, and the skin of his soles and heels cracked. He tore his clothes and wrapped his knees with the cloth. Standing like a crane, he leaned on the wall and cried in the Qin court. For seven days and seven nights, his crying never ceased. Lord Huan of Qin had always indulged himself in pleasures and had never cared about state affairs.[107] Shen Baoxu cried and sang, "Wu acts with no regard to the Way. It is like a big hog or a giant snake and gobbles up the noble states.[108] Its ambition is to conquer the world. Its attack began at Chu and my humble lord has run away to wild fields.[109] He sent me to inform you of this emergency." He did this for seven days and Lord Huan was greatly surprised,[110] saying, "Chu has such a virtuous officer, yet Wu still wants to destroy it. I, a man of little virtue, do not have any officer like him, so my demise is impending." He chanted the ode "Wuyi" to Shen Baoxu, and the lyric read: "How can you say you have no clothes, I will give you the same robes as my own. The king will mobilize his army, and with you face the same enemy."[111]

Shen Baoxu said, "I, your subject, have heard that a violent nature cannot be satisfied. If Your Majesty does not worry about the neighboring state, disaster along the borders will occur.[112] Given that Wu has not yet conquered the entirety of Chu, Your Majesty perhaps should claim a share of it. If Chu is completely destroyed, what benefit will this bring to Qin? This would mean the loss of your land.[113] I wish Your Majesty to use your divine power and save Chu so that, generation after generation, Chu will serve Your Majesty." The Marquis of Qin sent an envoy to reject this,[114] saying, "I, a man of little

---

106. Wu Zixu is saying that he is determined to gain revenge but is concerned that time passes too quickly; therefore, he is doing whatever fits his goal regardless whether it is in accordance with the rules.

107. According to *Shiji*, this should be Lord Ai of Qin 秦哀公, not Lord Huan. See *Shiji*, 40:665. See also *Shiji*, 66:2177.

108. These are the legendary beasts that brought harm to the people and were killed by the hero Yi 羿. See Major et al., *Huainanzi*, 275.

109. 政 (*zheng*) is a loan word for 征 (*zheng*), "to attack."

110. Again, this should be Lord Ai of Qin.

111. This poem from the state of Qin expresses comradeship and is found in the *Book of Songs*, the earliest anthology of poetry in Chinese history.

112. The neighboring state refers to Chu.

113. Chu's land could be obtained by Qin.

114. This is still Lord Huan of Qin. Qin was initially bestowed the rank of marquis by the Zhou king.

virtue, have heard your command. You, sir, should for now go to your lodging. I will consider this and then inform you." Shen Baoxu said, "My humble lord is now in the wild fields. I have not yet found out where he is hiding. How could I, your servant, dare to go and rest?" He again stood in the court, leaned against the wall and cried. Day and night his crying did not stop and no water passed his lips. The Marquis of Qin shed tears for him and then sent troops to accompany Shen Baoxu to Chu.[115]

4.26. 十年，秦師未出，越王元常恨闔閭破之檇里，興兵伐吳。吳在楚，越盜掩襲之。

4.26. In the tenth year (505 BCE), before the Qin troops had left the state, Yuanchang, king of Yue, hating Helü for his destruction of Zuili, mobilized troops and launched a military expedition against Wu. The Wu troops were in Chu at that time, so Yue, like a group of bandits, attacked them by surprise.

4.27. 六月，申包胥以秦師至，秦使公子子蒲、子虎率車五百乘救楚擊吳。二子曰：「吾未知吳道。」使楚師前與吳戰，而即會之，大敗夫概。

4.27. In the sixth month, Shen Baoxu arrived with Qin troops. Qin sent Gongzi Zipu and Gongzi Zihu to lead five hundred chariots to save Chu and attack Wu. The two Gongzi said, "We do not yet know the military strategy of Wu." They first sent Chu troops to engage in battle with Wu; they then quickly joined the Chu army and soundly defeated Fugai.[116]

4.28. 七月，楚司馬子成、秦公子子蒲，與吳王相守，私以間兵伐唐，滅之。子胥久留楚求昭王，不去。

4.28. In the seventh month, Sima Zicheng of Chu and Gongzi Zipu of Qin confronted the king of Wu. They secretly sent other troops to attack Tang and destroyed it.[117] Wu Zixu was in Chu for a long time pursuing King Zhao, and did not leave.

4.29. 夫概師敗，卻退。九月，潛歸，自立為吳王。闔閭聞之，乃釋楚師，欲殺夫概，奔楚，昭王封夫概於棠溪，闔閭遂歸。

---

115. This is adapted from *Zuozhuan*, Lord Ding 4. See Yang Bojun, 1548; Durrant, Li, and Schaberg, 1761.

116. Fugai is the younger brother of Helü. He won the battle in Boju. See *WYCQ*, 4.21. See also *Zuozhuan*, Lord Ding 5; Yang Bojun, 1551; Durrant, Li, and Schaberg, 1763.

117. Because Tang followed Wu and attacked Chu.

4.29. After Fugai's troops were defeated, he retreated. In the ninth month, he secretly returned to Wu and established himself as the king of Wu. Upon hearing this, Helü ceased his battle with Chu troops and wanted to kill Fugai. Fugai fled to Chu and was enfeoffed at Tangxi by King Zhao. Helü then returned to Wu.[118]

4.30. 子胥、孫武、白喜留，敗楚師於淮澨，秦師又敗吳師。楚子期將焚吳軍，子西曰：「吾國父兄身戰，暴骨草野焉，不收，又焚之，其可乎？」子期曰：「亡國失眾，存沒所在，又何殺生以愛死？死如有知，必將乘煙起而助我；如其無知，何惜草中之骨而亡吳國？」遂焚而戰，吳師大敗。

子胥等相謂曰：「彼楚雖敗我餘兵，未有所損我者。」孫武曰：「吾以吳干戈，西破楚，逐昭王而屠荊平王墓，割戮其屍，亦已足矣。」子胥曰：「自霸王以來，未有人臣報讎如此者也。行，去矣！」

4.30. Wu Zixu, Sun Wu, and Bo Pi stayed in Chu and defeated the Chu troops at Huaishi. The Qin troops again defeated the Wu army. Ziqi of Chu planned to attack by setting fire to the Wu troops, and Zixi remonstrated,[119] saying, "Our father and brothers sacrificed their lives fighting against Wu. Their bodies were exposed in the wild. We have already failed to retrieve them, is it acceptable to burn them?" Ziqi answered, "We have lost our capital and our people. Our survival or demise lies in this battle, how can we cherish the dead by letting the living die? If those who have died are conscious, they will certainly rise up with the smoke and assist us. If they are not conscious, why value the bones in the grass and let the Wu army escape?" Chu then set the fire and fought, and the Wu troops were soundly defeated.[120]

Wu Zixu and the others said to each other, "Although Chu has defeated our auxiliary troops, they did not do any real damage to us." Sun Wu said, "We, commanding the weapons of Wu, destroyed Chu to the west, chased King Zhao away, raided King Ping's tomb, and mutilated his corpse. That is already enough." Wu Zixu said, "Since the time of hegemons, no minister has taken revenge like this. Alright, let's leave."

---

118. See also *Shiji*, 31:1467; *Zuozhuan*, Lord Ding 5; Yang Bojun, 1551; Durrant, Li, and Schaberg, 1765.

119. This is the same Ziqi who planned to betray the Chu king when the king was fleeing. See *WYCQ*, 4.22. Zixi is also King Ping's son; stories of Zixi are found in *Zuozhuan*, Lord Ding 5; Yang Bojun, 1553–4; Durrant, Li, and Schaberg, 1765.

120. This is also recorded in *Zuozhuan*, Lord Ding 5. See Yang Bojun 1552; Durrant, Li, and Schaberg, 1765.

4.31. 吳軍去後，昭王反國。樂師扈子非荊王信讒佞，殺伍子奢、白州犁，而寇不絕於境，至乃掘平王墓，戮屍奸喜，以辱楚君臣；又傷昭王困迫，幾為天下大鄙，然已愧矣，乃援琴為楚作《窮劫之曲》，以暢君之迫厄之暢達也。其詞曰：「王耶王耶何乖烈，不顧宗廟聽讒孽，任用無忌多所殺，誅夷白氏族幾滅。二子東奔適吳越，吳王哀痛助忉怛，垂涕舉兵將西伐，伍胥、白喜、孫武決。三戰破郢王奔發，留兵縱騎虜荊闕，楚荊骸骨遭發掘，鞭辱腐屍恥難雪！幾危宗廟社稷滅，嚴王何罪國幾絕。卿士悽愴民惻悷，吳軍雖去怖不歇。願王更隱撫忠節，勿為讒口能謗褻。」昭王垂涕，深知琴曲之情，扈子遂不復鼓矣。

4.31. After the Wu troops had left, King Zhao returned to the capital. The musician Huzi blamed King Zhao of Chu for believing those slanderous and evil ministers, for killing Wu She and Bo Zhouli, and for causing constant invasions along their borders. He was even accountable for the digging up of King Ping's tomb, the flogging of his corpse, and the raping of the royal concubines as an insult to the ruler and ministers of Chu.[121] At the same time, Huzi also felt sorrow for the persecution and difficulty King Zhao had suffered, having almost become the lowliest man in the world, and having been embarrassed in these ways. He thereupon played the zither and composed a "Song of the Ravaging of Chu," in order to lament the difficulties the king suffered, and to sooth him. The lyrics read,

"Oh my king, oh my king, how absurd and cruel you are,
Neglecting your ancestral temple, listening to slander,
Trusting Bi Wuji, you killed many innocents,
And punished the Bo clan almost to the point of extinction.
The two sons fled east to Wu and Yue,[122]
The king of Wu was saddened by their grief and gave them aid.
Shedding tears, he mobilized his troops and prepared to invade the West,
With Wu Zixu, Bo Pi, and Sun Wu planning the strategy.
After three battles they conquered Ying and forced my king to flee,
They stationed their troops and loosed their horses, looting the Chu palace.
The Chu king's bones were dug up,
and the disgrace of flogging them was too much to wash away.

121. According to Lu Wenchao, the character 喜 (*xi*) should be 妻 (*qi*), wife.

122. The two sons are Wu Zixu and Bo Pi.

The ancestral temple was at risk, the altar and shrine of the state nearly destroyed.
What crime did King Zhuang commit to almost bring his state to its end?[123]
Ministers and officers bereft, the folk grievously sorrowful,
Although the Wu troops have gone, the horror still lingers.
I want my king to correct his faults, and console the loyal and dutiful,
And not let slanderers utter defaming words."[124]

King Zhao shed tears and deeply appreciated the feelings expressed in the song. Huzi never played the zither again.

4.32. 子胥等過溧陽瀨水之上，乃長太息曰：「吾嘗飢於此，乞食於一女子，女子飼我，遂投水而亡。將欲報以百金，而不知其家。」乃投金水中而去。

有頃，一老嫗行哭而來，人問曰：「何哭之悲？」嫗曰：「吾有女子，守居三十不嫁。往年擊綿於此，遇一窮途君子而輒飯之，而恐事泄，自投於瀨水。今聞伍君來，不得其償，自傷虛死，是故悲耳。」人曰：「子胥欲報百金，不知其家，投金水中而去矣。」嫗遂取金而歸。

4.32. When Wu Zixu and his army were passing the bank of the Lai River at Liyang, he sighed deeply, saying, "I once suffered hunger here and begged food from a woman; she fed me and then threw herself in the river and died. I wanted to repay her kindness with a hundred gold pieces, but I do not know where her family is." He then threw the gold in the river and left.[125]

Shortly afterward, an old lady came and cried. Some asked her, "Why do you cry so pathetically?" The old lady said, "I had a daughter who cherished her chastity and lived alone without getting married for thirty years. Several years ago when she came here to wash silk, she ran into a gentleman who was in dire straits and immediately gave him food. She was afraid this would be known by others and threw herself into the Lai River. Now I have heard that the gentleman Wu Zixu had come by, but I cannot obtain his reward. I feel sad because my daughter has died in vain, and I cry for this reason."

---

123. The character 嚴 (*yan*) here should be 莊 (*zhang*) and the king is King Zhuang of Chu, who brought Chu to the status of a hegemon. The use of 嚴 instead of 莊 is to avoid the taboo of Eastern Han Emperor Ming, whose name is Liu Zhuang 劉莊 (28–75).

124. The style of this poem is seven characters per line, a style that appeared at a much later time, beginning in the Han Dynasty. Consequently, this could not be an authentic work from the late Spring and Autumn period.

125. See *WYCQ*, 3.9.

The man said, "Wu Zixu wanted to repay a hundred gold pieces but did not know the whereabouts of your house, so he threw the gold in the water and left." The old lady then retrieved the gold and went home.

4.33. 子胥歸吳，吳王聞三師將至，治魚為鱠，將到之日，過時不至，魚臭。須臾子胥至，闔閭出鱠而食，不知其臭，王復重為之，其味如故。吳人作鱠者，自闔閭之造也。

4.33. Wu Zixu returned to Wu. The king of Wu heard that the three generals were about to arrive and ordered fish to be cooked and minced. On the day the generals were expected to arrive, they returned later than planned, and the fish spoiled. Shortly after this, Wu Zixu arrived. Helü presented the fish and served it to Wu Zixu. Wu Zixu did not notice the smell. The king repeated making this dish and its flavor tasted the same. The making of minced fish by the people of Wu began with Helü.

4.34. 諸將既從還楚，因更名閶門曰破楚門。復謀伐齊，齊子使女為質於吳，吳王因為太子波聘齊女。女少，思齊，日夜號泣，因乃為病。闔閭乃起北門，名曰望齊門，令女往遊其上。女思不止，病日益甚，乃至殂落。女曰：「令死者有知，必葬我於虞山之巔，以望齊國。」闔閭傷之，正如其言，乃葬虞山之巔。

4.34. After the generals returned from Chu, they renamed Chang Gate the "Gate of Destroying Chu." They furthermore planned to launch a military expedition against Qi. The marquis of Qi sent his daughter to Wu as a hostage. The king of Wu then married the daughter of Qi to the Heir Apparent Bo. The girl was young and she missed Qi. She cried day and night and consequently fell ill. Helü therefore constructed a northern gate at the capital and named it "Gate of Gazing at Qi" and let the girl wander on it. The girl's nostalgia did not cease and her illness became more severe day by day, and eventually she died. The girl had said, "If the dead have consciousness, please be sure to bury me at the top of Yu Mountain, so I can gaze at Qi." Helü was saddened by this. He buried her at the top of Yu Mountain, just as she had requested.[126]

4.35. 是時，太子亦病而死，闔閭謀擇諸公子可立者，未有定計。波太子夫差日夜告於伍胥曰：「王欲立太子，非我而誰當立？此計在君耳。」伍子胥曰：「太子未有定，我入則決矣。」

---

126. The Yu Mountain is located in Changshu 常熟 County. This is also mentioned in *Yue jue shu*. See Li Bujia, 35.

闔閭有頃召子胥，謀立太子，子胥曰：「臣聞：『祀廢於絕後，興於有嗣。』今太子不祿，早失侍御，今王欲立太子者，莫大乎波秦之子夫差。」闔閭曰：「夫愚而不仁，恐不能奉統於吳國。」子胥曰：「夫差信以愛人，端於守節，敦於禮義。父死子代，經之明文。」闔閭曰：「寡人從子。」

立夫差為太子，使太子屯兵守楚，留止自治宮室：立射臺於安平里，華池在平昌，南城宮在長樂里。闔閭出入游臥，秋冬治於城中，春夏治於城外，治姑蘇之臺。旦食組山，晝游蘇臺，射於鷗陂，馳於游臺，興樂石城，走犬長洲，斯止闔閭之霸時。

4.35. At that time, the Heir Apparent Bo also died due to illness. Helü consulted with the officers in order to choose one of his sons as successor, but the decision was not yet made. Bo's son Fuchai day and night talked to Wu Zixu,[127] saying, "The king wants to establish an Heir Apparent, if it is not me, who else should be established? The plan depends on you." Wu Zixu said, "The selection of the Heir Apparent has not been decided. It will be as soon as I have entered the palace."

Helü soon summoned Wu Zixu and consulted with him on the matter of establishing the Heir Apparent. Wu Zixu said, "I, your subject, have heard that 'a state sacrifice will become extinct because of a lack of posterity; it will become prosperous because of a line of successors.' Now the Heir Apparent died young and, at an early age, lost the opportunities to attend at your ritual services. Now, among the candidates from whom Your Majesty wants to establish as the Heir Apparent, no one in line is superior to the son of Bo."[128] Helü said, "Fuchai is unwise and not humane, I am afraid that he is incapable of carrying out the succession of the state." Wu Zixu said, "Fuchai is trustworthy and loves the people. His conduct is correct and he upholds the principles. He is sincere in observing the ritual rules. And it is clearly written in the classics that when a father dies his son succeeds him." Helü said, "I, a man of little virtue, follow your advice."

Helü established Fuchai as the Heir Apparent and sent him to command the troops guarding against Chu. The king himself stayed at the capital and constructed palace buildings. He built an archery terrace in the Anping District, a Hua Pond in the Pingchang District, and a Nancheng Palace in the Changle District. Helü moved in and out of the capital for excursions and rest. In autumn and winter he took care of government affairs in the city while in spring and summer he did this on Gusu Terrace outside of

127. There is a mistake here. Fuchai is also Helü's son, not his grandson.

128. The character 秦 (*qin*) does not make sense in this sentence. It has probably been inserted by mistake.

the city. In the mornings he enjoyed breakfast at Zu Mountain; daytimes he sought pleasure on Gusu Terrace. He hunted on the Ou river bank, rode horses on You Terrace, made merry at Shicheng, and raced dogs at Changzhou. This leisure began and ended during the time when Helü acted as the hegemon.

4.36. 於是太子定，因伐楚，破師，拔番。楚懼吳兵復往，乃去郢，徙于蔿若。當此之時，吳以子胥、白喜、孫武之謀，西破彊楚，北威齊晉，南伐於越。

4.36. At that time, because the Heir Apparent had already been chosen, Helü then launched a military expedition against Chu. He defeated the Chu army and conquered Po. The king of Chu was afraid that the Wu troops would return, and he then left Ying and relocated to Weiruo. At this time, the king of Wu adopted the strategies of Wu Zixu, Bo Pi, and Sun Wu: to the west he defeated the mighty Chu, to the north he threatened Qi and Jin, and to the south he attacked Yue.

吳越春秋夫差內傳第五

# Chapter 5

# The Inner Tradition of Fuchai

## Introduction

Fuchai was the last king of Wu. According to Sima Qian, Fuchai was a complicated and tragic figure who avenged his father's death, defeated Wu's longtime rival Yue, extended Wu's influence to the north, and led Wu to become a political hegemon among the states, but eventually brought about the demise of his state and himself because of his failure to listen to the advice of loyal ministers.

Instead of picturing the trajectory of Fuchai's life, the *WYCQ* chapter focuses on the fall of the king of Wu, highlighting Fuchai's obstinance, his trust of dishonest words, his executions of loyal ministers, and the eventual decline of his state. The chapter therefore omits the early successful years of King Fuchai and begins with the eleventh year of his rule, the year he ignored the most dangerous enemy Yue in the south and extended his power north by attacking the state of Qi. The consequences of his political ambition, compounded by his inability to distinguish the good from the crooked, dominate the narratives of the chapter. The chapter comes to an end with his reluctant suicide preceded by expressions of remorse for killing Wu Zixu and Gongsun Sheng. In order to stress its theme, this *WYCQ* chapter adopts many materials that are either not found in or contradict historical texts such as *Zuozhuan* and *Shiji*; these materials are more often fictional than historically accurate. For example, in this chapter, Fuchai's act of mutilating Wu Zixu's and Gongsun Sheng's bodies is probably influenced by folklore. Moreover, the reluctant death of Fuchai in the *WYCQ* chapter conflicts with the account in Sima Qian's writing, which records that Fuchai chose to commit suicide rather than live as a vassal to King Goujian of Yue.

Some of the stories in this chapter demonstrate strong Eastern Han *chenwei* 讖緯 characteristics. For example, Fuchai's dream before attacking Qi and the Chief Chancellor Bo Pi's and Gongsun Sheng's interpretations of the dream are typical of Han *chenwei* thought. Even Wu Zixu's admonition against Fuchai's plan to attack Qi is partly based upon *yinyang* divination.

Although many of the stories in this chapter are purely fictional, they create narrative tension that highlights Fuchai's obstinance and inability to heed loyal advice as the reasons for his fall. In addition to this moral lesson, the narrative of the chapter served to entertain readers with good stories that are dominated by outstanding characters, brilliant conversations, or dramatic conflicts. Sometimes this purpose is achieved by sacrificing historicity or even the integrity of the narratives. This is probably why the lengthy episode involving Zigong's clever persuasion of the rulers of Qi, Wu, Yue, and Jin is included in this chapter.

## Translation

5.1. 十一年，夫差北伐齊。齊使大夫高氏謝吳師，曰：「齊孤立於國，倉庫空虛，民人離散。齊以吳為彊輔，今未往告急而吳見伐，請伏國人於郊，不敢陳戰爭之辭，惟吳哀齊之不濫也。」吳師即還。

5.1. In the eleventh year of King Fuchai (485 BCE),[1] Fuchai launched a military expedition north against Qi. Qi sent Grand Minister Gao Wupi to entreat the Wu troops,[2] saying, "The ruler of Qi lacks support in the capital. His granaries and warehouses are empty and his people are scattered. The ruler of Qi relies upon Wu for its strong support. Now, before he comes to Wu in urgent need of help, he is attacked by Wu. He requests to prostrate his people at the suburb of the capital and dares not to mention any words

1. According to *Zuozhuan* and *Shiji*, there are several important events between the death of King Helü and the eleventh year of King Fuchai that are omitted by the *WYCQ*. These include: Bo Pi became the chief chancellor in 495 BCE. Fuchai defeated Goujian and agreed to make peace with Yue in 494 BCE. Wu invaded Chen in 494 and 489 BCE. Wu attacked Lu in 488 BCE and planned a military expedition against Qi in 486 BCE. Under Fuchai's rule, Wu quickly expanded its influence and began to compete with the states in the Central Plain.

2. Xu Tianhu argues that the grand minister was Gao Wupi. See Zhang Jue, 119n3.

pertaining to war.[3] He only wishes Wu would take pity on Qi, whose ruler never fails to be obedient."[4] The Wu troops therefore returned.[5]

5.2. 十二年，夫差復北伐齊。越王聞之，率眾以朝於吳，而以重寶厚獻太宰嚭。嚭喜，受越之賂，愛信越殊甚，日夜為言於吳王，王信用嚭之計。伍胥大懼，曰：「是棄吳也。」乃進諫曰：「越在，心腹之病。不前除其疾，今信浮辭僞詐而貪齊，破齊，譬由磐石之田，無立其苗也。願王釋齊而前越，不然，悔之無及。」吳王不聽，使子胥使於齊，通期戰之會。子胥謂其子曰：「我數諫王，王不我用，今見吳之亡矣。汝與吾俱亡，亡無為也。」乃屬其子於齊鮑氏而還。

太宰嚭既與子胥有隙，因讒之曰：「子胥為強暴力諫，願王少厚焉，」王曰：「寡人知之。」

未興師，會魯使子貢聘於吳。

5.2. In the twelfth year of King Fuchai (484 BCE), Fuchai again launched a military expedition north against Qi.[6] Upon hearing this, the king of Yue led his ministers to pay homage to Wu and presented many precious treasures to the Chief Chancellor Bo Pi.[7] Bo Pi was delighted by this and accepted the bribe from Yue. His fondness for and trust in Yue were extraordinary; day and night he spoke to the king of Wu on behalf of Yue. The king of Wu trusted Bo Pi and adopted his advice. Wu Zixu greatly feared this, saying, "This means the destruction of Wu."[8] He therefore presented his admonishment to the king, saying, "To Wu, the existence of Yue is as dangerous as disease in the heart and the stomach, yet Your Majesty fails to act and exterminate the disease. Now, you trusted high-sounding words and deceitful statements and covet Qi. Even if you were to conquer Qi, it would be the same as obtaining a field full of rocks, in which it is impossible to plant seeds. I wish Your Majesty would abort your expedition against Qi and move

3. This is a gesture of submission.

4. 濫 (*lan*) means excessive here. The Qi minister is saying that the ruler of Qi has never crossed the line as a subordinate to the king of Wu and his behaviors were not excessive in terms of proper ritual.

5. The event here is different from that in *Zuozhuan*, which records that in the tenth year of King Fuchai (486 BCE), Wu and Lu attacked Qi. The people of Qi defeated the Wu naval troops and Wu was forced to retreat. See *Zuozhuan*, Lord Ai 10; Yang Bojun, 1656; Durrant, Li, and Schaberg, 1893.

6. *Zuozhuan*, Lord Ai 11 reports that Wu and Lu launched a military expedition against Qi. On the twenty-seventh day of the fifth month, Qi and Wu battled at Ailing and Qi was defeated by Wu. *WYCQ* recorded this in the twelfth year of King Fuchai. For a detailed account of the battle at Ailing, see *Zuozhuan*, Lord Ai 11; Yang Bojun, 1661–63; Durrant, Li, and Schaberg, 1901.

7. This is King Goujian of Yue. In *WYCQ*, chaps. 6–10 focus on Goujian's stories.

8. *Wu* 吾, "me," is probably a mistake for 吳, *Wu*. *Shiji* also uses the character 吳 in this sentence. See *Shiji*, 31:1472.

against Yue first. Otherwise, it will be too late for you to repent."[9] The king of Wu refused to listen. He sent Wu Zixu to Qi as an emissary to negotiate an agreed upon date for the battle. Wu Zixu told his son, "I admonished the king several times but the king failed to listen to me. Now I can see the end of Wu. It is worthless for you to die with Wu."[10] He then entrusted his son to the Bao clan of Qi and returned.[11]

Because the Chief Chancellor Bo Pi bore a grudge against Wu Zixu, he took the chance to slander Wu Zixu to the king: "Wu Zixu's personality is rude and violent, and he is obstinate in admonishing. I wish Your Majesty to show him less favor." The king said, "I, a man of little virtue, know about this."[12]

Before the Wu troops had yet to mobilize, it happened that Lu sent Zigong to Wu for an official visit.[13]

5.3. 十三年，齊大夫陳成恆欲弑簡公，陰憚高、國、鮑、晏，故前興兵伐魯。魯君憂之，孔子患之，召門人而謂之曰：「諸侯有相伐者，丘常恥之。夫魯，父母之國也，丘墓在焉。今齊將伐之，子無意一出耶？」子路辭出，孔子止之；子張、子石請行，孔子弗許；子貢辭出，孔子遣之。

5.3. In the thirteenth year of King Fuchai (483 BCE), Chen Chenghuan, a minister of Qi, plotted to assassinate Lord Jian of Qi.[14] In his heart Chen Chenghuan was afraid of the Gao clan, Guo clan, Pao clan, and Yan clan,[15]

---

9. A more elaborate version of the admonishment of Wu Zixu is found in *Zuozhuan*, Lord Ai 11; Yang Bojun, 1664; Durrant, Li, and Schaberg, 1901.

10. See fn 8. 吾, "me," is a mistake for 吳, "Wu." See *Shiji*, 66:2179.

11. *Zuozhuan* and *Shiji* present conflicting accounts about to whom Wu Zixu entrusted his son. The biography of Wu Zixu in *Shiji* states it was Bao Mu 鮑牧; however, according to *Zuozhuan*, Bao Mu had already been killed by Lord Dao of Qi four years earlier in 487 BCE. It is difficult to decide which source is more reliable. See *Shiji*, 66:2179. *Zuozhuan*, Lord Ai 8; Yang Bojun, 1651; Durrant, Li, and Schaberg, 1885.

12. Both *Zuozhuan* and *Shiji* record that Fuchai ordered Wu Zixu to commit suicide after he returned from his mission to Qi. The *WYCQ*, however, reported the death as occurring in the following year. See *Shiji*, 66:2180. *Zuozhuan*, Lord Ai 11; Yang Bojun, 1664; Durrant, Li, and Schaberg, 1903.

13. Zigong was a disciple of Confucius. His surname was Duanmu 端木 and his first name was Ci 賜. Zigong was his style. The following accounts of Zigong visiting Qi, Wu, Yue, and Jin are adopted primarily from *Shiji* and *Yue jue shu*.

14. Chen Chenghuan was also called Tian Chang 田常 and was a minister of Qi. His ancestor Chen Wan 陳完 was the son of the lord of Chen. Chen Wan fled to Qi because of the political turmoil in Chen and changed his clan name to Tian. His descendants gradually gained power in Qi. At the time of Lord Jian of Qi 齊簡公, Tian Qi 田乞 seized the power of Qi. His son Tian Chang/Chen Chenghuan assassinated Lord Jian and established Lord Ping of Qi 齊平公 and appointed himself as the prime minister. The Tian clan thereby completely controlled Qi politics.

15. The Gao clan probably refers to Gao Wupi, see *WYCQ*, 5.1. The Guo clan refers to Guo Shu 國書, who was the chief general of the Qi army defeated by Wu at Ailing. The Bao clan refers to Bao Mu, to whom Wu Zixu entrusted his son. The Yan clan probably refers to Yan Yu 晏圉, son of the famous Qi minister Yan Ying 晏嬰.

he therefore mobilized troops and launched a military expedition against Lu. The ruler of Lu worried about this.[16] Confucius was also concerned about this, and he gathered his disciples and told them, "I, Qiu, often feel it is shameful that the lords attack each other.[17] As for Lu, it is the state where my parents lived and where my ancestral tombs are located. Now that Qi is going to attack it, do you have no intention of going to other states and seeking support for Lu?" Zilu announced his departure but was stopped by Confucius; Zizhang and Zishi requested to go on the mission but were not permitted by Confucius.[18] When Zigong made a request to leave, Confucius sent him on the mission.[19]

5.4. 子貢北之齊，見成恆，因謂曰：「夫魯者，難伐之國，而君伐，過矣。」

成恆曰：「魯何難伐也？」

子貢曰：「其城薄以卑，其池狹以淺，其君愚而不仁，大臣無用，士惡甲兵，不可與戰。君不若伐吳。夫吳，城厚而崇，池廣以深，甲堅士選，器飽弩勁，又使明大夫守之，此易邦也。」

成恆忿然作色，曰：「子之所難，人之所易；子之所易，人之所難，而以教恆，何也？」

子貢曰：「臣聞君三封而三不成者，大臣有所不聽者也。今君又欲破魯以廣齊，隳魯以自尊，而君功不與焉。是君上驕主心，下恣群臣，而求以成大事，難矣。且夫上驕則犯，臣驕則爭，此君上於王有遽，而下與大臣交爭。如此，則君立於齊危於累卵。故曰『不如伐吳。』且吳王剛猛而毅，能行其令，百姓習於戰守，明於法禁，齊遇為擒必矣。今君悉四境之甲，出大臣以環之，人民外死，大臣內空，是君上無彊敵之臣，下無黔首之士，孤主制齊者，君也。」

陳恆曰：「善！雖然吾兵已在魯之城下矣。吾去之吳，大臣將有疑我之心，為之奈何？」

子貢曰：「君按兵無伐，請為君南見吳王，請之救魯而伐齊，君因以兵迎之。」

陳恆許諾。

5.4. Zigong went north to Qi and received an audience from Chen Chenghuan. Taking a chance, Zigong told Chen Chenghuan, "Lu is a state that is hard to conquer, yet you attack it, this is your mistake."

16. This is Lord Ai of Lu (r. 494–467 BCE).

17. Confucius's surname is Kong 孔 and his first name is Qiu 丘. He is traditionally believed to have been born in 551 BCE and to have died in 479 BCE.

18. Zilu's name is Zhongyou 仲由; Zilu is his style. Both Zizhang and Zishi were students of Confucius. Their stories can be found in the "Tradition of the Disciples of Confucius" 仲尼弟子列傳 (*Zhongni dizi liezhuan*) in *Shiji*. See *Shiji*, 67: 2191–4, 2203–4, 2219.

19. This and the following persuasions of Zigong are also found in *Shiji*, 67:2197–2201, and *Yue jue shu*, chap. 9; see Li Bujia, 182–88; Milburn, 205–19.

Chen Chenghuan asked, "Why is Lu difficult to conquer?"

Zigong answered, "Because its city wall is thin and low, its city moat is narrow and shallow, its ruler is unwise and inhumane, its officers are not used, and its soldiers loathe the use of armor and weapons, so you should not fight against Lu. Rather, you should attack Wu. As for Wu, its city wall is thick and tall, its city moat is broad and deep, its armor is strong, its troops sharp, its weapons well-maintained, and its crossbows powerful;[20] it also has appointed talented officers to guard it. This is a city easy to conquer."

Chen Chenghuan's anger was apparent on his face. He said, "What you consider difficult is what others consider easy; what is easy to you is difficult to others. Yet you instruct me with these words, is there an explanation for this?"

Zigong replied, "I, your servant, have heard that you were enfeoffed three times but three times you failed, and this is because there were some officials who refused to follow you. Now you further plan to destroy Lu in order to broaden the land of Qi, and ruin Lu for the purpose of honoring yourself—you cannot find merit in doing this, because this, to those above, will cause the ruler to be haughty, for those below it will cause the many officials to be unruly. In this case it is impossible to hope to achieve greatness. Moreover, once a ruler is conceited he will mistreat people; once the officials are unruly they will be bellicose. Thus you harbor a grudge against the ruler above and contend for privilege with officials below. If this is the case, then your position in Qi is more dangerous than piling up eggs. This is the reason I said, 'You should attack Wu instead.' Moreover, the king of Wu is determined, fierce, and resolute; he is able to turn his orders into practice. His people are trained in offense and defense, and they are clear about laws and prohibitions. There is no doubt that Qi troops will be captured once they engaged in battle with Wu. Now if you bring out all the troops within the four corners of Qi and command officials to wear armor,[21] people will die fighting outside of the state and no officials will be left at court. Thus for those above there will be no mighty officials to act as your enemy, and among the folk below there will be no intelligent commoners to resist you. The only one who can isolate the ruler and control Qi is certainly you."

Chen Chenghuan said, "Excellent! However, my troops are already camped underneath the walls of the Lu capital. If I release Lu and invade Wu, it will incur officials' suspicion of me, what should I do about this?"

---

20. According to Zhang Jue, the *Siku quanshu* edition has a different sentence; it reads: 甲堅、器選、士飽、弩勁 (*jiajian, qixuan, shibao, nujin*), which means "armor strong, weapons maintained, soldiers well-fed and crossbows powerful." This makes more sense than the contents of the current edition. See Zhang Jue, 124n3.

21. 環 (*huan*) should be 擐 (*huan*), "to wear, to put on."

Zigong answered, "Please keep your troops from attacking, and please allow me to travel south to see the king of Wu on your behalf. I will ask him to save Lu and attack Qi, then you can confront Wu with your army."

Chen Chenghuan agreed.

5.5. 子貢南見吳王，謂吳王曰：「臣聞之，『王者不絕世，而霸者無彊敵。千鈞之重，加銖而移。』今萬乘之齊而私千乘之魯，而與吳爭彊，臣竊為君恐焉。且夫救魯，顯名也；伐齊，大利也，義存亡魯，害暴齊而威強晉，則王不疑也。」

吳王曰：「善。雖然，吾嘗與越戰，棲之會稽，入臣於吳，不即誅之，三年使歸。夫越君，賢主，苦身勞力，夜以接日，內飾其政，外事諸侯，必將有報我之心。子待我伐越而聽子。」

子貢曰：「不可。夫越之彊不過於魯，吳之彊不過於齊，王以伐越而不聽臣，齊亦已私魯矣。且畏小越而惡彊齊，不勇也；見小利而忘大害，不智也。臣聞仁人不因居，以廣其德；智者不棄時，以舉其功；王者不絕世，以立其義。且夫畏越如此，臣請東見越王，使出師以從下吏。」吳王大悅。

5.5. Zigong traveled south to see the king of Wu. He told the king of Wu, "I, your subject, have heard this: 'The kings of the world do not wish to have interrupted successions and hegemons do not want to have powerful rivals. Even for an object that weighs one thousand pounds, adding one ounce can change its balance.'[22] Now the ten-thousand-chariots-strong Qi wants to take the one-thousand-chariots-strong Lu as its own,[23] thus it can contend with Wu for dominance. I, your subject, in my heart am worried about this for you. Furthermore, saving Lu will bring you a good reputation and attacking Qi will bring you great benefits. Thus, nominally, you save Lu from its demise, while in reality you weaken violent Qi and cause powerful Jin to be awed by you; there will be no doubt that you will be a hegemon."

The king of Wu said, "Excellent! However, I fought against the king of Yue once and forced him to flee to the Kuaiji Mountains.[24] He came to Wu

22. 鈞 (*jun*) was a unit to measure weight in ancient times; thirty *jin* 斤 (roughly 33 pounds) make one 鈞. One thousand 鈞 suggests something is heavy. 銖 (*zhu*), on the other hand, is a smaller weight measure. One pound is approximately 240 銖.

23. During the Spring and Autumn Period the size of a state was often measured by the number of chariots its army possessed. According to the Zhou rule, the king of Zhou owns land of one thousand *li* and ten thousand chariots. A lord enjoys land of one hundred *li* and a thousand chariots. However, in the late Spring and Autumn period, some states annexed smaller neighboring states and actually had more than ten thousand chariots. Here Zigong suggests that Qi is already a large state.

24. This refers to an event that occurred in 494 BCE when Fuchai defeated Goujian, the king of Yue, and occupied the Yue capital. Goujian camped on Mount Kuaiji with only five thousand men; he finally submitted himself to Fuchai.

and served me as a servant.[25] I did not kill him at that time and sent him home three years later. The king of Yue is a wise ruler. He exerted himself, exhausted his strength, and day and night he set in order governmental affairs within the state and served the many lords outside of the state.[26] He certainly has the intention of seeking revenge against me. Please wait until after I attack Yue and then I will follow your words."

Zigong said, "This will not work. As for the strength of Yue, it does not overpower Lu, and the strength of Wu does not overpower that of Qi. If Your Majesty discards my suggestion and attacks Yue, Qi will have already seized Lu. Moreover, worrying about the small Yue and fearing the powerful Qi is not courageous; seeing only small benefit yet forgetting great danger is not wise. I, your subject, have heard, 'The humane does not leave people in a difficult situation,[27] thus he extends his virtue to more people; the wise does not give up opportunity, thus he can realize his achievement. The ruler of the world will not have interrupted successions, thus he can establish his principles.' If you are so worried about Yue, I sincerely request to go east to see the king of Yue, and I will make him dispatch troops to follow your expedition as your subordinates."[28]

The king of Wu was greatly delighted.

5.6. 子貢東見越王，王聞之，除道郊迎，身御至舍。問曰：「此僻狹之國，蠻夷之民，大夫何索然若不辱乃至於此？」

子貢 曰：「君處，故來。」

越王勾踐再拜稽首曰：「孤聞：『禍與福為鄰。』今大夫之弔，孤之福矣。孤敢不問其說。」

子貢曰：「臣今者見吳王，告以救魯而伐齊，其心畏越。且夫無報人之志而使人疑之，拙也；有報人之意而使人知之，殆也；事未發而聞之者，危也。三者，舉事之大忌也。」

越王再拜曰：「孤少失前人，內不自量，與吳人戰，軍敗身辱遁逃，上棲會稽，下守海濱，唯魚鱉見矣。今大夫辱弔而身見之，又發玉聲以教孤，孤賴天之賜也，敢不承教？」

子貢曰：「臣聞：『明主任人，不失其能；直士舉賢，不容於世。』故臨財分利則使仁，涉患犯難則使勇，用智圖國則使賢，正

25. *WYCQ*, chap. 7 records details of Goujian serving in Wu as a servant. This is also found in *Shiji*, chap. 41.

26. The character 飾 (*shi*) should be read as 飭 (*chi*), meaning "to regulate" and "to put in order."

27. According to *Yue jue shu*, 因居 (*yinju*) should be 困厄 (*kun'e*), "in a difficult situation." See Li Bujia, 184.

28. 下吏 (*xiali*) literally means lower-rank officials. Here it refers to the attendants of the king of Wu.

天下定諸侯則使聖。兵強而不能行其威勢，在上位而不能施其政令於下者，其君幾乎難矣！臣竊自擇可與成功而至王者，惟幾乎？今吳王有伐齊晉之志，君無愛重器以喜其心，無惡卑辭以盡其禮。而伐齊，齊必戰，不勝，君之福也；彼戰而勝，必以其兵臨晉。騎士銳兵弊乎齊，重寶、車騎、羽毛盡乎晉，則君制其餘矣。」

越王再拜，曰：「昔者吳王分其民之眾以殘吾國，殺敗吾民，鄙吾百姓，夷吾宗廟，國為墟棘，身為魚鱉。孤之怨吳，深於骨髓；而孤之事吳，如子之畏父，弟之敬兄。此孤之死言也。今大夫有賜，故孤敢以報情。孤身不安重席，口不嘗厚味，目不視美色，耳不聽雅音，既已三年矣；焦脣乾舌，苦身勞力，上事群臣，下養百姓；願一與吳交戰於天下平原之野。正身臂而奮吳越之士，繼踵連死，肝腦塗地者，孤之願也。思之三年，不可得也，今內量吾國不足以傷吳，外事諸侯而不能也。願空國，棄群臣，變容貌，易姓名，執箕帚，養牛馬以事之。孤雖知要領不屬，手足異處，四支布陳，為鄉邑笑，孤之意出焉。今大夫有賜，存亡國，舉死人，孤賴天賜，敢不待令乎？」

子貢曰：「夫吳王為人，貪功名而不知利害。」

越王慥然避位。

子貢曰：「臣觀吳王，為數戰伐，士卒不恩，大臣內引，讒人益眾。夫子胥為人，精誠中廉，外明而知時，不以身死隱君之過。正言以忠君，直行以為國，其身死而不聽。太宰嚭為人，智而愚，彊而弱，巧言利辭以內其身，善為詭詐以事其君，知其前而不知其後，順君之過以安其私，是殘國傷君之佞臣也。」

越王大悅。子貢去，越王送之金百鎰，寶劍一，良馬二。子貢不受。

5.6. Zigong traveled toward the east to see the king of Yue. Hearing of this, the king of Yue cleared the road, waited for Zigong in the suburb, and personally drove Zigong's chariot to the guest lodging.[29] He asked Zigong, "This is an isolated and small state, and its people are uncivilized. On what mission have you come, such as to disregard that coming to a state like mine is embarrassing?"

Zigong said, "This is the land of a princely man, and for this reason I came."[30]

29. This is probably the highest way to show respect to a guest.

30. Zigong is implying that the king of Yue is the princely man. *Yue jue shu*, however, records different words: 弔君，故來 (*diajun, gulai*), meaning "I grieve over your death, for this reason I came," which makes more sense when reading Goujian's response in the next line. See Li Bujia, 184; Milburn, 212.

Goujian, the king of Yue, bowed twice and lowered his head to the floor,[31] saying, "I, the orphan, have heard, 'Disaster resides next to fortune.' Now, your condolence is a fortune to me, the orphan. How dare I, the orphan, not ask for your explanation?"

Zigong replied, "At this time, I, your subject, went to see the king of Wu and suggested that he attack Qi in order to save Lu. In his heart, the king of Wu is afraid of Yue. Causing people's suspicion while having no intention of retaliating against them is inferior, having the intention of retaliating yet making people aware of it is unsafe, and having not carried out the scheme when people have already heard of it is dangerous. These three are the major threats to avoid in starting an uprising."

The king of Yue bowed twice again, saying, "I, the orphan, lost my father when I was young. In my heart I failed to measure myself properly and engaged in battle with Wu. My army was defeated and I, myself, was humiliated. Running up I hid in the Kuaiji Mountains, running down I defended myself at the coast, seeing only fishes and tortoises. Now you, the grand minister, condescend yourself and come to console me; moreover, you deliver words as valuable as jade to instruct me, the orphan. I, the orphan, consider this a heavenly bestowal, How could I dare not receive your teachings?"

Zigong said, "I, your subject, have heard, 'In employing people, a wise ruler will not misuse his talents; when an upright man recommends worthy people, he pays no attention to the opinions of the world.' Therefore when it comes to dealing with property and sharing benefits, the humane ones should be entrusted, when it comes to facing disaster and overcoming difficulty, the brave ones should be appointed, when it comes to using intelligence and making plans for the state, the worthy ones should be paid heed, and when it comes to rectifying the world and pacifying the many lords, the sagely ones should be employed. His army is strong yet he cannot execute his power, his status is highest but he cannot enforce his orders among those below him, a ruler like this is almost next to disaster. I, your subject, myself secretly examined who can achieve success with you and help you to arrive at the status of hegemon, and probably I am the only one qualified.[32] Now the king of Wu has the ambition of launching a military expedition against Qi and Jin. Your Majesty should not cherish precious treasures and present them

31. According to *Zhouli* 周禮, 稽首 (*qishou*) is the most ceremonious ritual performance to show respect. It requires one to lower one's head to the floor and pause for a little while before standing up. See Sun Yirang 孫詒讓, *Zhouli Zhengyi* 周禮正義 (Beijing: Zhonghua shuju, 1987), 2007.

32. The *Yue jue shu* sentence reads: 其惟臣幾乎 (*qi wei chen ji hu*). My translation is based upon the *Yue jue shu*. See Li Bujia, 185.

to the king of Wu in order to delight his heart, should not feel humiliated by expressing humble words, thus to honor the rituals you are obligated to perform for him. If he attacks Qi, Qi will fight against him.[33] If he does not win, then this is your fortune. If he engages in battle and wins, then he will certainly invade Jin with his army. His chariots and fine soldiers will be exhausted by Qi, his precious treasures, chariots, horses, flags, and banners will all be lost in Jin;[34] you can then command his remaining forces."

The king of Yue bowed twice, saying, "In the past the king of Wu mobilized his many people and damaged my state. He killed and defeated my people, humiliated my officials, and destroyed my ancestral temple.[35] My capital became a ruin filled with thorns and I hid myself among fishes and turtles.[36] My hatred of Wu penetrates into my bones and marrow. Yet my serving of Wu resembles a son's fear of his father and a younger brother's respect toward his older brother. I, an orphan, said these words at the risk of my death. Now you have given me your instruction, and for this reason I, an orphan, dare to report my sincere feelings. For three years my body did not reside on a double-layered mat,[37] my mouth did not taste rich flavors, my eyes did not look at beautiful women, and my ears did not listen to fine music. My lips were chapped and my tongue was dry, my body suffered from hardship and my strength was exhausted. In regard to those above, I served many officials; in regard to those below, I nourished my people. I wish one day to engage in battle with Wu in the broad and flat wild in the world. To stand with my body and arms straight and command the warriors of Wu and Yue to die one after another, and to smear their livers and brains on the ground are indeed wishes of mine.[38] I have been dreaming this for three years but have failed to achieve it. Now looking inward at my state, I have found it

33. 而 (*er*), "you," "yet," or "thereupon" should be rendered as 其 (*qi*), "he," referring to the king of Wu.

34. 羽毛 (*yumao*) here refers to flags and banners made of feathers, which are usually set up on the chariot of a ruler.

35. In early texts, *baixin* 百姓 usually refers to nobles or high officials, not commoners as the word suggests in later times.

36. The *Yue jue shu* sentence reads: "I, [Goujian], became food for fishes and turtles" 身為魚鱉餌 (*shen wei youbie er*). This is a euphemism for dying in the water. See Li Bujia, 185. Milburn translates 身 (*shen*) as "the bodies of [my people]," see Milburn, 213. In classical Chinese, when 身 is used by itself it usually refers to oneself.

37. In ancient times, the layers of a mat were determined by the status of the person. According to *Liji*, the son of heaven has five layers, the lords have three, and the ministers have two. See Sun Xidan, 632. The king of Yue sat on a single-layered mat in order to remind himself of the humiliations he suffered in Wu.

38. 肝腦塗地 (*gannao tudi*), "smearing livers and brains on the ground," is usually a metaphor in Chinese suggesting the devotion of one's life to a certain cause.

is not powerful enough to damage Wu; looking outward, I am not capable of serving the many lords. I wish to give up all the valuables of my state, abandon my officials, transform my appearance, change my name, hold dustpan and broom, and raise oxen and horses to serve whoever carries out revenge for me. Although I, an orphan, know doing this will cause my waist and neck to be severed,[39] my hands and feet scattered in different places, and my four limbs thrown in the four directions, and that I will be laughed at by my commoners, I still intend to realize my revenge. Now you, Grand Minister, confer upon me a plan to rescue my failing state and to save me from death. I, an orphan, rely upon this heavenly bestowal, how dare I not attend to your commands?"

Zigong said, "The king of Wu's personality is such that he is greedy about merit and reputation but fails to keep in mind that there are losses and gains."

The king of Yue was startled by this and moved away from his seat.[40]

Zigong said, "I, your subject, have noticed that the king of Wu engaged in several wars and military expeditions. His soldiers cannot rest,[41] his officials have retired from his court, and the slanderous comments are numerous. As a person, Wu Zixu, in his heart, is extremely loyal and upright. He is also intelligent about other matters and is aware of what is necessary at certain times. He would not ignore the faults of the ruler because of the fear of death. He uses his honest words to serve his ruler with loyalty, uses his straightforward deeds to serve the state, but up to death his words were not listened to.[42] The Chief Chancellor Bo Pi is cunning but unwise, imprudent, and weak. He advances himself by using artful language and honeyed words; he is good at using deceitful lies to serve his ruler. He only knows what happened in the past but is unable to foresee consequences, and he falls in with the wrongs of the ruler in order to secure his own benefit. He is a flattering courtier who ruins the state and harms the ruler."

The king of Yue was greatly delighted. Upon Zigong's departure, the king of Yue presented him one hundred *yi* of gold, a valuable sword, and two fine horses. Zigong did not accept them.

5.7. 至吳，謂吳王曰：「臣以下吏之言告於越王，越王大恐，曰：『昔者孤身不幸，少失前人。內不自量，抵罪於吳，軍敗身辱，逋逃出

---

39. 要 (*yao*) is a loan word for 腰 (*yao*), "waist." 領 (*ling*) refers to the neck and 屬 (*shu*) means to connect. The sentence literary means that neck and waist are not connected.

40. Moving away from one's seat was a gesture to show fear or respect in ancient times.

41. 恩 (*en*), "grateful," should be 息 (*xi*), "to rest." See Zhang Jue, 129.

42. There is a mistake in this sentence: Wu Zixu was not dead at that time. His death is described in section 5.19.

走，棲于會稽，國為墟莽，身為魚鱉。賴大王之賜，使得奉俎豆，修祭祀，死且不敢忘，何謀之敢？』其志甚恐，將使使者來謝於王。」

子貢館五日，越使果來，曰：「東海役臣勾踐之使者臣種，敢修下吏，少聞於左右：『昔孤不幸，少失前人，內不自量，抵罪上國，軍敗身辱，逋逃會稽，賴王賜，得奉祭祀，死且不忘。今竊聞大王興大義，誅彊救弱，困暴齊而撫周室，故使賤臣以奉前王所藏甲二十領，屈盧之矛，步光之劍，以賀軍吏。若將遂大義，弊邑雖小，請悉四方之內士卒三千人，以從下吏，請躬被堅執銳，以前受矢石，君臣死無所恨矣。』」

吳王大悅。乃召子貢曰：「越使果來，請出士卒三千，其君從之，與寡人伐齊。可乎？」子貢曰：「不可。夫空人之國，悉人之眾，又從其君，不仁也。受幣，許其師，辭其君即可。」

吳王許諾。

5.7. Zigong arrived at Wu and told the king of Wu, "I, your subject, as your humble official, spoke my words to the king of Yue. The king of Yue was greatly fearful, saying, 'Previously I, an orphan, was unfortunate. At a young age, I lost my father. In my heart, I failed to acquire proper understanding of myself and committed crimes against Wu. My army was defeated and I myself was humiliated. I fled and ran away from the capital and hid in the Kuaiji Mountains. My capital became a ruin covered by wild grass and I lived among fishes and tortoises. Because of Your Majesty's bestowal, I am able to hold the ceremonial vessel and offer ritual sacrifice.[43] I dare not to disobey you even if Your Majesty order me to commit suicide, what scheme dare I conceive?'[44] His facial expression looked deeply afraid; he will send an emissary to deliver his apology to you."

After Zigong lodged in Wu for five days, the Yue emissary indeed came and reported to Fuchai, "I, Wen Zhong,[45] your subject, emissary of Goujian, your servant living at the East Sea, dare to act as your junior officer to report some of my lord's words to your serving ministers on your left and right:[46] 'In the past I, an orphan, was unfortunate. At a young age I lost my father. In my heart I failed to acquire proper understanding of myself and so committed crimes against your prestigious state. My army was defeated and

43. 俎 (*zu*) and 豆 (*dou*) are sacrificial vessels. Here they are used to indicate a sacrificial ceremony.

44. A Song edition has the three characters "大王賜 *dawang ci*," "your majesty grants." See Zhang Jue, 132.

45. Wen Zhong was a key advisor in Goujian's revenge against Wu. Wen Zhong was a man from Chu. He helped Goujian destroy Wu but afterward was ordered to commit suicide by Goujian.

46. *Xiu* 修 means to "practice" and to "act" here. *Shao* 少 means "a little bit." Here Wen Zhong is saying that he represents the king of Yue and reports to the ministers of the king of Wu. Because the king of Yue is a subordinate to the king of Wu, he dares not to report too much. This is a humble expression in order to show respect to the king of Wu.

I was humiliated. I fled and ran away to the Kuaiji Mountains. Because of Your Majesty's kindness, I am able to continue my ancestral sacrifice. I dare not to disobey you even if you order me to commit suicide. Now, privately I have heard Your Majesty plans to promote justice, attack the aggressive and rescue the weak, restrain the violent Qi and pacify the Zhou clan.[47] For these reasons, Goujian sent me, your humble subject, to present before Your Majesty twenty suits of armor treasured by previous kings of Yue, a fine lance made by Qulu,[48] and the sword Buguang, thus to felicitate your soldiers and generals. If you are about to carry out justice, please allow us, a small and humble state, to mobilize all our soldiers within the four corners of our state, three thousand in number, to follow your junior officers. Goujian pledges to personally wear armor, holding weapons and braving arrows and stones in the front line. There is no regret even if he and his ministers die for you.'"

The king of Wu was greatly delighted. He then summoned Zigong, saying, "The emissary of Yue has come, as you expected. Yue pledged to send three thousand soldiers, together with their king, to follow me, a man of little virtue, to attack Qi; is this permissible?"

Zigong said, "This is not proper. It is not humane to empty one's state, recruit all of another's people, and let their ruler to follow you. It would be proper if you accept their gifts, permit the troops to follow, yet decline the request of the ruler."

The king of Wu agreed.

5.8. 子貢去晉，見定公曰：「臣聞：『慮不預定，不可以應卒；兵不預辦，不可以勝敵。』今吳齊將戰，戰而不勝，越亂之必矣；與戰而勝，必以其兵臨晉。君為之奈何？」定公曰：「何以待之？」子貢曰：「修兵伏卒以待之。」晉君許之。子貢返魯。

5.8. Zigong went to Jin and received an audience from Lord Ding of Jin, saying to the lord, "I, your subject, have heard that if thought is not given in advance, it is impossible to deal with sudden change;[49] if troops are not prepared in advance, it is impossible to defeat the enemy. Now Wu and Qi are about to engage each other on the battlefield. If Wu were to fight yet fail to win, its upheaval caused by Yue is unavoidable. If Wu fights and wins, it will definitely advance its troops to the border of Jin. What will you do

47. Lu's ancestor belonged to the Zhou royal family while Qi's did not. The founder of Wu was also a member of the Zhou household.

48. Qulu was a legendary master famous for making lances. Buguang was the name of a fine sword.

49. 卒 (*zu*) is the same as 猝 (*cu*), "sudden," here.

about this?" Lord Ding said, "How should I deal with it?" Zigong answered, "Sharpen your weapons, rest your soldiers, and wait for it." The ruler of Jin accepted his suggestion. Zigong returned to Lu.

5.9. 吳王果興九郡之兵，將與齊戰。道出胥門，因過姑胥之臺，忽晝假寐於姑胥之臺而得夢。及寤而起，其心恬然悵焉。乃命太宰嚭告曰：「寡人晝臥有夢，覺而恬然悵焉。請占之，得無所憂哉？夢入章明宮，見兩鬲蒸而不炊；兩黑犬嗥以南，嗥以北；兩鋘殖吾宮牆；流水湯湯，越吾宮堂；後房鼓震篋篋有鍛工；前園橫生梧桐。子為寡人占之。」

太宰嚭曰：「美哉！王之興師伐齊也。臣聞：章者，德鏘鏘也；明者，破敵聲聞，功朗明也。兩鬲蒸而不炊者，大王聖德，氣有餘也。兩黑犬嗥以南、嗥以北者，四夷已服，朝諸侯也。兩鋘殖宮牆者，農夫就成，田夫耕也。湯湯越宮堂者，鄰國貢獻，財有餘也。後房篋篋鼓震有鍛工者，宮女悅樂，琴瑟和也。前園橫生梧桐者，樂府鼓聲也。」

吳王大悅，而其心不已，復召王孫駱問曰：「寡人忽晝夢，為予陳之。」

王孫駱曰：「臣鄙淺於道，不能博大，今王所夢，臣不能占。其有所知者，東掖門亭長長城公弟公孫聖。聖為人少而好游，長而好學，多見博觀，知鬼神之情狀。願王問之。」

5.9. As expected, the king of Wu mobilized troops from nine prefects and planned to fight against Qi. He departed from the Xu Gate and therefore traveled past Guxu Terrace.[50] At Guxu Terrace, he unexpectedly took a nap during the daytime and had a dream.[51] When he woke up from the dream and got out of bed, he felt both happy and sorrowful. The king then summoned Chief Chancellor Bo Pi and told him, "I, an orphan, lay in bed in the daytime and had a dream. After I woke up I felt both happy and sorrowful. Please interpret it;[52] perhaps there is nothing worrisome in it. I dreamed that I entered the Zhangming Palace and I saw two cooking vessels that had steam rising from them but no fire under them,[53] two black dogs that barked toward the south and then barked toward the north, two shovels that were

50. This is the southern gate of the Wu capital. The terrace was built on Mount Guxu.

51. 假寐 (*jiamei*) means to sleep without taking off one's clothes. The following story of the Wu king's dream and the interpretations by Bo Pi and Gongsun Sheng are also found in *Yue jue shu*, "Wu wang zhanmeng" 吳王占夢 chapter. See Li Bujia, 283–85; Milburn, 257–71.

52. The origin of the character 占 (*zhan*) was related to divination using oracle bones and turtle shells.

53. These are cooking utensils shaped like cauldrons with three feet under them. *Yue jue shu* writes 見兩鬲炊而不蒸 (*jian liang li cui er bu zheng*) "saw two cooking vessels were put on the fire but no steam came out." See Li Bujia, 283.

planted on the palace wall, water flooded through the hall in my palace, in the back chamber there was the *qie qie* sound of a wind chest bellowing and metal workers,[54] in the front garden a firmiana tree stood horizontally. Please interpret this for me, an orphan."

Chief Chancellor Bo Pi said, "How wonderful is Your Majesty's mobilizing troops and attacking Qi. I, your subject, have heard this: '*Zhang* is the clanging sound of virtue.[55] *Ming*, brightness, means your reputation and the defeat of the enemy are both sound and distinguished.'[56] That there were two cooking vessels with steam but no fire underneath suggests Your Majesty's sagely virtue is abundant. As for two black dogs barking toward south and north, this represents the fact that four *yi* tribes will submit themselves and the many lords will pay homage at your court.[57] That two shovels were planted on the palace wall implies farmers will go to the field and plough there. That water flooding through the palace hall means there will be surplus treasures presented from neighboring states. That there was the *qie qie* sound of a wind chest bellowing and metal workers in the rear chamber indicates palace ladies are fond of music and playing zithers together. That a firmiana tree growing horizontally in the front garden is in fact the sound of drums in musical bureau songs."

The king of Wu was greatly delighted. Still his heart was not settled. He then summoned Wangsun Luo and asked him, "I, a man of little virtue, unexpectedly had a dream during the day, please explain it for me."

Wangsun Luo replied, "I, your subject, have shallow knowledge of the Way and I am not capable of having a broad perspective. Now, I cannot interpret what you, my king, had dreamt. Perhaps the one that can explain it is Gongsun Sheng, a student of the Older Yue, who serves as the village constable of the Dongye Gate.[58] Sheng was fond of traveling in his youth. When he grew up, he became diligent in the pursuit of learning. He is experienced and knowledgeable and knows about the matters of ghosts and spirits. I wish you, my king, would ask him."

---

54. Zhang Jue interprets 晨 (*zhen*) as 橐 (*tuo*), a "wind chest." See Zhang Jue, 135n9.

55. 章 (*zhang*) is in the name of the palace of which the king of Wu dreamed. The character also refers to the completion of a piece of music.

56. 明 (*ming*) is the other character in the name of the palace.

57. The four *yi* tribes refer to the *yi* people who lived in the east, the *rong* 戎 in the west, the *man* 蠻 in the south, and the *di* 狄 in the north. They were considered "barbarians" to the Chinese states.

58. *Tingzhang* 亭長 was the head of a small district called *duting* 都亭 or *menting* 門亭, located within the city wall or at the gate of the city wall during Qin and Han times. The *tingzhang* was in charge of public safety and lawsuits in his district. According to *Yue jue shu*, 城 (*cheng*) is a mistake for the character 越 (*yue*), which is the surname of the constable. See Li Bujia, 284.

5.10. 王乃遣王孫駱往請公孫聖，曰：「吳王晝臥姑胥之臺，忽然感夢，覺而悵然，使子占之，急詣姑胥之臺。」

公孫聖伏地而泣，有頃而起。其妻從旁謂聖曰：「子何性鄙！希睹人主，卒得急召，涕泣如雨。」

公孫聖仰天歎曰：「悲哉！非子所知也。今日壬午，時加南方，命屬上天，不得逃亡。非但自哀，誠傷吳王。」

妻曰：「子以道自達於主，有道當行，上以諫王，下以約身。今聞急召，憂惑潰亂，非賢人所宜。」

公孫聖曰：「愚哉！女子之言也。吾受道十年，隱身避害，欲紹壽命，不意卒得急召，中世自棄，故悲與子相離耳。」遂去，詣姑胥臺。

5.10. The king thereupon sent Wangsun Luo to go invite Gongsun Sheng, telling him, "The king of Wu napped on Guxu Terrace during the daytime and was suddenly affected by a dream. He felt sorrowful when he woke up from it and requested you to interpret it. Please hurry to see him at Guxu Terrace."

Gongsun Sheng threw himself on the ground and cried. After a while he stood up. His wife spoke to him from the side, saying, "How perverse is your disposition. You have long wished to see the king, all of a sudden you are urgently summoned and your tears stream down like raindrops."

Looking up the sky, Gongsun Sheng sighed, "How lamentable! This is not what you could comprehend. Today is the *renwu* day (the nineteenth day) and the time is noon.[59] The fates of the king and I are determined by the heaven, there is no escaping this. I am not self-pitying, truly, I feel sorrow for the king of Wu."

His wife said, "You have brought yourself to the king because of your specialty. If you have the knowledge, you should put it into practice. To the above you should use it to admonish the king, to those below you should use it to restrain yourself. Now hearing the urgent call you are deeply worried, hesitant, collapsed and confused, this is not appropriate for a virtuous man."

Gongsun Sheng said, "How foolish, these words of a woman! I have studied the art for ten years.[60] I hide myself and avoid danger in order to continue my destined years. I did not expect to receive this urgent summons. I have

59. *Renwu* 壬午 is the nineteenth day of the month. In *yinyang* cosmology, the twelve earthly branches are associated with twelves directions. The south is associated with noon and noon is associated with the character *wu* 午. In this case, the day is a 午 day and the time is also 午, because in the past the execution of criminals was at noon time 午時 (*wushi*), such a repetition of the date and time is therefore considered ominous.

60. The art of interpreting dreams.

abandoned my life in the middle of it. For this reason I lament. Now I bid you farewell." He then left home and went to Guxu Terrace.

5.11. 吳王曰：「寡人將北伐齊魯，道出胥門，過姑胥之臺，忽然晝夢，子為占之，其言吉凶。」

公孫聖曰：「臣不言，身名全，言之，必死百段於王前。然忠臣不顧其軀。」乃仰天歎曰：「臣聞：『好船者必溺，好戰者必亡。』臣好直言，不顧於命。願王圖之。臣聞：章者，戰不勝，敗走偉偟也。明者，去昭昭，就冥冥也。入門見鬲蒸而不炊者，大王不得火食也。兩黑犬嗥以南、嗥以北者，黑者，陰也，北者，匿也。兩鋘殖宮牆者，越軍入吳國，伐宗廟，掘社稷也。流水湯湯越宮堂者，宮空虛也。後房鼓震篋篋者，坐太息也。前園橫生梧桐者，梧桐心空，不為用器，但為盲僮，與死人俱葬也。願大王按兵修德，無伐於齊，則可銷也。遣下吏太宰嚭、王孫駱，解冠幘，肉袒徒跣，稽首謝於勾踐，國可安存也，身可不死矣。」

吳王聞之，索然作怒，乃曰：「吾天之所生，神之所使。」顧力士石番，以鐵鎚擊殺之。聖乃仰頭向天而言曰：「吁嗟！天知吾之冤乎？忠而獲罪，身死無辜以葬。我以為直者，不如相隨為柱，提我至深山，後世相屬為聲響。」於是吳王乃使門人提之蒸丘，「豺狼食汝肉，野火燒汝骨，東風數至，飛揚汝骸，骨肉縻爛，何能為聲響哉？」太宰嚭趨進曰：「賀大王喜，災已滅矣，因舉行觴，兵可以行。」

5.11. The king of Wu said, "I, a man of little virtue, was about to launch a military expedition north against Qi and Lu.[61] I followed the road out which took me to Xu Gate and past Guxu Terrace, when abruptly I took a nap and had a dream in the daytime. Please, will you, sir, interpret it for me and tell me if it is good or bad luck."

Gongsun Sheng answered, "If I, your subject, do not speak about it, I can preserve my body and name; if I speak I will be cut into one hundred pieces and die before you. However, a loyal minister should not only care for his own life." He then looked up at the sky and sighed, saying, "I, your subject, have heard this: 'Those who are fond of boating will certainly die from drowning, those who are fond of war will certainly perish.' I, your subject, like straight words and do not care about my life. I wish you, my king, to consider my saying this: I, your subject, have heard that *zhang*, to manifest,

61. The character 救 (*jiu*), "to rescue," is missing in the sentence before Lu. See Zhang Jue, 139n1.

means panic when defeated and running away.[62] *Ming*, brightness, suggests leaving the clear and entering the dark.[63] Entering the door and seeing cooking vessels steaming without fire implies you, the king, will not be able to eat cooked food. As for the two black dogs that barked south and then north, black is the color of *yin*, north is the direction of hiding.[64] That two shovels planted on the palace wall symbolize the Yue army's entry into Wu, where it attacks the ancestral temple and digs up the altar of land and the altar of grain. Water flooding through the palace wall and halls implies the palace is empty. The drum sound of *qie qie* in the back chamber suggests you sit and sigh. That a firmiana tree standing horizontally in the front garden—the firmiana tree is hollow inside and cannot be used except to make wooden human figures to be buried with the dead.[65] I wish you, great king, to halt your troops and cultivate your virtue. You should not launch the military expedition against Qi so the calamity can be dispelled. Moreover, you should command your subordinates, the Chief Chancellor Bo Pi and Wangsun Luo, to take off their caps, strip off their upper garments, and bare their feet,[66] kowtow and apologize to Goujian, thus the state can be safe and preserved and you will not die."

The king of Wu immediately became furious upon hearing this. He then said, "Heaven gave birth to me and spirits entrusted me with a mission." He ordered a strong man Shi Fan to kill Gongsun Sheng with an iron hammer. Gongsun Sheng lifted his head toward heaven and said, "Alas, heaven knows that I am innocent. Being loyal yet receiving punishment, I die without having committed any crime. Bury me then. Should I believe being upright is no more worthy than simply following? Set up a pillar for me and bring my corpse deep into the mountains. When I meet you later I will echo your sounds." The king of Wu then ordered the guard to carry Gongsun Sheng's corpse to Zhengqiu,[67] saying, "Jackals and wolves will eat your flesh, wildfire will burn your bones. When east winds blow, your remains will be scattered

62. 章 and 偉 share the same pronunciation, *zhang*, and the two characters are very close in appearance. Here, Gongsun Shen is using homophones to interpret different characters.

63. The characters 明, "brightness," and 冥, "darkness," have the same pronunciation: *ming*.

64. In Chinese cosmological thinking, north is associated with winter when creatures either hide or wither.

65. Xu Tianhu argues that the character 盲 (*mang*), "blind," is a mistake for the character 甬 (*yong*), "human-shaped burial figure." See Zhang Jue, 139n4. *Yue jue shu* also has the character 甬. See Li Bujia, 285.

66. In ancient times, people often took off their clothes and exposed their bodies to express respect or fear in situations such as a ritual sacrifice or offering an apology.

67. Mount Zheng is in modern-day Wu County, Jiangsu Province.

and your bones and flesh rotten, how can you echo with sounds?" Chief Chancellor Bo Pi moved forward quickly and said, "Congratulations, great king, on this joy, the calamity has been forestalled. Please then arrange the ritual of sharing the wine, so the troops can now march."

5.12. 吳王乃使太宰嚭為右校司馬，王孫駱為左校，及從勾踐之師伐齊。伍子胥聞之，諫曰：「臣聞興十萬之眾，奉師千里，百姓之費，國家之出，日數千金。不念士民之死，而爭一日之勝，臣以為危國亡身之甚。且與賊居不知其禍，外復求怨，徼幸他國，猶治救瘑疥而棄心腹之疾，發當死矣。瘑疥，皮膚之疾，不足患也。今齊陵遲千里之外，更歷楚趙之界，齊為疾其疥耳；越之為病，乃心腹也。不發則傷，動則有死。願大王定越而後圖齊。臣之言決矣，敢不盡忠！臣今年老，耳目不聰，以狂惑之心，無能益國。竊觀金匱第八，其可傷也。」吳王曰：「何謂也？」子胥曰：「今年七月，辛亥平旦，大王以首事。 辛，歲位也，亥，陰前之辰也。合壬子歲前合也，利以行武，武決勝矣。然德在合斗擊丑。丑，辛之本也。大吉為白虎而臨辛，功曹為太常所臨亥，大吉得辛為九醜，又與白虎并重。有人若以此首事，前雖小勝，後必大敗。天地行殃，禍不久矣。」

5.12. The king of Wu therefore appointed Chief Chancellor Bo Pi as the General of the Right Army, Wangsun Luo as the General of the Left Army, and led Goujian's troops to attack Qi. Hearing this, Wu Zixu remonstrated, saying, "I, your subject, have heard that when mobilizing ten thousand men to provide supply for troops a thousand *li* away, the cost to the people and the expense from the state amount to several thousand in cash every day. Disregarding the death of the soldiers and the people to fight for a temporary victory, I, your subject, consider this an extreme action that puts the state in danger and will cause your own demise. Moreover, living with a thief but not aware of the consequences,[68] yet causing hatred from outside by seeking luck in another state, these are similar to curing scabies while ignoring diseases of the heart and abdomen. When these illnesses make their presence known, death is inevitable. Scabies is a skin disease, and is not worth worrying about. Now Qi is declining a thousand miles away,[69] it is also blocked off by the states of Chu and Zhao.[70] If Qi is the disease, it is as minor as scabies. If Yue is the illness, it is a heart and stomach problem. We are hurt by them even if they do not show effects. Once they break out we will die. I wish you,

68. The thief refers to the Yue king Goujian and his troops.
69. The political power of Qi was in the hands of the Tian clan at that time.
70. Zhao should be Lu. The state of Zhao did not exist during that time.

great king, to pacify Yue and then make plans regarding Qi. I am resolute about what I just said. Dare I not be loyal? I, your subject, am advanced in age now. My eyes are not sharp and ears not keen. My delirious and muddled heart is of no benefit to the state. I privately read the eighth chapter of the *Jinkui* and realize that you will be harmed."[71] The king of Wu asked, "What do you mean by this?" Wu Zixu explained, "On the *xinhai* day (eleventh day), seventh month of this year, at dawn, you, great king, raised arms.[72] *Xin* is the turn of Jupiter of this year and *hai* is the Earthly Branch that precedes the arrival of *chen*, the *Beginning of Yin*.[73] Their corresponding day is *renzi*, which is the corresponding day before the arrival of the *taisui* constellation.[74] The date is auspicious for military actions, therefore a victory will be granted for our military expedition. However, although the heavenly stem of this day is in accordance with the corresponding date, the *dou* constellation moves to *chou*.[75] *Chou* generates *xin* and itself symbolizes great auspice, yet it is pressed by the White Tiger Constellation.[76] *Xin* represents the spirit of the

---

71. *Jinkui* is probably a book of divination that is lost now. The "Yiwen zhi" chapter of *Hanshu* mentions a text titled *Kanyu jinkui* 堪與金匱. In the Daoist encyclopedia *Daozang* 道藏 there is a collection titled *Huangdi jinkui yuheng jing* 黃帝金匱玉衡經 that might have some connection with this text.

72. 首事 (*shoushi*) here refers to mobilizing the army. Wu Zixu's divination is perplexing; scholars in the past have tried to make sense of it but it is still not clear what cosmological theory was involved.

73. *Suiwei* 歲位 means the position where *sui* 歲, Jupiter, is located. People in ancient times believed that Jupiter orbited every twelve years and they therefore used Jupiter to mark the year. However, because Jupiter moves from west to east, which is in the opposite direction of the twelve heavenly stems, people in ancient times created a *taisui* 太歲 constellation to correspond to Jupiter. The *taisui* moves from east to west and people marked the year by using the earthly branch in accordance with the location of the *taisui*. This is mixed with the *yinyang* theory. The thirteenth year of King Fuchai was the year of *xinmao* 辛卯, therefore Wu Zixu says that Jupiter is corresponding to *xin*. According to the ancient calendars found in the *Liuren daquan* 六壬大全, if the *yin* and *yang* are not in harmony, then the first day of the month is considered *yang* and is called the *Beginning of Yang* 陽建; the full moon is considered *yin* and is called the *Beginning of Yin* 陰建. The *Beginning of Yang* starts with the earthly branch *yin* 寅 while the *Beginning of Yin* starts with the earthly branch *xu* 戌. By this theory, in the seventh month, the *Beginning of Yang* is *shen* 申 and the *Beginning of Yin* is *chen* 辰. *Hai* is five earthly branches before *chen*; for this reason Wu Zixu says the date is before the arrival of *chen*, the *Beginning of Yin* of the month. See Zhang Jue, 141n10.

74. The heavenly stem *ren* and the earthly branch *zi* are both located in the northern sky and are in front of the location of Jupiter in the seventh month. According to the *liuren* calendar, this is called the *shuihe* 水合, "water correspondence," suggesting smoothness and successes in one's endeavor. Therefore Wu Zixu predicts that the Wu king Fuchai's military expedition will be successful.

75. In the Five Phases theory, heavenly stems are called *de* 德. *He* refers to *heri* 合日, corresponding date. *Xinmao* was a corresponding day. The *dou* constellation corresponds to the region where Yue is located; the *chou* constellation corresponds to the Wu region. *Dou* moving to *chou* suggests Yue invades Wu.

76. *Chou* is associated with earth and *xin* is associated with metal. According to the Five Phases theory, earth generates metal, thus Wu Zixu says *chou* generates *xin*. The White Tiger Constellation corresponds to the states of Lu and Jin. Wu Zixu is suggesting that Wu will be harmed by Lu and Jin.

clerk, it is compelled by the *taichang* spirit.[77] *Hai* symbolizes great fortune but it becomes the Nine Evils when counted together with *xin*; furthermore, it overlaps with the White Tiger Constellation.[78] If anyone takes up arms on this day, although he will gain minor victories at the beginning, he will suffer terrible defeat at the end. This is the misfortune brought upon us by heaven and earth; disaster is impending."

5.13. 吳王不聽，遂九月使太宰嚭伐齊。軍臨北郊，吳王謂嚭曰：「行矣！無忘有功，無赦有罪，愛民養士，視如赤子；與智者謀，與仁者友。」太宰嚭受命，遂行 。

5.13. The king of Wu did not listen to Wu Zixu. In the ninth month he then ordered Chief Chancellor Bo Pi to attack Qi. When the Wu troops arrived at the northern suburb of the capital, the king of Wu instructed Chief Chancellor Bo Pi, saying, "March on! Do not forget to award those who have provided great services; do not pardon those who have committed crimes. Love the people and nourish the soldiers, treating them with tenderness as if they are infants. Consult the wise and befriend the virtuous." Chief Chancellor Bo Pi received the command and left.

5.14. 吳王召大夫被離問曰：「汝常與子胥同心合志，并慮一謀，寡人興師伐齊，子胥獨何言焉？」被離曰：「子胥欲盡誠於前王，自謂老狂，耳目不聰，不知當世之所行，無益吳國 。」

5.14. The king of Wu summoned Grand Minister Beili and asked him, "You are often of one mind with Wu Zixu and strategize together with him. I, a man of little virtue, mobilized the troops to attack Qi, what did Wu Zixu say about this when he was alone?" Beili said, "Wu Zixu wants to be loyal to the former king. He said that he himself is old and addled. His eyes and ears are not sharp, he does not know the affairs of this time, therefore he is of no use to the state of Wu."

5.15. 王遂伐齊，齊與吳戰於艾陵之上，齊師敗績。吳王既勝，乃使行人成好於齊，曰：「吳王聞齊有沒水之慮，帥軍來觀，而齊興師蒲草，吳不知所安，設陣為備，不意頗傷齊師。願結和親而去。」

77. *Gongcao* 功曹 was originally an officer in Han government whose duty was recording other officers' merits. *Taichang* 太常 was a high-ranking minister in charge of ritual ceremonies. Here both the *gongcao* and *taichang* are names of gods in divination theories.

78. *Hai* itself is associated with collecting and gathering, therefore it is considered auspicious. If the heavenly stems *yi*, *wu*, *ji*, *xin*, and *ren* are matched individually with the earthly branches *zi*, *wu*, *mao*, and *you* then they are nine auspicious combinations. However, here *xin* is matched with *mao* and is not in accordance with the heavenly way, so it is considered evil and dangerous.

齊王曰：「寡人處此北邊，無出境之謀。今吳乃濟江淮喻千里而來我壤土，戮我眾庶，賴上帝哀存，國猶不至顛隕。王今讓以和親，敢不如命？」吳齊遂盟而去。

5.15. The king of Wu therefore attacked Qi. They fought at Ailing and Qi was soundly defeated.[79] After winning the battle, the king of Wu sent an emissary to Qi in order to make peace with Qi, saying, "The king of Wu has heard that Qi had concerns about flooding, he therefore led the troops to inspect the land. However, Qi hid its army among the calamus and grass; Wu did not know what else to do about this but deploy its troops in order to prepare. Wu did not intend to cause Qi so many casualties. Wu wishes to conclude a peace treaty with Qi and leave." The king of Qi said, "I, a man of little virtue, dwell in the northern land; I have no intention of sending troops out of my territory. Now Wu has come across the Yangzi and Huai rivers, traveled more than a thousand miles, arrived on my soil and killed many of my people. Because of the heavenly god's pity, my state was not altogether destroyed. Now that the king of Wu allows us to form a friendly relationship with Wu, dare I not follow his command?" Wu then made a covenant with Qi and retreated.

5.16. 吳王還，乃讓子胥曰：「吾前王履德明，達於上帝。垂功用力，為子西結彊讎於楚。今前王，譬若農夫之艾殺四方蓬蒿，以立名于荊蠻，斯亦大夫之力。今大夫昏耄而不自安，生變起詐，怨惡而出，出則罪吾士眾，亂吾法度，欲以妖孽挫衄吾師；賴天降衷，齊師受服。寡人豈敢自歸其功？乃前王之遺德，神靈之祐福也。若子於吳，則何力焉？」

伍子胥攘臂大怒，釋劍而對曰：「昔吾前王有不庭之臣，以能遂疑計惡，不陷於大難。今王播棄，所患外不憂，此孤僮之謀，非霸王之事。天之所棄，必趨其小喜，而近其大憂。王若覺寤，吳國世世存焉；若不覺寤，吳國之命斯促矣。員不忍稱疾辟易，乃見王之為擒。員誠前死，掛吾目於門，以觀吳國之喪。」

吳王不聽，坐於殿上，獨見四人向庭相背而倚，王怪而視之。群臣問曰：「王何所見？」王曰：「吾見四人相背而倚，聞人言則四分走矣。」子胥曰：「如王言，將失眾矣。」吳王怒曰：「子言不祥！」子胥曰：「非惟不祥，王亦亡矣。」後五日，吳王復坐殿上，望見兩人相對，北向人殺南向人。王問群臣：「見乎？」曰：「無所見。」子胥曰：「王何見？」王曰：「前日所見四人，今日

79. Both *Zuozhuan* and *Shiji* record that this battle occurred in the twelfth year of King Fuchai, not in the thirteenth year. See *Zuozhuan*, Lord Ai 11; Yang Bojun, 1664; Durrant, Li, and Schaberg, 1901; *Shiji*, 66:2179.

又見二人相對，北向人殺南向人。」子胥曰：「臣聞，四人走，叛也；北向殺南向，臣殺君也。」王不應。

5.16. As the king of Wu returned, he upbraided Wu Zixu, saying, "My deceased father demonstrated brilliant virtue and his deeds reached up to the heavens. He left a legacy and was devoted to this effort. For you he incurred the enmity of the powerful Chu state to the West. Now the former king can be likened to a farmer reaping the weeds and thistles on all sides, he established his reputation by defeating the Jing tribe,[80] this is also because of your, the grand minister's, assistance. Now you, the grand minister, are old and muddled, yet you are not content.[81] You stirred trouble and spread lies. Hatred and ill will come out of your mouth. When you came out to speak, you blamed my soldiers and people and disturbed my laws and regulations. You wanted to use abnormal phenomena to frustrate my troops.[82] Because of heaven's blessing, the Qi army was tamed. Dare I, a man of little virtue, attribute the victory to myself? This is possible by the remaining virtue of the former king and the protection of gods and spirits. As for you sir, what have you done for Wu?"

Wu Zixu bared his hands and became furious. He put down his sword and replied, saying, "In the past our former king had ministers who were given the privilege of not performing ritual;[83] because of this he could solve questions and measure problems, and avoid falling into great disasters. Now you, the king, have abandoned these ministers. To what you should be afraid of you give no thought and never worry.[84] This is the trick of an orphan and a child,[85] not the conduct of a hegemon. If one is abandoned by heaven, small joys will come to him, yet he moves closer to great disaster. If you, the king, would realize this, the state of Wu will exist generation after generation. If you cannot awaken to this, the fate of Wu will thus be shortened. I, Yun,[86] cannot bear to retreat and hide behind the excuse of illness and witness you, the king, being arrested. If indeed I, Yun, should die before that, please hang my eyes on the city gate so that I can observe the demise of the state of Wu."

---

80. The state of Chu was also called Jing. *Man* was the derogatory name for the tribes living in southern China during early times.

81. 耄 (*mao*) means "old in age."

82. This refers to Wu Zixu's prediction about Wu's eventual destruction by Yue. See the section above.

83. This is a special honor for respected ministers who are not required to bow or perform other court rituals before the ruler.

84. 外 (*wai*) means "to ignore."

85. The "Wuyu" 吳語 chapter in *Guoyu* has 孩童 (*haitong*), instead of 孤僮 (*gutong*). See Xu Yuangao, 544.

86. Wu Zixu's name is Wu Yun. Zixu is his style.

The king of Wu did not listen. He sat in the hall and he alone saw four men facing the courtyard and leaning back to back. The king felt strange about this and stared at them. The many officials asked him, saying, "What do you, the king, see?" The king said, "I saw four men leaning on each other's backs and who scattered away upon hearing people talking." Wu Zixu said, "If it is indeed like you, the king, said, you will lose the people." The king of Wu was angry, saying, "Your words are ominous." Wu Zixu said, "Not only is this not auspicious, but you, the king, will fall."

Five days later, the king of Wu again sat in the hall. He saw two men facing each other. The man facing north killed the one facing south. The king asked his many officials, "Have you seen this?" They replied, "We have not." Wu Zixu said, "What has the king seen?" The king answered, "Several days ago I saw four men. Today I once more saw two men facing each other. The man facing north killed the one facing south." Wu Zixu said, "I, your subject, have heard that the four men fleeing symbolize betrayal. The man facing north killing the one facing south means a minister assassinates his ruler."[87] The king did not respond to this.

5.17. 吳王置酒文臺之上，群臣悉在，太宰嚭執政，越王侍坐，子胥在焉。王曰：「寡人聞之，君不賤有功之臣，父不憎有力之子。今太宰嚭為寡人有功，吾將爵之上賞。越王慈仁忠信，以孝事於寡人，吾將復增其國，以還助伐之功。於眾大夫如何？」

群臣賀曰：「大王躬行至德，虛心養士，群臣並進，見難爭死；名號顯著，威震四海；有功蒙賞，亡國復存；霸功王事，咸被群臣。」

於是子胥據地垂涕，曰：「於乎，哀哉！遭此默默，忠臣掩口，讒夫在側；政敗道壞，諂諛無極；邪說偽辭，以曲為直，舍讒攻忠，將滅吳國：宗廟既夷，社稷不食，城郭丘墟，殿生荊棘。」吳王大怒，曰：「老臣多詐，為吳妖孽。乃欲專權擅威，獨傾吾國。寡人以前王之故，未忍行法，今退自計，無沮吳謀。」

子胥曰：「今臣不忠不信，不得為前王之臣。臣不敢愛身，恐吾國之亡矣。昔者桀殺關龍逢，紂殺王子比干，今大王誅臣，參於桀紂。大王勉之，臣請辭矣。」

5.17. The king of Wu threw a banquet on Wen Terrace; all his ministers attended. The Chief Chancellor Bo Pi was in charge of the banquet, the king of Yue was present and Wu Zixu also attended. The king said, "I, a man of little virtue, have heard this: 'The ruler does not despise a minister whose

87. The ruler sits facing south and the ministers facing north. Wu Zixu thereupon predicts that this indicates regicide.

services have been great; a father does not loathe a son who makes a great contribution.' Now the Chief Chancellor Bo Pi has provided great services to me, a man of little virtue. I will reward him with the highest award. The king of Yue is kind, humane, loyal, and trustworthy. He has served me, a man of little virtue, with filial deeds. I will return him to his country and increase his territory, as rewards for his merit in assisting my military expedition. What do you many grand officials think about this?"

All the ministers congratulated this, saying, "You, the great king, practice the ultimate personal virtue and nourish the talented with modesty. All ministers advance together and compete to die for you when encountering calamity. Your name and reputation are illustrious and your power awes the world. Those with achievements receive awards; and a destroyed state is rejuvenated.[88] The many ministers all benefit from your hegemonic merits and kingly deeds."[89]

At this moment Wu Zixu sat on the ground and shed tears,[90] saying, "Alas! Alas! How painful, and I encounter this silent moment.[91] The loyal minister holds his tongue and the slanderous man is at the side of the king. Governance is corrupted and the way destroyed. Flattering and toadying are endless. Evil sayings and false words make the crooked seem upright. Letting the slanderous go yet assailing the loyal will bring the state of Wu to ruin. The ancestral temple will be leveled and the altar of grain and the altar of earth will not receive sacrifice. The inner and outer cities will become ruins; thorns will grow in the palace halls."[92]

The king of Wu was furious, saying, "This old minister is full of deceit and has become a monster to Wu. He even wants to seize full power, hold authority, and destroy my state by himself. I, a man of little virtue, out of respect for the former king could not bear to put you under the law. Now you should retreat and think about this yourself. You should not halt the plan of Wu."

Wu Zixu said, "If I, your subject, am not loyal and not trustworthy, I did not deserve to be the subject of the former king. I dare not to cherish my own body; I am indeed afraid of the demise of my state. In the past Jie killed Guan Longpang and Zhou executed Prince Bigan.[93] Now if you, great king,

---

88. Refers to reinstating the king of Yue.

89. These lines, together with Wu Zixu's remonstration below, are all four syllables per line in Chinese. They are highly polished rhetorical speech, which is often seen in, for example, *Zuozhuan*.

90. Sitting on the ground is a very disrespectful gesture in a ritual ceremony.

91. Suggesting that loyal words are silenced.

92. Again, this is a speech consisting of lines with four syllables. The final words in each odd line rhyme. These finals all end with the sound "ɯg."

93. Guan Longpang was a minister of the Xia dynasty. He was killed by Jie, the last Xia king, because of his remonstration against the king's corrupt lifestyle. Prince Bigan was a loyal minister of the Shang dynasty. He was killed by King Zhou because of his criticism of the king.

kill your servant you will make three with Jie and Zhou. I wish you, great king, do your best. I, your subject, request to leave."

5.18. 子胥歸，謂被離曰：「吾貫弓接矢於鄭、楚之界，越渡江淮，自致於斯。前王聽從吾計，破楚見凌之讎。欲報前王之恩而至於此。吾非自惜，禍將及汝。」被離曰：「未諫不聽，自殺何益？何如亡乎？」子胥曰：「亡，臣安往？」

5.18. When Wu Zixu returned home, he said to Beili, "I have pulled my bow and caught arrows on the border between Zheng and Chu. I traveled across the Yangzi River and the Huai River and brought myself to this land. The former king followed my strategy and destroyed Chu, the enemy that had mistreated me. I wanted to repay the former king's kindness, yet I come to this situation. It is not that I pity myself, but the disaster will affect you." Beili said, "Although your further admonishments will not be listened to, what is the use of committing suicide? How about fleeing?" Wu Zixu said, "If I run away, where can I go?"

5.19. 吳王聞子胥之怨恨也，乃使人賜屬鏤之劍。子胥受劍，徒跣褰裳，下堂中庭，仰天呼怨，曰：「吾始為汝父忠臣，立吳，設謀破楚，南服勁越，威加諸侯，有霸王之功。今汝不用吾言，反賜我劍。吾今日死，吳宮為墟，庭生蔓草，越人掘汝社稷。安忘我乎？昔前王不欲立汝，我以死爭之，卒得汝之願，公子多怨於我。我徒有功於吳。今乃忘我定國之恩。反賜我死，豈不謬哉！」吳王聞之，大怒，曰：「汝不忠信，為寡人使齊，託汝子於齊鮑氏，有我外之心。」急令自裁：「孤不使汝得有所見。」子胥把劍，仰天歎曰：「自我死後，後世必以我為忠，上配夏殷之世，亦得與龍逢、比干為友。」遂伏劍而死。

吳王乃取子胥屍，盛以鴟夷之器，投之於江中，言曰：「胥，汝一死之後，何能有知？」即斷其頭，置高樓上，謂之曰：「日月炙汝肉，飄風飄汝眼，炎光燒汝骨，魚鱉食汝肉。汝骨變形灰，有何所見？」乃棄其軀，投之江中。子胥因隨流揚波，依潮來往，蕩激崩岸。

於是吳王謂被離曰：「汝嘗與子胥論寡人之短。」乃髡被離而刑之。

5.19. The king of Wu heard of Wu Zixu's hatred; he then sent a man to present Wu Zixu a Zhulou sword. Wu Zixu received the sword. Bearing his feet and lifting up his skirts,[94] Wu Zixu descended the hall and came to the courtyard. He looked up to the sky and shouted out his complaint,

94. These were gestures of anger or sorrow in ancient times.

saying, "From the beginning I have been a loyal minister of your father. I built the city for Wu, conceived the strategy that destroyed Chu. To the south I subdued the strong state of Yue and awed the many lords. I have the merit of establishing the king as the hegemon. Now you do not make use of my words, rather you present me with this sword. I will die today, yet the Wu palace will become ruin and the court will grow creeping weeds. The Yue people will dig up your altar of earth and altar of grain, would you not remember me then? Previously the former king did not want to enthrone you, I risked my life fighting for you. Eventually you have attained your wish, but the many sons of the former king bore grudges against me. In vain I have provided great services to Wu. Now you have already forgotten my merit of bringing peace to the state and to the contrary order me to commit suicide. Is this not absurd?" Hearing this, the king of Wu became greatly furious, saying, "You are not loyal and trustworthy. When you served as my envoy to Qi, you entrusted your son to the Bao clan of Qi; this shows your intention of betraying me." He hurriedly ordered Wu Zixu to commit suicide, saying, "I, a man of little virtue, will not allow you to be able to see." Holding the sword, Wu Zixu looked up to heaven and sighed, saying, "When I am dead, later generations will certainly consider me loyal. Tracing back and comparing the present to the times of Xia and Shang, I could be friends with Longpeng and Bigan." He then died under the sword.[95]

The king of Wu then took Wu Zixu's body and had it placed in a leather bag to be thrown in the river,[96] saying, "Zixu, once you are dead, how can it be that you are still able to perceive anything?" He then cut off Zixu's head, placed it on a tall building, and said to it, "Sun and Moon roast your flesh, whirling winds blow in your eyes, fire burns your bones, and fish and turtles eat your flesh. Your bones decay and your body becomes ash, what can you see?" He then threw the body into the river. Wu Zixu's body thereupon followed the current and stirred up waves. Following the tides, it went back and forth, clashing and crashing on the banks.

The king of Wu then told Beili, "You have discussed my faults with Wu Zixu." He then shaved Beili and punished him.[97]

5.20. 王孫駱聞之，不朝，王召而問曰：「子何非寡人而不朝乎？」駱曰：「臣恐耳。」曰：「子以我殺子胥為重乎？」駱曰：「大

95. *Zuozhuan* records Wu Zixu's death in the twelveth year of King Fuchai. See *Zuozhuan*, Lord Ai 11; Yang Bojun, 1665; Durrant, Li, and Schaberg, 1903.

96. 鴟夷 (*chiyi*) is a leather bag.

97. 髡 (*kun*) was a punishment involving shaving off a criminal's hair.

王氣高，子胥位下，王誅之。臣命何異於子胥？臣以是恐也。」王曰：「非聽宰嚭以殺子胥，胥圖寡人也。」駱曰：「臣聞人君者，必有敢諫之臣，在上位者，必有敢言之交。夫子胥，先王之老臣也，不忠不信，不得為前王臣。」吳王中心悏然，悔殺子胥：「豈非宰嚭之讒子胥？」而欲殺之。駱曰：「不可。王若殺嚭，此為二子胥也。」於是不誅。

5.20. Upon hearing of this, Wangsun Luo did not attend court. The king summoned him and asked, "Why do you avoid me and not attend the court?"[98] Wangsun Luo replied, "I, your subject, am simply afraid." The king said, "Do you regard my execution of Wu Zixu to be too harsh?" Wangsun Luo answered, "Your Majesty is high up and swaggering, Wu Zixu was subordinate to you, thus Your Majesty killed him. How different is my, your subject's, life from that of Wu Zixu's? For this I, your subject, am fearful." The king said, "It was not that I listened to Chancellor Bo Pi and killed Wu Zixu, it was because Wu Zixu had schemed against me, a man of little virtue." Wangsun Luo said, "I, your subject, have heard that the ruler of men must have ministers who dare to remonstrate, those at the upper rank must have friends who dare to speak out. As for Wu Zixu, he was a senior minister of the former king. If he was not loyal and trustworthy, he would not have been a minister of the former king." The king of Wu felt sorrowful in his heart and regretted killing Wu Zixu, saying, "Was that not because Chancellor Bo Pi slandered Wu Zixu?" He thereupon wanted to kill Chancellor Bo Pi. Wangsun Luo said, "You should not do this. If Your Majesty kills Chancellor Bo Pi, he will become the second Wu Zixu." Because of this Chancellor Bo Pi was spared.

5.21. 十四年，夫差既殺子胥，連年不熟，民多怨恨。吳王復伐齊。闕為闌溝於商魯之間，北屬蘄，西屬濟，欲與魯晉合攻於黃池之上。恐群臣復諫，乃令國中曰：「寡人伐齊，有敢諫者，死！」太子友知子胥忠而不用，太宰嚭佞而專政，欲切言之，恐罹尣也，乃以諷諫激於王。清旦，懷丸持彈從後園而來，衣袷履濡。王怪而問之，曰：「子何為袷衣濡履，體如斯也？」太子友曰：「適游後園，聞秋蜩之聲，往而觀之。夫秋蟬登高樹，飲清露，隨風撝撓，長吟悲鳴，自以為安，不知螳螂超枝緣條，曳腰聳距而稷其形。夫螳螂翕心而進，志在有利，不知黃雀緣茂林，徘徊枝陰，踙躍微進，欲啄螳螂。夫黃雀但知伺螳螂之有味，不知臣挾彈危擲，蹭蹬飛丸而集其背。今臣但虛心，志在黃雀，不知空埳其旁，闇忽埳中，陷於深井。臣故袷體濡

98. 非 (*fei*) means 違 (*wei*), "to avoid," here.

履，幾為大王取笑。」王曰：「天下之愚，莫過於斯：但貪前利，不睹後患。」太子曰：「天下之愚，復有甚者。魯承周公之末，有孔子之教，守仁抱德，無欲於鄰國，而齊舉兵伐之，不愛民命，惟有所獲。夫齊，徒舉而伐魯，不知吳悉境內之士，盡府庫之財，暴師千里而攻之。夫吳，徒知踰境征伐非吾之國，不知越王將選死士出三江之口，入五湖之中，屠我吳國，滅我吳宮。天下之危，莫過於斯也！」吳王不聽太子之諫，遂北伐齊。

5.21. In the fourteenth year (482 BCE), King Fuchai of Wu had already killed Wu Zixu and there had been no harvest for several years. Most of the people held ill will against the king who once more launched a military expedition against Qi. He dug a canal between Song and Lu;[99] to the north, connecting it to Qi River,[100] and to the west, connecting it to the Ji River—this was in order to engage in battle with both Lu and Jin in Huangchi.[101] Worried that the ministers would again remonstrate against this, the king then issued a command in his state, saying, "I, a man of little virtue, am launching a military expedition against Qi, anyone who dares to remonstrate shall be executed." The Heir Apparent You, knowing that Wu Zixu was loyal but not heeded and that Chief Chancellor Bo Pi was conniving yet held the power, desired to directly admonish the king about this but was afraid of receiving punishment. He then decided to remonstrate against the king in a roundabout way, hoping to rouse him.

In early morning, carrying pellets and holding a bow, the heir apparent came from the rear garden with his clothes wet and shoes soaked. Perplexed, the king asked him, "Why are your clothes wet, shoes soaked, and your body like this?" You, the heir apparent, replied, "Just now, I was wandering in the garden, heard the song of the autumn cicada, and went to look at it. The autumn cicada climbed on a tall tree; drank clear dew; swung along with the wind; made a long, shrill, and sorrowful sound; and thought itself safe. Yet it did not know that a mantis had leapt on a high branch and climbed along a twig, dragging its waist and lifting its claws with the intention of catching the cicada.[102] The mantis focused its mind and crawled, its attention fixed on gain, but it did not know that a yellow titmouse was relying upon the lush trees, and

---

99. This is probably the Hangou 邗溝, part of the Great Canal of China. Shang here refers to the state of Song, not the Shang dynasty. After Zhou destroyed Shang, the Zhou king enfeoffed Qi 啓, brother of the last Shang king, as the ruler of Song. So Song is the descendant of Shang and its capital was also in the location of one of the Shang capitals. Therefore Song was sometimes mentioned as Shang.

100. 蘄 (*qi*) is probably a mistake for 沂 (*yi*). The Qi River is in modern day Hubei Province; the Yi River is in modern day Shandong Province, up north in the Wu region.

101. In modern-day Fengqiu County, Henan Province.

102. Zhang Jue, citing from the *Taiping yulan*, argues that 而稷 (*erji*) should be 慾援 (*yuyuan*), "desire to catch." See Zhang Jue, 155.

lingered in the shadow of one. It gently lifted its claws and legs and stealthily moved forward, wanting to peck the mantis. The yellow titmouse only knew the testiness of the mantis but was unaware that I, your subject, was holding the pellet and shooting it up high. The bow had been pulled taut and the flying pellet was about to hit its back. At that moment, I, your subject, only knew to focus my mind and fix my intention on the yellow titmouse, I did not notice there was a hole beside me. In the dim light I suddenly fell into the hole and was stuck in a deep trap. For this reason I, your subject, got my body wet and shoes soaked and was almost laughed at by Your Majesty."[103]

The king said, "There is nothing in the world more foolish than this: coveting only the gain in front of one's eyes yet failing to see the danger behind it." The heir apparent said, "There are in the world things more foolish than this. Lu continued the heritage of Duke Zhou and received the teachings of Confucius.[104] It sticks to humaneness and cherishes virtue, desiring nothing from its neighboring states. Now Qi mobilized its troops to attack Lu. Qi did not value the life of the people and wished only to gain from the war. Qi simply mobilized to attack Lu; it did not realize that Wu sent all the men in its territory, exhausted the resources in its treasury, and stationed its troops over a thousand *li* in order to make its attack. Wu only knew to march across the border to punish and attack a state that did not belong to us, it did not realize that the king of Yue was about to select warriors who were not afraid of dying to come out from the delta of the three rivers and invade the five lakes.[105] They will annihilate our state of Wu and ruin our palaces. There is nothing in the world that is more dangerous than this." The king of Wu did not listen to the heir apparent's admonishment and attacked Qi to the north.

5.22. 越王聞吳王伐齊，使范蠡、洩庸率師屯海通江，以絕吳路。敗太子友於始熊夷，通江淮，轉襲吳，遂入吳國，燒姑胥臺，徙其大舟。

5.22. The king of Yue, upon hearing that the king of Wu attacked Qi, sent Fan Li and Yeyong to lead the troops to station along the coast and penetrate

103. This seems to have been a popular story during the Warring States and Han times. It appeared in the "Shanmu" 山木 chapter in *Zhuangzi*, and it was also recorded in *Hanshi waizhuan* 韓詩外傳 and Liu Xiang's 劉向 *Shuoyuan*. See Xiang Zonglu 向宗魯, *Shuoyuan jiaozheng* 說苑校證 (Beijing: Zhonghua shuju, 1987).

104. When the Zhou dynasty was established, Duke Zhou was enfeoffed in the state of Lu. Because King Cheng of Zhu was young, Duke Zhou stayed at the Zhou capital as the regent. His son Boqin 伯禽 then went to Lu and became the ruler of the state. Confucius was from Lu.

105. The three rivers probably refer to the Song River 松江, the Qiantang River 錢塘江, and the Puyang River 浦陽江. There are different explanations regarding what the five lakes refer to. In general, these are lakes in the Wu and Yue regions. Zhang Jue argues that "the five lakes" is actually another name of Taihu Lake, 太湖. See Zhang Jue, 157n24.

through the river, in order to cut the Wu army's retreat.[106] Yue defeated Heir Apparent You in Guxiongyi and penetrated inland following the river.[107] It then attacked Wu, invaded the Wu capital, burned Guxu Terrace, and took away Wu's grand boat.[108]

5.23. 吳敗齊師於艾陵之上，還師臨晉，與定公爭長，未合，邊候。吳王夫差大懼，合諸侯謀曰：「吾道遼遠，無會，前進，孰利？」王孫駱曰：「不如前進，則執諸侯之柄，以求其志。請王屬士，以明其令，勸之以高位，辱之以不從。令各盡其死。」

夫差昏秣馬食士，服兵被甲，勒馬銜枚，出火於造，闇行而進。吳師皆文犀長盾，扁諸之劍，方陣而行。中校之軍皆白裳、白髦、素甲、素羽之矰，望之若荼，王親秉鉞，戴旗以陣而立。左軍皆赤裳、赤髦、丹甲、朱羽之矰，望之若火。右軍皆玄裳、玄輿、黑甲、烏羽之矰，望之如墨。帶甲三萬六千，雞鳴而定陣,去晉軍一里。天尚未明，王乃親鳴金鼓，三軍譁吟，以振其旅，其聲動天徙地。

晉大驚,不出，反距堅壘，乃令童褐請軍，曰：「兩軍偃兵接好，日中為期。今大國越次而造弊邑之軍壘，敢請亂故？」吳王親對曰：「天子有命，周室卑弱，約諸侯貢獻，莫入王府，上帝鬼神而不可以告。無姬姓之所振，懼，遣使來告，冠蓋不絕於道。始周依負於晉，故忽於夷狄會晉，會晉今反叛如斯，吾是以蒲服就君。不肯長弟，徒以爭彊，孤進，不敢，去，君不命長，為諸侯笑。孤之事君，決在今日，不得事君，命在今日矣！敢煩使者往來，孤躬親聽命於藩籬之外。」童褐將還，吳王躡左足，與褐決矣。

及報，與諸侯、大夫列坐於晉定公前。既以通命，乃告趙鞅曰：「臣觀吳王之色，類有大憂，小則嬖妾、嫡子死，否則吳國有難；大則越人入，不得還也。其意有愁毒之憂，進退輕難，不可與戰。主君宜許之以前，期無以爭行而危國也。然不可徒許，必明其信。」趙鞅許諾。入謁定公，曰：「姬姓於周，吳為先老，可長，以盡國禮。」定公許諾。命童褐復命。

於是吳王愧晉之義，乃退幕而會。二國君臣並在，吳王稱公，前歃，晉侯次之，群臣畢盟。

5.23. After Wu defeated the Qi army near Ailing, it moved its troops and closed in on Jin, thus competing for hegemony with Lord Ding of Jin. Before

106. Fan Li was originally from the state of Chu. He served as a grand minister in Yue and helped Goujian, king of Yue, to destroy Wu. After that, he went to Qi and became a wealthy businessman. Yeyong was a minister of Yue.

107. According to *Guoyu*, 始熊夷 (*shixiongyi*) is a mistake for 姑熊夷 (*guxiongyi*); 江淮 (*jianghuai*) is also a mistake for 江 (*jiang*). See Zhang Jue, 158n3.

108. This is probably the Yuhuang boat mentioned in *WYCQ* 3.1.

its goal was achieved, its border scout arrived and reported Yue's trespass.[109] Fuchai, king of Wu, greatly feared this. He summoned his officials and discussed this,[110] saying, "Our return journey is far. Giving up the covenant and returning, or smearing the mouth with blood in oath-taking before Jin, which one is profitable?"[111] Wangsun Luo said, "We'd rather smear blood before Jin. Then we can wield command of the many lords in order to realize our wish. I request Your Majesty to gather your warriors, make clear to them your order, encourage them with high official positions, punish those who do not obey, and ensure that each one of them fights to the death."

At dusk Fuchai fed the horses and the soldiers. The soldiers carried their weapons, wore their armor, reined in the horses, held gags in their mouths,[112] emptied out the embers from the stove, and marched forward in darkness. The Wu troops were equipped with long shields made of patterned rhinoceros skin and Bianzhu swords;[113] they advanced in rows. The soldiers in the central column were all in white clothes, held white flags, wore white armor, and had short arrows with white feathers;[114] they looked like sow thistle flowers. The king of Wu personally held a wide-edged axe and stood in the line under a flag. The left column were all in red clothes, held red flags, wore red armor, and had short arrows with red feathers; they looked like fire. The right column were all in black clothes, drove black carriages, wore black armor, and held short arrows with black feathers; they looked like black ink. Armored warriors numbered thirty six thousand and formed the lines at dawn. Wu columns were only one *li* away from the Jin troops. When the sky had yet to grow bright, the king of Wu personally hit the metal drum and soldiers in the three columns all shouted in order to arouse the troops.[115] Their voices shocked the sky and shook the ground.

The Jin troops were greatly frightened and did not dare leave their camp. They defended and fortified the ramparts and sent Tong He to visit

109. According to *Guoyu*, the sentence should be 邊侯乃至，以越亂告. See Zhang Jue, 160.

110. 諸侯 (*zhuhou*), "many lords," is a mistake; it should be 諸臣 (*zhuchen*), "many officials."

111. Smearing blood on the mouth in oath-making was the tradition when entering into a covenant in early China. The order of smearing blood indicates the hierarchy among the participants.

112. In ancient times, when marching at night, soldiers were ordered to hold a small piece of wood in their mouths to make sure they moved quietly.

113. Bianzhu was the name of a sword. Duan Yucai 段玉裁 (1735–1815) argues that Bianzhu was the name of the decoration on a sword. See Duan Yucai 段玉裁, *Shuowen jiezi zhu* 說文解字註 (Shanghai: Shanghai guji, 1998), 655.

114. 髦 (*mao*) is 旄 (*mao*) here, which is a flag with a yak's tail on the top as a decoration. 矰 (*zeng*) is a short arrow.

115. Beating the drum was an order to advance the troops.

the Wu army,[116] saying, "Our two armies ceased military action, agreed to friendly terms, and scheduled a meeting at noon. Now your great state has come before the date and arrived at the military camp of our humble state. Dare I ask the reason for your twisting time?" The king of Wu personally responded, saying, "The son of heaven has commanded,[117] but the house of Zhou is humble and weak. It was agreed that the many lords should offer tribute to Zhou yet no items entered the treasury of the Zhou king. Because of this there was nothing to be offered to the high gods, ghosts, and spirits. The Zhou king has nothing to provide to the Ji clan,[118] he was afraid and sent emissaries to inform us of the urgency; the emissaries and their carriages lined up on the road. Previously Zhou relied upon Jin, therefore it ignored the Yi and Di people.[119] It happens that now Jin has disobeyed Zhou in this way, and for this reason I come crawling to you.[120] Jin refused to care for the younger ones but only competes with other states by force.[121] I, a man of little virtue, dare not transgress my former kings' rank. If I were to leave without being named hegemon by your lord, I will be laughed at by the many lords. That if I, a man of little virtue, can serve your lord depends on today; that if I cannot serve your lord, my fate is also decided today.[122] Dare I trouble you, emissary, to travel back and forth. I, a man of little virtue, will personally receive your lord's command outside of your battlement." When Tong He was about to depart, the king of Wu stepped on Tong He's left foot and bid Tong He farewell.[123]

When Tong He returned to make his report, he was sitting in a line in front of Lord Ding of Jin with the many lords and grand ministers. After he

---

116. Tong He was called Dong He 董褐 in *Guoyu*. In *Zuozhuan*, he was called "Officer in Charge of Chariot Yin," Sima Yin 司馬寅. Yin was his name. See Xu Yuangao, 550. See also *Zuozhuan*, Lord Ai 13; Yang Bojun, 1677; Durrant, Li, and Schaberg, 1915.

117. The son of heaven refers to the king of the Zhou, who was still the nominal king of all the states.

118. The surname of the Zhou royal family was Ji.

119. Yi and Di were often used as general names for the tribal people who lived outside of the central plain. Because Wu was on the southeastern coast, it was far from the central plain. Here Fuchai is using Yi and Di to refer to the state of Wu.

120. This is a humble way for King Fuchai to say that he was weak and powerless in front of the lord of Jin.

121. The states of Jin, Lu, and Wei were all founded by members of the Ji clan, all relatives of the Zhou household.

122. The king of Wu was implying that if Jin refused to agree to Wu's terms, Wu would engage in battle with Jin.

123. It is not clear why the king of Wu bid farewell to Tong He with such an intimate action. One possibility is that the king was deeply worried about the Yue invasion, so he did not pay attention to ritual distance when seeing Tong He off.

reported, he spoke to Zhao Yang,[124] saying, "I, your subject, have observed the expression of the Wu king; he seemed to have severe concerns. If it is a small matter, it could be that his favorite consort or the son born of his primary wife died. If not, then it must be that the state of Wu is in trouble. If it is a significant matter, it should be that the Yue people invaded Wu and the king of Wu is unable to return. Since there is worry and anger in his heart, he will consider little of the consequences of advancing and retreating, therefore we must not engage in battle with him. My lord should agree to his preference for blood smearing on the covenant, and I wish you not to endanger the state by competing for rank. However, we should not simply compromise; we must allow him to demonstrate his trustworthiness." Zhao Yang agreed. He entered the hall and received an audience with Lord Ding, saying to the lord, "As for the Ji clan of Zhou, the ancestor of Wu was the oldest.[125] The king of Wu therefore can first smear the blood, in order to comply with the ritual of the country." Lord Ding consented to this and ordered Tong He to report it to king of Wu.[126]

Because of this, the king of Wu was ashamed by Jin's righteousness and made a concession to covenant in a tent. The rulers and ministers of the two states were present. The king of Wu changed his title to duke and smeared the blood first and Lord Ding of Jin followed him. The many ministers all joined in the covenant.

5.24. 吳既長晉而還，未踰於黃池，越聞吳王久留未歸，乃悉士眾將踰章山，濟三江，而欲伐之。

吳又恐齊、宋之為害，乃命王孫駱告勞于周，曰：「昔楚不承供貢，辟遠兄弟之國，吾前君闔閭不忍其惡，帶劍挺鈹，與楚昭王相逐於中原。天舍其忠，楚師敗績。今齊不賢於楚，又不恭王命，以遠辟兄弟之國，夫差不忍其惡，被甲帶劍，徑至艾陵，天福於吳，齊師還鋒而退。夫差豈敢自多其功？是文武之德所祐助。時歸吳，不熟於歲，遂緣江泝淮，開溝深水，出於商魯之間而歸，告於天子執事。」

周王答曰：「伯父令子來乎？盟國，一人則依矣，余實嘉之。伯父若能輔余一人，則兼受永福，周室何憂焉？」乃賜弓弩、王阼，以增號謚。

吳王還歸自池，息民散兵。

5.24. After winning the upper hand over Jin, the king of Wu returned but did not pass Huangchi. The king of Yue, upon hearing that the king of Wu

124. Zhao Yang was a powerful Jin minister who actually held the power in Jin.

125. Taibo, the founder of Wu, was the oldest son of Gugong Danfu and the older brother of Jili, ancestors of the Zhou people. Therefore Zhao Yang says that Wu's ancestor was the oldest.

126. *Guoyu* records Tong He's reply to King Fuchai. See Xu Yuangao, 551–52.

had stayed out of the state for a long time and did not return, mobilized all his soldiers and men. He planned to pass the Zhang mountains,[127] cross the three rivers, and then invade Wu.

The king of Wu furthermore was afraid that Qi and Song would bring harm to Wu; therefore, he sent Wangsun Luo to report merit conduct to the Zhou king, saying, "Previously Chu refused to take responsibility for paying tribute to Zhou; it also caused estrangement among our sibling states.[128] Our former king, Helü, could not tolerate Chu's crimes; holding his sword and pulling out his knife,[129] he and king Zhao of Chu chased each other on the battlefield.[130] Heaven bestowed a blessing on him and the Chu army suffered defeat. Now Qi is worse than Chu, and furthermore it does not respect Your Majesty's commands and thereby estranges our sibling states. Fuchai could not tolerate Qi's crime, putting on his armor and holding his sword, he reached to Ailing. Heaven assisted Wu, the Qi army turned back their weapons and retreated. Dare Fuchai brag about his achievement? This is due to the protection and support of the virtue of King Wen and King Wu.[131] When he returned to Wu he found that the harvest of the year had failed, therefore he traveled down along the Yangzi River and traveled up along the Huai River, dug canals, deepened river channels, and marched the troops between Song and Lu before his return to Wu. Now he reports this to the servant of the son of heaven."[132]

The king of Zhou replied,[133] "Did my uncle Fuchai command you to come here?[134] You made a covenant with other states and I, the only one, can rely upon them.[135] I indeed appreciate this. If my uncle Fuchai can assist me, I will then at the same time be able to receive protection forever. What worries should the Zhou house have?"[136] Thereupon the Zhou king bestowed upon Fuchai a bow, a cross-bow, and the sacrificial meat presented to former Zhou kings.[137] He also gave Fuchai a title and honorific name.

127. Probably a mistake for the Chang Mountain 長山, located on the eastern shore of Taihu Lake.

128. States of Zhou descendants.

129. 鈹 (*pi*) was a weapon shaped like a long knife with blades on both sides.

130. 中原 (*zhongyuan*) is 原中 (*yuanzhong*), "battle field."

131. Founders of the Zhou dynasty. King Wen was the father of King Wu, who destroyed Shang.

132. This is a humble expression. Fuchai is saying that he dares not report directly to the king, so he reports to the servants of the king instead.

133. This is King Jing of Zhou 周敬王 (r. 519–476 BCE).

134. The king of Zhou usually called rulers of the state who were also from the Ji clan "uncles."

135. The son of heaven refers to himself as the "only one" 一人 (*yiren*).

136. The Wu report and the Zhou king's response are also found in *Guoyu*. See Xu Yuangao, 553–54.

137. The Zhou kings often shared sacrificial meat with rulers of states who were also Zhou descendants.

The king of Wu returned from Huangchi. He let the people rest and dismissed the army.

5.25. 二十年，越王興師伐吳。吳與越戰於檇李，吳師大敗，軍散，死者不可勝計。越追，破吳，吳王困急，使王孫駱稽首請成，如越之來也。越王對曰：「昔天以越賜吳，吳不受也；今天以吳賜越，其可逆乎！吾請獻勾甬東之地，吾與君為二君乎。」吳王曰：「吾之在周，禮前王一飯。如越王不忘周室之義，而使為附邑，亦寡人之願也。行人請成列國之義，惟君王有意焉。」大夫種曰：「吳為無道，今幸擒之，願王制其命。」越王曰：「吾將殘汝社稷，夷汝宗廟。」吳王默然。請成，七反，越王不聽。

5.25. In the twentieth year of King Fuchai (476 BCE), the king of Yue mobilized troops to attack Wu. Wu and Yue battled in Zuili and the Wu troops were soundly defeated. The Wu army dispersed and countless men died. Yue chased after them and destroyed Wu. The king of Wu was surrounded and in dire straits. He sent Wangsun Luo to kowtow before the king of Yue and begged for a truce, just as Yue had done previously. The king of Yue responded, saying, "Previously, heaven gave Yue to Wu but Wu did not receive it. Now heaven gives Wu to Yue, dare I disobey heaven's will? I make a request to present you the land of Gouzhang and that east of Yu River,[138] so your lord and I will be two rulers." The king of Wu said, "If I were at the Zhou court, according to the rites, the Zhou king should present me a feast before the king of Yue.[139] If the king of Yue has not forgotten the ritual of the Zhou royal family and allows me to become a vassal of Yue, this is what I, a man of little virtue, wish. My emissary entreats you to accept my request to remain a state, I wish Your Majesty to give consideration to it." Grand Minister Wen Zhong said, "The king of Wu's conduct does not accord with the Way. Now, fortunately, we can arrest him, and I wish Your Majesty to determine his fate." The king of Yue said, "I will ruin your altar of land and altar of grain and level your ancestral temple."[140] The king of Wu had nothing to say in response. The emissary traveled seven times to request a truce but the king of Yue refused to listen.

---

138. In modern day Zhejiang Province, Zhoushan 舟山 islands.

139. King Fuchai was the descendant of Taibo, older brother of the founder of Zhou. Goujian was the descendant of Yu, founder of the Xia dynasty, which was conquered by Zhou. Because of this, King Fuchai enjoyed higher status at the Zhou court than Goujian.

140. The altars and the ancestral temple are the symbols of a state. Goujian was saying that he would terminate the state of Wu.

5.26. 二十三年十月，越王復伐吳。吳國困，不戰，士卒分散，城門不守，遂屠吳。

吳王率群臣遁去，晝馳夜走，三日三夕，達於秦餘杭山，胸中愁憂，目視茫茫，行步猖狂，腹餒口飢，顧得生稻而食之，伏地而飲水。顧左右曰：「此何名也？」對曰：「是生稻也。」吳王曰：「是公孫聖所言『不得火食』、『走偉偟也』。」王孫駱曰：「飽食而去，前有胥山，西阪中可以匿止。」

王行有頃，因得生瓜，已熟，吳王掇而食之。謂左右曰：「何冬而生瓜，近道而人不食，何也？」左右曰：「謂糞種之物，人不食也。」吳王曰：「何謂糞種？」左右曰：「盛夏之時，人食生瓜，起居道傍，子復生，秋霜惡之，故不食。」吳王歎曰：「子胥所謂旦食者也。」

謂太宰嚭曰：「吾戮公孫聖，投胥山之巔，吾以畏責天下之慚，吾足不能進，心不能往。」太宰嚭曰：「死與生，敗與成，故有避乎？」王曰：「然。曾無所知乎？子試前呼之。聖在，當即有應。」吳王止秦餘杭山，呼曰：「公孫聖！」三反呼聖，從山中應曰：「公孫聖。」三呼三應。吳王仰天呼曰：「寡人豈可返乎？寡人世世得聖也。」

5.26. In the twenty-third year of King Fuchai (473 BCE), in the tenth month, the king of Yue again attacked Wu. People in the Wu capital were exhausted and did not fight. Wu soldiers scattered and no one guarded the gates, Yue therefore massacred those in the city.

The king of Wu led the many officials in running away. Day and night they fled. After three days and three nights, they arrived at Qinyuhang Mountain.[141] The king was deeply distressed and worried in his heart and his eyesight was blurred. He walked unsteadily, felt starving in his stomach and hungry in his mouth. He saw uncooked rice and ate it, then prostrated on the ground and drank water from it. Turning his head back, he asked his attendants, saying, "What is this?" They answered, "This is uncooked rice." The king of Wu said, "This is what Gongsun Sheng said, 'will not eat cooked food,' and 'run away in haste.'" Wangsun Luo said, "Eat enough and leave. There is Xu Mountain on the road ahead.[142] We can hide and rest on the west slope."

The king traveled for a while and then found a wild-growing melon that was already ripe. The king of Wu picked it up and ate it. He asked his attendants, "How does this melon grow in the winter? It was near the road, yet no one eats it; what is the reason for this?" The attendants said, "This is called 'a thing grown from excrement'; people do not eat it." The king of Wu

141. Also called Yang Mountain 陽山, in modern day Wu County, Jiangsu Province.

142. Also in Wu County, Jiangsu Province.

asked, "What is called the thing growing from excrement?" The attendants answered, "In midsummer, people eat unripe melons and then empty their bowels on the road side. The seeds grow again but are ruined by fall frost, therefore people do not eat it." The king of Wu sighed, saying, "This is the breakfast Wu Zixu had described."

The king told Chief Chancellor Bo Pi, "I executed Gongsun Sheng and threw his body on the top of Xu Mountain. Because I bear the shame that I am condemned by the people of the world, my feet cannot advance and in my heart I dare not walk onto the mountain." Chief Chancellor Bo Pi said, "Death and life, failure and success, are they indeed avoidable?" The king of Wu said, "Yes. Can it be possible that the dead do not have perception? You should try calling for him. If Gongsun Sheng is there, he should respond immediately." The king of Wu stopped at the Qinyuhang Mountain. Chief Chancellor Bo Pi called out, "Gongsun Sheng!" He called three times. Gongsun Sheng answered from the mountain, saying, "Gongsun Sheng." Three times Chief Chancellor Bo Pi called, three times Gongsun Sheng responded. The king of Wu looked up to heaven and cried, "Can I, a man of little virtue, return to my state? If so, forever I will serve Gongsun Sheng."

5.27. 須臾，越兵至，三圍吳。范蠡在中行，左手提鼓，右手操枹而鼓之。

吳王書其矢而射種、蠡之軍，辭曰：「吾聞狡兔以死，良犬就烹，敵國如滅，謀臣必亡。今吳病矣，大夫何慮乎？」

大夫種、相國蠡急而攻。大夫種書矢射之曰：「上天蒼蒼，若存若亡。越君勾踐下臣種敢言之：昔天以越賜吳，吳不肯受，是天所反。勾踐敬天而功，既得返國，今上天報越之功，敬而受之，不敢忘也。且吳有大過六，以至于亡，王知之乎？有忠臣伍子胥忠諫而身死，大過一也；公孫聖直說而無功，大過二也；太宰嚭愚而佞，言輕而讒諛，妄語恣口，聽而用之，大過三也；夫齊晉無返逆行，無僭侈之過，而吳伐二國，辱君臣，毀社稷，大過四也；且吳與越同音共律，上合星宿，下共一理，而吳侵伐，大過五也；昔越親戕吳之前王，罪莫大焉，而幸伐之，不從天命，而棄其仇，後為大患，大過六也。越王謹上刻青天，敢不如命？」

大夫種謂越君曰：「中冬氣定，天將殺戮，不行天殺，反受其殃。」越王敬拜曰：「諾。今圖吳王，將為何如？」大夫種曰：「君被五勝之衣，帶步光之劍，仗屈盧之矛，瞋目大言以執之。」越王曰：「諾。」乃如大夫種辭吳王曰：「誠以今日聞命！」言有頃，吳王不自殺。越王復使謂曰：「何王之忍辱厚恥也？世無萬歲之君，死生一也。今子尚有遺榮，何必使吾師眾加刃於王？」吳王仍未肯自殺。勾踐謂種蠡曰：「二子何不誅之？」種蠡曰：「臣，人臣之位，不敢加誅於人主。願主急而命之：『天誅當行，不可久留。』」越王復瞋目怒曰：「死者，人之所惡。惡者，無罪於天，不負於人。今君抱六過之罪，不知愧辱而欲求生，豈不鄙哉？」吳王乃太息，四顧而望，言曰：「諾。」乃引劍而伏之死。越王謂太宰嚭曰：「子為臣不忠無信，亡國滅君。」乃誅嚭并妻子。

吳王臨欲伏劍，顧謂左右曰：「吾生既慚，死亦愧矣。使死者有知，吾羞前君地下，不忍睹忠臣伍子胥及公孫聖；使其無知，吾負於生。死必連繄組以罩吾目，恐其不蔽，願復重羅繡三幅，以為掩明，生不昭我，死勿見我形，吾何可哉？」

越王乃葬吳王以禮於秦餘杭山卑猶。越王使軍士集于我戎之功，人一隰土以葬之。宰嚭亦葬卑猶之旁。

5.27. Soon the Yue troops arrived and surrounded the king of Wu in three circles. Fan Li remained with the troops; with drum in his left hand and drumstick in his right hand, he beat the drum for advancing.

The king of Wu tied his letter on an arrow and shot it into Wen Zhong's and Fan Li's army. The letter read, "I have heard that: 'After the cunning hare is killed, the hound is boiled. If the rival state is destroyed, the ministers planning for it will certainly face demise.' Now Wu is in dire straits, what consideration should you, grand ministers, have?"

Grand Minister Wen Zhong and Prime Minister Fan Li hurried the attack. Grand Minister Wen Zhong tied his letter on an arrow and shot it to the king of Wu, saying, "Heaven is vast and without boundaries. It saves some states but destroys the others. Wen Zhong, the humble minister of the king of Yue, Goujian, dares to tell you the following: 'Previously heaven gave Yue to Wu but Wu refused to accept it, this disobeyed heaven. Goujian respected heaven and pacified his people, thereupon he was able to return to his state. Now heaven has rewarded the king of Yue's merit, he must respectfully accept this and dare not ignore it. Furthermore, Wu has committed six major crimes and thus came to its demise. Are you, the king, aware of them? You had loyal minister Wu Zixu, who remonstrated with honesty but was killed; this is the first major crime. Gongsun Sheng admonished you with sincerity but you did not listen; this is the second major crime. Chief Chancellor Bo Pi is unwise but cunning in words, he is frivolous and slanderous, his words absurd and speech reckless, yet you listened to him and used him; this is the third major crime. As for Qi and Jin, they did not commit perverse deeds, nor did they commit the crimes of usurping or being lavish in their conduct. Yet Wu attacked these two states, humiliated their lords and ministers, and destroyed their altar of land and altar of grain; this is the fourth major crime. Furthermore, Wu and Yue share the same tone and pitch, correspond to the same constellation above, and belong to the same celestial demarcation below,[143] yet Wu invaded and attacked Yue; this is the fifth major crime of Wu. In the past, the king of Yue personally killed the former king of Wu,[144] there is no crime worse than this. Wu attacked Yue and luckily won, yet you freed your enemy without following the command of heaven,[145] which later caused big trouble for Wu; this is the sixth major crime. The king of Yue reverently and carefully follows the will of heaven, dare he not obey heaven's command?'"

Grand Minister Wen Zhong said to the lord of Yue, "In the midwinter the *qi* ceases to grow and heaven conducts its killing. If we fail to follow heaven's will to kill, we will suffer disaster in return." The king of Yue respectfully bowed, saying, "Assented. Now we should make plans for the king of Wu. What should we do about him?" Grand Minister Wen Zhong answered, "My lord wears the cloth with the pattern of the five phases overcoming each other,[146] carries the Buguang sword, and holds the Qulu lance. Glare at him, shout angrily, and arrest him." The king of Yue said, "Alright." He then followed Grand Minister Wen Zhong's words and told the king of Wu, "I sincerely want to hear your fate today." After the words had been delivered, for a while, the king of Wu did not commit suicide. The king of Yue again sent someone to the king of Wu, saying, "Why does Your Majesty tolerate humiliation and such shamelessness? There is no lord who can survive for ten thousand years; death and life are the same. Now you, sir, still have remaining dignity, why must Your Majesty cause our soldiers to put blades in you?" The king of Wu was still not willing to kill himself. Goujian told Wen Zhong and Fan Li, "Why do you two not kill him?" Wen Zhong and Fan Li answered, "We, your subjects, are in the position of ruler's ministers and we dare not execute a lord of men. We wish Your Majesty to hurriedly

---

143. The five tones are: *gong* 宫, *shang* 商, *jue* 角, *zhi* 徵, and *yu* 羽. The *yinyang* and Five Phases theories associated the five tones with five directions: *gong* was associated with the center, *shang* with west, *jue* with east, *zhi* with south, and *yu* with north. Wu and Yue were both located in the southeast and they share corresponding tones. People in ancient times also associated twenty-eight constellations with states. The states of Wu and Yue corresponded to the division of the constellations *dou* 斗, *niu* 牛, and *nü* 女.

144. This refers to the battle of Wu and Yue in 496 BCE, during which Yue defeated Wu and injured King Helü. King Helü died soon after the battle. See *Zuozhuan*, Lord Ding 14; Yang Bojun, 1596; Durrant, Li, and Schaberg, 1817.

145. This refers to Fuchai's defeat of Goujian in 494 BCE. Goujian begged for a truce and served as a servant in Wu; Fuchai returned Goujian to Yue in 492 BCE.

146. The five phases are: metal, wood, water, fire, and earth. There are two theories describing the relationships among the five phases. One theory is that the five phases generate each other: wood feeds fire, fire creates earth (ash), earth bears metal, metal enriches water, and water nourishes wood. The other order is that the five phases overcome each other: wood parts earth, earth dams water, water extinguishes fire, fire melts metal, and metal chops wood.

command him, saying, 'The punishment of heaven must be executed, it cannot be further delayed.'" The king of Yue again glared and spoke angrily, saying, "Death is what all men detest. But anyone though disliking death should not offend heaven, should not betray others. Now, Your Majesty committed six crimes. You do not know about shame and humiliation but seek life, is this not disgraceful?" The king of Wu then sighed deeply. Turning back and looking around, he said, "I concede." He then drew his sword and committed suicide. The king of Yue told Chief Chancellor Bo Pi, "As a servant of your lord, you, sir, are not loyal and trustworthy. You caused the demise of your state and the death of your ruler." He then executed Bo Pi and his wife and children.

Before the king of Wu killed himself with the sword, he looked to his attendants and said, "I am ashamed when I am alive and I will feel guilty even after my death. If the deceased are sentient, then I am ashamed to face my former king in the grave, and I cannot bear to meet the loyal ministers Wu Zixu and Gongsun Sheng. If the deceased are not sentient, I still failed the living. After I die, you must cover my eyes with woven silk ribbons. Being afraid that this may not completely cover my eyes, I wish you furthermore to blind my sight with three pieces of folded silk cloth to ensure the living do not appear before my eyes and the dead do not see my body. What else could be proper for me?"

The king of Yue thereupon buried the king of Wu at Biyou in Qinyuhang Mountain according to ritual. The king of Yue ordered each soldier who had achieved merits in this battle to bury the king of Wu using dirt dug from low and moist ground.[147] Chief Chancellor Bo Pi was also buried near Biyou.[148]

---

147. The dirt of a tomb should be dry. The king of Yue purposely ordered the solders to bury the king of Wu with dirt from low and moist ground as an action of contempt.

148. Both the "Hereditary Household of Wu" 吳世家 chapter and the "Hereditary Household of Yue" 越世家 chapter in *Shiji* report that Goujian executed Chief Chancellor Bo Pi right after the death of Fuchai. However, *Zuozhuan* records that Bo Pi served Goujian and was trusted by the Yue king after the fall of Wu. See *Zuozhuan*, Lord Ai 24; Yang Bojun, 1723; Durrant, Li, and Schaberg, 1977.

# 吳越春秋越王無余外傳第六

## Chapter 6

# The Outer Tradition of King Wuyu of Yue

## Introduction

This is the first chapter of the second half of the text, which focuses on the histories and stories of Yue, especially the legends of the Yue king Goujian.

Although the title of the chapter refers to King Wuyue of Yue, it in fact consists of the myths and tales of Yu, the legendary ruler from high antiquity and the ancestor of the Yue people. The chapter begins with the mythical birth of Yu, whose mother was impregnated by swallowing a pearl barley grain and gave birth to Yu by opening her side. Again we see *chenwei* source texts dominate the story of Yu; Yu's dream of a spirit who told him the location of the mountain god's text for regulating flooding and the nine-tailed white fox who helped Yu make his marriage decision were probably adopted from lost Han *chenwei* writings. Sima Qian's biography of Yu in the *Shiji*, interestingly, is not used as a primary source.

The language of the *WYCQ* chapter is also different from the language in Sima Qian's record of Yu. Sima Qian relied heavily upon *Shangshu* 尚書, *The Book of Antiquity*, and the language of his record is old, plain, and difficult to understand. By comparison, the language of this *WYCQ* chapter is more ornamented and descriptive, with attention to details and the moods of the characters. While the *Shangshu* essay "Yugong" 禹貢 is completely copied in

Sima Qian's *Shiji*, it is not included in *WYCQ*, probably because the essay is a plain record of the geographical differences between the nine regions Yu settled, and offers little joy to readers.

## Translation

6.1. 越之前君無余者，夏禹之末封也。禹父鯀者，帝顓頊之後。鯀娶於有莘氏之女，名曰女嬉。年壯未孳。嬉於砥山得薏苡而吞之，意若為人所感，因而妊孕，剖脅而產高密。家於西羌，地曰石紐。石紐在蜀西川也。

6.1. Wuyu, the former ruler of Yue, was an enfeoffed descendant of Yu of the Xia dynasty.[1] Gun, Yu's father, was the descendant of Lord Zhuanxu. [2] Gun took a daughter of the Youshen clan as his wife and her name was Nüxi. [3] She passed the age of maturity without a child.[4] When she was playing at Mount Di, Nüxi found a pearl barley grain and swallowed it.[5] In her heart she felt that she was touched by someone and thereupon was impregnated. She opened her side and gave birth to Yu.[6] Gun resided in the western Qiang region; the place was called Shiniu, which is in present day Xichuan County in the Shu Commandery.[7]

6.2. 帝堯之時，遭洪水滔滔，天下沉漬，九州閼塞，四瀆壅閉。帝乃憂中國之不康，悼黎元之罹咎。乃命四嶽，乃舉賢良，將任治水。自中國至於條方，莫薦人。帝靡所任，四嶽乃舉鯀而薦之於

1. Yu was a legendary tribal leader. In early myth, Yu controlled the floods and established the Xia dynasty. His stories can be found in "Xia benji" 夏本紀 (Basic Annals of Xia) in Sima Qian's *Shiji*. The earliest record of Yu is found in a Western Zhou (1046–771 BCE) bronze vessel *suigong xu* 遂公盨. See Li Xueqin 李学勤, "Suigong Ying yu DaYu zhishui chuanshuo" 遂公盈与大禹治水传说, *Zhongguo shehui kexueyuan yuanbao* 中国社会科学院院报 (2003): 1–23. For an English translation of "Xia benji," see William Nienhauser, ed., *The Grand Scribe's Records* (Bloomington: Indiana University Press, 1994), 1:21–40.

2. Zhuanxu was one of the mythical Five Emperors 五帝 (*wudi*). He was said to be the grandson of the Yellow Emperor. See the "Wudi benji" 五帝本紀 (Basic Annals of the Five Lords) in Sima Qian's *Shiji*. See also Nienhauser, *The Grand Scribe's Records*, 1:5.

3. The Youshen tribe lived near present-day Heyang 郃陽 County in Shaanxi Province.

4. In ancient times the age of thirty was regarded as the age of maturity (*zhuangnian* 壯年). See the "Quli" 曲禮 chapter in *Liji*, Sun Xidan, 12.

5. The Xia royal family's surname was 姒 (*si*), which shares the same radical with 苡 (*yi*), the barley that Nüxi swallowed. Thus, the Xia clan's name is probably related to this myth.

6. Gaomi was possibly another name for Yu. Another theory argues that Gaomi was the state where Yu was enfeoffed.

7. Qiang is an ethnic group that lives in southwestern China. Shiniu is in modern-day Wenchuan 汶川 County, Sichuan Province.

堯。帝曰：「鯀負命毀族，不可。」四嶽曰：「等之群臣，未有如鯀者。」堯用治水，受命九載，功不成。帝怒曰：「朕知不能也。」乃更求之，得舜，使攝行天子之政，巡狩。觀鯀之治水無有形狀，乃殛鯀於羽山。鯀投於水，化為黃能，因為羽淵之神。

6.2. At the time of Lord Yao,[8] it happened there was a great flood and the world sank deep into the water. The Nine Regions were separated and the Four Rivers blocked.[9] Lord Yao was worried that the Central Plain would not be at peace and pitied the people suffering from disaster; he then commanded the Four Advisers to recommend a worthy and able man to be entrusted with flood control.[10] From the Central Plain all the way to the far border area,[11] no one was recommended. Lord Yao had no one to appoint, so the Four Advisers then recommended Gun and introduced him to Yao. Lord Yao said, "Gun disobeyed an order and injured good people, he cannot be used." The Four Advisers said, "Comparing the many ministers, none is more capable than Gun." Yao thus used him to control the flood; nine years after receiving the command, the project had still not succeeded. Lord Yao was angry, saying, "I knew he was not capable." Thereupon Yao further sought and found Shun.[12] Yao let Shun act on behalf of the son of heaven in governing and toured the land to inspect it. Seeing the failure of Gun's flood control, Shun thereupon exiled Gun to Mount Yu. Gun threw himself into the river and transformed into a yellow bear,[13] and he therefore became the god of the Yu Yuan depths.[14]

---

8. Yao was one of the legendary Five Lords. See Sima Qian's "Basic Annals of the Five Lords" in *Shiji*, 1:15–30.

9. According to the legend, after Yu controlled the floods, he divided China into nine administrative regions, so the Nine Regions often refer to China as a whole. The Four Rivers are the Yangzi River, the Huai River, the Yellow River, and the Ji River.

10. 四岳 (*siyue*) has multiple meanings. It refers to four famous mountains (Mount Tai 泰山 in the east, Mount Hua 華山 in the west, Mount Heng 衡山 in the south, and Mount Heng 恆山 in the north). It also refers to the four advisors of Lord Yao. According to legend, Xizhong 羲仲, Xishu 羲叔, Hezhong 和仲, and Heshu 和叔 took charge of the four seasons and patrolled major mountains of the four directions.

11. 條 (*tiao*) means 遠 (*yuan*), "far." Another explanation for 條方 (*tiaofang*) is that it refers to 鳴條 (*mingtiao*), located in modern-day Shandong Province.

12. Shun was one of the three legendary wise rulers (Yao, Shun, and Yu). Shun succeeded Yao and commanded Yu to control the floods. Shun eventually abdicated the throne to Yu.

13. There are two explanations of the character 能 (*neng*). One is that it is same as 熊 (*xiong*), "a bear"; the other is that it is a character for a soft-shelled turtle. See Zhang Jue, 178n15.

14. 淵 (*yuan*) means a deep pool. 羽 (*yu*) here refers to Mount Yu. This is a deep pool in the river beneath Mount Yu where Gun was exiled.

6.3. 舜與四嶽舉鯀之子高密。四嶽謂禹曰：「舜以治水無功，舉爾嗣，考之勳。」禹曰：「俞，小子敢悉考績，以統天意。惟委而已。」

禹傷父功不成，循江，泝河，盡濟，甄淮，乃勞身焦思以行，七年，聞樂不聽，過門不入，冠掛不顧，履遺不躡。功未及成，愁然沉思。乃案《黃帝中經曆》，蓋聖人所記曰：「在於九山東南天柱，號曰宛委，赤帝在闕。其巖之巔，承以文玉，覆以磐石，其書金簡，青玉為字，編以白銀，皆瑑其文。」

禹乃東巡，登衡嶽，血白馬以祭，不幸所求。禹乃登山，仰天而嘯，忽然而臥，因夢見赤繡衣男子，自稱玄夷蒼水使者，聞帝使文命於斯，故來候之。非厥歲月，將告以期，無為戲吟。故倚歌覆釜之山，東顧謂禹曰：「欲得我山神書者，齋於黃帝巖嶽之下三月，庚子登山發石，金簡之書存矣。」禹退又齋，三月庚子，登宛委山，發金簡之書。案金簡玉字，得通水之理。復返歸嶽，乘四載以行川。始於霍山，徊集五嶽，詩雲：「信彼南山，惟禹甸之。」

遂巡行四瀆。與益、夔共謀，行到名山大澤，召其神而問之山川脈理、金玉所有、鳥獸昆蟲之類，及八方之民俗、殊國異域、土地裏數，使益疏而記之，故名之曰《山海經》。

6.3. Shun and the Four Advisers recommended Gun's son Yu. The Four Advisers spoke to Yu, saying, "Shun, because of Gun's failure in controlling the floods, has promoted you to continue your deceased father's work." Yu said, "Alas! Could I, the humbled, presume to exhaust my strength to plan for the will of heaven? I am simply commissioned."

Yu was saddened that his father's work had not succeeded, and he thereupon traveled down the Yangzi River and up the Yellow River, visited all the Ji River regions, and inspected the Huai River. He thus exhausted his body, wearied his mind, and worked outside of his home. For seven years, he never listened when hearing music, never entered his home when passing by, never looked back when his cap was caught by a tree branch, and never picked up his shoes when they fell, but the work was yet to be successful. Distressed, he thought about it deeply and then examined *The Calendar of the Yellow Emperor's Middle Classic*,[15] which was recorded by sages, and it said, "On Mount Tianzhu southeast of Mount Jiuyi, there is a mountain called Wanwei and the Vermillion Emperor lives in the palace at its peak.[16] On the top of the cliff there is a text, which is kept in a patterned jade box and

15. This is a *chenwei* text attributed to the Yellow Emperor.

16. Mount Jiuyi is in modern-day Ningyuan 寧遠 County in Hunan Province. Mount Tianzhu is in Zhejiang Province and it is also called Mount Wanwei. The Vermillion Emperor was one of the five heavenly emperors; he was the god of the south.

hidden by a massive rock. The text consists of gold slips and its characters are made of green jade pieces. It is bonded by silver threads and characters protrude on the slips."

Yu thereupon traveled east and ascended Mount Heng.[17] He killed a white horse and offered its blood as sacrifice but failed to obtain what he was searching for. Yu therefore climbed to the top, looked up, and whistled. In a trance, he laid down to rest and dreamed of a man in red embroidered cloth who identified himself as the emissary of the god Xuanyicangshui, saying, "I have heard that Lord Shun sent Yu here and for this reason I am waiting for you.[18] It is not yet the time to look at the text, but I will tell you the date for it. Do not jest and groan and purposely lean on Mount Fufu and sigh."[19] Looking back toward the east, he told Yu, "If you want to obtain the book of my mountain god, you must fast under the Yellow Emperor Peak. On the *gengzi* day of the third month, you climb Mount Wanwei and lift the rock, the text on the gold slips will be there." Yu retreated and fasted. On the *gengzi* day of the third month, he ascended Mount Wanwei, found the text on the gold slips, examined the jade characters on the gold slips, and learned the principle of regulating the floods.

Yu returned to Mount Heng and rode in four kinds of vehicles to inspect the rivers.[20] He started from Mount Huo and toured the Five Mountains.[21] The *Book of Songs* says, "Long and winding is the Southern Hill, Yu had managed it."[22]

Yu then toured and inspected the four rivers and made arrangements with Yi and Kui.[23] When he traveled to large mountains and large lakes, he summoned the gods there and asked them about the ranges and valleys of the mountains and rivers; the gold and jade they contained; the birds, beasts, and insects of the place; the customs of all the areas; and the land and extent

---

17. This is Mount Kuaiji located in Zhejiang Province, different from Mount Heng in Hunan Province.

18. 文命 (*wenming*) is also Yu's name.

19. Mount Fufu is Mount Kuaiji.

20. According to *Shiji*, Yu rode on a boat when traveling on the rivers, rode on a chariot when traveling on the land, rode on a sled when traveling in the mud, and wore a pair of clogs when climbing the mountains. See *Shiji*, 2:51.

21. These are Mount Song 嵩山, Mount Tai, Mount Hua, Mount Heng in the south, and Mount Heng in the north.

22. This is the poem "xin nanshan" 信南山 from *The Book of Songs*, the first anthology of poetry in Chinese history; it contains 305 poems dating between the eleventh and seventh centuries BCE.

23. According to the legend, Yi assisted Yu in flood control and was selected as the successor of Yu. However, after Yu died, Yu's son Qi succeeded Yu and killed Yi. Kui was an officer of music for Yao and Shun.

of different countries and regions. He asked Yi to record these respectively and accordingly entitled these records *The Classic of Mountains and Seas*.[24]

6.4. 禹三十未娶，行到塗山，恐時之暮，失其度制，乃辭云：「吾娶也，必有應矣。」乃有白狐九尾造於禹。禹曰：「白者，吾之服也。其九尾者，王之證也。塗山之歌曰：『綏綏白狐，九尾痝痝。我家嘉夷，來賓為王。成家成室，我造彼昌。天人之際，於茲則行。』明矣哉！」禹因娶塗山，謂之女嬌。取辛、壬、癸、甲，禹行。十月，女嬌生子啟。啟生不見父，晝夕呱呱啼泣。

6.4. Yu was thirty years old but had yet to take a wife. When he traveled to Mount Tu,[25] he was afraid he would get married too late, in contravention of the marriage rules. He therefore made an announcement, saying, "If I am to marry, there must be a sign for it." Thereupon a nine-tailed white fox came to Yu. Yu said, "White is the color of my cloth. That the fox has nine tails is the sign of a king. The song of Mount Tu says,

'Solitary is the white fox,[26]
big and fluffy are its nine tails.
Happy and auspicious is my family,
and all the guests are kings.
Becoming a family and becoming a couple,
my arrival brings prosperity to him.
Following this word,
the relation between heaven and man will be unimpeded.'

"The sign is clear!" Yu thereupon married a woman from Mount Tu and called her Nüjiao. After the *xin*, *ren*, *gui*, and *jia* days following the marriage, Yu left.[27] Ten months later, Nüjiao gave birth to a son, Qi. After Qi was born, he did not see his father and cried day and night.

---

24. *The Classic of Mountains and Seas* (*Shanhai jing* 山海經) is a Chinese classic text that records early geography and myth. Its early form can be dated back to the fourth century BCE but its final version was probably compiled during the Han Dynasty. See Anne Birrell, ed., *The Classic of Mountains and Seas* (London: Penguin Books, 1999).

25. The location of Mount Tu is controversial. Some believe it is in Anhui Province, others argue it is either in Sichuan Province or in Zhejiang Province.

26. 綏綏 (*suisui*), solitary but looking for a mate. In the *Book of Songs* there is a poem titled "You hu" 有狐 that contains the following lines: "There is a fox, solitary, at the bank of the Qi River. My heart is sad, that man has no lower cloth." See Cheng Junying 程俊英, *Shijing yizhu* 詩經譯註 (Shanghai: Shanghai guji chubanshe, 1995), 117–18.

27. These are four consecutive days.

6.5. 禹行使大章步東西，豎亥度南北，暢八極之廣，旋天地之數。

禹濟江，南省水理，黃龍負舟，舟中人怖駭，禹乃啞然而笑，曰：「我受命於天，竭力以勞萬民。生，性也；死，命也。爾何為者？」顏色不變。謂舟人曰：「此天所以為我用。」龍曳尾舍舟而去。

南到計於蒼梧，而見縛人，禹拊其背而哭。益曰：「斯人犯法，自合如此，哭之何也？」禹曰：「天下有道，民不罹辜；天下無道，罪及善人。吾聞，『一男不耕，有受其飢；一女不桑，有受其寒。』吾為帝統治水土，調民安居，使得其所，今乃罹法如斯，此吾得薄，不能化民證也。故哭之悲耳。」

於是周行宇內，東造絕跡，西延積石，南踰赤岸，北過寒谷；徊崑崙，察六扈，脈地理，名金石；寫流沙於西隅，決弱水於北漠；青泉、赤淵，分入洞穴；通江東流，至於碣石；疏九河於涽淵，開五水於東北；鑿龍門，闢伊闕；平易相土，觀地分州。殊方各進，有所納貢；民去崎嶇，歸於中國。

堯曰：「俞！以固冀於此。」乃號禹曰伯禹，官曰司空，賜姓姒氏，領統州伯，以巡十二部。

6.5. Yu continued his tour. He sent Taizhang to survey the length from east to west, and Shuhai to survey the length from south to north.[28] They fully measured the range of the eight directions and learned their astronomic and geographic data.[29]

When Yu was crossing the Yangzi River to inspect the waterways of the South, a yellow dragon carried the boat on its back. People in the boat were very frightened; Yu nevertheless laughed, saying, "I received the command from heaven and exhausted my strength taking care of all the people. Life is what human nature desires, yet death is determined by fate. What do you, yellow dragon, intend to do?" He did not change his facial expression. Yu said to the people in the boat, "This dragon is given by heaven in order to be used by me." The dragon dragged its tail, gave up the boat, and left.[30]

When Yu traveled south to Mount Cangwu to inspect the officials,[31] he saw a man who was tied up. Yu stroked the man's back and cried. Yi asked,

28. Taizhang and Shuhai are ministers of Yu. This is also found in *Huainanzi*. See He Ning, *Huainanzi jishi*, 321.

29. According to the *Book of Changes*, there are twenty-five heavenly numbers and thirty earthly numbers. The total number together therefore is fifty-five, and these numbers can be used to deduce the changes in both the human world and the natural world.

30. This appears to be a famous story in pre-Qin and Han times. It is also found in *Huainanzi*, the "jingshen xun" 精神訓 chapter in He Ning, *Huainanzi jishi*, 533–34; the "zhifen" 知分 section in Xu Weiyu, *Lüshi chunqiu jishi*, 554; and Huang Hui, *Lunheng jiaoshi*, 224.

31. This mountain is also called Mount Jiuyi, located in modern-day Ningyuan County, Hunan Province.

"This man violated the law and deserves this. Why are you crying for him?" Yu said, "If the world follows the Way, people do not suffer from punishment. If the world does not follow the Way, punishment affects good people. I have heard that 'if one man does not work in the field, someone will suffer from hunger; if one woman does not tend the silkworms, someone will suffer from coldness.'[32] I manage the rivers and lands for Lord Shun; I must look after the people, see that they live contentedly, and ensure everyone has his proper position. Now they commit crime like this! This is evidence that my virtue is not great enough to transform people. For this reason I have cried and felt sorrowful."

After this, Yu traveled to every place in the world. To the east he went to the coast,[33] to the west he arrived at Mount Jishi,[34] to the south he came across Mount Chi'an, and to the north he passed Mount Hangu.[35] He traveled back and forth among the Kunlun Mountains,[36] inspected Xuanhu,[37] investigated closely their terrain, and inscribed the stones. In the western border region he cleaned the floating sand and dredged the Ruo River in the northern desert area.[38] He channeled the green underground spring water and red water into separate deep valley gorges, cleaned rivers and aided them in flowing all the way east to Mount Jieshi,[39] in muddy whirlpools he dredged nine tributaries of the Yellow River, and channeled five rivers to the northeast.[40] He bored through Mount Longmen and cut open Mount Yique.[41] He leveled the ground and examined the soil. He inspected the terrain and divided the districts. Each region thus presented different products and had their portions to pay. The people left rugged mountains and became residents of the central plain.

---

32. This is also a popular Han saying. It is found in Jia Yi's 賈誼 (200–168 BCE) *Xinshu* 新書. Wang Fu's 王符 (83–170) *Qianfu lun* 潛夫論. See: Yan Zhenyi 閻振益 and Zhong Xia 鍾夏, *Xinshu jiaozhu* 新書校註 (Beijing: Zhonghua shuju, 2015), 163. Peng Duo 彭鐸, *Qinfu lunjian jiaozheng* 潛夫論箋校正 (Beijing: Zhonghua shuju, 2004), 156.

33. 絕跡 (*jueji*) literally means "where the footprints stop"; here it refers to the coast.

34. There are two mountains named Jishi, one is called the Big Jishi Mountain and is located in Qinghai Province, the other is the Small Jishi Mountain in Gansu Province. Both are in northwest China.

35. Mount Chi'an is probably located in Jiangsu Province. Mount Hangu is in modern-day Miyun 密雲 County, southwest of Beijing.

36. The Kunlun Mountains are located in northwest China between Xinjiang and Tibet. This is where the Yellow River originates.

37. 六 (*liu*) is a mistake for 玄 (*xuan*). Xuanhu is the Xuanhu Mountain, located in southern Shaanxi Province.

38. The Ruo River is also called the Zhangye 張掖 River, located in modern-day Gansu Province.

39. Mount Jieshi is located in modern-day Changli 昌黎 County, Hebei Province.

40. The five rivers refer to the five tributaries of the Yangzi River.

41. Mount Longmeng is located between Hancheng 韓城 County, Shaanxi Province, and Hejin 河津 County, Shanxi Proince. Mount Yique is near Luoyang, in Henan Province.

Yao said, "Excellent! I had expected these to be done!" He then named Yu as Boyu, appointed him to the position titled Supervisor of Construction,[42] and bestowed upon him the clan name of Si so that he could lead an inspection tour of the twelve regions.

6.6. 堯崩，禹服三年之喪，如喪考妣，晝哭夜泣，氣不屬聲。

堯禪位于舜，舜薦大禹，改官司徒，內輔虞位，外行九伯。

舜崩，禪位命禹。禹服喪三年，形體枯槁，面目黎黑，讓位商均，退處陽山之南，陰阿之北。萬民不附商均，追就禹之所，狀若驚鳥揚天，駭魚入淵，晝歌夜吟，登高號呼，曰：「禹棄我，如何所戴？」禹三年服畢，哀民，不得已，即天子之位。三載考功，五年政定，周行天下，歸還大越。登茅山，以朝四方群臣，觀示中州諸侯，防風後至，斬以示眾，示天下悉屬禹也。乃大會計治國之道。內美釜山州慎之功，外演聖德以應天心，遂更名茅山曰會稽之山。因傳國政，休養萬民，國號曰夏后。封有功，爵有德，惡無細而不誅，功無微而不賞，天下喁喁，若兒思母、子歸父。而留越，恐群臣不從，言曰：「吾聞食其實者，不傷其枝，飲其冰者，不濁其流。吾獲覆釜之書，得以除天下之災，令民歸於里閭。其德彰彰若斯，豈可忘乎？」乃納言聽諫，安民治室；居靡山，伐木為邑；晝作印，橫木為門；調權衡，平斗斛，造井示民，以為法度。鳳凰棲於樹，鸞鳥巢於側，麒麟步於庭，百鳥佃於澤。

遂已耆艾將老，歎曰：「吾晏歲年暮，壽將盡矣，止絕斯矣。」命群臣曰：「吾百世之後，葬我會稽之山，葦槨桐棺，穿壙七尺，下無及泉，墳高三尺，土階三等。葬之後，田無改畝，以為居之者樂，為之者苦。」

禹崩之後，眾瑞並去。天美禹德而勞其功，使百鳥還為民田，大小有差，進退有行，一盛一衰，往來有常。

6.6. When Yao died, Yu remained in mourning for three years, as if he had lost his parents.[43] Day and night he cried and was choked with sobs.

Yao abdicated the position to Shun. Shun recommended Yu and changed Yu's post to Supervisor of Land. At court Yu assisted Shun, outside of court he supervised the heads of the Nine Districts.

Before Shun died, he abdicated the position to Yu. Yu remained in mourning for three years. His body looked haggard and his face dark. He yielded his position to Shangjun and retreated to reside on the south side of Mount Yang

42. 司空, *Sikong*, was a high official in charge of construction works.

43. Three years of mourning (twenty-five months, in fact) is the longest ritual mourning period; it is usually reserved for children mourning their parents.

and the north side of Yin hill.[44] People did not submit to Shangjun but instead ran to Yu's place. They looked like startled birds flying up into the sky, scared fish diving into deep water. They sung during daytime and chanted at night and climbed up the mountain and cried, saying, "Yu has abandoned us. How can we show that we love and support him?" After Yu had completed his three years of mourning, he commiserated with the people having no one to turn to, and so ascended to the position of the son of heaven.

Yu spent three years assessing his officials' administrative merits, and in five years the governmental situation was settled. He toured all over the world and then returned to the great Yue region. Ascending Mount Mao,[45] Yu received homage from the many ministers from the four directions and ordered the lords from the central plain to meet there. Fangfeng was late for the meeting;[46] Yu then executed Fangfen and showed this to the public, demonstrating that the world under heaven completely belonged to him. Yu then broadly appraised the methods of governing the states. Inwardly he prized the god of Mount Fufu's merit for his assistance in pacifying the regions, and outwardly he displayed sagely virtue in order to correspond to heavenly will and thus renamed Mount Mao as Mount Kuaiji. Moreover, he issued government policies, let many people rest and recuperate, and named the state Xia. He enfeoffed those with merit and granted honorific ranks to the worthies. No wrongdoing escaped punishment no matter how trivial it was, no achievement failed to be rewarded regardless of how insignificant it was. All the people under heaven looked up to him and stayed in Yue as children who missed their mother and sons returned to their father. Yu worried that the many ministers did not follow him and spoke to them, saying, "I have heard 'Eat fruit but do not damage its branches; drink water but do not pollute its stream.'[47] I received the text of Mount Fufu and thereupon I am able to end the disasters of the world and let people return to their villages. My merits being this apparent, how can they be forgotten?" Yu therefore adopted the officials' advice and followed their suggestions. He settled the people down, constructed houses, went to the mountains and cut trees to build cities, marked wood pieces as tallies, and installed beams for gates. He adjusted measurements and rectified

---

44. Shangjun was Shun's son. Both Mount Yang and Yin hill are located in Dengfeng 登封 County, Henan Province.

45. Mount Mao is another name for Mount Kuaiji.

46. Fangfeng was the name of a legendary tribal leader. He was said to be extremely tall. The story of Yu killing Fangfeng has circulated in many early texts, including the "Shixie" 飾邪 chapter in *Hanfeizi*, the "Luyu xia" 魯語下 chapter in *Guoyu*, the "Bianwu" 辨物 chapter in *Shuoyuan*, the "Bianwu" chapter in *Kongzi jiayu* 孔子家語, and the "Kongzi shijia" 孔子世家 chapter in *Shiji*.

47. 冰 (*bing*), ice, should be 水 (*shui*), "water," here.

dry measures. Yu also showed the people how to dig wells and used these as the rules for the people to follow.[48] Phoenixes rested in the trees and *luan* birds nested in neighboring trees.[49] Unicorns strolled in court and hundreds of birds pecked in the marsh.[50]

Yu soon was in his fifties and sixties and was getting old.[51] He sighed, saying, "My years are many and my life is about to end. I am going to die here." He ordered his officials, saying, "After I die, bury me in Mount Kuaiji. Use reeds as the outer coffin and paulownia wood for the inner coffin; dig my tomb seven *chi* deep but not reaching to the underground springs. My tomb should be three *chi* high with three levels of mud stairs. After the burial, do not change the ridges between plots of farming fields. Do not let the farmers suffer in order to make the deceased enjoy residing there."

After Yu died, all the auspicious signs disappeared. The heavenly god praised Yu's virtue and rewarded his achievements, so he let the many birds return and till the land for the people. The birds were different in size and moved in lines. Gathering and scattering, they came and went at regular times.

6.7. 禹崩，傳位與益。益服三年，思禹未嘗不言。喪畢，益避禹之子啟於箕山之陽，諸侯去益而朝啟，曰：「吾君，帝禹子也。」啟遂即天子之位，治國於夏。遵《禹貢》之美，悉九州之土以種五穀，累歲不絕。啟使使以歲時春秋而祭禹於越，立宗廟於南山之上。

6.7. After Yu died, Yi ascended to the throne. He mourned Yu for three years during which he never ceased to mention his remembrance of Yu. When the mourning period was completed, Yi yielded the position to Yu's son Qi and moved to the south of Mount Qi.[52] The many lords left Yi and sought to be received in audience by Qi, saying, "Qi was the son of our ruler, Lord Yu's son." Qi thereupon assumed the position of the son of heaven and governed the Xia kingdom. He followed the policies recorded in "Yugong" and cultivated the entire land of the Nine Regions in order to plant the five grains;[53] this continued for years. In each season, Qi, in accordance with the

48. A different interpretation of 井 (*jing*) is that it is an interchangeable word for 刑 (*xing*), "punishment." The sentence therefore could be: Yu established punishments and showed them to the people, using these as the rules for them to follow.

49. These are all auspicious birds. *Luan* is a mythical bird that looks like a chicken with colorful feathers.

50. In Chinese myth, the unicorn is a humane beast that only appears when the world is at peace.

51. Sixty years old is 耆 (*qi*), fifty years old is 艾 (*ai*).

52. Probably located in Dengfeng County, Henan Province.

53. "Yugong" is a chapter in the *Book of Documents* 尚書. It contains two parts. The first part is a description of the Nine Regions and the improvements Yu made to each region. The second part

sacrificial holidays, sent emissaries to Yue to offer a sacrifice to Yu and built an ancestral temple on the south side of Mount Kuaiji.

6.8. 禹以下六世而得帝少康。少康恐禹祭之絕祀，乃封其庶子於越，號曰無余。余始受封，人民山居，雖有鳥田之利，租貢纔給宗廟祭祀之費。乃復隨陵陸而耕種，或逐禽鹿而給食。無余質朴，不設宮室之飾，從民所居。春秋祠禹墓於會稽。

6.8. Six generations after Yu there was Lord Shaokang.[54] Shaokang, worrying that the sacrifice to Yu would not be continued, enfeoffed a son of his concubine in Yue and named him Wuyu.[55] At the beginning, when Wuyu was enfeoffed, people of Yue lived in the mountains. Although they benefitted from birds planting the fields, yet with the taxes they could merely afford the expense of the sacrifices at the ancestral temple. Wuyu therefore let the people cultivate hills and lands, or chase birds and deer in order to provide food for themselves. Wuyu was simple and sincere; he did not adorn his palace and halls but lived in the same kind of dwelling as the people. Each year he offered sacrifices at Yu's tomb in Kuaiji.

6.9. 無余傳世十餘，末君微劣，不能自立，轉從眾庶為編戶之民，禹祀斷絕。十有餘歲，有人生而言語，其語曰鳥禽呼：嚥喋嚥喋。指天向禹墓曰：「我是無余君之苗末，我方修前君祭祀，復我禹墓之祀，為民請福於天，以通鬼神之道。」眾民悅喜，皆助奉禹祭，四時致貢，因共封立，以承越君之後，復夏王之祭，安集鳥田之瑞，以為百姓請命。自後稍有君臣之義，號曰無壬。

6.9. Wuyu's offspring continued to govern for more than ten generations. The last ruler was weak, base, and could not establish himself; instead, he followed the masses and became a registered commoner. The sacrifice to Yu was thus terminated. Ten years later, there was a man who began to talk at birth and his words were: "Birds are chirping *yandie yandie*." Pointing his finger at the sky and looking at Yu's tomb, he said, "I am the descendant of Lord Wuyu. I am going to reinstate the sacrifice to the former lords and resume the sacrifice at the tomb of our Yu in order to pray to heaven for fortune for

---

describes Yu's survey of the rivers. Traditionally, it was believed to be authored by Yu; scholars now generally agree that it was probably written around the fifth century BCE or later. There are different explanations for what the five grains are. Here it refers to all grains.

54. Shaokang was mentioned in the "Basic Annals of Xia" in *Shiji*. Stories of Shaokang are also found in *Zuozhuan*, Lord Xiang 4 and Lord Ai 1. See *Shiji*, 2:86; Yang Bojun, 938, 1606; Durrant, Li, and Schaberg, 917, 1835.

55. 庶子 (*shuzi*) is a son birthed by a concubine, or any son birthed by the primary wife after the first son.

the people and connect with the way of ghosts and spirits." The people were pleased by this and all helped offer sacrifice to Yu. For four seasons they paid tribute to Yu and then together vested this man as the inheritor of rule of the Yue lords. He resumed the sacrifices to Yu and the king of Xia, secured the auspices of birds ploughing the fields, and prayed to heaven on behalf of the people. After this, he gradually reformed the ritual between ruler and subjects. He was titled Wuren.

6.10. 壬生無睪，擇專心守國，不失上天之命。無擇卒，或為夫譚。夫譚生元常，常立，當吳王壽夢、諸樊、闔閭之時。越之興霸自元常矣。

6.10. Wuren begot Wuyi. Wuyi was determined to guard his state and never failed the command of heaven. After Wuyi died, he was probably succeeded by Futan. Futan begot Yuanchang. When Yuanchang was established, it was during the period when Wu kings Shoumeng, Zhufan, and Helü ruled. Yue's rise and hegemony began from the time of Yuanchang.

# 吳越春秋勾踐入臣外傳第七

## Chapter 7

# The Outer Tradition of Goujian as a Servant

## Introduction

Starting from this chapter, *WYCQ* focuses on Goujian, the king of Yue who destroyed Wu and became a hegemon among the state rulers. Stories of Goujian are divided into four chapters in *WYCQ*: chapter seven concerns Goujian living in Wu as a servant after he was defeated by Fuchai; chapter eight is an account of Goujian's return to Yue; chapter nine describes Goujian's preparation to attack Wu; and Goujian's conquest of Wu and his obstinance after the victory are portrayed in the final chapter, chapter ten.

When Goujian's father had died and Goujian had just ascended the throne as the king of Yue, Helü, the king of Wu, took the opportunity to attack Yue. Goujian defeated Helü and severely wounded him. The latter died soon afterward and was succeeded by his son Fuchai. In the action of avenging the death of his father, Fuchai defeated Goujian and besieged him at Mount Kuaiji. Following his ministers' advice, Goujian decided to surrender himself to Fuchai and went to Wu as a servant to the Wu king, hoping one day he could return to Yue and wash off his humiliation by destroying Wu. The *WYCQ* chapter omits this part of the history and begins from the moment Goujian departs for Wu. The reason behind such an authorial choice is not very clear. Most likely, the narrator is more interested in portraying the characters than truthfully reporting the historical realities.

In addition to this, many events recorded in this chapter in *WYCQ* are not found in *Zuozhuan*, and they are different from Sima Qian's reports as well. Chapter seven does demonstrate some connection to the "Yue yu" 越語 section in *Guoyu*. The language styles of the two texts are also similar; like *Guoyu*, which places emphasis on conversations, this *WYCQ* chapter relies upon dialogue and songs to unfold the stories and portray characters. At the same time, tensions and conflicts are also created through discussions and heated debates at the Wu court on the issue of releasing Goujian back to Yue. Goujian's ability to endure difficulty and humiliation, Chief Chancellor Bo Pi's avarice and deceitfulness, Fuchai's irresolution and tendency to fall for cunning words, and Wu Zixu's anger and frustration toward Fuchai are all vividly demonstrated through the characters' own words.

## Translation

7.1. 越王勾踐五年五月，與大夫種、范蠡入臣於吳，群臣皆送至浙江之上。臨水祖道，軍陣固陵。大夫文種前為祝，其詞曰：「皇天祐助，前沉後揚。禍為德根，憂為福堂。威人者滅，服從者昌。王雖牽致，其後無殃。君臣生離，感動上皇。眾夫哀悲，莫不感傷。臣請薦脯，行酒二觴。」

越王仰天太息，舉杯垂涕，默無所言。種復前祝曰：「大王德壽，無疆無極，乾坤受靈，神祇輔翼。我王厚之，祉祐在側。德銷百殃，利受其福。去彼吳庭，來歸越國。觴酒既升，請稱萬歲。」

7.1. In the fifth month of the fifth year of King Goujian of Yue (492 BCE),[1] when the king and his ministers Wen Zhong and Fan Li were about to enter service to Wu, all the king's officials saw him off on the bank of Zhe River.[2] Facing the river, they offered a sacrifice to the gods of the road and lined up the troops in Guling.[3] Grand Minister Wen Zhong moved forward and made a prayer. His words were: "With the blessing and assistance of High Heaven, we will rise up even if we fell previously. Disaster creates the root of fortune and hardship the hall of happiness. The one who oppresses others will be destroyed, yet the obedient will thrive. Although Your Majesty is forced to go to Wu, have no worries after that. Deeply moved is the high god by the

1. A couple of major events occurred before the fifth year of King Goujian. In 496 BCE, upon hearing of the death of the Yue king Yuanchang, the Wu king Helü attacked Yue but was defeated by Goujian. Helü soon died of injuries from the battle. In 494 BCE, Wu king Fuchai defeated Goujian and invaded Yue. Goujian submitted himself as a servant to Fuchai.

2. According to *Guoyu*, Goujian went to Wu with Fan Li, Wen Zhong stayed in Yue.

3. In ancient times, people usually offered sacrifices to the gods before embarking on long-distance travel.

separation in life between our lord and his ministers. All the people are grieving and saddened, none of them do not feel wounded. I, your subject, respectfully present you with dry meat and urge everyone to drink a cup or two."[4]

Looking at the sky, the king of Yue sighed deeply. He lifted up his cup and shed tears. Remaining silent, he did not say a word. Wen Zhong again moved forward and prayed, "The virtue and life of Your Majesty are beyond boundary and limit. Heaven and earth grant you blessings; gods in the heaven and spirits on earth assist you.[5] The virtue of our king is profound, and fortune and blessings accompany you. Your virtue will dispel all kinds of disasters and give you the advantage of receiving fortune. Though now you are going to the Wu court, you will return to the land of Yue. A cup of wine has been raised, let us all shout 'long live the king!'"

7.2. 越王曰：「孤承前王餘德，守國於邊，幸蒙諸大夫之謀，遂保前王丘墓。今遭辱恥，為天下笑，將孤之罪耶，諸大夫之責也？吾不知其咎，願二三子論其意。」

大夫扶同曰：「何言之鄙也？昔湯繫於夏臺，伊尹不離其側；文王囚於石室，太公不棄其國。興衰在天，存亡繫於人。湯改儀而媚於桀，文王服從而幸於紂；夏殷恃力而虐二聖，兩君屈己以得天道。故湯王不以窮自傷，周文不以困為病。」

越王曰：「昔堯任舜、禹而天下治，雖有洪水之害，不為人災。變異不及於民，豈況於人君乎？」

大夫若成曰：「不如君王之言。天有曆數，德有薄厚。黃帝不讓，堯傳天子。三王臣弒其君，五霸子弒其父。德有廣狹，氣有高下。今之世猶人之市，置貨以設詐。抱謀以待敵。不幸陷厄，求伸而已。大王不覽於斯，而懷喜怒？」

越王曰：「任人者不辱身，自用者危其國。大夫皆前圖未然之端，傾敵破讎，坐招泰山之福。今寡人守窮若斯，而云湯、文困厄後必霸，何言之違禮儀？夫君子爭寸陰而棄珠玉，今寡人冀得免於軍旅之憂，而復反係獲敵人之手，身為傭隸，妻為僕妾，往而不返，客死敵國。若魂魄有，愧於前君，其無知，體骨棄捐。何大夫之言不合於寡人之意？」

於是大夫種、范蠡曰：「聞古人曰：『居不幽，志不廣；形不愁，思不遠。』聖王賢主皆遇困厄之難，蒙不赦之恥。身拘而名尊，軀辱而聲榮；處卑而不以為惡，居危而不以為薄。五帝德厚，而窮厄之恨，然尚有泛濫之憂。三守暴困之辱，不離三獄之囚，泣涕而受冤，行哭而為隸，演《易》作卦，天道祐之。時過於期，否

4. The speech is in four syllables per line, a highly polished style imitating the *Book of Songs*.

5. 神 (*shen*) is the heavenly god; 祇 (*qi*) is the earthly god.

終則泰，諸侯並救，王命見符，朱鬣玄狐。輔臣結髮，拆獄破械，反國修德，遂討其讎。擢假海內，若覆手背，天下宗之，功垂萬世。大王屈厄，臣誠盡謀，夫截骨之劍，無削剟之利；臽鐵之矛，無分髮之便；建策之士，無暴興之說。今臣遂天文，案墜籍，二氣共萌，存亡異處，彼興則我辱，我霸則彼亡。二國爭道，未知所就。君王之危，天道之數，何必自傷哉！夫吉者，凶之門；福者，禍之根。今大王雖在危困之際，孰知其非暢達之兆哉？」

大夫計研曰：「今君王國於會稽，窮於入吳，言悲辭苦，群臣泣之。雖則恨悷之心，莫不感動。而君王何為謾辭譁說，用而相欺？臣誠不取。」

7.2. The king of Yue said, "I, the orphan, inherited the virtue passed down by the previous kings and guarded the state at its borders. Fortunately I received advice from all of you, my ministers, and was able to protect the tombs of previous kings. Now I have suffered humiliation and shame and was laughed at by the world. Is this my own fault? Or is it you, my ministers, who should be responsible for it? I do not know whom I shall blame; I wish you to express your comments."

Grand Minister Futong said, "Why are your words so base? In the past, Tang was jailed at Xia Terrace, but Yi Yin did not leave his side;[6] King Wen was imprisoned in a stone chamber, yet Taigong did not abandon his country.[7] Rise and decline are decided by the heavens; survival or fall, however,

---

6. Tang was the leader of the Shang people. He destroyed the Xia dynasty and established the Shang dynasty. Tang was once imprisoned by Jie, the last Xia king. Legends say that Yi Yin was Tang's prime minister, and had previously been a slave in Tang's bride's family. Tang realized Yi Yin's talent and trusted him, and Yi Yin helped Tang destroy Xia. For more information on Yi Yin, see Mayvis L. Marubbio, "Yi Yin, Pious Rebel. A Study of the Founding Minister of the Shang in Early Chinese Texts" (PhD diss., University of Minnesota, 2000), 45–55. See also Cai Zhemao 蔡哲茂, "Yin buci 'Yi Yin qishi' kao—jian lun tashi" 殷卜辭伊尹啓示考—兼論它事, *Zhongyang yanjiuyuan lishi yuyan yanjiusuo jikan* 中央研究院歷史語言研究所集刊 58, no. 4 (1987): 755–808. The Qinghua University bamboo document "Chihu zhi ji Tang zhi wu" 赤鵠之集湯之屋 contain an interesting story of Yi Yin in which Yi Yin was cursed by Tang but was later rescued by a shaman crow. Yi Yin overheard from the crows' conversation the secret behind the Xia king's illness and treated the king accordingly. For the Qinghua University bamboo document chapter, see Huang Dekuan 黃德寬, "Qinghua jian 'Chihu zhi ji Tang zhi wu' yu xian Qian xiaoshuo" 清華簡赤鵠之集湯之屋與先秦小說, *Fudan xuebao* 復旦學報, no. 4 (2013): 81–86. See also Liu Chengqun, "Qinghua jian 'Chihu zhi ji Tang zhi wu' wenti xingzhi zai tan" 清華簡赤鵠之集湯之屋文體性質再探, *Xueshu luntan* 學術論壇 39, no. 8 (2016): 100–10, 129. For an introduction to the Qinghua bamboo slips, see Liu Guozhong, *Introduction to the Tsinghua Bamboo-Strip Manuscripts*, ed. Christopher J. Foster and William N. French (Leiden, Brill, 2016).

7. King Wen was the father of King Wu, founder of the Zhou dynasty. He was once jailed by Zhou, the last Shang king. Taigong's name was Jiang Shang 姜尚. According to legend, at the age of seventy, Taigong was still a fisherman by the Wei River. King Wen followed a divination and found Taigong at the river and appointed Taigong as an advisor. Taigong assisted King Wu and destroyed the Shang. He was enfeoffed as the ruler of the state of Qi. See "Qi taigong shijia" 齊太公世家 in

depends on the people. Tang changed his demeanor in order to please Jie. King Wen acted obediently and was favored by Zhou. Xia and Yin relied upon their power and maltreated these two sages,[8] but the two rulers made concessions in order to receive the heavenly way. For this reason King Tang did not lament his hardship and King Wen did not consider his distress shameful."

The king of Yue said, "In the past, Yao appointed Shun and Yu and the world was in order. Although there was damage from the flood it did not extend to the people. The abnormal natural phenomena did not harm the people, let alone harm the ruler."

Grand Minister Kucheng said, "It was not like what Your Majesty has concluded. Heaven has its heavenly order, but man's virtue varies and may be great or little. The Yellow Emperor did not abdicate his position, but Yao handed down the title of son of heaven to Shun. The founding king of the Three Dynasties committed regicide while he was still a minister and, as sons, the five hegemons murdered their father.[9] Virtue varies in terms of broadness and narrowness, man's dispositions differ by loftiness and baseness. Nowadays the world is just like a market, where people display goods in order to set traps, conceive schemes in order to deal with enemies. If we unfortunately fall into distress, then we just seek to outlast it. Your Majesty failed to see this but entertained the mood of anger."

The king of Yue said, "Those who appoint people will not allow themselves to be humiliated; those who do not accept advice will endanger their state. All you ministers should plan in advance, before any situation reaches the point of reality. You should also topple the enemy and destroy the foe, thus let the ruler sit at ease while enjoying a fortune as big as Mount Tai. Now I, a man of little virtue, fall into such a distress, yet you talk about Tang and King Wen who were bound to be hegemons after hardship, how your words violate the rites! Furthermore, a gentleman seizes every moment but discards pearls and jade.[10] Now I, a man of little virtue, wish I could escape from the worries of war, yet I am captured by the enemy. I myself

---

*Shiji*, 12:1477–1515. See also Long Jianchun 龍建春, "'Taigong' xingshi minghao kaolun" "太公"姓氏名號考論, *Taizhou xueyuan xuebao* 台州學院學報, no. 2 (2003): 24–28.

8. Shang was also called Yin.

9. The founding kings are Yu of Xia, Tang of Shang, and King Wen and King Wu of Zhou. One legend says that Yu exiled Shun. Tang exiled Jie of Xia. King Wu defeated Zhou of Shang and cut off his head. Usually, the five hegemons are listed as Lord Huang of Qi 齊桓公, Lord Wen of Jin 晉文公, Lord Mu of Qin 秦穆公, Lord Xiang of Song 宋襄公, and King Zhuang of Chu 楚莊王. The source of the story of the five hegemons' patricide is not clear. It is not mentioned in any extant early text. An alternative reading of this is: "During the Three Dynasties, there were ministers who committed regicide; in the era of the Five Hegemons there were sons who committed patricide."

10. One's lifespan is limited and therefore a gentleman values it over treasures.

have become a servant and my wife a maid. I leave the homeland without returning to it and will die as a foreigner in a rival state. If a man's soul has perception after death, I will be ashamed to face the former kings; if the soul does not have perception, my body and bones will be abandoned. Why are your words not in accord with my feelings?"

To this the Grand Ministers Wen Zhong and Fan Li answered: "We have heard that a man of antiquity had said, 'One's view will not be broad if one does not live in difficult circumstances; one's sight will not be profound if one's body does not suffer from sorrow.' Sagely kings and virtuous rulers all faced difficulties in dire straits and suffered unwashable shame. Their person was detained yet their reputation was still high; their body was humiliated yet their fame was still glorious. They stayed in low positions but did not consider them vile; they lived in dangerous times but did not regard them as precarious. The Five Lords' virtues were great such that they were free from adversity caused by difficulties, yet they still had the worries caused by the flood.[11] King Wen of Zhou suffered from the humiliation of being mistreated and detained and could not free himself from several imprisonments.[12] He shed tears but bore the injustices; he walked and cried but served as a slave. He deduced the *Book of Changes* and created the diagrams;[13] he was protected by the will of heaven. When the time of adversity had reached its end, it was followed by joy. The many lords came to his aid and his destiny to become a king was demonstrated by signs. A horse with a crimson mane and a fox with black fur were found. His assisting ministers, acting like loyal wives, tore down the jail and broke the shackles.[14] King Wen thus returned to his state and governed it with virtue. He then attacked his foe, and he conquered and controlled the world as easily as turning over his palm. The entire world respected him as the ruler and his achievement was honored by ten thousand generations. Your Majesty now meets with hardship, yet we, your subjects, are indeed making plans

11. There were different theories on who the Five Lords were. A popular theory is that the Five Lords were the Yellow Emperor, Zhuangxu 顓頊, Lord Ku 帝嚳, Yao, and Shun. Here, reference to the Five Lords probably only refers to Yao and Shun, as the sentence says that they were worried about the flood.

12. Zhang Jue argues that the character *san* 三 is a mistake for *wang* 王 and that the character *wen* 文 is missing before 王. Thus the subject of the sentence is allegedly *Wenwang* 文王, King Wen. See Zhang Jue, 203n24.

13. *Book of Changes* was an ancient divination book. According to Sima Qian, King Wen edited the book while he was imprisoned by Zhou. See *Shiji*, 4:119.

14. 結髮 (*jiefa*) was originally a ritual performed during a wedding ceremony; the hair of the bride and groom were tied up together as a symbol of their marriage. Here it suggests that the ministers serve King Wen as a wife serves her husband.

for you. A bone-cutting sword does not do well for paring and scraping, an iron-piercing spear has no use in splitting a hair, and a policy-making advisor does not make false speeches of sudden rises to power. Now we, your subjects, study the patterns of heaven and investigate the classics of our land. We have noticed that the *yin* and *yang* forces germinate together, and survival and demise are found in different places. If they, the Wu people, are prosperous, we then will be humiliated; if we become dominant, then they will be destroyed. As for we two states competing for the heavenly Way, it is still yet to be known on which side the will of heaven will reside. Your Majesty's difficulty is destined by the Way of heaven, so why should you cry for yourself? Auspiciousness is the gateway to evil; fortune is the root of disaster.[15] Although Your Majesty is in the midst of difficulty, who can be sure that this is not the sign of success and fulfillment?"

Grand Minister Ji Yan said,[16] "Now Your Majesty has settled his capital on Mount Kuaiji, and, in a desperate situation, is going to Wu. Your words are sorrowful and speeches sad; your many ministers shed tears for this. Even those who are fierce and malicious-hearted are touched by it. I truly do not see the point in Your Majesty's using deceitful statements and callous words to fool everyone."

7.3. 越王曰：「寡人將去入吳，以國累諸侯大夫，願各自述，吾將屬焉。」

大夫皋如曰：「臣聞大夫種忠而善慮，民親其知，士樂為用。今委國一人，其道必守，何順心佛命群臣？」

大夫曳庸曰：「大夫文種者，國之梁棟，君之爪牙。夫驥不可與匹馳，日月不可並照。君王委國於種，則萬綱千紀無不舉者。」

越王曰：「夫國者，前王之國。孤力弱勢劣，不能遵守社稷，奉承宗廟。吾聞父死子代，君亡臣親。今事棄諸大夫，客官於吳，委國歸民以付二三子。吾之由也，亦子之憂也。君臣同道，父子共氣，天性自然。豈得以在者盡忠，亡者為不信乎？何諸大夫論事，一合一離，令孤懷心不定也？夫推國任賢，度功績成者，君之命也；奉教順理，不失分者，臣之職也。吾顧諸大夫以其所能而云委質而已。於乎，悲哉！」

計研曰：「君王所陳者，固其理也。昔湯入夏，付國於文祀，西伯之殷，委國於二老。今懷夏將滯，志在於還。夫適市之妻，教嗣

15. This is from the famous sentence in chapter 58 of *Dao de jing*: "Bad fortune is what good fortune leans on, good fortune is what bad fortune hides in." Lao Tzu, *Tao Teh Ching*, trans. John C. H. Wu (Boston: Shambala, 2005), 119.

16. Ji Yan is also called Ji Ran 計然 in *Shiji* and Ji Ni 計倪 in *Yue jue shu*. See *Shiji*, 129:3256. *Yue jue shu*, "Ji Ni neijing" 計倪內經 chapter, Li Bujia, 109–126.

糞除，出亡之君，敕臣守禦。子問以事，臣謀以能。今君王欲士之所志，各陳其情，舉其能者，議其宜也。」

越王曰：「大夫之論是也。吾將逝矣，願諸君之風。」

7.3. The king of Yue said, "I, a man of little virtue, am about to leave and travel to Wu and I trouble you many ministers with the duty of the state.[17] I wish each of you to speak your mind and I will entrust you with state affairs."

Grand Minister Gaoru said, "I, your subject, have heard that Grand Minister Wen Zhong is loyal and excels in making plans. The people trust his wisdom and the talented are happy to be used by him.[18] Now entrusting the state to him alone he will certainly act in accordance with the right way of governance. Why appoint as many ministers as your heart dictates?"[19]

Grand Minister Yeyong said,[20] "Grand Minister Wen Zhong is the ridgepole and beams of the state, the claws and teeth of Your Majesty.[21] Fast horses cannot be ridden bridle to bridle; the sun and the moon cannot shine at the same time. If Your Majesty entrusts the state to Wen Zhong, all regulations and principles will be carried out."

The king of Yue said, "The state is the former king's state.[22] My strength is weak and my situation perilous. I cannot protect the altars of the earth and the grain, cannot offer sacrifices to the ancestral temple. I have heard that 'if the father dies, the son replaces him; if the ruler is out of the state, ministers take over the administration.' Now I abandon the governance to you ministers and serve outside of the state as a servant of Wu.[23] I will entrust my state and turn my people over to you gentlemen,[24] this is what I will do and it is also what you gentlemen should be concerned about.[25] That the ruler and ministers follow the common principle, and father and son share the same disposition is a natural quality determined by the heavens. How can it happen that one is loyal when the ruler is in the state and deceitful when the ruler is away? Why in discussions do you ministers sometimes

17. 諸侯大夫 (*zhuhou dafu*), lords and ministers, is probably a mistake for 諸大夫 (*zhu dafu*), many ministers.

18. In this sentence 知 (*zhi*, "to know") is a loan word for 智 (*zhi*), "wisdom."

19. According to Xu Tianhu, in this sentence 怫 (*fu*) means 大 (*da*), "big." See Zhang Jue, 207.

20. Yeyong also appears in *WYCQ*, 5.2. Gaoru and Yeyong are mentioned in *Zuozhuan*, Lord Ai 26. See Yang Bojun, 1727; Durrant, Li, and Schaberg, 1989.

21. 棟梁 (*dongliang*), "ridgepole and beams," is a common metaphor meaning pillar of the state. 爪牙 (*zhuaya*), "claws and teeth," is a metaphor for a capable assistant of a ruler.

22. Goujian is saying that he inherited the state from the previous kings of Yue.

23. Zhang Jue believes that 客 (*ke*, "guest") is a mistake for 宦 (*huan*), a "servant" or a "subject." See Zhang Jue, 207n9.

24. 二三子 (*er san zi*) is a polite and also intimate way of addressing close friends, ministers, or students.

25. 由 (*you*) means 行 (*xing*), "action."

accord with each other yet sometimes disagree with each other so that my heart is disturbed? Sharing governance, appointing the worthy, evaluating the merits, and reviewing achievements are the duties of the ruler; carrying out regulations and following principles without being delinquent are the responsibilities of the ministers. My trust in you ministers is based upon your abilities, yet you simply say you will die for the sake of loyalty.[26] Alas, how pitiful that is!"

Ji Yan said, "What Your Majesty stated is certainly reasonable. In the past when Tang went to Xia court, he entrusted the state to Wen Si.[27] When the Earl of the West went to Yin, he entrusted his state to the two elders.[28] Now summer is coming and Your Majesty is departing for Wu,[29] but your wish is to return to your home state. For a wife who is going to the market, she will instruct her son to clean the house;[30] for a ruler who is compelled to leave the state, he will command his ministers to guard the land.[31] A son should ask about what housework needs to be done, and, based upon their abilities, ministers should make plans for the ruler. Now Your Majesty wishes to learn everyone's will and asks everyone to state their mind and explain their talent, and it is appropriate for everyone to discuss."

The king of Yue said, "What the minister remarked was right. I am about to leave and I wish to learn all you gentlemen's plans."[32]

7.4. 大夫種曰：「夫內修封疆之役，外修耕戰之備，荒無遺土，百姓親附：臣之事也。」

26. According to Fu Qian's 服虔 commentary cited in Zilu's 子路 biography in the *Shiji*, in ancient times, ministers wrote their names on bamboo slips when they began to serve the ruler, which meant that they would devote their lives to the ruler and would be willing to die for him. See *Shiji*, 67:2191.

27. This refers to the legend that Tang was summoned and then imprisoned by King Jie of Xia. Wen Si was Tang's minister.

28. The Earl of the West is King Wen of Zhou. This refers to the famous story that King Wen was imprisoned by King Zhou of Yin at Youli 羑里, probably modern-day Tangyin 湯陰 County, Henan Province. The "two elders" might refer to San Yisheng 散宜生 and Hong Yao 閎夭.

29. These four characters, 懷夏將滯 (*huai xia jiang zhi*), are difficult to understand. Lu Wenshao reads 夏 (*xia*) as a mistake for 憂 (*you*); if so, 懷夏 is therefore 懷憂, which means to carry sorrow or worries. However, Sun Yirang argues that 懷 (*huai*) should be 遝 (*ta*), meaning "to approach." 懷夏 then is understood as "when summer comes." At the same time, Jiang Guangxu 蔣光煦 (1813–1860) notes that according to the Song 宋 edition of *WYQC*, the character 滯 (*zhi*) was 遰 (*di*), which means "to depart." In this case the sentence should be read as "the summer is coming and your majesty will depart for Wu." For detailed discussion, see Zhou Shengchun, *Wu Yue Chunqiu jijiao huikao*, 118–9.

30. 糞除 (*fenchu*) means "to clean."

31. 敕 (*chi*) means "to warn" or "to command."

32. Xu Tianhu argues that there should be the word 聞 (*wen*), "to listen to," after 愿 (*yuan*), "to wish." See Zhang Jue, 208n23.

大夫范蠡曰：「輔危主，存亡國，不恥屈厄之難，安守被辱之地，往而必反，與君復讎者：臣之事也。」

大夫苦成曰：「發君之令，明君之德，窮與俱厄，進與俱霸，統煩理亂，使民知分：臣之事也。」

大夫曳庸曰：「奉令受使，結和諸侯，通命達旨，賂往遺來，解憂釋患，使無所疑，出不忘命，入不被尤：臣之事也。」

大夫皓進曰：「一心齊志，上與等之，下不違令，動從君命；修德履義，守信溫故；臨非決疑，君誤臣諫，直心不撓；舉過列平，不阿親戚，不私於外，推身致君，終始一分：臣之事也。」

大夫諸稽郢曰：「望敵設陣，飛矢揚兵，履腹涉屍，血流滂滂，貪進不退；二師相當，破敵攻眾，威凌百邦：臣之事也。」

大夫皋如曰：「修德行惠，撫慰百姓；身臨憂勞，動輒躬親；弔死存疾，救活民命；蓄陳儲新，食不二味；國富民實，為君養器：臣之事也。」

大夫計研曰：「候天察地，紀歷陰陽，觀變參災，分別妖祥，日月含色，五精錯行，福見知吉，妖出知凶：臣之事也。」

越王曰：「孤雖入於北國，為吳窮虜，有諸大夫懷德抱術，各守一分，以保社稷，孤何憂焉？」遂別於浙江之上。群臣垂泣，莫不咸哀。越王仰天歎曰：「死者，人之所畏。若孤之聞死，其於心胸中曾無怵惕？」遂登船徑去，終不返顧。

7.4. Grand Minister Wen Zhong said, "Setting in order military service so as to guard the border within the state, preparing for warfare out against the enemy, making sure that no state land is neglected, and that the people love and follow the king—these are my, your subject's, responsibilities."

Grand Minister Fan Li said, "Assisting the ruler in dangerous situations, saving a state that is failing, not being shamed by the hardships of humiliation and distress, peacefully staying in the place where insult is inevitable, and, while going to Wu, making sure to return and seek revenge with the king against the enemy—these are my, your subject's, responsibilities."

Grand Minister Kucheng said, "Publicizing the king's orders, illustrating the king's virtue, going through difficulty with the king when he is in distress, completing the achievements of a hegemon with the king as he advances, taking charge of varied affairs, putting chaotic affairs in order, and ensuring the people know their duties—these are my, your subject's, responsibilities."

Grand Minister Yeyong said, "Receiving the order and serving as an envoy to other states, making friends with many lords, reporting the commands and conveying the will of the king, presenting and receiving gifts,[33] relieving

33. 遺 is pronounced as "wèi" here, meaning "to give as a gift." 賂 (*luo*) also means "presenting gifts."

his concerns and making the king worry-free, keeping in my heart the commands of the king when going abroad, receiving no criticism when returning to the state—these are my, your subject's, responsibilities."

Grand Minister Hao moved forward and said,[34] "Being of one mind and being in accordance with the king above, violating no order when serving as a subordinate, following the commands of the king in every action, cultivating my virtue, putting righteousness into practice, keeping my promises, reviewing the past, dispelling doubts when confronting unusual situations, remonstrating as a subject when the king makes mistakes, being upright and never being bent, informing against wrongs and governing with fairness,[35] never being partial to relatives and never collaborating with a foreign state, devoting myself to the king, and being loyal all the time—these are my, your subject's, responsibilities."

Grand Minister Zhuji Ying said,[36] "Inspecting enemy troops and arranging the order of battle; shooting arrows and wielding weapons; stepping on bellies and advancing across bodies in the field where blood flows like a river; desiring only to charge forward, not retreat; coordinating the troops on the left and right destroying the rival state and defeating its army; holding all states in awe—these are my, your subject's, responsibilities."

Grand Minister Gaoru said, "Cultivating virtue, being kind to the people and soothing them, personally experiencing worries and pains and carrying out everything by actual efforts,[37] mourning the deceased and comforting the ill, saving the people's lives, storing up old rice and reserving the new grains, never eating more than one food at a meal, making the state rich and the people wealthy, educating the talented for the king—these are my, your subject's, responsibilities."[38]

---

34. Both Huang Rensheng and Zhou Shengchun read this minister's name as 皓進 (*Haojin*). However, in *WYCQ*, 8.8, the minister is mentioned as 大夫浩, Grand Minister Hao. Because of this his name is probably Hao, but 進 (*jin*) should be rendered as a verb meaning "to move forward." See Huang Rensheng, 224; Zhou Shengchun, 119. See also Zhang Jue, 210.

35. 撓 (*nao*) is the loan word of 橈 (*nao*) here, which means "to yield to," "to bend to." 列 (*lie*) means 治 (*zhi*), "to rule," "to govern."

36. In *Guoyu*, Goujian asked Zhuji Ying to seek a truce with Fuchai after Goujian was defeated. See Xu Yuangao, 538, 540.

37. Gaoru is saying that he will share the pain and worries of the people and personally carry out everything.

38. 器 (*qi*) refers to a talented man. In the *Analects*, Confucius says that "the gentleman is not a vessel 君子不器 (*junzi buqi*)." 器 is a vessel that is designed to serve a specific function; here Confucius uses it metaphorically, referring to men with specialized training or skill. This, however, might reflects the transformation in governmental institutions from late Spring and Autumn to the Warring States as more and more specialists were needed in each state.

Grand Minister Ji Yan said, "Observing the sky and inspecting the land; calculating the calendar; reckoning *yin* and *yang*; observing anomalies and watching for signs of disaster;[39] differentiating and distinguishing between the ominous and the auspicious, whether the sun and the moon present an unusual color, or the five planets move irregularly;[40] knowing it is auspicious when a good sign appears, that it is ominous when an anomaly shows up—these are my, your subject's, responsibilities."

The king of Yue said, "Although I, the orphan, am going north and am becoming a desperate slave of Wu, with you many ministers' innate virtue and talents and each of you taking care of your duties to protect the altar of earth and the altar of grain, what worry do I, the orphan, have?" He then bid farewell to the ministers on the bank of the Zhe River. The ministers all shed tears and none of them did not feel sorrowful. The king of Yue looked up to the sky and lamented, "Death is what man fears; yet now if I hear about death I will have no fear at all in my heart." He then ascended onto the boat and left directly, not looking back.

7.5. 越王夫人乃據船而哭，顧見烏鵲啄江渚之蝦，飛去復來，因哭而歌之，曰：「仰飛鳥兮烏鳶，淩玄虛號翩翩。集洲渚兮優恣，啄蝦矯翮兮雲間，任厥兮往還。妾無罪兮負地，有何辜兮譴天？颿颿獨兮西往，孰知返兮何年？心惙惙兮若割，淚泫泫兮雙懸。」

又哀今曰：「彼飛鳥兮鳶鳥，已迴翔兮翕蘇。心在專兮素蝦，何居食兮江湖？徊復翔兮游颺，去復返兮於乎！始事君兮去家，終我命兮君都。終來遇兮何幸，離我國兮去吳。妻衣褐兮為婢，夫去冕兮為奴。歲遙遙兮難極，冤悲痛兮心惻。腸千結兮服膺，於乎哀兮忘食。願我身兮如鳥，身翱翔兮矯翼。去我國兮心搖，情憤惋兮誰識？」

越王聞夫人怨歌，心中內慟，乃曰：「孤何憂？吾之六翮備矣。」

7.5. The wife of the king of Yue then leaned against the boat and cried. Looking back, she saw crows pecking shrimp at the islet; they flew away and then came back. She thereupon cried and composed a song about this, singing,

Looking up, I see crows and kites flying.[41]
High above in the sky, they swiftly soar.[42]

39. 參 (*can*) means "to observe."

40. 五精 (*wujing*) refers to the five planets of Venus, Jupiter, Mercury, Mars, and Saturn.

41. 鳶 (*yuan*) is a black-eared kite or hawk.

42. Xu Tianhu argues that the word 號 (*hao*) is a mistake for 兮 (*xi*), which is a modal particle that slows down the pace of a line in Han poems. See Zhang Jue, 213n3.

Perching at the islet, they are free and at ease.
They peck shrimp and flutter their wings among the clouds.[43]
Flying up and down as they please.[44]
I have not committed any crime,
nor have I betrayed the earth,
for what offense am I punished by heaven?[45]
Hurried and rushed I travel to the west alone,[46]
who could know in which year I can return?
My heart is so painful, as if it is cut by a knife.[47]
Tears flow from my eyes down my cheeks.[48]

Again she chanted with sorrow:[49]

Kites are the flying birds,
resting their wings after soaring.[50]
Their minds concentrate on the white shrimp,
why do they live and feed by the rivers and lakes?
Coming back and forth they fly and flutter, alas!
They leave and return.
In the beginning I left my family to serve you, my lord,
and I spent my life at my lord's capital.
What crime have I committed to eventually meet this,[51]
leaving my state and entering Wu.
The wife wears coarse cloth and serves as a maid;
the husband takes off his crown and works as a slave.
Long and distant are the many years to endure;
grievance, sorrow and pain sadden my heart.
Oh how my chest is so overwhelmed

---

43. 翮 (*he*) refers to the feathers of birds.

44. Xu Tianhu believes that there is a word missing after 任厥 (*renjue*). 厥 is the same as 其 (*qi*), referring to the birds. Zhang Jue, however, argues that there are in total seven words missing after 任厥. Zhang Jue is probably correct, considering that the poem is highly regulated in form and there should be seven more words to constitute the stanza. See Zhang Jue, 213n6; Huang Rensheng, 229n7.

45. 譴 (*qian*) is a passive verb here, meaning "punished by."

46. 颿颿 (*fan*) is an adjective describing a horse galloping.

47. 惙惙 (*chuochuo*) is a description of worry.

48. 泫泫 (*xuanxuan*) is an adjective describing water or tears flowing.

49. According to the Ming edition, 今 (*jin*) should be 吟 (*yin*), "to chant." See Huang Rensheng, 229n12; Zhang Jue, 212.

50. 翕 (*xi*), means "to close their wings." 蘇 (*su*) suggests "to rest."

51. 幸 (*xing*) is a loan word for 辜 (*gu*), which means "crime," "fault" or "offence."

with sorrow and longing that I forget to drink and eat.[52]
I wish that I could be the bird,
spreading my wings I would fly up high.
My heart shakes when leaving the state,
who would know my anger and regret?"

Hearing his wife's sorrowful song, the king of Yue was deeply saddened in his heart, but he said, "What should I, the orphan, worry about? My strong wings are indeed ready."[53]

7.6. 於是入吳，見夫差稽首再拜稱臣，曰：「東海賤臣勾踐，上愧皇天，下負后土，不裁功力，污辱王之軍士，抵罪邊境。大王赦其深辜，裁加役臣，使執箕帚。誠蒙厚恩，得保須臾之命，不勝仰感俯愧。臣勾踐叩頭頓首。」吳王夫差曰：「寡人於子亦過矣。子不念先君之讎乎？」越王曰：「臣死則死矣，惟大王原之。」伍胥在旁，目若熛火，聲如雷霆，乃進曰：「夫飛鳥在青雲之上，尚欲繳微矢以射之，豈況近臥於華池，集於庭廡乎？今越王放於南山之中，游於不可存之地，幸來涉我壤土，入吾梐梱，此乃廚宰之成事食也，豈可失之乎？」吳王曰：「吾聞誅降殺服，禍及三世。吾非愛越而不殺也，畏皇天之咎，教而赦之。」太宰嚭諫曰：「子胥明於一時之計，不通安國之道。願大王遂其所執，無拘群小之口。」夫差遂不誅越王，令駕車養馬，祕於宮室之中。

7.6. The king of Yue thereupon arrived in Wu and received an audience from Fuchai. He kowtowed twice and called himself a servant, saying, "Goujian, the humble subject from the east sea, feels shame facing the heavenly god above, and fails the god of earth below.[54] Being ignorant of my own strength, I insulted your soldiers and warriors, my king, and committed crime along the border. Your Majesty pardoned my severe misdeeds, and sentenced me to be a labor servant and allowed me to clean your palace with broom and dust pan. Truly because I am indebted to you, I am able to preserve my transitory life. Looking up, I cannot express enough my gratitude to you; looking down I cannot say enough how shameful I feel about myself. Touching my head to the ground, your servant, Goujian, kowtows in front of you." The king of Wu, Fuchai, said, "I, a man of little virtue, have

52. Zhang Jue interprets 服 (*fu*) as 腷 (*bi*), "pent-up emotion," "oppression," etc. 膺 (*ying*) is "chest." Huang Rensheng reads 服膺 as "remembering in the heart." Considering the context, Zhang Jue's interpretation is likely accurate. See Zhang Jue, 213n18; Huang Rensheng, 229n21.

53. 六翮 (*liuhe*) refers to strong wings. Here it is used as a metaphor for many able ministers.

54. 皇天 (*huangtian*), "heavenly god," and 后土 (*houtu*), "god of earth," often appear in texts as a pair.

also treated you wrongly. Have you, sir, not remembered the feud with my deceased lord?"[55] The king of Yue said, "If I, your servant, should die, then I will die. I only wish Your Majesty pardon me." Wu Zixu was next to the Wu king; his eyes sparkling like fire and his voice like thunder.[56] Moving forward, he said, "If a bird is flying above the blue sky, a man still wants to shoot at it with a short arrow fastened to a skill string,[57] not to mention those that nest close by in the Hua pond,[58] and perch in the courtyard roof. The king of Yue was let free in the mountains in the south, wandering in places that are difficult to find.[59] Now luckily he stepped onto our soil and entered our fence,[60] this is just like a dish that can be cooked by a chef only, how can we lose him?" The king of Wu said, "I have heard that 'by murdering a man who has already surrendered himself, disaster will continue for three generations.' It is not that I love the king of Yue or that I do not want to kill him. I am afraid of heaven's blame, so I instruct him and pardon him." Chief Chancellor Bo Pi admonished the king, saying, "Wu Zixu is brilliant in planning for a certain event, he does not understand the way of stabilizing the state. I wish Your Majesty would fulfill Goujian's wish of holding a broom and dust pan, and not be restrained by the sayings of petty men." Fuchai thereupon did not kill the king of Yue. He ordered him to drive the carriage and tend the horses, housing him secretly in a stone chamber.

7.7. 三月，吳王召越王入見，越王伏於前，范蠡立於後。吳王謂范蠡曰：「寡人聞：『貞婦不嫁破亡之家，仁賢不官絕滅之國。』今越王無道，國已將亡，社稷壞崩，身死世絕，為天下笑。而子及主俱為奴僕，來歸於吳，豈不鄙乎？吾欲赦子之罪，子能改心自新，棄越歸吳乎？」范蠡對曰：「臣聞：『亡國之臣，不敢語政，敗軍之將，不敢語勇。』臣在越不忠不信，今越王不奉大王命號，用兵與大王相持，至今獲罪，君臣俱降。蒙大王鴻恩，得君臣相保，願得入備掃除，出給趨走，臣之願也。」此時越王伏地流涕，自謂遂失范蠡矣。吳王知范蠡不可得為臣，謂曰：「子既不移其志，吾復置子於石室之中。」范蠡曰：「臣請如命。」吳王起，入宮中，越王、范蠡趨入石室。

55. According to Sima Qian, Fuchai's father Helü was defeated by Yue and died because of it. His last words to Fuchai were: "Have you forgotten that Goujian killed your father?" Fuchai promised his father that he dared not to forget the enmity. Now, when King Fuchai does not execute Goujian, he betrays his father's wish. This is why Fuchai says he treated Goujian wrongly. See *Shiji*, 31:1468.

56. These are to describe Wu Zixu's anger.

57. 繳 (*zhuo*) is a string fastened to an arrow so the weapon can be retrieved after shooting.

58. The Hua pond was mentioned in *WYCQ*, 4.35. It was a place Helü enjoyed.

59. This refers to when Goujian was hidden at Mount Kuaiji after Wu conquered the Yue capital.

60. This is the fence set up in front of government buildings in order to block people and horses.

7.7. After three months, the king of Wu summoned the king of Yue to the palace for an audience. The king of Yue prostrated himself before the king of Wu while Fan Li stood behind the king of Yue. The king of Wu spoke to Fan Li, saying, "I, a man of little virtue, have heard that 'a chaste woman will not marry into a debased family, and a humane and virtuous man will not take office in a disintegrating state.' Now the king of Yue does not follow the Way. His state is already falling apart, the altars of earth and grain are ruined and collapsed. If he dies his lineage will end, and he will be laughed at by the world. Yet both you and your lord became servants and came to submit yourselves to Wu; isn't this despicable? I want to pardon your punishment; can you change your heart, renew yourself, give up Yue, and render your loyalty to Wu?" Fan Li responded, saying, "I, your subject, have heard that 'an official from a destroyed state dares not talk about governance; a general defeated in battle dares not speak of courage.' When I, your subject, was in Yue, I was not loyal and trustworthy. Now the king of Yue did not follow the command from Your Majesty, but used military forces to confront Your Majesty, which caused punishments; and we, the ruler and minister, both surrendered. Thanks to Your Majesty's great kindness, we, as ruler and minister, are able to preserve ourselves. I wish I could clean for you when you are in the palace, run for you and be used by you when you go out, these are my, your subject's, wishes." At this moment the king of Yue prostrated on the floor and shed tears, believing that he was about to lose Fan Li. The king of Wu realized that he could not persuade Fan Li to become his minister; he then told Fan Li, "Since you sir cannot change your mind, I will again place you in the stone chamber." Fan Li said, "I, your subject, request to follow your order." The king of Wu rose up and entered the palace. The king of Yue and Fan Li entered the stone chamber in haste.

7.8. 越王服犢鼻，著樵頭。夫人衣無緣之裳，施左關之襦。夫斫剉養馬，妻給水、除糞、灑掃。三年，不慍怒，面無恨色。吳王登遠臺，望見越王及夫人、范蠡坐於馬糞之旁，君臣之禮存，夫婦之儀具。王顧謂太宰嚭曰：「彼越王者，一節之人；范蠡，一介之士，雖在窮厄之地，不失君臣之禮。寡人傷之。」太宰嚭曰：「願大王以聖人之心，哀窮孤之士。」吳王曰：「為子赦之。」

7.8. The king of Yue wore a loincloth and a turban;[61] his wife wore an unhemmed skirt and a left-lapeled top jacket.[62] The husband cut grass for

61. Both the loincloth and the turban were the dress of people of modest means.

62. In ancient times, the edges of clothes were usually made of cloth that was of a different textile from the dressing garment. An unhemmed skirt suggests low social status. The top jacket of

raising horses while the wife watered the horses, cleaned out the manure, sprayed water on the ground, and swept it. For three years they had been doing these chores without resentment, nor did they wear a facial expression of hatred. The king of Wu ascended a distant tower and saw from there the king of Yue and his wife and Fan Li sitting beside horse manure, but their ritual as the ruler and minister remained and the etiquette between the husband and wife was perfect. Looking back at Chief Chancellor Bo Pi, the king of Wu said, "That king of Yue is a man of integrity; Fan Li is a man of moral fortitude. Although in a desperate situation, they did not ignore the ritual between the ruler and the minister. I, a man of little virtue, feel sad for them." Chief Chancellor Bo Pi said, "I wish Your Majesty would pity these men in distress in your sagely heart." The king of Wu said, "I will pardon them for you, sir."

7.9. 後三月，乃擇吉日而欲赦之，召太宰嚭謀曰：「越之與吳，同土連域。勾踐愚黠，親欲為賊。寡人承天之神靈，前王之遺德，誅討越寇，囚之石室。寡人心不忍見，而欲赦之，於子柰何？」太宰嚭曰：「臣聞：『無德不復。』大王垂仁恩加越，越豈敢不報哉？願大王卒意。」

越王聞之，召范蠡告之曰：「孤聞於外，心獨喜之，又恐其不卒也。」范蠡曰：「大王安心，事將有意，在《玉門》第一。今年十二月，戊寅之日，時加日出。戊，囚日也；寅，陰後之辰也。合庚辰，歲後會也。夫以戊寅日聞喜，不以其罪罰日也。時加卯而賊戊，功曹為騰蛇而臨戊，謀利事在青龍，青龍在勝先而臨酉，死氣也；而剋寅。是時剋其日，用又助之。所求之事，上下有憂。此豈非天網四張，萬物盡傷者乎？王何喜焉？」

果子胥諫吳王曰：「昔桀囚湯而不誅，紂囚文王而不殺，天道還反，禍轉成福。故夏為湯所誅，殷為周所滅。今大王既囚越君而不行誅，臣謂大王惑之深也。得無夏殷之患乎？」

吳王遂召越王，久之不見。范蠡、文種憂而占之，曰：「吳王見擒也。」有頃，太宰嚭出見 大夫種、范蠡，而言越王復拘於石室。

伍子胥復諫吳王曰：「臣聞王者攻敵國，克之則加以誅，故後無報復之憂，遂免子孫之患。今越王已入石室，宜早圖之，後必為吳之患。」太宰嚭曰：「昔者，齊桓割燕所至之地以貺燕公，而齊君獲其美名；宋襄濟河而戰，《春秋》以多其義：功立而名稱，軍敗而德存。今大王誠赦越王，則功冠於五霸，名越於前古。」吳王曰：「待吾疾愈，方為大宰赦之。」

---

the people from the central states was right-lapeled. A left-lapeled jacket indicates association with "barbarians."

7.9. Three months later, the king of Wu then chose an auspicious day and planned to pardon the king of Yue. He summoned Chief Chancellor Bo Pi and discussed it with him, saying, "Yue and Wu are in the same region and our borders connect. Goujian is foolish yet cunning; he personally wanted to harm me. I, a man of little virtue, blessed by the heavenly spirits and the virtue left by the former kings, punished and attacked the Yue enemy and imprisoned him in the stone chamber. I, a man of little virtue, in my heart cannot bear to see him distressed in such a situation and want to pardon him; what, sir, is your opinion on this?" Chief Chancellor Bo Pi said, "I, your subject, have heard that 'no virtuous deeds fail to receive reward.' Your Majesty bestows humaneness and favor upon Yue, dare Yue not repay this? I wish Your Majesty would act on your thought."

Upon hearing this, the king of Yue summoned Fan Li and said to him, "I, the orphan, heard this elsewhere, but in my heart I am secretly delighted by it, and at the same time I am afraid it won't be realized." Fan Li said, "Your Majesty, please calm your heart, there will be some doubts in this matter,[63] because it corresponds to the first category of the *Jade Gate*.[64] You heard the news on the *wuyin* day, the fifteenth day, in the twelfth month of this year,[65] and the hours were when the sun was rising.[66] The day of *wu* suggests imprisonment; *yin* is the earthly branch following the arrival of the Great *Yin*.[67] Their combining date is *gengchen*,[68] which is a combining date after the Great *Yin* has passed.[69] That Your Majesty heard the good news on a *wuyin* day suggests that heaven does not punish the heavenly stems because of the day's reference to imprisonment.[70] But that the hours were at *mao* nevertheless caused harm to *wu*,[71] and the spirit on duty was the flying snake

63. 意 (*yi*), "intention," is a loan word for 疑 (*yi*), "doubtful."

64. 玉門 (*yumen*), *Jade Gate*, is probably a book or a technique of divination.

65. This was the third year after Goujian came to Wu, which was 490 BCE. The *wuyin* day was the fifteenth day of the month.

66. Again, in ancient China, people used the twelve earthly branches to mark the hours. The hours of sunrise are *maoshi* 卯時, corresponding to five o'clock to seven o'clock in the morning. Fan Li is using the *liuren* divination technique here.

67. For explanations of *yin* and *chen* 辰, see *WYCQ* 5.12, 193n73 陰後之辰 (*Yinhou zhichen*) refers to the earthly branches that the Great *Yin* has passed. Since on that day the Great *Yin* was at the location of *bingshu* 丙戌 and *wuyin* was eight days ahead of it, therefore the *yin* day was called the branch that the Great *Yin* has passed.

68. For the meaning of 合 (*he*) and 會 (*hui*), combination day, see *WYCQ* 5.12, 195n75. *Genyin* was the third day of that month.

69. This combination is considered ominous.

70. The *wu* day was the day of imprisonment.

71. In the Five Phases theory, *mao* is associated with wood and *wu* with earth. According to the overcoming theory, wood overcomes earth, and therefore Fan Li says that *mao* brings harm to *wu*.

which pressed on toward the *wu* position,[72] thus the planning of advantageous things is determined by Jupiter.[73] Now Jupiter has passed noon and it is close to the *you* hours, this means deadly *qi*, and it also conquers *yin*.[74] In this way, not only did the hours overcome the day of *wuyin*,[75] but also the movement of Jupiter aided the problem.[76] The matter Your Majesty is praying for appears worrisome by either the heavenly stems or the earthly branches. Isn't this the time when the heavenly net is open at its four corners and all things will be damaged? What is my lord happy about?"

As expected, Wu Zixu admonished the king of Wu, saying, "In the past, Jie put Tang in jail but did not execute him, Zhou imprisoned King Wu but did not kill him. The way of heaven changed quickly and disaster became fortune. Therefore Xia was destroyed by Tang, and Yin was annihilated by Zhou. Now, Your Majesty has already kept the lord of Yue in custody but failed to execute him. I, your subject, believe Your Majesty is greatly confused. Perhaps you will have the same trouble as Xia and Yin?"

The king of Wu then summoned the king of Yue but did not come out to see him for a while. Fan Li and Wen Zhong were worried about this and made a divination, and the result read, "The king of Wu arrests us."[77] After a short while, Chief Chancellor Bo Pi walked out. He saw Grand Ministers Wen Zhong and Fan Li and told them that the king of Yue would be detained in the stone chamber again.

Wu Zixu again admonished the king of Wu, saying, "I, your subject, have heard that when a king attacks a rival state, if he defeats them he will then execute their ruler, thus he can free his descendants from worries. Now the king of Yue has already been put into the stone chamber, we'd better make a plan for him as early as possible; otherwise he certainly will make trouble for Wu." Chief Chancellor Bo Pi said, "In the past, Lord Huan of Qi ceded the areas where Lord Zhuang of Yan had traveled to see him off and gave

---

72. For explanation of *gongcao* 功曹, see *WYCQ* 5.12, 195n77. Flying snake symbolizes killing.

73. *Qinglong*, green dragon, refers to Jupiter here.

74. Sun Yirang explains that noon is called *shengxian* (勝午). Since the Great *Yin* was at the location of *bingshu*, the location of Jupiter should be at *wushen* 戊申, which means that Jupiter has passed noon and was close to *you*. *Shen* resembles destruction and *you* resembles danger, therefore the time was not auspicious. Also, in the Five Phases theory, *shen* and *you* are associated with metal while *yin* with wood. Thus according to the overcoming theory, metal overcomes wood. See Zhang Jue, 220nn14–15.

75. Hours overcoming days are especially inauspicious.

76. Zhang Jue reads 用 (*yong*) as 行 (*xing*); Huang Rensheng, however, argues that 用 is a special divination word, which means the practice or the embodiment. See Zhang Jue, 221n17 and Huang Rensheng, 238n12.

77. 見 (*jian*) means 我 (*wo*), "us," here. See Zhang Jue, 221n19. According to previous paragraphs, Wen Zhong did not accompany Goujian to Wu. This is probably a mistake.

them to Lord Zhuang of Yan,[78] the lord of Qi then received a good reputation. Lord Xiang of Song did not fight against the Chu troops until they crossed the river, the *Spring and Autumn Annals* praised his righteousness.[79] Lord Huan of Qi accomplished his achievement and his name was extolled; Lord Xiang of Song lost the battle yet his virtue spread. Now if Your Majesty really frees the king of Yue, your achievement then surpasses the five hegemons and your fame exceeds that of anyone in the past." The king of Wu said, "Wait until I have recovered from my illness, then I will free him for you, Chief Chancellor."

7.10. 後一月，越王出石室，召范蠡，曰：「吳王疾，三月不愈。吾聞人臣之道，主疾臣憂，且吳王遇孤恩甚厚矣。疾之無瘳，惟公卜焉。」范蠡曰：「吳王不死明矣，到己巳日當瘳，惟大王留意。」越王曰：「孤所以窮而不死者，賴公之策耳，中復猶豫，豈孤之志哉？可與不可，惟公圖之。」范蠡曰：「臣竊見吳王，真非人也。數言成湯之義，而不行之。願大王請求問疾，得見，因求其糞而嘗之，觀其顏色，當拜賀焉，言其不死，以瘳起日期之。既言信後，則大王何憂？」

7.10. One month later, the king of Yue walked out of the stone chamber and summoned Fan Li, saying, "The king of Wu is ill. He has not recovered for three months. I have heard the way of being a subject of someone is this: when the ruler is ill, the subject worries for him. Moreover, the king of Wu's treatment of me, the orphan, indeed shows great kindness. I am afraid that his illness will not turn better; I only wish you, sir, to divine on this." Fan Li said, "That the king of Wu will not die is clear.[80] He will feel better when *yisi* day arrives. I wish Your Majesty would keep this in mind." The king of Yue said, "The reason that I, the orphan, am still alive in a desperate situation is

78. Lord Huan of Qi was the first of the five hegemons of the Spring and Autumn period. According to Sima Qian, the state of Yan was attacked by the *rong* people. Lord Huan of Qi attacked the *rong* in order to rescue Yan. Lord Zhuang of Yan, with gratitude, escorted Lord Huan to Qi. Because, according to ritual, the many lords should not leave their own states in seeing off other rulers, Lord Huan of Qi gave the areas where the Yan ruler has passed to Yan. See *Shiji*, 32:1488.

79. Lord Xiang of Song refused to attack the Chu troops while they were crossing the river and waited until they formed lines. He was defeated and personally injured by Chu. The *Spring and Autumn Annals* was the earliest historical text of China. It is an important Confucian canonical text and, traditionally, has three commentaries attached to it, the *Zuo Commentary*, the *Gongyang Commentary*, and the *Guliang Commentary*. The *Guliang Commentary* praises Lord Xiang's decision as righteous. See *Zuozhuan*, Lord Xi 22; Yang Bojun, 397; Durrant, Li, and Schaberg, 357.

80. Zhang Jue cites chapter seven in *Taiping yulan*, which states that there should be twenty-two words in Fan Li's speech before this sentence: "Today's heavenly stems and earthly branches and *yin* and *yang* are all harmonious above and below; none of them overcomes others. The divination text says that 'once rescued by the heaven, what worries should one have?'" See Zhang Jue, 223.

simply because of your, sir, advice. Now you are hesitant while speaking, how can this be what I, the orphan, wish?[81] No matter whether it is feasible or not, I only wish you, sir, to plan on it." Fan Li said, "I, your subject, personally believe the king of Wu is not a kind person. He talked about Tang's righteousness several times but cannot practice it. I wish Your Majesty would make a request to visit him while he is ill. If you are able to see him, take the chance to ask for his excrement and taste it. You observe his facial expression, then you should kneel and congratulate him, saying that he will not die and promising him on that day he will feel better. After your words are confirmed, what worries should Your Majesty have?"

7.11. 越王明日謂太宰嚭曰：「囚臣欲一見問疾。」太宰嚭即入言於吳王，王召而見之。適遇吳王之便，太宰嚭奉溲、惡以出，逢戶中。越王因拜：「請嘗大王之溲，以決吉凶。」即以手取其便與惡而嘗之。因入曰：「下囚臣勾踐賀於大王，王之疾至己巳日有瘳，至三月壬申病愈。」吳王曰：「何以知之？」越王曰：「下臣嘗事師聞糞者，順穀味、逆時氣者死，順時氣者生。今者臣竊嘗大王之糞，其惡味苦且楚酸。是味也，應春夏之氣。臣以是知之。」吳王大悅，曰：「仁人也。」乃赦越王，得離其石室，去就其宮室，執牧養之事如故。越王從嘗糞惡之後，遂病口臭。范蠡乃令左右皆食岑草，以亂其氣。

7.11. The next day, the king of Yue spoke to Chief Chancellor Bo Pi, saying, "I, the imprisoned subject, would like to receive audience from the king of Wu and ask about his illness." Chief Chancellor Bo Pi then entered the palace and reported this to the king of Wu. The king of Wu summoned the king of Yue and was about to meet him. It happened that the king of Wu went to relieve himself and Chief Chancellor Bo Pi held the urine and excrement and walked out, running into the King of Yue at the door.[82] The king of Yue then bowed, saying, "I request to taste his majesty's excrement in order to decide whether the result of the illness is auspicious or not." After this he picked up some urine and excrement by hand, tasted it, and entered the room, saying to the king of Wu: "Goujian, your humble imprisoned subject, congratulates Your Majesty. Your Majesty's illness will turn better on *yisi* day and you will completely recover on *renshen* day in the third month." The king of Wu asked, "How do you know?" The king of Yue said, "Your

81. Goujian was disappointed that Fan Li did not give him clear advice on what to do; Fan Li simply said Goujian should keep this in mind. Goujian was concerned about the possibility of being released by Fuchai.

82. This is probably the door to Fuchai's bedroom.

humble subject once studied with a master and learned that if the excrement tastes like grain but different from the taste of the season,[83] the patient will die; if it tastes the same as that of the season, the patient will survive. Now I, your subject, secretly tasted Your Majesty's excrement, its taste is bitter and sour. This taste corresponds to the *qi* of spring and summer. I, your subject, thus know you will recover."[84] The king of Wu was greatly delighted, saying, "How humane you are!" He then pardoned the king of Yue, letting him leave the stone chamber and come to the king of Wu's palace where he took charge of the duty of raising horses as he did before. After the king of Yue tasted the excrement he suffered from halitosis. Fan Li thus ordered all the attendants on the left and right to eat houttuynia to cover the smell.[85]

7.12. 其後，吳王如越王期日疾愈，心念其忠，臨政之後，大縱酒於文臺。吳王出令曰：「今日為越王陳北面之坐，群臣以客禮事之。」伍子胥趨出，到舍上，不御坐。酒酣，太宰嚭曰：「異乎！今日坐者，各有其詞，不仁者逃，其仁者留。臣聞：『同聲相和，同心相求。』今國相，剛勇之人，意者內慚至仁之存也，而不御坐，其亦是乎？」吳王曰：「然。」於是范蠡與越王俱起，為吳王壽，其辭曰：「下臣勾踐、從小臣范蠡，奉觴上千歲之壽，辭曰：皇在上令，昭下四時，并心察慈，仁者大王。躬親鴻恩，立義行仁。九德四塞，威服群臣。於乎休哉，傳德無極上感太陽，降瑞翼翼。大王延壽萬歲，長保吳國。四海咸承，諸侯賓服。觴酒既升，永受萬福！」於是吳王大悅。

7.12. After that, the king of Wu recovered from his illness by the date that the king of Yue had predicted, so he kept thinking about the king's loyalty in his heart. One day when he had finished handling government affairs, he held a sumptuous drinking banquet on Wen Terrace. The king of Wu issued a command, saying, "Today we arrange a seat facing north for the king of

83. This means that the grain was not completely digested. According to the Five Phases theory, each season is associated with certain tastes.

84. There seems to have been a medical practice of examining excrement in order to diagnose a patient. In later tradition, this was transformed into an action of filial piety. In the famous Twenty-four Filial Stories, a Southern Qi 南齊 (479–502) official Yu Qianlou 庾黔婁 (ca. 470–510) also tasted his ill father's excrement as a filial deed. See his biography in *Nanshi* 南史. See Li Yanshou 李延壽 (fl. 7th century), chap. 50 in *Nanshi* (Beijing: Zhonghua shuju, 1975), 1245. In *Xin Tangshu* 新唐書, the biography of cruel official "Kuli zhuan" 酷吏傳, Guo Hongba 郭弘霸 tasted minister Wei Yuanzhong's 魏元忠 excrement when Wei was sick in order to show his loyalty to Wei. See Ouyang Xiu 歐陽修, *Xin Tangshu* 新唐書 (Beijing: Zhonghua shuju, 1975), 134:5911. In some regional medicine, excrement was used as an antidote for food poisoning. Another medicine made of excrement, *huanglong tang* 黃龍湯, was recorded in several medical canons such as *Zhouhou fang* 肘後方 and *Bencao gangmu* 本草綱目 for curing typhoid fever.

85. The plant has a strong fishy smell.

Yue;[86] ministers should serve him in accordance with the ritual for serving a guest." Wu Zixu hurriedly walked out and returned home; he did not sit in company. When they were drinking to their heart's content, Chief Chancellor Bo Pi said, "How strange it is! Today at the seating, everyone has his words to say. The unworthy one runs, while the worthy stays. I, your subject, have heard that 'same sounds correspond to each other; same thoughts search for each other.' Now the prime minister is a tough and brave man. I suppose that if in one's heart one is ashamed by the presence of the ultimate humane person, one does not dare to sit in his company. Perhaps this is also the reason for the prime minister's absence?" The king of Wu said, "You are right." At that time, Fan Li and the king of Yue both stood up to congratulate the king of Wu and wish him a long life, and their words were: "Your humble subject Goujian and his attendant, your small subject Fan Li, hold up the wine cup and wish Your Majesty a life of a thousand years." They chanted, "Brilliant is your command from above, it shines as the four seasons below. You are sincere, sharp, and kind. Virtuous is Your Majesty. Personally you bestow upon us your great compassion, you have established righteousness and conduct yourself with humaneness. Your nine virtues fill the world and all ministers submit to your authority.[87] Alas! How magnificent! The virtue you pass on is boundless. To the above it touches the sun, which sends down numerous blessings. Your Majesty will spread your life over ten thousand years, forever will you protect the state of Wu. All in the world come to salute you, and the many lords render homage. The cups have been lifted up, we wish you to forever enjoy endless bliss." The king of Wu therefore was greatly delighted.

7.13. 明日，伍子胥入諫曰：「昨日大王何見乎？臣聞：『內懷虎狼之心，外執美詞之說，但為外情以存其身。豺不可謂廉，狼不可親。』今大王好聽須臾之說，不慮萬歲之患，放棄忠直之言，聽用讒夫之語；不滅瀝血之仇，不絕懷毒之怨。猶縱毛爐炭之上幸其焦，投卵千鈞之下望必全，豈不殆哉？臣聞：『桀登高自知危，然不知所以自安也；前據白刃自知死，而不知所以自存也。惑者知返，迷道不遠。』願大王察之。」

吳王曰：「寡人有疾三月，曾不聞相國一言，是相國之不慈也；又不進口之所嗜，心不相思，是相國之不仁也。夫為人臣不仁不

86. Rulers in ancient times sat facing south and ministers facing north.

87. The term 九德 (*jiude*) appears in many pre-Qin and Han texts and there are different interpretations of the meanings. For example, the *Yi Zhoushu* 逸周書 explains that these virtues are loyalty, trustworthiness, reverence, rigidness, flexibility, harmony, firmness, integrity, and reasonableness. See Huang Huaixin 黃懷信, Zhang Maorong 張懋鎔 and Tian Xudong 田旭東, *Yi Zhoushu huijiao jizhu* 逸周書匯校集注 (Shanghai: Shanghai guji chubanshe, 2007), 53.

慈，焉能知其忠信者乎？越王迷惑，棄守邊之事，親將其臣民來歸寡人，是其義也；躬親為虜，妻親為妾，不慍寡人，寡人有疾，親嘗寡人之溲，是其慈也；虛其府庫，盡其寶幣，不念舊故，是其忠信也。三者既立，以養寡人，寡人曾聽相國而誅之，是寡人之不智也，而為相國快私意耶，豈不負皇天乎？」

子胥曰：「何大王之言反也？夫虎之卑勢，將以有擊也；狸之卑身，將求所取也。雉以眩移拘於網，魚以有悅死於餌。且大王初臨政，負《玉門》之第九，誡事之敗，無咎矣。今年三月甲戌，時加雞鳴。甲戌，歲位之會將也。青龍在酉，德在土，刑在金，是日賊其德也。知父將有不順之子，君有逆節之臣。大王以越王歸吳為義，以飲溲食惡為慈，以虛府庫為仁，是故為無愛於人，其不可親。面聽貌觀以存其身。今越王入臣於吳，是其謀深也；虛其府庫，不見恨色，是欺我王也；下飲王之溲者，是上食王之心也；下嘗王之惡者，是上食王之肝也。大哉，越王之崇吳，吳將為所擒也。惟大王留意察之，臣不敢逃死以負前王。一旦社稷丘墟，宗廟荊棘，其悔可追乎？」

吳王曰：「相國置之，勿復言矣。寡人不忍復聞。」

7.13. The next day, Wu Zixu entered the palace and remonstrated, saying, "What has Your Majesty seen yesterday? I, your subject, have heard that 'if one hides inside a heart of a tiger or wolf, yet decorates himself outside with speeches of flattering words, he is merely putting on emotions at the surface level in order to save himself. A jackal cannot be incorruptible and a wolf cannot be kept too close.' Now Your Majesty likes to listen to words for a moment of pleasure but ignores the worries of ten thousand years. You neglected loyal and upright advice but believe slanderers' speech. You did not exterminate the foe you swore to avenge with your blood and did not eradicate the enemy you hated. These are the same as putting hair on the stove charcoal yet wishing it would not burn, throwing an egg beneath an object weighing a thousand *jun* while expecting it will not be crushed; aren't these dangerous?[88] I, your subject, have heard that when Jie climbed high he knew he was in danger, but he did not know how to make himself safe; when he was close to the edge of a weapon in front of him, he knew he would die, but he did not know how to save himself. If the confused knows to turn back, then he would not have gone too far on the way to being lost. I wish Your Majesty would investigate this."

The king of Wu said, "I, a man of little virtue, was sick for three months; during that time I have not heard a word from you, Prime Minister; this

88. *Jun* 鈞 was an ancient unit of weight. One *jun* is roughly 33 pounds.

shows that you, Prime Minister, are not benevolent. Moreover, you did not bring the food I am fond of and you were not concerned about me; this shows that you, Prime Minister, are not humane. If one as a subject is not benevolent and humane, how can people know he is loyal and trustworthy? The king of Yue was once lost and confused, but he forsook the matter of guarding the border and personally led his subjects to surrender to me, a man of little virtue; this shows his righteousness. He serves as a slave himself and his wife as a maid personally, but they were never resentful toward me, a man of little virtue. When I, a man of little virtue, was suffering from illness, he tasted my excrement with his own mouth; this shows his benevolence. He emptied his treasury, presented all his valuables but does not hold grudges; this shows his loyalty and trustworthiness. He has already possessed these three characteristics and has been serving me, a man of little virtue, with them. If I, a man of little virtue, followed you, Prime Minister, and killed him, I, a man of little virtue, am not acting wisely but simply satisfying your, Prime Minister, personal desire. Isn't this failing the will of heaven?"

Wu Zixu said, "How absurd are Your Majesty's words! If a tiger lowers its head, it is because the tiger is about to attack; if a wildcat presses down its body, it is because the cat will soon get what he desires. A pheasant is trapped in a net because it is dazzled by shining feathers; a fish dies on the hook for going after what intrigues it. Moreover, when Your Majesty began to resume your governing, you violated the ninth category described in the *Jade Gate*. This indeed indicates that things are bound to fail and there is no use in blaming anyone. It was on the *jiashu* day (28th day), in the third month of this year, that you resumed attending court, and the hours were at *yin* (3 to 5 a.m.) when the rooster crows. *Jiashu* is an inauspicious combining date after the Great *Yin* has passed;[89] it hinders you.[90] The Green Dragon is at *yiyou*,[91] which means the heavenly stem corresponds to the earth and the earthly branch corresponds to metal,[92] thus the *jiashu* day caused damage to your heavenly stem.[93] Therefore I know that a father will have an unfilial son and a ruler will have a traitorous subject. Your Majesty considers the submission of the

89. See *WYCQ* 5.12, 194n73 for the meaning of 歲後 (*suihou*).

90. An alternative reading of this sentence is: "On the *jiawu* day, the location of Jupiter will overlap with the movement of the third month at *Kui* constellation." See Huang Rensheng, 247.

91. The Green Dragon refers to Jupiter here.

92. 德 (*de*) refers to heavenly stems while 刑 (*xing*) refers to earthly branches. Jupiter was in the location of *yiyou*, therefore the heavenly stem is *yi*, which is associated with earth, and the earthly branch is *you*, which is associated with metal.

93. In Five Phases theory, *jia* is associated with wood. According to the overcoming theory, wood overcomes earth, therefore *jia* overcomes *yi*. Thus the heavenly stem of the day overcomes the heavenly stem of the year, this symbolizes that subordinates overcome superiors, and it is inauspicious.

king of Yue as righteous, his tasting your excrement as benevolent, his emptying his treasury as humane. I, nevertheless, because of these actions believe that he never loved his people and thus should not be close to you. But you listened to the words he put on, saw his false expression, and saved his life. Moreover, that the king of Yue came to Wu and served as a slave is because of his artful stratagem: that he emptied his treasury without showing any resentful expression means he is deceiving Your Majesty; that he drank Your Majesty's urine below is in fact eating Your Majesty's heart above; that he tasted your excrement below is indeed devouring Your Majesty's liver above. How devious is the king of Yue's worship of Wu! Wu will be conquered by him. I wish Your Majesty would pay attention and investigate him. I, your subject, dare not run away from a death sentence and thus betray the former king. Once the altars of earth and grain have become ruins and thorns grow in the ancestral temple, is there any use in repenting?"

The king of Wu said, "The prime minister should put this aside and not speak about it again. I, a man of little virtue, cannot bear to hear this again."

7.14. 於是遂赦越王歸國，送於蛇門之外，群臣祖道。吳王曰：「寡人赦君，使其返國，必念終始。王其勉之。」越王稽首曰：「今大王哀臣孤窮，使得生全還國，與種蠡之徒，願死於轂下。上天蒼蒼，臣不敢負。」吳王曰：「於乎！吾聞：『君子一言不再。』今已行矣，王勉之。」越王再拜跪伏，吳王乃引越王登車，范蠡執御，遂去。至三津之上，仰天歎，淚下沾襟，曰：「嗟乎！孤之屯厄，誰念復生渡此津也？」謂范蠡曰：「今三月甲辰，時加日昳，孤蒙上天之命，還歸故鄉，得無後患乎？」范蠡曰：「大王勿疑，直視道行。越將有福，吳當有憂。」至浙江之上，望見大越，山川重秀，天地再清。王與夫人歎曰：「吾已絕望，永辭萬民，豈料再還，重復鄉國？」言竟掩面，涕泣闌干。此時萬姓咸歡，群臣畢賀。

7.14. The king of Wu then freed the king of Yue and allowed him to return to his state. He saw him off outside of the Snake Gate and his ministers set up a farewell dinner. The king of Wu said, "I, a man of little virtue, pardoned you, sir, and let you return to your state; you must forever keep this in mind. I wish Your Majesty to try your best to do this." The king of Yue lowered his head to the ground and said, "Today Your Majesty pities me, your subject, being lonely and desperate, and lets me preserve my life and return to my state. I, together with my ministers Wen Zhong and Fan Li, am willing to die for you. May the grand heaven be my witness; I, your subject, dare not betray you." The king of Wu said, "Alas! I have heard that a gentleman does not make the same promise twice. You should have already departed. I wish

Your Majesty to try your best." The king of Yue bowed twice and prostrated himself on the ground. The king of Wu then supported the king of Yue in ascending into the carriage; with Fan Li serving as the driver, the king of Yue then departed. When the king arrived at the ferry on the bank where three rivers merged, he looked up to the sky and sighed. His tears dropped down and wet his clothing, and he said, "Alas, I, the orphan, was in difficulty and adversity, who would have thought I would have survived and am about to cross on this ferry again!" He spoke to Fan Li, saying, "Today is the *jiachen* day of the third month and the hours are at *wei* (1 to 3 p.m.).[94] I, the orphan, received the mandate from the heaven above and return to my homeland. I hope there will not be any future worries!" Fan Li said, "Your Majesty should not be confused. Look at the path ahead and follow the road. Yue will be fortunate and Wu will have trouble." When they arrived at the Zhe River, they saw in the distance the vast land of Yue, where mountains and rivers once more presented beauty, heaven and earth became clean and bright again. The king of Yue and his wife sighed, saying, "We had already given up hope and thought we would never see the people again. We did not expect to come back again and return to our village and state." After saying this, they covered their faces and tears fell down abundantly. At this moment, the king's people were all full of joy; his ministers all came to congratulate him.

---

94. This cannot be the same third month. There must be a mistake here. The *jiachen* day is thirty days after the *jiawu* day.

# 吳越春秋勾踐歸國外傳第八

## CHAPTER 8

# The Outer Tradition of Goujian's Return to His State

## Introduction

The theme of this chapter is Goujian's reconstruction of Yue, covering the two- or three-year period after he returned from his time as a captive in Wu. The chapter opens with the people of Yue welcoming Goujian's return and encouraging him to strive to become a hegemon. This sets the tone for the whole chapter; the paragraphs are therefore organized around Goujian's efforts to rebuild Yue, reform his governance, and plan revenge against Wu.

Goujian's rejuvenation of the state clearly resembles what we have already seen in the chapter concerning King Helü in the *WYCQ*. Interestingly, both Goujian and Helü's paths to hegemony begin with the construction of their capital cities, designed and supervised by their chief advisors, Fan Li and Wu Zixu, respectively.

Goujian's efforts in reviving his state also involve governmental reform, bribing Wu, and seeking revenge upon his rival, Fuchai. The chapter uses both dialogues and descriptions to present Goujian's strategies to the reader. The tone of this chapter is no longer depressive and sorrowful as in the previous chapter that recounted Goujian's captivity in Wu. Instead, the sentences in this chapter are usually short and thus the pace of the narrative is fast, creating a bright and positive feeling. The words of Goujian's ministers also display strong confidence.

Influences from a variety of modes of philosophical thought popular from pre-Qin to Han times are also reflected in this chapter. The most apparent are still the Han *yinyang* and Five Phases ideas, which serve as the reference for the auspicious hour for Goujian's return to the state and the right date for Goujian to resume his rule, as well as providing the guiding principle in constructing the Yue capital city. Another important Han political school, Huanglao, is apparent in Wen Zhong's response to Goujian on the question of proper governance. The lengthy conversations between Goujian and his ministers on policies for dealing with Wu clearly demonstrate the characteristics of the military strategist school that was popular during the Warring States period.

## Translation

8.1. 越王勾踐臣吳，至歸越，勾踐七年也。百姓拜之於道，曰：「君王獨無苦矣！今王受天之福，復於越國，霸王之跡，自斯而起。」王曰：「寡人不慎天教，無德於民，今勞萬姓擁於岐路，將何德化以報國人？」顧謂范蠡曰：「今十有二月，己巳之日，時加禺中，孤欲以此到國，何如？」蠡曰：「大王且留，以臣卜日。」於是范蠡進曰：「異哉，大王之擇日也！王當疾趨，車馳人走。」越王策馬飛輿，遂復宮闕。吳封地百里於越，東至炭瀆，西止周宗，南造於山，北薄於海。

8.1. Goujian, the king of Yue, served as a servant in Wu; when he returned to Yue it was already the seventh year after he had been enthroned (490 BCE). The people saluted him on the road, saying, "Our lord finally is free from hardship. Now Your Majesty has received a blessing from heaven and returned to the state of Yue. Your path toward becoming a hegemon starts from here." The king said, "I, a man of little virtue, was not cautious in following the command of heaven and have not left any benignity for the people. Now I have troubled people from ten thousand households who crowd onto the crossroads, what kind deeds should I do in order to repay the people of my state?" He looked back and told Fan Li, "Today is the *yisi* day (27th day) in the twelfth month, and the hours are in *si* (9 to 11 a.m.). I, the orphan, want to arrive at the capital during these times, how can I do this?" Fan Li said, "Your Majesty, please give me a moment and let me, your subject, make a divination on the date." After he had done so, Fan Li walked toward the king and said, "How unique is the date Your Majesty chose.[1]

---

1. According to the "tianwen xun" 天文訓 chapter in *Huainanzi*, *chen* suggests fullness and *si* implies balance, together they indicate survival and generating (辰為滿，巳為平，主生). See Zhang Jue, 234n5.

Your Majesty should immediately race in the chariot and have the attendants run." The king of Yue then whipped his horses and sped up his chariot; he then returned to the palace. Wu had granted over a hundred *li* of land to Yue, which stretched east from Tandu, west to Zhouzong,[2] south to Mount Gousheng,[3] and north, close to the East Sea.

8.2. 越王謂范蠡曰：「孤獲辱連年，勢足以死，得相國之策，再返南鄉。今欲定國立城，人民不足，其功不可以興。為之柰何？」范蠡對曰：「唐虞卜地，夏殷封國，古公營城周雒，威折萬里，德致八極，豈直欲破彊敵，收鄰國乎？」越王曰：「孤不能承前君之制，修德自守，亡眾，棲於會稽之山，請命乞恩，受辱被恥，囚結吳宮。幸來歸國，追以百里之封，將遵前君之意，復於會稽之上，而宜釋吳之地。」范蠡曰：「昔公劉去邰，而德彰於夏；亶父讓地，而名發於岐。今大王欲國樹都，并敵國之境，不處平易之都，據四達之地，將焉立霸王之業？」越王曰：「寡人之計未有決定。欲築城立郭，分設里閭，欲委屬於相國。」

8.2. The king of Yue spoke to Fan Li, saying, "I, an orphan, suffered humiliation in the past years and the situation was severe enough to end my life. Fortunately I was assisted by your plan and am able to return to my home in the south. Now I want to settle the capital and erect the city wall, but I do not have enough manpower, so the project cannot be carried out. What can I do about it?" Fan Li responded, saying, "Yao and Shun chose capitals by means of divination,[4] Yu and Tang piled up earth to make their borders, and Gugong Danfu built a city at Zhou.[5] Their authority caused people to submit from ten thousand *li* away and their virtues reached to the most distant places in the eight directions. They did not simply want to destroy a strong enemy and conquer the neighboring states." The king of Yue said, "Our previous lord Wuyu set the capital on the south side of Mount Qinwang; the altar of earth, the altar of grain, and the ancestral temple on the south bank of the lake.[6] I did not continue the policies of the former king, did not

2. Both places are in modern-day Shaoxing 紹興, Zhejiang Province.

3. In modern-day Zhuji 諸暨, Zhejiang Province.

4. This refers to Yao and Shun choosing capital locations to avoid the flood.

5. Yu is the founder of the Xia dynasty and Tang established the Shang dynasty. Gugong Danfu was the ancestor of the Zhou people; his story is also mentioned in *WYCQ*, 1.3. Gugong Danfu led his people and relocated from Bin 豳 to Mount Qi 岐山 because of the attacks from the Rong and Di tribes. They finally settled at Zhouyuan 周原 at the foot of Mount Qi and were thus called the Zhou people. Luoyang was the capital of Eastern Zhou and was built by Duke Zhou, not by Gugong Danfu.

6. This sentence is not found in extant *WYCQ*. Xu Naichang 徐乃昌 (1869–1946) added this sentence based upon a *WYCQ* quotation found in *Shuijing zhu*. Xu Naichang is certainly correct,

cultivate my virtue and protect myself; I caused the people to flee and I hid on Mount Kuaiji,[7] begging for my life to be spared and beseeching favors from others. I suffered humiliation and endured shame and was imprisoned at the palace in Wu. Fortunately I returned to my state; and the king of Wu gave me one hundred *li* of land as redemption. I will follow the will of my former king and return to Mount Kuaiji. I therefore should give up the land Wu gave me." Fan Li said, "In the past, Gongliu left Tai but his virtue was illustrated in Xia,[8] Gugong Danfu yielded land and his reputation began to spread from Qi.[9] Now Your Majesty wants to settle his capital and erect the city, giving up the land from the enemy. If you do not settle in a flat place, with an easily accessible city that is central to all directions, how will you accomplish your goal of being a hegemon?" The king of Yue said, "I, a man of little virtue, have not decided my plan. I want to build the inner city and set up the outer wall, divide the districts and alleys. I would like to entrust this to you, Prime Minister."

8.3. 於是范蠡乃觀天文，擬法於紫宮，築作小城，周千一百二十二步，一圓三方。西北立龍飛翼之樓，以象天門，東南伏漏石竇，以象地戶；陵門四達，以象八風。外郭築城而缺西北，示服事吳也，不敢壅塞，內以取吳，故缺西北，而吳不知也。北向稱臣，委命吳國，左右易處，不得其位，明臣屬也。城既成而怪山自生者，琅琊東武海中山也。一夕自來，故名怪山。范蠡曰：「臣之築城也，其應天矣，崑崙之象存焉。」越王曰：「寡人聞崑崙之山，乃天地之柱，上承皇天，氣吐宇內，下處后土，稟受無外。滋聖生神，嘔養帝會。故帝處其陽陸，三王居其正地。吾之國也，扁天地之壤，乘東南之維，斗去極北。非糞土之城，何能與王者比隆盛哉？」范蠡曰：「君徒見外，未見於內。臣乃承天門制城，合氣於后土，嶽象已設，崑崙故出。越之霸也。」越王曰：「苟如相國之言，孤之命也。」范蠡曰：「天地卒號，以著其實。」名東武，起游臺其上。東南為司馬門，立增樓，冠其山巔，以為靈臺。起離宮於淮陽，中

---

considering the logic between the added sentence and Goujian's words that follow. See both Zhang Jue, 235; Huang Rensheng, 258n12.

7. A Song dynasty edition of *WYCQ* has 毀軍 (*huijun*), "army to collapse," after 亡衆 (*wangzhong*), "people to flee." See Zhang Jue, 235; Huang Rensheng, 258n13.

8. Gongliu was also an ancestor of the Zhou people. Gongliu lived first in Tai in modern-day Wugong County, Shaanxi Province, and was forced to relocate to Bin because of the political trouble among the Xia people. The poem "Gongliu" in the *Book of Songs* praises Gongliu's leadership and his decision to relocate his people. The story of Gongliu is also mentioned in *WYCQ*, 1.1.

9. According to legend, Gugong Danfu was attacked by the neighboring Rong and Di and moved from Bin to Mount Qi. The people of Bin all followed him and many tribes also considered him their leader. His son Taibo became the founder of Wu. See *Shiji*, 4:113–14. See also *WYCQ*, 1.3.

宿臺在於高平，駕臺在於成丘，立苑於樂野，燕臺在於石室，齋臺在於襟山。勾踐之出游也，休息石台，食於冰廚。

8.3. Fan Li then observed the pattern of the stars; he imitated the *ziwei* constellation and built a small city.[10] The perimeter was one thousand one hundred and twenty two paces, with one round and three square corners. On the northwest side a tower was erected with roofs bent like birds' wings, symbolizing the heavenly gate.[11] At the foot of the southeast corner a stone water drainage channel was built, symbolizing the earthly entrance. All gates on the ground faced in one of the four directions, symbolizing the eight winds.[12] A wall was built to form the outer city but left the northwest corner open; this was to show that Yue served Wu as a subject and dared not set up any defense. However, in their hearts, this gap left on the northwest corner was intended to symbolize the conquest of Wu, but Wu was not aware of this. Yue declared itself a vassal to Wu to the north and entrusted its fate to Wu, therefore it switched the left and right sides of the city and placed the buildings in inappropriate places, in order to show that Yue belonged to Wu. After the construction of the city had been completed, a strange mountain appeared by itself.[13] It was a mountain from the sea near Dongwu County in Langye Commandery.[14] It arrived one night and was thus named Mount Strange.[15] Fan Li said, "I, your subject, constructed this city probably in accordance with the will of heaven; so the pattern of Mount Kunlun is

---

10. Ancient Chinese astronomers divide the celestial sphere into asterisms or constellations, which are further divided into four groups: the Twenty-Eight Mansions (*ershiba xiu* 二十八宿) along the ecliptic, and the Three Enclosures (*sanyuan* 三垣) of the northern sky. The *ziwei* constellation (the Purple Forbidden Enclosure) is one of the Three Enclosures and is believed to be the palace of the High God, which corresponds to the ruler's palace in the human world. For more information on Chinese constellations, see Joseph Needham, "Astronomy in Ancient and Medieval China," *Philosophical Transactions of the Royal Society of London, series A, Mathematical and Physical Sciences* 276, no. 1257 (1974): 67–82. See also Xiaochun Sun and Jacob Kistemaker, *The Chinese Sky During the Han: Constellating Stars and Society*, Sinica Leidensia 38 (Leiden: Brill, 1997).

11. A *Taiping yulan* quotation of *WYCQ* contains the following sentence after this: "Two small dragon shapes were made entwining the ends of the ridge, symbolizing dragon horns." (為兩蟉繞棟，以象龍角). See Zhang Jue, 237.

12. Xu Naichang reads 陵門 (*lingmen*) as 陸門 (*lumen*), "gate on the ground." Huang Rensheng interprets 陵 as "tall." See Huang Rensheng, 259n30. However, in *Yue jue shu*, the "dizhuan" (Tradition on geography of Yue) chapter records that Goujian's small city has "four ground gates and one water gate" (陸門四，水門一). Xu Naichang's reading is probably correct. For the *Yue jue shu* record, see Li Bujia, 222. For the meaning of "eight winds," see *WYCQ*, 4.2n11.

13. 生 (*sheng*), "to grow," should be a mistake for 至 (*zhi*), "to come, to arrive".

14. Langye Commandery is in modern-day Jiaonan 膠南 and Zhucheng 諸城 counties in Shandong 山東 Province.

15. A *Taiping yulan* quotation of *WYCQ* contains more description of this mountain: "It arrived one night by itself; the people felt strange about it and thus named it Mount Strange. Its shape resembled that of a turtle and thus it was also called Mount Turtle." See Huang Rensheng, 259n37.

found in it."[16] The king of Yue said, "I, a man of little virtue, have heard that Mount Kunlun is the primary pillar between heaven and earth. Above, it holds the great heaven and circulates *qi* in the universe. Below, it is the dwelling of the god of earth and there is nothing it does not support. It gives birth to sages, produces gods; and it is the hub that cultivates and nourishes emperors. Thus the Five Lords resided on its south land while the Three Kings lived in front of it.[17] As for our state, it is in a remote place between heaven and earth, located at the southeast corner, and the Northern Dipper and the Pole Star are faraway in the north.[18] Isn't it a humble city? How can it compare in prosperity with the city where the kings lived?" Fan Li said, "My lord has only seen the outside but not the inside. I, your subject, modeled it after the heavenly gate when constructing this city; it also combines the *qi* of the earthly god. The pattern of great mountains has already been set up so the pattern of Mount Kunlun appears from it; this shows Yue will become a hegemon." The king of Yue said, "If indeed it is what you, Prime Minister, just said, this is then my, the orphan's, fate." Fan Li said, "Any object between heaven and earth needs a title in order to indicate its substance." He then named the strange mountain Mount Dongwu and built a touring terrace on it. Southeast of it he built Sima Gate and added buildings on it, such as the Spiritual Terrace. A temporary palace was constructed in Huaiyang. Zhongsu Terrace was built in Gaoping, Jia Terrace in Chengqiu, a hunting garden in Yueli, Yan Terrace in Shishi, and Zhai Terrace on Mount Ji. When Goujian went out on excursions, he rested at Yan Terrace and dined from the larder.[19]

8.4. 越王乃召相國范蠡、大夫種、大夫郢問曰：「孤欲以今日上明堂，臨國政，專恩致令，以撫百姓，何日可矣？惟三聖紀綱維持。」范蠡曰：「今日丙午日也。丙，陽將也。是日吉矣，又因良時，臣愚以為可。無始有終，得天下之中。」大夫種曰：「前車已覆，後車必戒。願王深察。」范蠡曰：「夫子故不一二見也。吾王今以

16. Mount Kunlun is in modern-day Xinjiang 新疆. In early Chinese myth, Mount Kunlun is where the gods live.

17. Here *di* 帝 should be *wudi* 五帝, "Five Lords," as 五帝 usually appears in parallel with mention of *sanwang* 三王, "Three Kings" — *sanwang wudi*. There are different theories as to whom the Five Lords refer to. Some believe they represent the Yellow Emperor, Zhuanxu, Lord Ku 帝嚳, Yao, and Shun; others argue that they are Fuxi 伏羲, Shennong 神農, Yellow Emperor, Yao, and Shun. The same controversy applies to the Three Kings as well. They can be either Yu, Tang, and King Wen of Zhou; or Yu, Tang, and King Wu of Zhou.

18. The *dou* 斗 constellation is one of the seven northern constellations and it marks the border between Wu and Yue in Chinese astronomy. The Northern Dipper and the Pole Star were believed to be located in the middle of the sky and thus symbolized authority. For example, in the *Analects*, Confucius says that "one who rules through the power of Virtue is analogous to the Pole Star: it simply remains in its place and receives the homage of the myriad lesser stars." See Confucius, *Analects*, 8.

19. This is a cellar stored with ice in order to preserve food.

丙午復初臨政，解救其本，是一宜；夫金制始，而火救其終，是二宜；蓄金之憂，轉而及水，是三宜；君臣有差，不失其理，是四宜；王相俱起，天下立矣，是五宜。臣願急升明堂臨政。」越王是日立政，翼翼小心。出不敢奢，入不敢侈。

8.4. The king of Yue then summoned Prime Minister Fan Li, Grand Minister Wen Zhong, and Grand Minister Zhuqi Ying and asked them, "Now I, the orphan, want to ascend the Bright Hall to govern the state affairs,[20] bestow benevolence and issue orders,[21] thus to settle the people. Which day is appropriate for this? I wish you, my three sagely ministers,[22] to assist me in planning and managing governmental affairs." Fan Li said, "Today is day *bingwu* (22nd day). Because *bing* is the chief general of *yang*, it is an auspicious day.[23] Moreover, the hours are lucky too; I, your subject, foolishly believe it is appropriate. It has a completion even though it does not have a beginning; and it stays in the center of the world."[24] Grand Minister Wen Zhong said, "The overturning of the carriage ahead offers lessons to those that follow.[25] I wish Your Majesty would thoroughly investigate it." Fan Li said, "You, sir, indeed see less than one or two parts of the whole picture. Our majesty resumes governance today, a *bingwu* day, in order to save the root of Yue; this is the first proper reason.[26] The beginning day was

---

20. The Bright Hall is the central building in the palace where rulers in ancient times held court meetings, offered sacrifices, and performed other important state ceremonies. The term *mingtang* 明堂 was first mentioned in the "kaogong ji" 考功記 chapter in *Zhouli* 周禮 (*Rites of Zhou*).

21. Both *Taiping yulan* and *Yiwen leiju* 藝文類聚 quotations contain 布 (*bu*), "to bestow," instead of 專 (*zhuan*), "to focus, to be in charge of." See Zhang Jue, 241; Huang Rensheng, 263n3.

22. Referring to Wen Zhong, Fan Li, and Zhuqi Ying. 聖臣 (*shengchen*) means "sagely minister." The "chendao" 臣道 (The way to be a minister) chapter in *Xunzi* explains that a "sagely minister" is one who "can revere his lord above while also being able to care for the people below. His governmental orders and educational influence take form among his subordinates like a shadow following a body. He adapts completely to unexpected occurrences and changes as quickly as an echo following a sound. He knows how to extend categories and connect types in order to handle cases without a precedent. In every area, he brings about the phenomena of order." (上则能尊君，下则能爱民，政令教化，刑下如影，应卒遇变，齐给如响，推类接誉，以待无方，曲成制象，是圣臣者也) See *Xunzi*, trans. Eric L. Hutton (Princeton: Princeton University Press, 2014), 133.

23. In *yinyang* theory, the days of *jia*, *bing*, *wu*, *geng* 庚, and *ren* 壬 are considered *yang* days and the hours of *zi*, *yin*, *chen*, *wu*, *shen*, and *xu* are defined as *yang* hours. The date *bingwu* therefore contains both the *yang* day and the *yang* hour; it is purely *yang* so is called the "general of *yang*."

24. In ancient times, the hours were marked by the twelve earthly branches, which begin from *zi* and end with *hai*. The current hour is *wu*, which is the seventh branch, located in the middle of the twelve branches.

25. This appears to be a popular saying in early China. It can be found in the chapter "chengxiang" 成相 in *Xunzi*, the "lianyu" 連語 chapter in *Xinshu*, and Cai Yong's 蔡邕 biography in *Hou Hanshu*. See Wang Xianqian, *Xunzi jijie* 荀子集解 (Beijing: Zhonghua shuju, 2015), 550; Yan Zhenyi and Zhong Xia, *Xinshu jiaoshu*, 198; and *Hou Hanshu* 60:1986.

26. *Bing* is the general of *yang*. *Wu* is associated with peace and settlement. In Five Phases theory, *bingwu* is associated with fire, south, brightness, and kingship, thus it is auspicious to resume governance on a *bingwu* day.

the day before today, which corresponds to metal, and *bingwu* corresponds to fire, which saves another day of metal, the final day after today; this is the second proper reason.[27] The concern of accumulating the virtue of metal is overturned by the virtue of water; this is the third proper reason.[28] There are hierarchical differences between the ruler and the ministers yet the appropriate ritual is not neglected; this is the fourth proper reason. The king and the prime minister all rise up from difficulties, the order of the world can be established; this is the fifth proper reason. I, your subject, wish your majesty to hurriedly ascend the Bright Hall and govern." The king of Yue administered the government on that day. He was very cautious,[29] and did not dare to be lavish when going out or to be extravagant when staying inside.

8.5. 越王念復吳讎非一旦也，苦身勞心，夜以接日。目臥，則攻之以蓼；足寒，則漬之以水。冬常抱冰，夏還握火。愁心苦志，懸膽於戶，出入嘗之，不絕於口。中夜潸泣，泣而復嘯。於是群臣咸曰：「君王何愁心之甚？夫復讎謀故，非君王之憂，自臣下急務也。」

8.5. There had not been one day that the king of Yue had not thought about revenge against Wu. He exerted his body and exhausted his mind working day and night. When his eyes were tired he stimulated them with smartweed. When his feet were cold he warmed them with water. In winter time he often embraced ice; in summer time he nevertheless held fire. In order to keep his mind on revenge and sharpen his will, he hung a gallbladder at the door and never was there a time he did not lick it when going in or out of the door. He often cried silently at midnight and then moaned afterwards. His many ministers then said, "Why has our lord been troubled

27. *Shi* 始 refers to *zi* day, as *zi* is the beginning earthly branch. The *zi* day before *bingwu* is a *gengzi* 庚子 day. *Geng* is associated with metal, thus Fan Li says that the date begins with metal. The last of the twelve branches is *hai* 亥. The *hai* day after *bingwu* is *xinhai* 辛亥. *Xin* is also associated with metal. Because in Five Phases theory metal is related to weapons and therefore killing, it is not auspicious. However, *bingwu* corresponds to fire and in the overcoming theory fire overcomes metal, so *bingwu* then "saves" the inauspicious *gengzi* and *xinhai*.

28. Because the beginning and final dates are all associated with metal and killing, these cause worry. However, the day after *xinhai* is *renzi* 壬子, which corresponds to water, and for this reason Fan Li says it is overturned by water. In Five Phases theory, water is associated with north and harvest and is auspicious.

29. There is a reference to 翼翼小心 (*yiyi xiaoxin*) in the poem "Daming" 大明 in the *Book of Songs*, which describes King Wen of Zhou in the following lines: "This king Wen, watchfully and reverently, with his entire intelligence served God, and so secured the great blessing. His virtue was without deflection; and in consequence he received [the allegiance of] the States from all quarters." (維此文王、小心翼翼。昭事上帝、聿懷多福。厥德不回、以受方國) Translation adapted from Legge, *The She King*, 236.

so much? As for seeking revenge and planning against the foe, these are not the concerns of our lord but indeed the urgent tasks of his subordinates."

8.6. 越王曰：「吳王好服之離體，吾欲采葛，使女工織細布獻之，以求吳王之心，於子何如？」群臣曰：「善。」乃使國中男女入山采葛，以作黃絲之布，欲獻之。

未及遣使，吳王聞越王盡心自守，食不重味，衣不重綵，雖有五臺之游，未嘗一日登翫。「吾欲因而賜之以書，增之以封，東至於勾甬，西至於檇李，南至於姑末，北至於平原，縱橫八百餘里。」

越王乃使大夫種索葛布十萬，甘蜜九党，文笥七枚，狐皮五雙，晉竹十廋，以復封禮。

吳王得之曰：「以越僻狄之國無珍，今舉其貢貨而以復禮，此越小心念功，不忘吳之效也。夫越，本興國千里，吾雖封之，未盡其國。」子胥聞之，退臥於舍，謂侍者曰：「吾君失其石室之囚，縱於南林之中，今但因虎豹之野而與荒外之草，於吾之心，其無損也？」

吳王得葛布之獻，乃復增越之封，賜羽毛之飾、机杖、諸侯之服。越國大悅。

采葛之婦，傷越王用心之苦，乃作苦之詩，曰：「葛不連蔓棻台台，我君心苦命更之。嘗膽不苦甘如飴，令我采葛以作絲。女工織兮不敢遲。弱於羅兮輕霏霏，號絺素兮將獻之。越王悅兮忘罪除，吳王歡兮飛尺書。增封益地賜羽奇，机杖茵褥諸侯儀。群臣拜舞天顏舒，我王何憂能不移？」

8.6. The king of Yue said, "The king of Wu is fond of clothes that are loosely cut. I plan to collect kudzu and let the maids weave them into fine clothes and present them to him, thus to gain favor from the king of Wu.[30] What do you gentlemen think?" The many ministers said, "Excellent!" The king of Yue then sent men and women in his state to go to the mountains to collect kudzus and used them to make clothes with yellow fibers.[31] He planned to present them to the king of Wu.

Before he had time to send the emissary, the king of Wu had already heard that the king of Yue was full-heartedly content with his situation and

30. Kudzu fiber can be used to make cloth. The making of kudzu cloth can be dated back to high antiquity. Pieces of kudzu cloth were found in a Neolithic site in Caoxieshan 草鞋山 near Suzhou 蘇州. See Nanjing Museum 南京博物院, "Jiangsu Wuxian Caoxieshan yizhi" 江苏吴县草鞋山遗址, *Wenwu ziliao congkan* 文物资料丛刊, no. 3 (1980): 1–24. *Hanfeizi* describes the legendary Yao as wearing deerskin in winter and kudzu clothes in summer. The *Zhouli* also mentions an official in charge of kudzu cloth (*zhangge* 掌葛). In the *Book of Songs* there is a love song titled "Caige" 采葛 (Gathering kudzu). See Chen Qiyou, 1041. See also Sun Yirang, 1214–15. For the *Book of Songs* poem, see Legge, *The She King*, 120.

31. *Yue jue shu* identifies this mountain as *geshan* 葛山, Mount Kudzu. See Li Bujia, 226.

that he never ate more than two kinds of food at a time,[32] never wore cloth made of more than two different fibers; though he had five terraces to tour, there was never a day he ascended them for enjoyment. The king of Wu said, "I would like to send him a letter because of this and increase his fief east to Gouyong,[33] west to Zuili,[34] south to Gumo, and north to Pingyuan,[35] a region that spans more than eight hundred *li*."

The king of Yue thereupon sent Grand Minister Wen Zhong, who delivered ten thousand rolls of cloth made of kudzu, nine buckets of sweet honey, seven decorated square bamboo containers,[36] five sets of fox fur, and ten boats of arrow bamboo as gifts to repay the king of Wu for increasing his fief.[37]

The king of Wu received the gifts and said, "I thought Yue was a remote and small state that did not have valuables,[38] but now it has exhausted its tributary articles in order to repay my favor. This is a demonstration that the king of Yue sincerely remembers my kindness and dares not to forget Wu. Yue was a thousand *li* wide when its state was established. Although I have granted him some lands, I have not completely reinstalled its territory." Hearing this, Wu Zixu returned from the court and lay down at home. Talking to his attendant, he said, "Our lord released the criminal jailed in the stone chamber and let him free in the forest south. Now if he only relies upon the wild where tigers and leopards roam and the plants from far remote areas, in my view he will not be able to cause any damage."[39]

After the king of Wu received the tribute of the kudzu clothes, he again added a fief to the king of Yue and bestowed upon him a feathered banner, a small table, a cane, and the dress of a lord.[40] Yue was greatly delighted.

---

32. This expression 食不重味 (*shibu chongwei*), "there is no more than one flavor consumed at a time," appears in many early texts including, for example, the "Shangren" 上仁 chapter in *Wenzi* 文子, the "Zhushu xun" 主朮訓 chapter in *Huainanzi*, *Shiji* "yuxia liezhuan" 遊俠列傳, and *Hanshu* "Xue Xuan Zhu Bo zhuan" 薛宣朱博傳.

33. In modern-day Zhoushan islands 舟山, Zhejiang Province. See *WYCQ* 5.25.

34. In modern-day Jiaxing County, Zhejiang Province. In 486 BCE, Yue defeated Wu in Zuili and Fuchai's father Helü died of injury during the battle. In 476 BCE, Fuchai was defeated by Goujian in Zuili and committed suicide. See *WYCQ*, 4.17 and 5.25.

35. Gumo is in modern-day Quzhou 衢州, Zhejiang Province. Pingyuan should be Wuyuan 武原, in modern-day Haiyan 海鹽, Zhejiang Province.

36. 笥 (*si*) is a square-shaped container for clothes or food; it is usually made of bamboo.

37. 廋 (*sou*), "to hide," should be 艘 (*sou*), which is a boat.

38. 狄 (*Di*), name of an ancient tribe, is a mistake for 狹 (*xia*), "narrow."

39. Meaning that Wu Zixu will consider Goujian dangerous if he relies upon his ministers instead of local products.

40. The small table was for seniors resting at home and the cane was for them to walk outside. Bestowing a small table and cane was a ritual of showing care and respect to the old. Since Goujian had defeated Fuchai's father in the battle at Zuili, there is a chance that Goujian is older than Fuchai.

The women collecting kudzu were sympathetic to the king of Yue's hard efforts and made a song titled "Poem of Great Effort," singing,[41]

The kudzu flowers connect with vine,
luxuriant and dense are they.[42]
Our lord lay himself out and fate changed him.
Tasting gall he did not complain it was bitter,
rather he felt it is as sweet as sugar.
He ordered us to collect kudzu and make string and thread.
The maids weaved and weaved,
and dared not to delay.[43]
The kudzu clothes were softer than silk
and so light that they whirled in the air.
They were named "refined white"[44]
and were ready to be presented to the king of Wu.
So delighted was the king of Yue
that he forgot that he was a released criminal.
The king of Wu enjoyed them
and sent a letter promptly.
He added to our king's fiefs and increased his land;
he bestowed upon him a feathered banner, small table,
cane, cushion, and dress of a lord.
The ministers bowed and danced in celebration;
smiles appeared on our king's face.
What worries of our king are there
that cannot be removed?

8.7. 於是越王內修其德，外布其道，君不名教，臣不名謀，民不名使，官不名事。國中蕩蕩，無有政令。越王內實府庫，墾其田疇，民富國彊，眾安道泰。越王遂師八臣與其四友，時問政焉。大夫種曰：「愛民而已。」越王曰：「柰何？」種曰：「利之無害，成之

41. *Taiping yulan* has different titles for this song: "ruohe zhige" 若何之歌 (Song of what to do) or "kuhe zhige" 苦何之歌 (Song of the cause of sorrow). See Zhang Jue, 245n16; Huang Rensheng, 266n19.

42. 不 (*bu*) is 柎 (*fu*), flower petal.

43. Xu Tianhu cites *Wenxuan* and argues that there is a line before this: "No time to eat even when we were hungry, and our four limbs were exhausted." 飢不遑食四體疲 (*ji bu huangshi siti pi*). See Zhang Jue, 246n19; Huang Rensheng, 277n22.

44. The poem "Getan" 葛覃 in the *Book of Songs* describes gathering kudzu and making both refined and coarse kudzu cloths (為絺為綌 *weichi weixi*). See Legge, *The She King*, 7.

無敗，生之無殺，與之無奪。」越王曰：「願聞。」種曰：「無奪民所好則利也，民不失其時則成之，省刑去罰則生之，薄其賦斂則與之，無多臺游則樂之，靜而無苛則喜之；民失所好則害之，農失其時則敗之，有罪不赦則殺之，重賦厚斂則奪之，多作臺游以罷民則苦之，勞擾民力則怒之，臣聞善為國者，遇民如父母之愛其子，如兄之愛其弟。聞有飢寒為之哀，見其勞苦為之悲。」越王乃緩刑薄罰，省其賦斂，於是人民殷富，皆有帶甲之勇。

8.7. The king of Yue thereupon cultivated his virtue at court; outside of court he publicized his way of governance: the ruler does not claim responsibility for educating the people,[45] the ministers do not say their duties are conceiving strategy, the people do not consider their work forced labor, and the officials do not regard their job as serving the ruler. Meanwhile, in the state, public matters took their own course and there were no policies or laws.[46] Within the state, the king of Yue filled the treasury and his weaponry warehouses,[47] and opened up land for farming; the people were rich and the state strong, the multitude was content and his governance was carried out. The king of Yue then took the eight ministers and their friends as his teachers and often asked them about governance.[48] Grand Minister Wen Zhong said, "The way of governing is simply to love the people." The king of Yue said, "What exactly should I do?" Wen Zhong replied, "Bring them benefit

45. 名 (*ming*), "name," is read here as 命 (*ming*), "to claim, to name."

46. This is saying that everything is in perfect order and runs its own course so there is no need to control the state and its people by laws.

47. 府 (*fu*) is "treasury" and 庫 (*ku*) usually refers to a weaponry warehouse.

48. The eight ministers are Wen Zhong, Fan Li, Kucheng, Yeyong, Hao, Zhuji Ying, Gaoru, and Ji Yan. They are the ministers to whom Goujian entrusted the state before he left for Wu and served as a slave there. See *WYCQ*, 7.2–7.4. 四友, "four friends," seems to be a popular term in Eastern Han texts. The "Wen Kong" 問孔 (Inquiry about Confucius) chapter in *Lunheng* says that Confucius has 四友, four students/friends, but does not specify who they are. *Fengsu tongyi* 風俗通義 mentions that Ran You is one of the four. Yan Yuan 顏淵, Zigong 子貢, Zizhang 子張, and Zilu 子路 are identified as the four in *Kongcongzi* 孔叢子. Later texts such as Zhang Hua's 張華 *Bowu zhi* 博物志 state that Nangong Kuo 南宮括, Sanyi Sheng 散宜生, Hong Yao 閎夭, and Taidian 太顛 are the four friends/advisors of King Wen. The term 四友 is further adopted between the time of Wei-Jin to Tang. *Sanguo zhi* 三國志 records Zhuge Ke 諸葛恪, Zhang Xiu 張休, Gu Tan 顧譚, and Chen Biao 陳表 as the four friends of Sun Deng 孫登, the heir apparent of Wu. *Jinshu* also mentions that Wang Yan 王衍 has four friends. *Xintang shu* 新唐書 reports that Cui Rong 崔融, Li Qiao 李嶠, Su Weidao 蘇味道, and Du Shenyan 杜審言 are called 四友. At the same time, the four treasured items people used in their studies—brush, ink, paper, and ink stone—are also called "the four friends in the study." Probably starting from Yuan, the pine tree, bamboo, plum tree, and orchid are grouped as the "four friends of winter" (*suihan siyou* 歲寒四友). See Huang Hui, *Lunheng jiaoshi*, 419; Wang Liqi 王利器, *Fengsu tongyi jiaozhu* 風俗通義校註 (Beijing: Zhonghua shuju, 2015), 245; Wang Junlin 王鈞林 and Zhou Haisheng 周海生, trans., *Kongcongzi* 孔叢子 (Beijing: Zhonghua shuju, 2012), 27; Zhu Hongjie 祝鴻傑, *Bowu zhi quanyi* 博物志全譯 (Guiyang: Guizhou renmin chubanshe, 1990), 140; Chen Shou 陳壽 *Sanguo zhi* 59:1363; Fang Xuanling, *Jinshu* 43:1239; Ouyang Xiu, *Xintang shu*, 201:5736.

instead of harming them, make them successful instead of failing them, allow them to survive instead of killing them, and provide for them instead of robbing them." The king of Yue said, "I would like to listen to more explanation." Wen Zhong answered, "Do not take away what the people like, this brings them benefit. Do not cause the people to miss the right season, this makes them successful. Reduce laws and free the people from punishment, this allows them to survive. Lessen their taxes, this benefits them. Do not build many terraces for entertainment, this makes them joyful. Be peaceful and not relentless, this makes them happy. If the people lose what they like, then they are harmed. If the peasants miss the seasons, then they are failed. If they commit crimes but are not pardoned, then they are killed. If they are heavily taxed and levied, then they are robbed. If the ruler builds many terraces and entertains on them so that he exhausts the people, then they suffer. If the people's strength is exhausted and disturbed, then they are angry. I, your subject, have heard that those who are good at governing treat the people in the same way as parents loving their sons and older brothers loving their younger brothers, who feel sorrowful when they hear they are hungry and cold, feel saddened when seeing they are tired and suffering." The king of Yue therefore loosened the law, lessened the punishment, and reduced the taxes. Because of this the people prospered, and they were all brave enough to wear armor and fight.

8.8. 九年正月，越王召五大夫而告之曰：「昔者越國遁棄宗廟，身為窮虜，恥聞天下，辱流諸侯。今寡人念吳，猶躄者不忘走，盲者不忘視。孤未知策謀，惟大夫誨之。」

扶同曰：「昔者亡國流民，天下莫不聞知。今欲有計，不宜前露其辭。臣聞：『擊鳥之動，故前俯伏，猛獸將擊，必餌毛帖伏；鷙鳥將搏，必卑飛戢翼；聖人將動，必順辭和眾。』聖人之謀，不可見其象，不可知其情。臨事而伐，故前無剽過之兵，後無伏襲之患。今大王臨敵破吳，宜損少辭，無令泄也。臣聞吳王兵彊於齊晉，而怨結於楚。大王宜親於齊，深結於晉，陰固於楚，而厚事於吳。夫吳之志猛，驕而自矜，必輕諸侯而凌鄰國。三國決權，還為敵國，必角勢交爭。越承其弊，因而伐之，可克也。雖五帝之兵，無以過此。」

范蠡曰：「臣聞：『謀國破敵，動觀其符。』孟津之會，諸侯曰可，武土辭之。方今吳楚結讎，構怨不解，齊雖不親，外為其救；晉雖不附，猶效其義。夫內臣謀而決讎其策，鄰國通而不絕其援，斯正吳之興霸，諸侯之上尊。臣聞：『峻高者隤，葉茂者摧，日中則移，月滿則虧，四時不並盛，五行不俱馳，陰陽更唱，氣有盛衰。故溢堤之水，不淹其量，熻乾之火，不復其熾；水靜則無漚瀴之怒，火消則無熹毛之熱。』今吳乘諸侯之威，以號令於天下，不知德薄而恩淺，道狹而怨廣，權懸而智衰，力竭而威折，兵挫而軍退，士散而眾解。臣請按師整兵，待其壞敗，隨而襲之，兵不血刃，士不旋踵，吳之君臣為虜矣。臣願大王匿聲，無見其動，以觀其靜。」

大夫苦成曰：「夫水能浮草木，亦能沉之；地能生萬物，亦能殺之；江海能下谿谷，亦能朝之；聖人能從眾，亦能使之。今吳承闔閭之軍制，子胥之典教，政平未虧，戰勝未敗。大夫嚭者，狂佞之人，達於策慮，輕於朝事；子胥力於戰伐，死於諫議。二人權，必有壞敗。願王虛心自匿，無示謀計，則吳可滅矣。」

大夫浩曰：「今吳，君驕臣奢，民飽軍勇；外有侵境之敵，內有爭臣之震，其可攻也。」

大夫句如曰：「天有四時，人有五勝。昔湯武乘四時之利而制夏殷，桓繆據五勝之便而列六國。此乘其時而勝者也。」

王曰：「未有四時之利，五勝之便，願各就職也。」

8.8. In the ninth year (488 BCE), first month, the king of Yue summoned his five ministers and told them, "Previously the state of Yue abandoned the ancestral temple and fled. I, myself, became a desperate prisoner. All in the world have heard about my humiliation and the story of my shame was spread among the lords. Now I, a man of little virtue, desire to seek revenge against Wu, just like a cripple cannot forget about running,[49] a blind man cannot forget about seeing. I, the orphan, do not know the scheme and strategy and I wish you ministers to instruct me on this."

Futong said, "Previously our state was destroyed and people drifted away; none in the world did not know about this. If now we want to make any plan we should not reveal any words. I, your subject, have heard that when a fighting bird moves, it first lowers its body on the ground; when a fierce wild beast is about to strike, it will contract its fur and lies flat on the ground tamely; when a bird of prey is about to fight, it will certainly fly low and fold its wings; and when a sage is about to act, he definitely will use smooth words and bond with people. As for the planning of a sage, no one can see its trace and know its details. The sage attacks just before the battle begins, thus before him there are no troops to check him and no worry of being ambushed afterwards. Now Your Majesty faces your foe and wants to destroy Wu, you'd better speak less about it, and thus not let it become exposed. I, your subject, have heard that the king of Wu is using his troops to struggle

49. 躃 (*bi*), "unable to walk." The "Wangzhi" 王制 chapter in the *Liji* states that "the mute, the deaf, the crippled, unable to walk, mutilated, and dwarf were all fed in accordance with what work they fit" (瘖、聾、跛、躃、斷者、侏儒，百工各以其器食之). See Sun Xidan, 388.

for hegemony against Qi and Jin;[50] he is also at odds with Chu. Your Majesty should be close to Qi, make strong connections with Jin, secretly strengthen our relationship with Chu and serve Wu lavishly. The king of Wu is fierce, arrogant, and conceited, he will definitely slight the many lords and bully neighboring states. The three states, Qi, Jin, and Chu, will judge the situation and quickly become Wu's enemy, they will definitely contest its power and compete in battle with Wu. When Wu is exhausted, Yue can take the opportunity to attack it. Wu can be conquered. Even the Five Lords' use of troops does not surpass this."

Fan Li said, "I, your subject, have heard that when making plans on another state and destroying an enemy, one must observe auspicious signs while taking action.[51] For this reason, when making a covenant in Mengjing, although the many lords said Zhou could be attacked, King Wu declined the proposal.[52] Now Wu and Chu have enmity toward each other and their hatred cannot be reconciled; however, although Qi is not in a close relationship with Wu, it will nevertheless provide aid to Wu. Although Jin does not attach itself to Wu, it still acts in accordance with its duty to Wu.[53] That within the state of Wu there are ministers making plans and deciding on their policy, neighboring states connect with it and do not discontinue their aid. These exactly demonstrate that Wu is establishing its hegemon status and the many lords are showing respect to the king of Wu. I, your subject, have heard that lofty and tall mountains will collapse, trees with lavish leaves will break, once passing noon the sun moves down, and after its full shape the moon wanes.[54] The four seasons do not dominate at the same time and the Five Phases do not run together. *Yin* and *yang* take turns to lead,[55] and *qi* has its own rise and fall. Therefore if water overflows a bank there is nothing to control its discharge, if the fire burns out there is nothing to restore its

50. 強 (*qiang*), "strong," should be read as a verb here: "to compete, to strike for dominance."

51. 符 (*fu*) originally was a military tally made of bamboo pieces, here it means auspicious signs.

52. This refers to King Wu's attack on Shang. Legends say that King Wu made a covenant with eight hundred lords at Mengjing before his final conquest of Shang. *Shiji* reports that during the meeting all of the lords proposed that it was the right time to attack the Shang king Zhou but King Wu believed that heaven had not issued the mandate yet. See *Shiji*, 4:120. Mengjing is located in modern-day Meng County, Henan Province.

53. The ruling houses of Jin and Wu were both descendants of the Zhou royal family. Taibo, the founder of Wu, was the son of Gugong Danfu, whose grandson King Wu established Zhou. King Wu's son Shuyu 叔虞 was enfeoffed in Tang, in modern-day Yicheng 翼城, Shanxi Province, thus began the state of Jin.

54. This is a popular saying that appears in quite a few early texts, including, for example, the "Shouruo" 守弱 chapter in *Wenzi* and *Shiji*. See *Shiji*, 79:2422. See also Wang Liqi 王利器, *Wenzi shuyi* 文子疏義 (Beijing: Zhonghua shuju, 2015), 159.

55. 唱 (*chang*), "to sing," should be 倡 (*chang*), "to lead."

heat. When the water settles down there will be no land-drowning, roaring waves;[56] when the fire dies out there will be no hair-scorching heat. Now the king of Wu relies upon the power of the lords and issues his commands to the world, yet he fails to realize that his virtue is superficial, his kindness shallow, his path narrow, but the hatred he causes broad. He wields power but his intelligence has declined, his strength is exhausted and his authority undermined, his troops are defeated and his army has retreated, his soldiers run away and his followers scatter. I, your subject, request to prepare our troops and strengthen the soldiers, we wait until Wu becomes corrupt and declines and then take the chance to attack it by surprise. In this way, without our weapons smearing with blood and our soldiers turning back their heels,[57] the king and ministers of Wu will become our slaves. I, your subject, wish Your Majesty hide your words, do not let people see your movement, only show them your inaction."

Grand Minister Kucheng said, "Water can float grass and wood, it can also sink them. Earth can grow all things, it can also kill them. Rivers and oceans can stay below valleys, they can also cause the streams of the valleys to flow toward them. A sage can follow the people, he can also command them. Now Wu has continued Helü's military system and the regulation and education set up by Wu Zixu, its government is stable and has not declined, it has won battles and has not been defeated. Grand Minister Bo Pi is arrogant and flattering, he is familiar with scheming but thinks little of governmental affairs. Wu Zixu devotes his strength in military attack and risks his life in admonishing the king. When these two compete there certainly will be damage and failure to the state. I wish Your Majesty to be modest and conceal your intention, you should not reveal your plan, in this way Wu can be destroyed."[58]

---

56. 漚 (*ou*), "to soak in water;" 瀴 (*ying*), "flooding, waving water."

57. This is another popular saying that is found in many early texts, for example, the "Yibing" 議兵 chapter in *Xunzi*, the "Wugong" 勿躬 section in *Lüshi chunqiu*, the "Yuzeng" 語增 chapter in *Lunheng*, and the "Taizu xun" 泰族訓 chapter in *Huainanzi*. See Wang Xianqian, *Xunzi jijie*, 331; Xu Weiyu, *Lüshi chunqiu jishi*, 452; Huang Hui, *Lunheng jiaoshi*, 342, 344, 346; He Ning, *Huainanzi jishi*, 1404.

58. The advice given by Wen Zhong, Fan Li, and Kucheng all emphasizes, besides patiently waiting for Wu's internal turmoil, concealing Yue's military intentions. The "Taizu xun" chapter in *Huainanzi* states that if a ruler has the intention of attacking another state, animals such as dogs, roosters, and horses will show unusual behaviors: "Therefore if the ruler holds the intention of attacking another state, the town dogs will howl together, roosters cry at night, war horses will be startled once the weapons in the arsenals are moved" (故人主有伐國之志，邑犬羣嘷，雄雞夜鳴，庫兵動而戎馬驚). According to *Huainanzi*, this is due to the fact that the *qi* has been disturbed by the ruler's military intention and the animals' unsettled behaviors correspond to the *qi*. See He Ning, *Huainanzi jishi*, 1400. The *Book of Changes* also cautions on the importance of keeping secret: "The Master said

Grand Minister Hao said, "Currently the king of Wu is arrogant and its ministers wasteful. Its people are well fed and its soldiers reckless. Outside of the state there are enemies caused by Wu's border invasion, inside the state there are power-strutting ministers usurping authority; it can be conquered."

Grand Minister Gouru said, "There are four seasons in nature and there are the Five Phases in the human world.[59] In the past, Tang and King Wu relied upon the advantage of the alternation of the four seasons and conquered Xia and Yin respectively. Lord Huan of Qi and Lord Mu of Qin relied upon the benefits of the overcoming of the Five Phases and put six states in order.[60] They are the ones who gained victory by taking opportunities."

The king of Yue said, "We do not yet possess the advantage of the alternations of the four seasons and the benefit of the overcoming of the Five Phases, I wish you all to return to your posts."

---

on this: 'When disorder arises, it will be found that (ill-advised) speech was the steppingstone to it. If a ruler do not keep secret (his deliberations with his minister), he will lose that minister. If a minister do not keep secret (his deliberations with his ruler), he will lose his life. If (important) matters in the germ be not kept secret, that will be injurious to their accomplishment. Therefore the superior man is careful to maintain secrecy, and does not allow himself to speak." (子曰：亂之所生也，則言語以為階。君不密，則失臣；臣不密，則失身；幾事不密，則害成。是以君子慎密而不出也。) See James Legge, *The Yî King*, in *Sacred Books of the East*, vol. 16, *The Sacred Books of China*, vol. 2 of 6, Part II of *The Texts of Confucianism* (Oxford: Clarendon Press, 1882), 363.

59. 五勝 (*wusheng*) refers to the overcoming relationships of the Five Phases: metal overcomes wood, wood overcomes earth, earth overcomes water, water overcomes fire, and fire overcomes metal. This overcoming theory was often adopted by the *fangshi* in the Qin and Han eras to explain the rise and fall of a dynasty. For example, the First Emperor of Qin believes that Zhou corresponds to fire and Qin corresponds to water, so Qin replaces Zhou. See *Shiji*, 6:237.

60. Lord Huan of Qi was one of the Five Hegemons of the Spring and Autumn period. See his biography in the "Qitaigong shijia" 齊太公世家chapter in *Shiji*, 32:1485–94. Lord Mu of Qin was also one of the hegemons of the Spring and Autumn period. See "Qin benji" 秦本紀 in *Shiji*, 5:185–95.

# 吳越春秋勾踐陰謀外傳第九

## CHAPTER 9

# The Outer Tradition of Goujian's Secret Plots

## Introduction

This chapter continues to recount Goujian's chain of actions aimed at retaliating and destroying Wu. While the main topic of the previous chapter is Goujian's efforts to empower Yue, the current chapter details the many strategies and schemes Goujian applies for the purpose of weakening Wu and for preparing his final attack against his enemy.

The chapter begins with a statement that Yue had become a rich state but that Goujian was still disappointed because no one was as eager to seek revenge upon Wu as he was. Goujian's minister, Ji Yan, criticizes him and suggests that he should attempt to truly understand and trust his ministers. The chapter then turns to Goujian's pursuit of advice from worthy men and woman of different areas of expertise. The most important advice given to Goujian is Wen Zhong's Nine Schemes, which are designed to strengthen Yue and weaken Wu. Three of the Nine Schemes are adopted by Goujian, causing the king of Wu to indulge himself in women and a lavish lifestyle while neglecting his state. The narratives in this chapter present a sharp contrast between Goujian and Fuchai in their ability to listen to suggestions and criticism. While Goujian seeks worthies and uses their talents, Fuchai repeatedly rejects Wu Zixu's loyal admonishments, thus making himself a victim of Yue's tricks.

From a literary perspective, the language of this chapter resembles the style found in the *Zhanguo ce* and *Guoyu*. Some interesting stories are recorded in the chapter, such as that in which Yue borrows grain from Wu and returns cooked seeds in order to cause famine in Wu. The tale of a Yue maiden's sword fight with a white monkey that appears in this chapter inspired many later stories and dramas. The ancient song about shooting animals quoted by Chen Yin in his discussion on archery is often regarded by scholars as one of the earliest poems in Chinese literary history.

## Translation

9.1. 越王勾踐十年二月，越王深念遠思，侵辱於吳，蒙天祉福，得越國。群臣教誨，各畫一策，辭合意同，勾踐敬從，其國已富。

9.1. In the tenth year of King Goujian of Yue (487 BCE), second month, the king of Yue thought deeply and remembered the past invasion and humiliation brought by Wu. Because of the blessings granted by heaven, he was about to return to Yue.[1] All his ministers instructed and advised him; each of them conceived a plan for him, their words agreeable and ideas shared. Goujian respectfully followed their advice and his state therefore became wealthy.

9.2. 反越五年，未聞敢死之友。或謂諸大夫愛其身、惜其軀者。乃登漸臺，望觀其群臣有憂與否。相國范蠡、大夫種、句如之屬，儼然列坐，雖懷憂患，不形顏色。

越王即鳴鍾驚檄而召群臣，與之盟，曰：「寡人獲辱受恥，上愧周王，下慚晉楚。幸蒙諸大夫之策，得返國修政，富民養士。而五年未聞敢死之士，雪仇之臣，柰何而有功乎？」群臣默然，莫對者。越王仰天歎曰：「孤聞主憂臣辱，主辱臣死。今孤親被奴虜之厄，受囚破之恥，不能自輔，須賢任仁，然後討吳，重負諸臣，大夫何易見而難使也？」

於是計研年少官卑，列坐於後，乃舉手而趨，蹈席而前進曰：「謬哉，君王之言也！非大夫易見而難使，君王之不能使也。」

越王曰：「何謂？」

計研曰：「夫官位、財幣、金賞者，君之所輕也；操鋒履刃，艾命投死者，士之所重也。今王易財之所輕，而責士之所重，何其殆哉？」

1. According to Xu Tianhu, there is a character, 返 (*fan*), "to return," missing in the sentence. See Zhang Jue, 254; Huang Rensheng, 279.

9.2. Five years after Goujian had returned to his state,[2] he had not yet heard of anyone who was brave enough to die for him.[3] Some told him that the ministers all value their lives and cherish their bodies, and he therefore ascended the terrace overseeing the water and observed from a distance whether his ministers had the look of worry.[4] Ministers such as Prime Minister Fan Li and Grand Ministers Wen Zhong and Gaoru solemnly sat in order. Although they were worried at heart, this was not expressed in their visages.

The king of Yue then struck the bell as a call to arms and called the many ministers. He swore an oath with them, saying, "I, a man of little virtue, received insults and suffered from humiliation. I am ashamed to face the king of Zhou above,[5] I feel embarrassed to meet with the rulers of Jin and Chu below. Fortunately, because of the plans I received from all you ministers, I was able to return to my state and reform my governance. I brought prosperity to the people and cultivated the talented. However, over five years I have not heard of any gentleman who dares to die for me, nor any officials willing to avenge my humiliation. How can my intention be realized?" The many ministers remained silent and none of them responded. The king of Yue looked up to the sky and sighed, saying, "I, the orphan, have heard that 'the minister would feel ashamed if his ruler is worried; the minister would rather die than see his ruler insulted.'[6] Now I, the orphan, personally endured the hardship of being a servant and suffered the humiliations of being captured and my state being destroyed. I cannot assist myself, I seek the worthy and employ the humane and then will attack Wu. I deeply rely upon all you ministers, but why are you grand ministers easy to recruit yet difficult to use?"[7]

---

2. It has, in fact, only been three years since Goujian returned to Yue.

3. According to Zheng Xuan 鄭玄, people who share the same will and belief are called 友 (*you*). See Zheng Xuan's commentary for the "Dasitu" 大司徒 chapter in *Zhouli*. See Sun Yirang, *Zhouli Zhengyi*, 748.

4. There are quite a few records of 漸臺 (*jiantai*) in early texts. King Zhao of Chu 楚昭王, King Xuan of Qi 齊宣王, Emperor Wen and Emperor Wu of Han, and Wang Mang 王莽 (46 BCE-23CE) are all said to have had 漸臺 in their palaces. Emperor Wu's biography in *Shiji* reports that in the Jianzhang 建章 palace the emperor ordered the digging of a big pond and building of a tall terrace next to it. *Lienü zhuan* 列女傳 tells the story that King Zhao of Chu left his wife on the 漸臺 terrace, and later, when a flood crashed the terrace, the wife drowned and died. It is then clear that 漸臺 refers to a terrace built next to water. See Liu Xiang, *Gu Lienü zhuan*, 109–110. See also *Shiji*, 12:482.

5. This is King Jing of Zhou, 周敬王 (r. 519–476 BCE).

6. This also appears in *Shiji*, the biography of Fan Li and the biography of Fan Sui 范雎. See *Shiji*, 41:1752; *Shiji*, 79:2417. See also Li Bujia, 269; Milburn, 248.

7. 見 (*jian*), "to see; to meet," should be 得 (*de*), "to recruit, to obtain." See Zhang Jue, 256n8; Huang Rensheng, 279n13.

At that time Ji Yan was young and his position was low; he sat at the back row by order.[8] He however raised his hand and hastened to step onto the mat and walk to the front, saying, "How absurd are the words of my king! It is not that the grand ministers are easy to recruit but difficult to use. It is you, my king, who are unable to use them."[9]

The king of Yue asked, "What do you mean?"

Ji Yan said, "Official posts, wealth, and awards of gold, these are things that the ruler regards as of little consequence. Holding a sharp weapon, stepping on the blade, giving up one's life, and dying for others are what an officer regard as weighty.[10] Now Your Majesty changes the slightness with which he regards wealth,[11] but seeks officers to do what they regard as weighty,[12] how dangerous is this!"

9.3. 於是越王默然不悅，面有愧色，即辭群臣，進計研而問曰：「孤之所得士心者何等？」

計研對曰：「夫君人，尊其仁義者，治之門也。士民者，君之根也。開門固根，莫如正身。正身之道，謹左右。左右者，君之所以盛衰者也。願王明選左右，得賢而已。昔太公，九聲而足，磻溪之餓人也，西伯任之而王；管仲，魯之亡囚，有貪分之毀，齊桓得之而霸。故傳曰：『失士者亡，得士者昌。』願王審於左右，何患群臣之不使也？」

越王曰：「吾使賢任能，各殊其事，孤虛心高望，冀聞報復之謀，今咸匿聲隱形，不聞其語，厥咎安在？」

計研曰：「選賢實士，各有一等，遠使以難，以效其誠；內告以匿，以知其信；與之論事，以觀其智；飲之以酒，以視其亂；指之以使，以察其能；示之以色，以別其態。五色以設，士盡其實，人竭其智。知其智，盡實，則君臣何憂？」

越王曰：「吾以謀士效實，人盡其智，而士有未盡進辭有益寡人也。」

計研曰：「范蠡明而知內，文種遠以見外。願王請大夫種與深議，則霸王之術在矣。」

8. The admonishment of Ji Yan is probably adopted from *Yue jue shu*. See Li Bujia, 269–70, Milburn, 248–52

9. A parallel sentence is found in *Hanshi waizhuan*, chap. 7, the conversation between Song Yan 宋燕 and Chen Rao 陳饒. See Xu Weiyu, *Hanshi waizhuan jishi*, 261.

10. 艾 (*ai*) means 刈 (*yi*), "to cut."

11. 易 (*yi*) means "to manage" here.

12. Similar sentences concerning the different attitudes toward awards and death between the ruler and ministers are found in several early texts, including *Hanshi waizhuan*, *Zhanguo ce*, and *Shuoyuan*. See Xu Weiyu, *Hanshi waizhuan jishi*, 262; *Zhanguo ce*, 421; Xiang Zenglu, *Shuoyuan jiaozheng*, 191.

9.3. Without a word, the king of Yue thereupon became depressed; a look of embarrassment appeared on his face. He then dismissed the many ministers and called Ji Yan up front and asked him, "What are the things that I, the orphan, can use to win officers' hearts?"

Ji Yan replied, saying, "When ruling the people, valuing humaneness and righteousness are the doors to good governance. Officers and the people are the roots of the ruler. As for opening the doors and consolidating the roots, nothing can compare with rectifying the self. The way of rectifying the self is to carefully choose the ones close to you.[13] The favorite ministers are the reasons for a ruler's rise or fall. I wish Your Majesty would wisely choose your assistants and employ only the worthy. In the past Jiang Taigong failed to achieve anything, at the age of ninety he was still a starving man by the Pan Stream.[14] However, the Earl of the West employed him and became the king.[15] Guan Zhong was a prisoner running away to Lu and bore a reputation for being greedy.[16] Yet Lord Huan recruited him and became a hegemon. Therefore the commentary says that 'losing the worthy leads to fall; obtaining the worthy brings prosperity.' I wish Your

---

13. This sentence is probably adopted from the "Ji Yan" chapter in *Yue jue shu*, see Li Bujia, 269; Milburn, 249.

14. Jiang Taigong, personal name Jiang Shang 姜尚 (fl. eleventh century BCE), was the first marquis of the state of Qi. He was also called Lü Shang 呂尚 or Lü Wang 呂望. His style name was Jiang Ziya 姜子牙. Legends tell that Jiang Shang was very old and lived as a recluse near the Wei River 渭河. King Wen of Zhou ran into Jiang Shang and recognized his worthiness and talent. King Wen hired Jiang Shang as an advisor. After King Wen died, Jiang Shang assisted King Wu and destroyed the Shang dynasty. He was enfeoffed in Qi and became the founder of the state of Qi. See *Shiji*, 32:1477–81. The military text *Liutao* 六韜 was attributed to him. However, in Chinese popular culture he is often described as a Daoist figure. He was one of the dominant characters in the Ming novel *Fengshen yanyi* 封神演義. The *WYCQ* text states that Jiang Taigong was "skilled in all nine tones" (九聲而足). The nine tones refer to the ancient Chinese musical tones: *gong* 宮, *shang* 商, *jue* 角, *zhi* 徵, *yu* 羽, *gongqing* 宮清, *shangqing* 商清, *jueqing* 角清, and *zhiqing* 徵清. However, there is no mention of Jiang Taigong's skill in music in early texts. On the contrary, *Yue jue shu*, *Hanshi waizhuan*, and *Shuoyuan* all tell the story that Jiang Taigong had failed to achieve anything even by the time he was ninety years old. So, "skilled in nine tones" should, in fact, be "achieved nothing by the age of ninety." See Zhang Jue, 257n1. For a study of the development of Jiang Taigong, see Sarah Allan, "The Identities of Taigong Wang in Zhou and Han Literature," *Monumenta Serica* 30 (1972–1973): 57–99.

15. The Earl of the West became King Wen of Zhou. His name was Ji Chang 姬昌 and he was probably the leader of the tribes in the western region of Shang.

16. Guan Zhong, whose personal name was Guan Yiwu 管夷吾, was a famous politician in the early Spring and Autumn period. Guan Zhong ran to Lu due to political turmoil in Qi, accompanying the rival of the future Lord Huan of Qi. Eventually Lord Huan recognized Guan Zhong's talent and entrusted him with governance. He helped Lord Huan of Qi become the first hegemon of the Spring and Autumn period. Stories of Guan Zhong can be found in the "Qi shijia" as well as in his biography in *Shiji*. See *Shiji*, 32:1485–93, 62:2131–34. Guan Zhong was traditionally considered a Legalist. The Legalist text *Guanzi* is attributed to him.

Majesty would inspect those close to you. Why do you worry that the many ministers are not used by you?"

The king of Yue said, "I employed the worthy, appointed the talented, and divided their duties. I, the orphan, humbly looked up to them, wishing I would hear from them their plan of revenge against Wu. Now they have all silenced their voices and hidden their traces, and I cannot hear a word from them. What is my fault in this?"

Ji Yan said, "As for selecting the worthy and knowing the talent of the officers, each has its individual principle: send them far away as emissaries with challenging matters in order to examine their loyalty, tell them secrets at court in order to learn if they are trustworthy, discuss issues with them in order to appreciate their wisdom, provide them drinks in order to see if they upset their presence of mind,[17] engage them in matters in order to investigate their ability, show them your facial expression in order to distinguish their attitude. When the facial expressions are all shown,[18] officers then present their true ability and the talented devote their intelligence. If you know their intelligence and completely understand their ability, what worries should Your Majesty have?"[19]

The king of Yue said, "I have already asked officers to present their ability and the talented to devote their wisdom, yet there are still officers who have not done their utmost to submit suggestions benefiting me, a man of little virtue."

Ji Yan said, "Fan Li is wise and understands domestic affairs. Wen Zhong has foresight and knows situations outside of the state. I wish Your Majesty would invite Grand Minister Wen Zhong and thoroughly discuss with him; you will then find the method for becoming a hegemon."

9.4. 越王乃請大夫種而問曰：「吾昔日受夫子之言，自免於窮厄之地。今欲奉不羈之計，以雪吾之宿讎，何行而功乎？」

大夫種曰：「臣聞：『高飛之鳥，死於美食；深泉之魚，死於芳餌。』今欲伐吳，必前求其所好，參其所願，然後能得其實。」

越王曰：「人之所好，雖其願，何以定而制之死乎？」

大夫種曰：「夫欲報怨復讎，破吳滅敵者，有九術，君王察焉？」

17. Excessive drinking had been a concern probably since Shang. The Zhou people viewed the demise of Shang as a result of the drinking problems of the Shang kings. However, Zhou people themselves also fell victim to overindulgence in alcohol. The *Analects* records that Confucius "would only enjoy wine without limit, though never to the point of disorderliness." See Confucius, *Analects*, 103.

18. 五色 (*wuse*), "five colors," here refers to facial expressions.

19. 君臣 (*junchen*), "ruler and minister," should be 君王 (*junwang*), "ruler."

越王曰：「寡人被辱懷憂，內慚朝臣，外愧諸侯，中心迷惑，精神空虛，雖有九術，安能知之？」

大夫種曰：「夫九術者。湯、文得之以王，桓、穆得之以霸。其攻城取邑，易於脫屣。願大王覽之。」種曰：「一曰尊天事鬼以求其福；二曰重財幣以遺其君，多貨賄以喜其臣；三曰貴糴粟槁以虛其國，利所欲以疲其民；四曰遺美女以惑其心而亂其謀；五曰遺之巧工良材，使之起宮室以盡其財；六曰遺之諛臣，使之易伐；七曰彊其諫臣，使之自殺；八曰君王國富而備利器；九曰利甲兵以承其弊。凡此九術，君王閉口無傳，守之以神，取天下不難，而況於吳乎？」

越王曰：「善。」

9.4. The king of Yue therefore invited Grand Minister Wen Zhong and asked him, saying, "Previously I have followed your advice and was able to avoid finding myself in a desperate situation. Now I desire to receive your superb strategy in order to avenge myself on my old foe.[20] What should I do to be successful?"

Grand Minister Wen Zhong said, "I, your subject, have heard that 'birds flying high above die when they swoop down for delicious food; fishes in deep springs die when they rise for fragrant bait.' Now if you want to attack Wu, you must first find out what the king of Wu favors and, with reference to his desire, then you can obtain his land and wealth."[21]

The king of Yue said, "How can you be sure that you can use one's preference, even if it is what one desires, and doom one to demise?"

Grand Minister Wen Zhong said, "If you want to wipe out your hatred, seek revenge on your foe, destroy Wu and exterminate your enemy, there are nine schemes to be used. Does Your Majesty know about these?"[22]

The king of Yue said, "I, a man of little virtue, suffer from humiliation and bear worries in my heart. In the state I feel ashamed facing the ministers at court. Out of the state I am embarrassed meeting the many lords. I am confused in my heart and empty in my spirit. Although there are nine schemes, how do I know them?"

---

20. 不羈 (*buji*) here means "unrestrained talent." The "Zizhi" 資質 chapter in *Xinyu* describes people with unrestrained talent (懷不羈之能) who suffer from poverty due to the lack of recommendations. See Wang Liqi, *Xinyu jiaozhu*, 122.

21. 實 (*shi*), "fruit," refers to "loot," "land," and "wealth" here. The "Aigong wen" 哀公問 chapter in *Liji* reports Confucius's criticism that "gentlemen nowadays are never satisfied with their fondness for wealth (今之君子好實無厭)," see Sun Xidan, 1259. The "Yuandao xun" 原道訓 in *Huainanzi* says that "beasts step with their feet on the land and run (獸蹠實而走)." See He Ning, *Huainanzi jishi*, 34.

22. The biography of Goujian in *Shiji* records seven schemes (*qishu*, 七術) instead of nine schemes. See *Shiji*, 41:1747.

Grand Minister Wen Zhong said, "As for the nine schemes, Tang and King Wen became kings by using them;[23] Lord Huan of Qi and Lord Mu of Qin became hegemons by following them. Using them to attack cities and conquer towns is easier than taking off shoes. I wish Your Majesty to examine them." Wen Zhong continued, "The first one is to be reverent to heaven and serve the ghosts and spirits in order to seek their blessings.[24] The second is to add more valuable goods and present them to the enemy ruler, and increase bribes in order to please his ministers. The third is to buy provisions and fodder at high prices from the enemy in order to create food shortages in their state, and luring the ruler to follow his desires in order to exhaust his people. The fourth is to present to the ruler beautiful ladies in order to delude his mind and undermine his plans. The fifth is to offer the ruler skillful craftsmen and fine lumber, letting him construct palaces and buildings in order to drain his wealth. The sixth is to send to him flattering ministers, causing him to be reckless in launching military expeditions.[25] The seventh is to induce his admonishing ministers to be more intransigent and cause them to commit suicide. The eighth is to enrich Your Majesty's state and equip your troops with sharp weapons. The ninth is to prepare your armory and train your soldiers, taking advantage of them when they are weak and attacking them. For all of these nine schemes, Your Majesty should close your mouth and not reveal them. Holding onto them with your heart, it is then not difficult to conquer the world, not to mention destroy Wu."[26]

The king of Yue said, "Excellent!"

9.5. 乃行第一術，立東郊以祭陽，名曰東皇公，立西郊以祭陰，名曰西王母。祭陵山於會稽，祀水澤於江州。事鬼神一年，國不被災。越王曰：「善哉，大夫之術！願論其餘。」

9.5. The king of Yue then carried out the first scheme. He established a shrine in the eastern suburb to offer sacrifices to the god of *yang*, whose name was Grandiose Lord of the East.[27] A shrine was established in the western

23. Tang was the founder of the Shang dynasty. King Wen's son, King Wu, destroyed Shang and established Zhou.

24. Xu Tianhu argues that the word 神 (*shen*), "spirit," belongs after 鬼 (*gui*), "ghost," in the sentence. In the following section it says that "after a year serving the ghosts and spirits, his state was free from natural disasters." Based on this context, Xu Tianhu is probably correct. See *WYCQ*, 9.5.

25. An alternative reading of 伐 (*fa*) is "bragging about one's merits." The sentence is then "sending to him flattering minister and causing him to be unrestrained in self-aggrandizing."

26. These nine schemes are also found in *Yue jue shu*, the "Jiushu" 九術 (Nine schemes) chapter. See Li Bujia, 321; Milburn, 299–300.

27. 東皇公 (*Dong huanggong*) was also called 東王公 (*Dong wanggong*) and 東王父 (*Dong wangfu*), and became a Taoist deity after the Tang dynasty. A text titled *Shenyi jing* 神異經, which is probably

suburb to offer sacrifices to the god of *yin*, whose name was Queen Mother of the West.[28] He offered sacrifices to Yu's tomb on Mount Kuaiji and worshiped gods of rivers and lakes on the isle of the Zhe River. After a year serving the ghosts and spirits, his state was free from natural disasters. The king of Yue said, "Excellent is this scheme of yours, Grand Minister! I wish you would discuss the other schemes."

9.6. 種曰：「吳王好起宮室，用工不輟。王選名山神材，奉而獻之。」

越王乃使木工三千餘人入山伐木，一年，師無所幸。作士思歸，皆有怨望之心，而歌《木客之吟》。一夜，天生神木一雙，大二十圍，長五十尋。陽為文梓，陰為楩柟，巧工施校，制以規繩，雕治圓轉，刻削磨礱，分以丹青，錯畫文章，嬰以白璧，鏤以黃金，狀類龍蛇，文彩生光。

乃使大夫種獻之於吳王，曰：「東海役臣，臣孤勾踐使臣種，敢因下吏聞於左右：賴大王之力，竊為小殿，有餘材，謹再拜獻之。」

吳王大悅。

子胥諫曰：「王勿受也。昔者，桀起靈臺，紂起鹿臺，陰陽不和，寒暑不時，五穀不熟，天與其災，民虛國變，遂取滅亡。大王受之，必為越王所戮。」

吳王不聽，遂受而起姑蘇之臺。三年聚材，五年乃成，高見二百里。行路之人，道死巷哭，不絕嗟嘻之聲：民疲士苦，人不聊生。

越王曰：「善哉，第二術也！」

9.6. Wen Zhong said, "The king of Wu is fond of building palaces and he never stops using craftsmen. Your Majesty should select rare lumber from famous mountains and respectfully present it to him."

The king of Yue therefore sent more than three thousand woodworkers to enter the mountains to cut trees.[29] A year passed and the men had not

---

from the Jin dynasty, describes this Lord of the East as having a human body, the face of a bird, and a tiger tail. He was said to be the leader of all male gods. This 東皇公 is different from the god 東皇太一 (*Donghuang taiyi*) as seen in Qu Yuan's poem. 東皇太一 is the divinity in the worship of the Taiyi (Great Unity) that can be traced back to early the Warring States; it is originally the name of a star. For more on 東皇公, see Huang Rensheng, 288n19. For the Taiyi in *Chuci* 楚辭 and Han dynasty Taiyi worship, see Gopal Sukhu, *The Shaman and the Heresiarch: A New Interpretation of the Li Sao* (Albany, NY: SUNY Press, 2012), 197–98.

28. 西王母 (*Xi wangmu*), Queen Mother of the West, is a goddess in Chinese religion and folktales. The earliest reference to Queen Mother of the West can be traced back to oracle bone inscriptions. There are many stories about her in Chinese mythology and folk culture. She is often regarded as a Taoist divinity. For more information on her, see Suzanne E. Cahill, *Transcendence and Divine Passion: The Queen Mother of the West in Medieval China* (Stanford: Stanford University Press, 1993).

29. The following story of the woodworkers' complaint and the mysteriously appearing trees are not found in *Yue jue shu*.

found the rare trees they desired.[30] The workers wanted to go home and everyone was resentful in their hearts.[31] They thus chanted the "Song of Woodworkers."[32] One night, mysteriously, a pair of divine trees grew. They were twenty *wei* around and fifty *xun* tall.[33] The one on the south side was a catalpa ovata tree with a pattern on it; the one on the north side was a phoebe nanmu tree.[34] Skillful workers measured them and trimmed them by using compasses and marking lines.[35] They carved the trees round and then cut them, trimmed them, and rubbed them. Colors were applied and complicated patterns were painted.[36] White jade plates were attached on the trees,[37] gold was engraved on them, shaped like dragons and snakes and illuminating lights.

The king of Yue then sent Grand Minister Wen Zhong to present the trees to the king of Wu, saying, "Your servant from the East Sea, Goujian, your subject, sent Wen Zhong, your subject, through your low officials, to dare to report to your attendants on the left and right: relying upon your power, I secretly built a small hall. There is some lumber left and I respectfully bow twice and present it to you."

The king of Wu was greatly delighted.[38]

---

30. 師 (*shi*) refers to the workers. 幸 (*xing*) serves here as the verb "to favor."

31. In the *Book of Documents*, the legendary ruler Shun 舜 appointed Gao Yao to serve as Minister of Law (汝作士 *ru zuoshi*). This is probably the earliest reference to the term 作士. However, the *Zhouli* reports on a position called *sishi* 司士, "Overseer of Officers," whose duty includes sending officers to accompany the king when the king is attending a covenant (凡會同，作士從). Here 作 is used as a verb meaning "to cause, to make." In the *WYCQ* sentence, 作 shares the same meaning as that seen in the *Zhouli* and 作士 therefore refers to the workers dispatched into the mountains to cut trees. See Sun Xingyan 孫星衍, *Shangshu jinguwen zhushu* 尚書今古文註疏 (Beijing: Zhonghua shuju, 1986), 65. See also Sun Yirang, *Zhouli zhengyi*, 2469.

32. Presumably, this is a song composed by the woodworkers.

33. *Wei* was an ancient unit of measure for circumference. There were different definitions of the length of a *wei*. It could be either 5 inches, or the more approximate circumference of arms encircling something. *Xun* was also a unit for measuring length; one Han *xun* is approximately 3.2 feet long. Thus, the trees were about eight feet in circumference and 160 feet tall.

34. Both are rare and valuable trees. *Yin* and *yang* refer to locations here.

35. 規 (*gui*) is a compass and 繩 (*sheng*) means a marking line with ink on it.

36. 丹青 (*danqing*) is a word for "color" in Chinese. 錯 (*cuo*) is a verb here, meaning "to paint with color." 文章 (*wenzhang*) refers to mixed patterns of colors. The alternation of red and green is called 文 while the alternation of red and white is 章 (*zhang*).

37. 嬰 (*ying*) means "to wrap, to coil around".

38. Xu Tianhu found this speech and the Wu king's reaction absurd. Xu points out that this is rare and valuable lumber, yet Wen Zhong says it is leftover wood from a hall Goujian built for himself. The Wu king Fuchai should be enraged about this rather than delighted. See Zhang Jue, 263n12; Huang Rensheng, 288n38.

Wu Zixu remonstrated against this, saying, "You majesty should not accept it. In the past Jie built Ling Terrace and Zhou constructed Deer Terrace.[39] These caused the imbalance of *yin* and *yang*, winter and summer came at the wrong times, and the five grains failed to ripen.[40] Heaven sent down to them disasters. Their people were poor, realms suffered misfortune, and eventually they met their demise. If Your Majesty accepts this you will certainly be killed by the king of Yue."

The king of Wu did not listen; instead he accepted the lumber and built the Gusu Terrace. Three years were spent collecting materials; the project was completed after five years. On the top of the terrace one could see as far as two hundred *li* away. People were forced to leave home and participate in the construction, they died on the way and cried in the alleys, and none of them could stop sighing. People were tired and the officers were miserable. They could barely survive.

The king of Yue said, "Excellent! The second scheme!"

9.7. 十一年，越王深念永思，惟欲伐吳，乃請計研問曰：「吾欲伐吳，恐不能破，早欲興師，惟問於子。」

計研對曰：「夫興師舉兵，必且內蓄五穀，實其金銀，滿其府庫，勵其甲兵。凡此四者，必察天地之氣，原於陰陽，明於孤虛，審於存亡，乃可量敵。」

越王曰：「『天地』、『存亡』，其要柰何？」

計研曰：「天地之氣，物有死生。原陰陽者，物貴賤也；明孤虛者，知會際也；審存亡者，別真偽也。」

越王曰：「何謂『死生』、『真偽』乎？」

計研曰：「春種八穀，夏長而養，秋成而聚，冬畜而藏。夫天時有生而不救種，是一死也；夏長無苗，二死也；秋成無聚，三死也；冬藏無畜，四死也。雖有堯舜之德，無如之何。夫天時有生，勸者老，作者少，反氣應數，不失厥理，一生也；留意省察，謹除苗穢，穢除苗盛，二生也；前時設備，物至則收，國無逋稅，民無失穗，三生也；倉已封塗，除陳入新，君樂臣歡，男女及信，四生也。夫陰陽者，太陰所居之歲，留息三年，貴賤見矣。夫孤虛者，謂天門地戶也。存亡者，君之道德也。」

越王曰：「何子之年少，於物之長也？」

計研曰：「有美之士，不拘長少。」

39. Jie was the last king of the Xia dynasty; Zhou was the last king of Shang. Both were infamous for their corruption and cruelty.

40. The five grains refer to soybeans, wheat, broomcorn, panicled millet, and hemp.

越王曰：「善哉，子之道也！」乃仰觀天文，集察緯宿，曆象四時。以下者上，虛設八倉，從陰收著，望陽出糴，筴其極計，三年五倍，越國熾富。勾踐歎曰：「吾之霸矣。善！計研之謀也。」

9.7. In the eleventh year of King Goujian (486 BCE), the king of Yue was deeply concerned and, for long, had been thinking of his only desire, to attack Wu. He then called Ji Yan and asked him, saying, "I want to attack Wu but I am concerned that I am not able to destroy it. I have long been thinking of mobilizing the troops and I only discuss this with you, sir."

Ji Yan responded, saying, "To raise the army and mobilize the troops, you must store up the five grains in your state, save your gold and silver, fill up your granary and armory, and prepare your armor and weapons. For each of these four you must inspect the *qi* of heaven and earth, reason out *yin* and *yang*, understand the good and bad fortunes indicated by the heavenly stems and earthly branches, and investigate the circumstances for survival and demise,[41] and you can then compete with the enemy."

The king of Yue asked, "What are the principles for the *qi* of heaven and earth and the circumstances for survival and demise?"

Ji Yan said, "The *qi* of heaven and earth is responsible for the death and life of all creatures. Reasoning out *yin* and *yang* can distinguish things between noble and base. Understanding the good and bad fortunes indicated by the heavenly stems and earthly branches can help one foresee chances and opportunities. Investigating the circumstances for survival and demise can differentiate truth and falsehood."

41. 孤虛 (*guxu*) was a type of divination in early China. It was mainly used to decide whether a certain date and hours were auspicious and whether military actions would be successful. If the divination result is 孤虛, this foreshadows the failure of the action. The *Shiji* chapter on divination, "Guice liezhuan" 龜策列傳, states that if "the heavenly stems and earthly branches are not complete, therefore there is *guxu* (日辰不全，故有孤虛)." See *Shiji*, 128:3237. The earliest record of 孤虛 is found in *Weiliaozi* 尉繚子 where the author criticizes military generals relying only upon divinations such as 孤虛 while ignoring the talented. See Liu Yin 劉寅 (*jinshi* in 1371), *Weiliaozi jijie* 尉繚子直解 (Yangzhou: Jiangsu guji chubanshe, 1998), 89. Shashi 沙市 zhoujiatai 周家台 Qin bamboo strips #355 and #361 record the technique of using the 孤虛 method to detect from which direction a thief would come and in which direction the owner should search for stolen livestock. For example, if the ten days (*xun* 旬) starts with a *jiazi* 甲子 day, the *xu* and *hai* days are considered *gu* 孤 and the *chen* and *si* hours are *xu* 虛. In these days and hours, the thief is likely coming from the southeast and the stolen animals will be found hidden in the northwest (甲了旬，戌亥为孤，辰巳为虚，道东南入 . . . 甲子亡马牛，求西北方). See Hubei sheng jingzhou shi zhouliang yuqiao yizhi bowuguan 湖北省荆州市周梁玉橋遺址博物館 ed., *Guanju QianHan mu jiandu* 关沮秦汉墓简牍 (Beijing: Zhonghua shuju, 2001), 133. For further discussion on the 孤虛 method, see Long Yongfang 龍永芳, "Gudai guxu shu xiaoyi—jianlun Zhoujiatai Qinjian zhong de guxu fa" 古代孤虚术小议—兼论周家台秦简中的孤虚法, *Jingmen zhiye jishu xueyuan xuebao* 荊門職業技術學院學報 22, no. 2 (2007): 85–9.

The king of Yue asked, "What do you mean by death and life, truth and false?"

Ji Yan said, "Eight grains are planted in the spring.[42] When they grow up in the summer you nourish them. You collect them when they are ripe in the fall and save them and store them in the winter. However, if the natural season is ready for sprouting but you did not plant the seeds,[43] this is the first reason for death. In the summer the grains should grow but if there are no seedlings, this is the second reason for death. When the grains are ripe during fall but are not harvested, this is the third reason for death. In the winter the grains should be stored but if they are not saved, this is the fourth reason for death. Even one as virtuous as Yao or Shun can do nothing about these. When the natural season is ready for life, with the encouragement of the seniors and the labor of the young, follow the *qi* of heaven and earth and be in accordance with its principles,[44] and do not violate the natural way of the grains;[45] this is the first way of survival. Pay attention to checking and inspection, and carefully weed the grasses among the seedlings; once the grasses are weeded sprouts can flourish, this is the second way of survival. Get ready before the harvest, when the grains are collected they are then stored. No one in the state avoids tax payment and the people do not lose their grain; this is the third way of survival. Granaries are sealed, old grains are cleaned and new ones stored, the ruler is delighted and the ministers happy, men and women trust them; this is the fourth way of survival. As for *yin* and *yang*, this means during the years when Jupiter is the corresponding constellation you cease activities and rest for three years;[46] thus the difference between noble and base is clear. As for good and bad fortune, this refers to the heavenly gate and earthly entry. The circumstances of survival and demise are related to the virtue of the ruler."

The king of Yue asked, "Why, sir, are you so young yet have knowledge of these things?"

Ji Yan said, "People of virtue are not limited by age."[47]

The king of Yue said, "Excellent are your explanations!" He then looked up and observed the pattern of heaven, focused and examined the stars and

42. The eight grains are: common millet, panicled millet, glutinous millet, spiked millet, tarrow, wheat, beans, and rice.

43. 救種 (*jiuzhong*) means "working on the seeds."

44. 反 (*fan*) here means "to follow."

45. 厥 (*jue*) refers to the eight grains.

46. 太陰 (*taiyin*) is also called 太歲 (*taisui*), Jupiter. In ancient divination, the location to which Jupiter moves was considered inauspicious and construction in that area should be avoided.

47. 美 (*mei*) here suggests one's inner qualities such as profound knowledge and virtue.

constellations,[48] decided the calendar and the time of the seasonal changes, correlated the earthly events with the heavenly phenomena, established eight granaries in response to the Eight Grains Constellation,[49] collected and stored grains in accordance with *yin* and sold them by following the changes of *yang*.[50] Best plans were conceived and the store of grain increased fivefold in three years. The state of Yue became rich and flourished. Goujian sighed, "I will become a hegemon. How wonderful are Ji Yan's strategies!"

9.8. 十二年，越王謂大夫種曰：「孤聞吳王淫而好色，惑亂沉湎，不領政事，因此而謀，可乎？」

種曰：「可破。夫吳王淫而好色，宰嚭佞以曳心，往獻美女，其必受之。惟王選擇美女二人而進之。」

越王曰：「善。」

乃使相者國中得苧蘿山鬻薪之女，曰西施、鄭旦。飾以羅穀，教以容步，習於土城，臨於都巷。三年學服而獻於吳。

乃使相國范蠡進曰：「越王勾踐竊有二遺女，越國洿下困迫，不敢稽留，謹使臣蠡獻之。大王不以鄙陋寢容，願納以供箕帚之用。」

吳王大悅，曰：「越貢二女，乃勾踐之盡忠於吳之證也。」

子胥諫曰：「不可！王勿受也。臣聞；『五色令人目盲，五音令人耳聾。』昔桀易湯而滅，紂易文王而亡，大王受之，後必有殃。臣聞越王朝書不倦，晦誦竟夜，且聚敢死之士數萬，是人不死，必得其願；越王服誠行仁，聽諫進賢，是人不死，必成其名；越王夏被毛裘，冬御絺綌，是人不死，必為對隙。臣聞賢士國之寶，美女國之咎：夏亡以妹喜，殷亡以妲己，周亡以褒姒。」

吳王不聽，遂受其女。

越王曰：「善哉，第三術也。」

9.8. In the twelfth year of King Goujian (485 BCE), the king of Yue spoke to Grand Minister Wen Zhong, saying, "I, the orphan, have heard that the king of Wu indulges himself in carnal pleasure and is fond of women. He is delirious and drinks uninhibitedly and does not care about governmental affairs. Can we then take advantage of this and make plans?"

48. 緯 (*wei*) refers to Mercury, Venus, Mars, Jupiter, and Saturn. 宿 (*xiu*) are the Twenty-Eight Mansions, which are part of the Chinese constellation system. In the ancient Chinese constellation system, the sky ecliptic is divided into four regions and each region contains seven mansions. Each mansion corresponds to a geographic location.

49. These are the eight stars in the Purple Forbidden Enclosure and they correspond to the eight grains.

50. Huang Rensheng interprets *yin* as winter and *yang* as summer: collected and stored in winter, and sold the food in summer. See Huang Rensheng, 293,nn22–23.

Wen Zhong answered, saying, "We can take advantage of this and destroy Wu. The king of Wu is licentious and lewd; Chief Chancellor Bo Pi manipulates his mind through flattery.[51] If we go and present beautiful ladies he will certainly accept them. I wish Your Majesty to selected two beautiful women and present them to him."

The king of Yue said, "Excellent!"

He then ordered physiognomists to search the state and they found girls selling firewood in Mount Zhuluo,[52] with the names Xishi and Zheng Dan.[53] He dressed them with silk gauze and crepe,[54] instructed them on facial expressions and styles of walking,[55] and let them practice in Tucheng and observe people in the alleys in the capital.[56] After three years they learned and became accustomed to these things, and Goujian thus offered them to the king of Wu.

Therefore Goujian sent Prime Minister Fan Li to present them to the Wu king, saying, "The king of Yue, Goujian, privately holds two girls bestowed by heaven.[57] The state of Yue is low in altitude and is in a poor situation. The king of Yue dared not to let them stay; he respectfully sent me, Fan Li, your subject, to present them to Your Majesty. If Your Majesty does not detest that

---

51. 曳 (*ye*) means "to drag," "to pull."

52. The *Taiping yulan* quotation of this contains the verb 索 (*suo*), "to search," after 相工 (*xianggong*), "physiognomists." See Zhang Jue, 268. Physiognomy was used as a way to read the body for political purposes from at least the Spring and Autumn period. There are many stories of using physiognomy to read the female body in *Hanshu* and *Hou Hanshu*. For example, Wang Zhengjun's 王政君 father hired a physiognomist to predict her future and then presented her to the palace. Wang Zhengjun later became the wife of Emperor Yuan of Han 漢元帝 (r. 48–33 BCE). See *Hanshu* 97: 3964, 98: 4015. Mount Zhuluo is in modern-day Zhuji County, Zhejiang Province.

53. Xi Shi was probably the most famous beauty in ancient China. Her name appears in almost all pre-Qin philosophical texts, as well as in many Han writings. For example, she was mentioned in the "Zhenglun" 正論 chapter in *Xunzi*, the "Qinshi" 親士 section in *Mozi* 墨子, the "Qiwu lun" 齊物論 and "Tianlun" 天論 chapters in *Zhuangzi* 莊子, the "Xianxue" 顯學 chapter in *Hanfeizi*, and several Chuci poems.

54. 羅 (*luo*) is silk gauze with patterns on it. 縠 (*hu*) is crepe.

55. Facial expressions and walking styles were important bodily performances in court ritual in early China. The "Xiangdang" 鄉黨 chapter in the *Analects*, for example, describes Confucius's exemplary bodily performances. *Liji* contains many rules and regulations on how one acts and behaves in different social circumstances. The *Shiji* chapter on Confucian scholars, "Rulin liezhuan" 儒林列傳, records that Scholar Xu of Lu was good at court ritual performance (容, *rong*) and served as grand minister in charge of ritual during Emperor Wen's time. His grandson Xu Xiang 徐襄 was born with good bodily features that allowed him to be good at court ritual performance, but Xu Xiang could not understand the *Book of Rites* (鲁徐生善为容。孝文帝时，徐生以容为礼官大夫。传子至孙延、徐襄。襄，其天姿善为容，不能通礼经). See *Shiji*, 121:3126.

56. Tucheng is in modern-day Shaoxing, Zhejiang Province.

57. *Yue jue shu* states: "Previously King Goujian of Yue privately had Xi Shi and Zheng Dan, who were bestowed by heaven" (昔者越王勾踐，竊有天之遺西施、鄭旦). See Li Bujia, 322; Milburn, 301.

they are ignorant and unattractive,[58] we wish you would accept them for the purpose of cleaning."

The king of Wu was greatly delighted, saying, "Yue offered tribute of two girls, this is certainly a testimony of Goujian's unbounded loyalty to Wu."

Wu Zixu admonished against this, saying, "It is not right. Your Majesty should not accept them. I, your subject, have heard that 'five colors make people blind; five tones cause people to become deaf.'[59] In the past Jie thought little of Tang and was destroyed;[60] Zhou slighted King Wen and was killed.[61] If Your Majesty accepts them, misfortune will definitely follow. I, your subject, have heard that the king of Yue writes tirelessly in the daytime and reads overnight. Moreover, he gathers tens of thousands of men who are not afraid of dying. If this man does not die, he will definitely realize his ambition. The king of Yue acts with sincerity and carries out humane governance. He listens to remonstration and promotes the worthy. If this man does not die, he will definitely establish his name. The king of Yue wears a fur coat in the summer but puts on linen clothes in the winter. If this man does not die, he will definitely become our enemy. I, your subject, have heard that 'the virtuous is the treasure of the state yet the beautiful is its disaster.' Xia fell because of Moxi,[62] Yin came to the end because of Daji, and Zhou met its demise because of Baosi."[63]

The king of Wu did not listen but accepted the girls right away.

The king of Yue said, "Excellent! The third scheme!"

58. 㾛 (*qin*), "ugly." The Han minister Tian Fen's 田蚡 biography in *Shiji* records that Tian Fen was "ugly but was born into a very noble family" (貌㾛，生貴甚). See *Shiji*, 107:2844.

59. This is a famous saying in the *Daode jing*. See Lao Tzu, *Tao Teh Ching*, 25. A similar phrase is also found in the "Jiushou" chapter in *Wenzi*. See Wang Liqi, *Wenzi shuyi*, 117.

60. Jie was the last king of Xia. Tang was the founder of Shang, which replaced Xia. This refers to the legend that Jie once jailed Tang on Xia Terrace but, feeling that Tang was not a real threat to him, he released Tang. Later Tang attacked Jie and destroyed Xia. Jie was regretful for not killing Tang before he died in exile. See *Shiji*, 2:88.

61. Similar to the story above, Zhou, the last king of Shang, arrested the future King Wen of Zhou but allowed him to return to his people. King Wen's son, King Wu, terminated Zhou's rule and forced the latter to commit suicide. See *Shiji*, 3:106–8.

62. According to *Guoyu*, Moxi was a daughter of the Youshi tribe (有施氏). Xia King Jie attacked the Youshi tribe, who presented Moxi to Jie. Moxi was favored by Jie; however, she conspired with Yi Yin and destroyed Xia from inside. See Xu Yuangao, 250.

63. When the last Shang king Zhou attacked the Yousu tribe (有蘇氏), he took Daji, a daughter of the Yousu tribe, as his wife. Daji was favored by Zhou, but she allied with Jiaoge 膠鬲 and undermined Shang. Baosi was another "dangerous woman" in early Chinese texts. Again, a daughter from a tribe attacked by the last Zhou king, she was favored by the king yet colluded with Guo Shifu 虢石甫, causing the fall of Zhou. See Xu Yuangao, 250.

9.9. 十三年，越王謂大夫種曰：「孤蒙子之術，所圖者吉，未嘗有不合也。今欲復謀吳，柰何？」種曰：「君王自陳:『越國微鄙，年穀不登。願王請糴，以入其意。』天若棄吳，必許王矣。」

越乃使大夫種使吳，因宰嚭求見吳王。辭曰：「越國洿下，水旱不調，年穀不登，人民飢乏，道荐飢餒，願從大王請糴，來歲即復太倉，惟大王救其窮窘。」

吳王曰：「越王信誠守道，不懷二心，今窮歸愬，吾豈愛惜財寶，奪其所願？」

子胥諫曰：「不可。非吳有越，越必有吳。吉往則凶來。是養生寇而破國家者也。與之不為親，不與未成冤。且越有聖臣范蠡，勇以善謀，將有修飾攻戰，以伺吾間。觀越王之使使來請糴者，非國貧民困而請糴也，以入吾國伺吾王間也。」

吳王曰：「寡人卑服越王而有其眾，懷其社稷以愧勾踐。勾踐氣服，為駕車，卻行馬前，諸侯莫不聞知。今吾使之歸國，奉其宗廟，復其社稷，豈敢有反吾之心乎？」

子胥曰：「臣聞：『士窮非難，抑心下人，其後有激人之色。』臣聞越王飢餓，民之困窮，可因而破也，今不用天之道，順地之理，而反輸之食，固君之命，狐雉之相戲也。夫狐卑體而雉信之，故狐得其志而雉必死。可不慎哉？」

吳王曰：「勾踐國憂，而寡人給之以粟，恩往義來，其德昭昭，亦何憂乎？」

子胥曰：「臣聞：『狼子有野心，仇讎之人不可親。』夫虎不可餧以食，蝮蛇不恣其意。今大王捐國家之福，以饒無益之讎，棄忠臣之言，而順敵人之欲，臣必見越之破吳，豸鹿游於姑胥之臺，荊榛蔓於宮闕。願王覽武王伐紂之事也。」

太宰嚭從旁對曰：「武王非紂王臣也？率諸侯以伐其君，雖勝殷，謂義乎？」

子胥曰：「武王即成其名矣。」

太宰嚭曰：「親戮主以為名，吾不忍也。」

子胥曰：「盜國者封侯，盜金者誅。令使武王失其理，則周何為三家之表？」

太宰嚭曰：「子胥為人臣，徒欲干君之好，咈君之心以自稱滿，君何不知過乎？」

子胥曰：「太宰嚭固欲以求其親，前縱石室之囚，受其寶女之遺。外交敵國，內惑於君，大王察之，無為群小所侮。今大王譬若浴嬰兒，雖啼，無聽宰嚭之言。」

吳王曰：「宰嚭是。子無乃聞寡人言，非忠臣之道，類於佞諛之人？」

太宰嚭曰：「臣聞：『鄰國有急，千里馳救。』是乃王者封亡國之後，五霸輔絕滅之末者也。」

吳王乃與越粟萬石而令之曰：「寡人逆群臣之議而輸於越，年豐而歸寡人。」

大夫種曰：「臣奉使返越，歲登誠還吳貸。」

大夫種歸越，越國群臣皆稱萬歲。即以粟賞賜群臣，及於萬民。

9.9. In the thirteenth year of King Goujian (484 BCE), the king of Yue spoke to Grand Minister Wen Zhong, saying, "I, the orphan, benefited from your strategies, sir, everything I have planned has met with good fortune and none of them has failed. Now I desire to once more make plans for Wu, what should I do?" Wen Zhong said, "My lord should report this to Wu by yourself: 'The state of Yue is small and lies afar. Our harvest has failed this year. I wish Your Majesty would allow me to buy grain.'[64] And use this to test his intention.[65] If heaven abandons Wu, the king of Wu will definitely allow Your Majesty."

The king of Yue thereupon sent Grand Minister Wen Zhong to travel to Wu as an emissary. Through Chief Chancellor Bo Pi he requested an audience from the king of Wu, and his words read: "The land of the state of Yue is low. Its drought and flood are unbalanced and the harvest failed. Its people are hungry and exhausted, and starving people have crowded onto the roads.[66] I wish to buy grain from Your Majesty. I will immediately return it to your grand granaries next year. I implore Your Majesty to save us from poverty and difficulty."

The king of Wu said, "The king of Yue is trustworthy, honest, and stands by the Way. He does not harbor any thought of disloyalty. Now he is in a desperate situation and comes to appeal to me.[67] How can I cherish valuables and not fulfill his wishes?"

---

64. 籴 (*di*) is the same as 糴 (*di*), which specifically means "to buy grain"; the opposite is 糶 (*tiao*), "to sell grain." The left bottom parts of the two characters contain the character 米 (*mi*), rice. On the top of 米 are the characters 入 (*ru*), "to enter," and 出 (*chu*), "to leave," respectively. Thus they indicate buying (bringing in) and selling (sending out) grains. These are a pair of terms that are often used together. For example, the "Kenling" 墾令 chapter in *Shangjun shu* 商君書 warns of the consequences of a situation where "merchants could not buy grains and peasants could not sell grains" 使商無得籴，農無得糶. See Jiang Lihong 蔣禮鴻, *Shangjun shu zhuizhi* 商君書錐指 (Beijing: Zhonghua shuju, 2015), 8.

65. 入 (*ru*), "to enter," is a mistake for 卜 (*bu*), "to make divination on." The "Yue shijia" chapter in *Shiji* reads 以卜其意 (*yi bu qiyi*), "in order to test his intention." See *Shiji*, 41:1743.

66. Zhang Jue cites Du Yu's 杜預 commentary to a *Zuozhuan* sentence "狄戎荐居 (*Di Rong jianjun*)" and interprets 荐 (*jian*) as 聚 (*ju*), "to gather together, to crowd." See Zhang Jue, 272n3.

67. 愬 (*su*), "to report, to complain, to appeal." The poem "Bozhou" in the *Book of Songs* contains the following line: "If I go and complain to them, I meet with their anger" (薄言往愬，逢彼之怒). See Legge, *The She King*, 38. *Shishuo xinyu* 世說新語 has an interesting story about this line. It says that the servants and maids in the household of the famous Eastern Han scholar Zheng Xuan 鄭玄 (127–200) were all able to read. Once a maid upset Zheng Xuan and he was about to lash her as a punishment. The maid continued to appeal for mercy, but this enraged Zheng Xuan, who then

Wu Zixu remonstrated against this, saying,[68] "It is not right! If it is not Wu conquering Yue it must be Yue conquering Wu. If fortune goes to Yue then misfortune befalls Wu. Selling them food is feeding the enemy and destroying the state. Even if we give them food they will not become close to us; if we do not give them food it will not cause hatred. Moreover, Yue has a sagely minister, Fan Li, who is brave and good at strategy. He will cover up their attempts at invasion and use food buying as an excuse in order to spy on us for opportunities.[69] I notice that the king of Yue's sending an emissary to come buy food is not because his state is poor and his people are suffering, he is using this to enter our state and prey on Your Majesty's mistake."

The king of Wu said, "I, the orphan, have caused the king of Yue to humble himself and surrender to me. I controlled his people, seized his altars of land and grain, and humiliated him. Goujian yielded willingly. He readied my carriage, and walked backward to lead my horses.[70] None of the lords has not heard of this. Now I have sent him to return to his state so that he can offer sacrifice to his ancestral temple and regain his altars of land and grain, how dare he harbor any thought of betraying me?"

Wu Zixu said, "I, your subject, have heard that if a man is in a desperate situation it is not difficult for him to lower himself in front of people, but after that he will have the look of aspiration.[71] I, your subject, have heard that the king of Yue is suffering from famine and his people experience hardship and distress; we can take advantage of this and destroy him. Now if we do not follow the way of heaven and obey the principle of the earth but supply them with food instead, then indeed Your Majesty's fate resembles the trick the fox played on the pheasant: the fox lowered down its body humbly and

---

ordered her to be dragged through the mud. Soon after, another maid came and asked the punished one, quoting the line from the poem "Shiwei" 式微 in the *Book of Songs*, "Why should we be here in the mire?" The punished maid answered, citing lines from the poem "Bozhou:" "I went and complained to him, I met with his anger." (鄭玄家奴婢皆讀書。嘗使一婢，不稱旨，將撻之。方自陳說，玄怒，使人曳箸泥中。須臾，復有一婢來，問曰："胡為乎泥中？"答曰："薄言往愬，逢彼之怒。") See Xu Zhen'e 徐震堮, *Shishuo xinyu jiaojian* 世說新語校箋 (Beijing: Zhonghua shuju, 2001), 105.

68. *Yue jue shu* includes more elaborate discussions among the Wu ruler and his ministers on this issue of selling grain to Yue. See the "Qing di" 請糴 chapter in *Yue jue shu*. Li Bujia, 127–29; Milburn, 165–70.

69. 間 (*jian*), "gap, opportunity."

70. 却行 (*quexing*) means "walk backward." This is a way of showing deep respect. Liu Bang's biography in *Shiji* records that after Liu Bang became the emperor, his father held a broom and walked backward at the home gate to welcome Liu Bang's visit. See *Shiji*, 8:382.

71. *Yue jue shu* has a clearer argument on this. Wu Zixu says that "I, your subject, have heard that when a sage is in an urgent situation he is not ashamed to serve as slave and servant but his will and aspiration are still seen by people" (臣聞聖人有急，則不羞爲人臣僕，而志氣見人). See Li Bujia, 128; Milburn, 168.

the pheasant trusted it. Therefore the fox achieved its goal and the pheasant inevitably died. How can we not be cautious about this?"

The king of Wu said, "Goujian's state is in trouble and I, a man of little virtue, will supply him with grain. The kindness I give him he will return with loyalty. My virtue is illustrious so what worries should I have?"

Wu Zixu said, "I, your subject, have heard that a wolf cub has a wild heart and a foe should not be kept close.[72] One should not feed a tiger with food; one should not allow a viper to crawl as it pleases. Now Your Majesty abandoned the fortune of the state and enriched the enemy that brings no benefit to us; you disregarded the words of a loyal minister yet submitted to the will of the foe. I, your subject, will certainly witness Yue destroying Wu, snakes and deer wandering at the Gusu Terrace,[73] and thorns and bushes spread within the palace. I wish Your Majesty would review the event of King Wu attacking Zhou."[74]

Chief Chancellor Bo Pi commented nearby, saying, "Wasn't King Wu a subject of King Zhou? He led the many lords to attack his ruler, how can he be considered righteous even if he conquered Yin?"[75]

Wu Zixu said, "But King Wu established his fame from this."

Chief Chancellor Bo Pi said, "Establishing his fame via killing his ruler by his own hand, I cannot tolerate this."

---

72. "The wolf cub has a wild heart" 狼子野心 (*langzi yexin*) is a proverb cited at least twice in *Zuozhuan*, see Lord Xun 4 and Lord Zhao 28. This was cited when two newborn children were deemed evil. See Yang Bojun, 679, 1493; Durrant, Li, and Schaberg, 1687.

73. Xu Tianhu cites *Erya* 爾雅 and interprets 豸 (*zhi*) as a footless insect. See Zhang Jue, 272n16.

74. King Wu's attack on Zhou, the last king of Shang, is recorded in both "Basic Annals of Yin" 殷本紀 and "Basic Annals of Zhou" 周本紀 in *Shiji*. King Wu defeated Zhou in Muye 牧野. Zhou wore his robe decorated with treasures and threw himself into a fire and died. King Wu cut the head off of Zhou's corpse and hung it on a white flag. See *Shiji*, 3:108, 4:124.

75. The question of the legitimacy of Tang's destroying Xia king Jie and King Wu's killing of Shang king Zhou was at the center of many political discussions in pre-Qin and Han times. The *Book of Changes* confirms that Tang's and King Wu's actions in overthrowing tyrants were in line with the will of heaven and the people's demands (湯武革命，順乎天而應乎人). When King Hui of Liang 梁惠王 questions the rightfulness of Tang's and King Wu's killing of their former rulers, Mencius responds that Jie and Zhou mutilated humaneness and crippled righteousness and they were simply outcasts (*yifu* 一夫); therefore Tang and King Wu only punished the "outcasts," not their former lords. Xunzi agrees with Mencius and confirms that killing Jie and Zhou was killing "outcasts." Even in Western Han, this was still a controversy among elites. The "Rulin liezhuan" 儒林列傳 chapter in *Shiji* records a heated debate between Yuangu sheng 轅固生 and Huang sheng 黃生 in front of Emperor Jing 景帝 over the question of whether Tang and King Wu committed regicide. When the arguments lead to the question of whether the Han founder Emperor Gaozu's 漢高祖 replacement of Qin should be considered regicide, Emperor Jing has to stop the debate. See *Shiji*, 121:3122–23. See also Kong Yingda 孔穎達 (574–648), *Zhouyi Zhengyi* 周易正義 (Beijing: Zhonghua shuju, 1982), 60. For Mencius, see *Mencius*, 23. For Xunzi, see Wang Xianqian, *Xunzi jijie*, 325.

Wu Zixu said, "He who steals the state makes himself a lord; he who steals money gets killed.[76] If King Wu has lost the Way, why then did Zhou honor the three men Qizi, Bigan, and Shangrong?"[77]

Chief Chancellor Bo Pi said, "Wu Zixu is a minister, yet he only wants to interfere with the ruler's preferences and resist the ruler's heart in order to satisfy himself.[78] How could the ruler not know his own faults?"

Wu Zixu said, "Chief Chancellor Bo Pi just wants to take this opportunity to seek favor from the king of Yue. In the past he released the prisoner from the stone cave,[79] and accepted money and beauties from Yue. Outside of the state he befriends a hostile state and in the state he misguides the ruler. Your Majesty must investigate this, do not be played by pitiful men. Now Your Majesty is in the same situation as bathing a baby; even if he is crying, you should not listen to Chief Chancellor Bo Pi's words."

The king of Wu said, "Chief Chancellor Bo Pi is right. You, sir, seem unable to listen to my words.[80] This is not the way of a loyal minister but is similar to that of a slanderer."

Chief Chancellor Bo Pi said, "I, your subject, have heard that 'when the neighboring state has an urgent situation one should travel a thousand *li* a day to the rescue.' This is why those who become king enfeoff the descendants of the conquered realm and the Five Hegemons help the offspring of the destroyed states."[81]

The king of Wu thereupon gave Yue ten thousand piculs of grain and issued an order to Wen Zhong, saying, "I, a man of little virtue, disregarded the ministers' suggestion and supplied food to Yue. You must return the grain to me, a man of little virtue, after harvest."

---

76. This is adopted from *Zhuangzi*, where Zhuangzi criticizes the Confucian promotion of the "sagely way" 聖人之道 (*shengren zhidao*): "The one who steals a hook is put to death for it; the one who steals a state becomes its ruler" (竊鉤者誅, 竊國者諸侯). See the "Quqie" 胠篋 chapter in *Zhuangzi*; see Guo Qingfan, *Zhuangzi jishi*, 359. This phrase is also quoted by Sima Qian in his biography of the knights, "Youxia liezhuan" 遊俠列傳; see *Shiji*, 124:3182.

77. These are three loyal ministers of the Shang king Zhou. Because of their remonstrations, Zhou put Qizi in jail, cut out Bigan's heart, and removed Shangrong from his post. After King Wu conquered Shang, he released Qizi and honored Bigan and Shangrong posthumously. See the "Basic Annals of Yin" chapter and the "Basic Annals of Zhou" chapter in *Shiji*. *Shiji*, 3:108, 4:126.

78. 咈 (*fu*), "to disobey."

79. Referring to Goujian who was detained in a stone cave in Wu.

80. 乃 (*nai*) means 能 (*neng*), "able," here.

81. According to *Shiji*, after Tang destroyed Xia he enfeoffed the descendants of the Xia kings. King Wu of Zhou also gave land to Zhou's sons to allow them to continue the Shang sacrifices. See *Shiji*, 2:88, 4:126.

Grand Minister Wen Zhong said, "I, your subject, receive your commend and return to Yue. Once there is a harvest we definitely will pay back Wu's food."

Grand Minister Wen Zhong returned to Yue. All the ministers of Yue shouted, "Long live the king!" The king of Yue then bestowed the grain to all the ministers, and further to all the people.

9.10. 二年，越王粟稔，揀擇精粟而蒸，還於吳，復還斗斛之數，亦使大夫種歸之吳王。王得越粟長太息謂太宰嚭曰：「越地肥沃，其種甚嘉，可留使吾民植之。」於是吳種越粟，粟種殺而無生者，吳民大飢。越王曰：「彼以窮居，其可攻也？」大夫種曰：「未可，國始貧耳，忠臣尚在，天氣未見，須俟其時。」

9.10. The next year (483 BCE), after the grain was ripe, the king of Yue selected fine grain, steamed it, and returned it to Wu, repaying the same amount of piculs.[82] He again sent Grand Minister Wen Zhong to return the grain to Wu. The king of Wu received the grain from Yue, and he gave a long sigh and addressed Chief Chancellor Bo Pi, saying, "The land of Yue is fertile and their seeds are very good. We can save the seeds and let our people plant them." Therefore Wu planted the grain from Yue; the seeds were dead and none of them grew. The people of Wu suffered from a great famine. The king of Yue then said, "They are already in a difficult situation; they can be attacked." Grand Minister Wen Zhong said, "Not yet. The hardship has just begun in their state and their loyal ministers are still alive.[83] The heavenly *qi* has yet to appear,[84] so we must wait for the right time."

9.11. 越王又問相國范蠡曰：「孤有報復之謀，水戰則乘舟，陸行則乘輿，輿舟之利，頓於兵弩。今子為寡人謀事，莫不謬者乎？」范蠡對曰：「臣聞古之聖君，莫不習戰用兵，然行陣隊伍軍鼓之事，吉凶決在其工。今聞越有處女，出於南林，國人稱善。願王請之，立可見。」越王乃使使聘之，問以劍戟之術。

處女將北見於王，道逢一翁，自稱曰袁公。問於處女：「吾聞子善劍，願一見之。」女曰：「妾不敢有所隱，惟公試之。」於是袁公即拔箖箊竹，竹枝上枯槁，未折墮地，女即捷末。袁公操其本而刺處女。處女應即入之，三入，因舉杖擊袁公。袁公則飛上樹，變為白猿。遂別去，見越王。

82. Both 斗 (*dou*) and 斛 (*hu*) are dry measures used in the past. Roughly ten 斗 equals one 斛.

83. According to *Zuozhuan*, Wu Zixu had already died by 484 BCE, see Lord Ai 11. Yang Bojun, 1664; Durrant, Li, and Schaberg, 1903.

84. This refers to the heavenly *qi* indicating the fall of Wu.

越王問曰：「夫劍之道則如之何？」女曰：「妾生深林之中，長於無人之野，無道不習，不達諸侯。竊好擊之道，誦之不休。妾非受於人也，而忽自有之。」越王曰：「其道如何？」女曰：「其道甚微而易，其意甚幽而深。道有門戶，亦有陰陽。開門閉戶，陰衰陽興。凡手戰之道，內實精神，外示安儀，見之似好婦，奪之似懼虎，布形候氣，與神俱往，杳之若日，偏如滕兔，追形逐影，光若彿彷，呼吸往來，不及法禁，縱橫逆順，直復不聞。斯道者，一人當百，百人當萬。王欲試之，其驗即見。」越王大悅，即加女號，號曰「越女。」乃命五校之隊長、高才習之，以教軍士。當此之時皆稱越女之劍。

9.11. The king of Yue further asked Prime Minister Fan Li, saying, "I, the orphan, have a plan for revenge against Wu: we will sail in a boat if the battle occurs in the river; ride chariots if marching on land. However, the advantages of using chariots and boats are undermined by weapons and crossbows. Now you, sir, made plans for me, the orphan, and perhaps there are errors in your idea?" Fan Li answered, saying, "I, your subject, have heard that in ancient times sagely rulers were all familiar with war and the deployment of troops. However, as for arranging the lines, commanding the troops, and beating the drum for advance and retreat,[85] victory and defeat are determined by people with expertise.[86] Now I have heard that there is a maiden who was born in the Southern Grove in Yue and people in the state praise her skill. I wish for Your Majesty to invite her; you will see her skill right away." The king of Yue therefore sent an emissary to invite her and asked her about the art of the sword and halberd.

The maiden was about to travel north to receive an audience from the king. On her way she ran into an old man who called himself Senior Yuan.[87] He asked the maiden, "I have heard that you are good with a sword; I wish I could observe this." The girl said, "I dare not hide it; I wish for you, old sir, to test me." Senior Yuan thereupon pulled up a Linyu bamboo shoot.[88] The top of the branch withered so that its tip broke and dropped on the ground.[89] The girl then immediately picked up the tip.[90] Senior Yuan held the branch and executed a strike as a feint at the maiden. The maiden then let him strike. After three attempts she then raised the stick to fence Senior

85. Drums and gongs were used to command soldiers to advance and retreat in the past.

86. 工 (*gong*) here refers to experts and people with specific skills.

87. The surname Yuan is a pun on the word "*yuan*" 猿, an ape.

88. The name of this bamboo appears first in the *WYCQ* story and is then mentioned often in later literary works because of the influence of the *WYCQ* story.

89. 未 (*wei*), "not, yet," should be a mistake for 末 (*mo*), "tip, end."

90. 捷 (*jie*), "fast, to speed," should be 接 (*jie*), "to pick up."

Yuan. Senior Yuan immediately jumped up into a tree and transformed into a white monkey. The maiden thereupon bid farewell to him and went to see the king of Yue.[91]

The king of Yue asked the maiden, "What, indeed, is the way of swordsmanship?" The girl answered, "I was born in the deep woods and grew up in the uninhabited wild. I have no access to learning and I am not known by the lords.[92] Privately I am fond of the art of fencing so I study it consistently. It is not that I have learned from someone, I just acquired the art all of a sudden." The king of Yue said, "What is the way of fencing?" The girl said, "Its way is subtle but simple, yet its thought is very deep and profound. It has both a correct path and crooked practices;[93] it also contains the aspects of *yin* and *yang*. Open the right path and close the twisted way, then *yin* will decline and *yang* will rise up.[94] In general, the principle of fighting with a weapon is filling your body with energy yet displaying a composed posture. You look like a gentle lady but fight like a terrifying tiger. Observe your *qi* to ready your body accordingly, and advance together with your mind. Be as lofty as the sun but as swift as a jumping hare. Chase the body and the shadow of your enemy as quickly as light. In the space of a breath, advance and retreat, no

---

91. The story of the white monkey testing the maiden's swordsmanship skill has become a famous anecdote among later generations. Wang Chong's *Lunheng* mentions the Yue maiden as a master of swordsmanship. By Jin times, the story had already become a well-known literary allusion. Tang and Song encyclopedias such as *Yiwen leiju* and *Taiping yulan* also quote the story in several categories. The popularity of the story can be attested by its frequent appearance in not only poems and essays but also in epitaphs for military men in the Tang and Song eras. Qian Zhongshu 錢鍾書 includes a list of literary works citing this story in his *Guanzhui bian* 管錐編. In the Ming dynasty, the story was adapted into a novel titled *Jianxia zhuan* 劍俠傳 (*Legends of Sword Masters*), as well as by Feng Menglong 馮夢龍 (1574–1646) in his *Dongzhou lieguozhi yanyi* 東周列國志演義. A portrait of this maiden, mistakenly labeled as the Maiden of Zhao, is the first portrait of the Qing artist Ren Xiong's 任熊 series *Sasan jianke tu* 卅三劍客圖 (Portraits of Thirty-Three Swordsmen). More recently, the famous modern *wuxia* 武俠 (martial arts and chivalry) writer Jin Yong's 金庸 (Louis Cha Leung-yung) short novel *Yuenü jian* 越女劍 was also developed from the *WYCQ* story. The novel was later made into a twenty-episode Hong Kong TV series by ATV in 1985. For more on Wang Chong, see Huang Hui, *Lunheng jiaoshi*, 597. For information on Qian Zhongshu, see Qian Zhongshu, *Guanzhui bian* (Beijing: Zhonghua shuju, 1979), 1530.

92. 道 (*dao*), "means, access." 不 (*bu*) functions as 而 (*er*), indicating "by which means."

93. 門 (*men*) is a pair of doors that swing open in the middle; 戶 (*hu*) is half of a door pair. 門 and 戶 here are used as metaphors, referring to a correct path and a narrow path.

94. The maiden's description of the Way resembles that of Daoist mystery philosophy. However, her suggestion regarding opening and closing doors in order to control *yin* and *yang* bears the mark of the "New Text" school popular in Han times. As recommended in *Chunqiu fanlu* 春秋繁露, a text traditionally attributed to Dong Zhongshu, rain can be caused by males hiding inside and females being in full spirit, as male and female are associated with *yang* and *yin*, respectively. Similarly, in order to stop excessive rain, females should be prohibited from entering the market place and should hide themselves inside. The idea is that in a correlative universe, rain, which is a *yin* element, can be manipulated by adjusting the proportion of *yin* and *yang* in the human world. See Su Yu 蘇輿, *Chunqiu fanlu yizheng* 春秋繁露義證 (Beijing: Zhonghua shuju, 2015), 431.

law or regulation can detain you. Going left and right, back and forth, no one can hear you. Mastering this art, one can defeat one hundred men, and one hundred can defeat ten thousand. If Your Majesty wishes to test it, its effect will show immediately." The king of Yue was greatly delighted. He bestowed the maiden with a title right away and called her the "Maiden of Yue." He thereupon ordered colonels of all units and elite warriors to learn from her and then teach the soldiers.[95] At that time everyone praised the Maiden of Yue's art of the sword.

9.12. 於是范蠡復進善射者陳音。音，楚人也。越王請音而問曰：「孤聞子善射，道何所生？」

音曰：「臣，楚之鄙人，嘗步於射術，未能悉知其道。」

越王曰：「然，願子一二其辭。」

音曰：「臣聞弩生於弓，弓生於彈，彈起古之孝子。」

越王曰：「孝子彈者柰何？」

音曰：「古者人民朴質，飢食鳥獸，渴飲霧露，死則裹以白茅，投於中野。孝子不忍見父母為禽獸所食，故作彈以守之，絕鳥獸之害。故歌曰：『斷竹，續竹，飛土，逐肉』遂令死者不犯鳥狐之殘也。於是神農、黃帝弦木為弧，剡木為矢，弧矢之利，以威四方。黃帝之後，楚有弧父。弧父者，生於楚之荊山，生不見父母，為兒之時，習用弓矢，所射無脫。以其道傳於羿，羿傳逄蒙，逄蒙傳於楚琴氏，琴氏以為弓矢不足以威天下。當是之時，諸侯相伐，兵刃交錯，弓矢之威不能制服。琴氏乃橫弓著臂，施機設樞，加之以力，然後諸侯可服。琴氏傳之楚三侯，所謂句亶、鄂、章，人號麋侯、翼侯、魏侯也。自楚之三侯傳至靈王，自稱之楚累世，蓋以桃弓棘矢而備鄰國也。自靈王之後，射道分流，百家能人用，莫得其正。臣前人受之於楚，五世於臣矣。臣雖不明其道，惟王試之。」

越王曰：「弩之狀何法焉？」

陳音曰：「郭為方城，守臣子也；教為人君，命所起也；牙為執法，守吏卒也；牛為中將，主內裹也；關為守禦，檢去止也；錡為侍從，聽人主也；臂為道路，通所使也；弓為將軍，主重負也；弦為軍師，禦戰士也；矢為飛客，主教使也；金為穿敵，往不止也；衛為副使，正道里也；又為受教，知可否也；縹為都尉，執左右也。敵為百死，不得駭也，鳥不及飛，獸不暇走，弩之所向，無不死也，臣之愚劣，道悉如此。」

95. 五校 (*wujiao*) is a Han military term which refers to the colonels of the five armies that include both infantry and cavalry. These are: Colonel of Garrison Cavalry 屯騎 (*tunji*), Colonel of Elite Cavalry 越騎 (*yueji*), Colonel of Infantry 步兵 (*bubing*), Colonel of Zhang River (encampment) 長水 (*changshui*), and Colonel of Shooters at Sounds 射聲音 (*she shengyin*).

越王曰：「願聞正射之道。」

音曰：「臣聞正射之道，道眾而微。古之聖人射，弩未發而前名其所中。臣未能如古之聖人，請悉其要。夫射之道，身若戴板，頭若激卵，左蹉，右足横，左手若附枝，右手若抱兒，舉弩望敵，翕心咽煙，與氣俱發，得其和平，神定思去，去止分離，右手發機，左手不知，一身異教，豈況雄雌？此正射持弩之道也。」

「願聞望敵儀表，投分飛矢之道。」

音曰：「夫射之道，從分望敵，合以參連。弩有斗石，矢有輕重，石取一兩，其數乃平，遠近高下，求之銖分。道要在斯，無有遺言。」

越王曰：「善。盡子之道，願子悉以教吾國人。」

音曰：「道出於天，事在於人，人之所習，無有不神。」

於是乃使陳音教士習射於北郊之外，三月，軍士皆能用弓弩之巧。

陳音死，越王傷之，葬於國西山上，號其葬所曰陳音山。

9.12. At that time Fan Li also recommended a man named Chen Yin who was good at archery. Chen Yin was a native of Chu. The king of Yue invited Chen Yin and asked him, "I, the orphan, have heard you, sir, are good at archery. Where did you learn your skill?"

Chen Yin said, "I, your subject, am a man from the remotest place of Chu. I once learned the art of archery but am not able to completely understand its way."[96]

The king of Yue said, "Even so, I still wish you, sir, to introduce it in one word or two."

Chen Yin said, "I, your subject, have heard that the crossbow was developed from the bow, the bow came from the slingshot, and the slingshot was invented by filial sons in the ancient times."

The king of Yue asked, "Why did the filial sons invent the slingshot?"

Chen Yin said, "In ancient times people were simple and unsophisticated. They ate birds and beasts when they were hungry, drank dew when thirsty. After they died they were wrapped in white grass and thrown into the wild.[97]

---

96. 步 (*bu*), "step" or "to step in." Chen Yin is being modest in saying that he only has a little knowledge of archery.

97. 白茅 (*baimao*), "white grass," was often used for sacrificial purposes. For example, *Yi Zhoushu* records that when King Wu enfeoffed the lords, he presented them with earth of a specific color corresponding to their land and wrapped the earth in white grass. See Niu Hong'en 牛鴻恩, *Xinyi yi zhoushu* 新譯逸周書 (Taipei: Sanmin shuju, 2015), 368. 白茅 was also used to filter wine that was offered in sacrifice. *Zuozhuan*, Lord Xi 4 records Lord Huan of Qi attacking Cai and Chu; the reason for Qi's attack on Chu, as stated in the words of Guan Zhong, was that Chu failed to pay its tribute—the white grass—so there was nothing to filter the wine and the Zhou king's sacrifice was not supplied. See Yang Bojun, 290; Durrant, Li, and Schaberg, 265.

Filial sons could not bear to see deceased parents be eaten by birds and beasts, whereupon they made slingshots and guarded the bodies in order to prevent harm from the birds and beasts.[98] For this reason the ancient men sung, 'Cut off the bamboo and tie it with wood; shoot clay balls to chase away animals.'[99] This thus ensured that the deceased would not be damaged by birds and foxes. After this, Shen Nong and the Yellow Emperor bound string to a branch and made a bow;[100] they chopped wood and made arrows. Relying upon the power of the bow and arrow, they awed the whole world.[101] After the Yellow Emperor, there was Hufu from Chu. Hufu was born on Mount Jing in Chu. From birth he had never seen his parents.[102] When he was a child he was skillful in using a bow and arrow, and none of the animals he shot could escape. He taught his skill to Yi,[103] Yi taught Pangmeng, and Pangmeng taught Qinshi of Chu.[104] Qinshi thought that a bow and arrow were not powerful enough to awe the world. At that time, the lords attacked each other, blades of weapons crossed together, and the power of the bow

---

98. This is adapted from a story in *Mencius* in which Mencius argues that filial piety comes from children's innate desire to protect the bodies of their deceased parents from being mutilated by animals. Mencius says, "Presumably there must have been cases in ancient times of people not burying their parents. When the parents died, they were thrown in the gullies. Then one day the sons passed the place and there lay the bodies, eaten by foxes and sucked by flies. A sweat broke out on their brows, and they could not bear to look. Their sweating was not put on for others to see. It was an outward expression of their innermost heart. They went home for baskets and spades. If it was truly right for them to bury the remains of their parents, then it must also be right for all dutiful sons and benevolent men to do likewise." 蓋上世嘗有不葬其親者。其親死，則舉而委之於壑。他日過之，狐狸食之，蠅蚋姑嘬之。其顙有泚，睨而不視。夫泚也，非為人泚，中心達於面目。蓋歸反虆梩而掩之。掩之誠是也，則孝子仁人之掩其親，亦必有道矣。See *Mencius*, 63.

99. Chinese scholars often regard this as one of the earliest songs from high antiquity and seldom question its authenticity.

100. Shen Nong is a legendary ruler in Chinese mythology. He was credited with many inventions associated with agriculture. For example, Shen Nong was said to have invented the hoe, plow, axe, and irrigation. He taught the people how to farm and was also believed to be the founder of traditional Chinese medicine. The Yellow Emperor is probably the most important figure in Chinese mythology and religion. Generally he is regarded as the founder of Chinese civilization and is credited with numerous inventions. Sima Qian's *Shiji* begins with legends of the Yellow Emperor. See *Shiji*, 1:1–10.

101. This is adapted from the *Book of Changes*: "Bound string to a branch and made a bow, and chopped wood and made arrows. Relying upon the power of the bow and arrow, they commanded the world." (弦木为弧，剡木为矢，弧矢之利，以威天下) See Kong Yingda, *Zhouyi Zhengyi*, 75.

102. It is interesting that the Maid of Yue also claims that she is an orphan.

103. Yi, also called Houyi, was a legendary archer in Chinese mythology. In Chinese folklore, there were once ten suns scorching the earth, and Yi shot down nine of them and left one in the sky.

104. Pangmeng was a student of Yi. According to Mencius, Pangmeng killed Yi after he had completed his learning: "Pangmeng learned archery from Yi, and, having learned everything Yi could teach, thought to himself that in all the world Yi was the only archer superior to himself. Thereupon he killed Yi." (逄蒙学射于羿，尽羿之道，思天下惟羿为愈己，于是杀羿。) Translation adopted from *Mencius*, 92.

and arrow could not subdue the enemy. Qinshi therefore placed the bow horizontally and attached it to a barrel, equipped it with a trigger and added a sight, which increased the power of the bow and thereby he prevailed over the many lords.[105] Qinshi passed this on to the three marquises of Chu, the so-called Goutan, E, and Zhang, whom people called Marquis Mi, Marquis Yi, and Marquis Wei.[106] From the three marquises of Chu, the crossbow was handed down to King Ling, who proclaimed that for generations Chu would use bows made of peach tree wood and arrows made of buckthorn to guard against neighboring states.[107] After King Ling, the arts of archery split into different schools; each of the hundred schools had capable men using bows and arrows but none had mastered the right way. These ancestors of mine, your subject, learned this in Chu for five generations until it was passed down to me. Although I do not understand the art of it, I wish Your Majesty to test me."

The king of Yue asked, "What is the shape of a crossbow modeled after?"

Chen Yin said, "The sight, *guo*, resembles a square-shaped city wall, which protects the ministers and the people. The trigger, *jiao*, resembles the ruler of man, from whom orders are issued. The latch, *ya*, resembles law officers, who take charge of clerks and soldiers. The cow tendon, *niü*, resembles officers, who are in charge of internal affairs. The trigger reset, *guan*, resembles the guards, controlling coming and going. The crossbow holder, *qi*, is the attendant, who listens to the ruler. The barrel, *bi*, is the path, through which emissaries pass. The limb, *gong*, is the general, bearing the heavy load. The string, *xian*, is the tactician, commanding the warriors. The arrow, *shi*, is the flying messenger, responsible for receiving and carrying out the order. The arrowhead, *jin*, is the vanguard, dashing forward without stopping. The

---

105. For a discussion on the history of the crossbow, see Joseph Needham, *Science and Civilisation in China*, vol. 5, part 6 (Cambridge: Cambridge University Press, 2004), 135. The earliest crossbow bolt was found in a fifth-century BCE Chu tomb in modern-day Yutaishan 雨臺山, in Jiangling 江陵 County, Hubei Province. See Donald B. Wagner, *Iron and Steel in Ancient China* (Leiden: Brill, 1996), 157.

106. These were three sons of the Chu ruler Xiongqu 熊渠: Xiongkang 熊康, Xionghong 熊紅, and Xiongzhici 熊執疵 who were all enfeoffed as King Goutan, King E, and King Yuezhang by their father. Later on, afraid that King Li of Zhou would attack Chu because he had given his sons the title of king, a title that could only enjoyed by the Zhou kings, Xiongqu changed their title to marquis. See *Shiji*, 40:1692.

107. In *Zuozhuan*, Lord Zhao 12, Chu minister Zige 子革 speaks to the Chu king, saying, "In the past our former king Xiongyi dwelt far off in the wilds of Mount Jing. Riding in a rugged wooden cart and clad in tattered hemp, he lived in the grasses of the plain. He trod over mountains and forests to serve the Son of Heaven, and all he had was a bow of peach wood and arrows of thorn to present as tribute to the royal court." 昔我先王熊绎，辟在荆山，筚路蓝缕，以处草莽，跋涉山林，以事天子，唯是桃弧棘矢，以共御王事. See Yang Bojun, 1339. Translation adapted from Durrant, Li, and Schaberg, 1483.

fletchings, *wei*, are the assistant emissaries, who correct the direction of the way. The nock, *you*, is the one receiving command who knows whether or not the plan will be carried out. The foregrip, *piao*, is the commander, leading the attendants left and right. The arrowpoint, *di*, hits the target with every shot and cannot be disturbed. Once it is shot, birds are not able to fly away and beasts have no chance to run. Of that which the crossbow is aimed at, nothing will survive. I, your subject, am foolish and base, these are what I have learned."

The king of Yue said, "I would like to hear the proper way of archery."

Chen Yin said, "I, your subject, have heard that the proper way of archery is complicated but subtle. Sagely men of ancient times could tell which target the arrow would hit before the crossbow was triggered. I, your subject, am not able to be like the sagely men of the past, please allow me to introduce all the essentials. The ways of archery are as follows: The body should stand straight as if it is tied on a board. The head should rise up as if it is of high spirits.[108] The left foot stands longitudinally and the right foot laterally.[109] The left hand clutches the crossbow as if holding a branch; the right hand grips the trigger as if holding an infant. Lift up the crossbow and aim at the enemy, concentrate yourself, and abate your breath. The arrow should be released together with your breath, so it can be as peaceful and calm as the breath. Your mind is still and your distracting thoughts are gone. The shooting or holding of the arrow must be clear. When your right hand pulls the trigger, your left hand is not aware of this. All the parts of the body follow different orders, as needless to say, men are different from each other.[110] These are the right ways of operating the crossbow and shooting the arrow.

The king of Yue beseeched, "I wish to hear the methods of looking at the enemy and aiming at the target, as well as shooting together and individually."

Chen Yin said, "The way of shooting is this: Shooting individually depends on the situations of observing and aiming at the enemy. Shooting together uses three consecutive draws.[111] Crossbows are of strong and weak strengths;[112] the arrows are light or heavy. When drawing a crossbow with

---

108. 卯 (*luan*), "an egg," is probably a mistake for 卬 (*ang*), "rise up." In a Ming edition, it is written as 激卬 (*ji'ang*) instead of 激卯 (*jiluan*). See Huang Rensheng, 313n30.

109. The *Taiping yulan* quotes this as 左足縱，右足橫 (*zuozu zong, youzu heng*). See Zhang Jue, 280; Huang Rensheng, 313n31.

110. 雄 (*xiong*), "male," and 雌 (*ci*), "female," here refer to different persons.

111. 叁連 (*sanlian*) was one of the five ways of shooting mentioned in *Zhouli*. The commentary of *Zhouli* explains that 叁連 means to shoot one arrow first, followed by three arrows. See Zhang Jue, 283n50; Huang Rensheng, 313n35.

112. 斗 (*dou*) and 石 (*dan*) were units of weight in the past; they were also used to measure the strength of a bow. Ten Western Han 斗 equal one 石, which is roughly 66 pounds.

one *shi* strength, one uses arrows weighted one *liang*,[113] thus the proportion is balanced. As for the difference of far and near, high or low targets, this can be adjusted by using arrows with slight weight differences.[114] All of the essentials of archery are introduced here, I have not missed any words."

The king of Yue said, "Excellent! You, sir, have presented all your knowledge. I wish you, sir, to teach all of this to my people."

Chen Yin said, "The principles are created by heaven but the learning depends on man. If men practice repeatedly, they will all be sharp."

The king of Yue thereupon ordered Chen Yin to teach soldiers to practice archery outside of the northern suburb. After three months, the soldiers all mastered the skills of the crossbow.

The king of Yue was sad when Chen Yin died. He buried Chen Yin on the mountain west of the capital and named the place of burial Mount Chen Yin.[115]

---

113. One Western Han 两 (*liang*) is roughly 0.55 of an ounce.

114. 銖 (*zhu*) and 分 (*fen*) were smaller units of weight. One Western Han 銖 is approximately 0.022 of an ounce. One Western Han 分 is about 0.002 of an ounce.

115. In modern-day Shaoxing County, Zhejiang Province.

# 吳越春秋勾踐伐吳外傳第十

## CHAPTER 10

# The Outer Tradition of Goujian Attacking Wu

## Introduction

This chapter covers the period from Goujian's defeat of Wu to the end of his own state of Yue, focusing primarily on Goujian's destruction of Wu and his deteriorating relationship with his ministers. Events and materials included in this *WYCQ* chapter are different from those in Sima Qian's *Shiji*, which provides details on King Wujiang's competition with Chu and the legend of Fan Li.

The current chapter follows a chronological order and begins with Goujian's resolution to attack Wu. Goujian's preparation involves consulting with many ministers and wisemen, mobilizing the people and establishing law and order. The sentences in these paragraphs often repeat their patterns, creating a mixed air of tension, eagerness, prudence, and vengeance.

Description of the actual military expedition is, however, very brief. The narrator is more interested in entertaining the reader with the mystical story of Wu Zixu's spirit scaring away the Yue troops. After the fall of Wu, the chapter quickly changes to an ominous tone, starting with the description of the Yue King Goujian's dissatisfaction with his ministers during the celebration banquet. The Yue king's ambition and his personal faults alienate Fan Li, who wisely chooses to leave the king. The narrative then focuses on the execution of Wen Zhong, whose loyalty was wrongfully doubted by Goujian.

The account of Goujian's old age in this chapter consists of myth and anecdotes. Stories of spirits appear two times in the narrative, first with Wu Zixu floating in the air with Wen Zhong, and then with the spirit of King Yuanchang's disapproval of relocating his tomb. The episode in which Confucius presents ritual and music to Goujian is purely literary and does not align with any possible historical reality. The chapter ends with a genealogy of the Yue royal family.

## Translation

10.1. 勾踐十五年，謀伐吳。謂大夫種曰：「孤用夫子之策，免於天虐之誅，還歸於國。吾誠已說於國人，國人喜悅。而子昔日云:『有天氣即來陳之，』今豈有應乎？」

種曰：「吳之所以彊者，為有子胥。今伍子胥忠諫而死，是天氣前見，亡國之證也。願君悉心盡意，以說國人。」

越王曰：「聽孤說國人之辭：『寡人不知其力之不足以大國報讎，以暴露百姓之骨於中原。此則寡人之罪也。寡人誠更其術。』於是乃葬死問傷，弔有憂，賀有喜，送往迎來，除民所害。然後卑事夫差，往宦士三百人於吳。吳封孤數百里之地，因約吳國父兄昆弟而誓之曰：『寡人聞古之賢君，四方之民歸之若水。寡人不能為政，將率二三子夫婦以為藩輔。』令壯者無娶老妻，老者無娶壯婦。女子十七未嫁，其父母有罪；丈夫二十不娶，其父母有罪。將免者以告於孤，令醫守之。生男二，貺之以壺酒、一犬，生女二，賜以壺酒、一豚。生子三人，孤以乳母；生子二人，孤與一養。長子死，三年釋吾政，季子死，三月釋吾政，必哭泣葬埋之，如吾子也。令孤子、寡婦、疾疹、貧病者，納官其子，欲仕，量其居，好其衣，飽其食而簡銳之。凡四方之士來者，必朝而禮之。載飯與羹以游國中，國中僮子戲而遇孤，孤餔而啜之，施以愛，問其名。非孤飯不食，非夫人事不衣。七年不收，國民家有三年之畜。男即歌樂，女即會笑。今國之父兄日請於孤曰：『昔夫差辱吾君王於諸侯，長為天下所恥。今越國富饒，君王節儉，請可報恥。』孤辭之曰：『昔者我辱也，非二三子之罪也。如寡人者，何敢勞吾國之人，以塞吾之宿讎？』父兄又復請曰：『誠四封之內，盡吾君子，子報父仇，臣復君隙，豈敢有不盡力者乎？臣請復戰，以除君王之宿讎。』孤悅而許之。」

大夫種曰：「臣觀吳王得志於齊晉，謂當遂涉吾地，以兵臨境。今疲師休卒，一年而不試，以忘於我，我不可以怠。臣當卜之於天，吳民既疲於軍，困於戰鬥，市無赤米之積，國廩空虛，其民必有移徙之心，寒就蒲贏於東海之濱。夫占，兆人事，又見於卜筮。

王若起師，以可會之，利犯吳之邊鄙，未可往也。吳王雖無伐我之心，亦雖動之以怒，不如詮其間，以知其意。」

越王曰：「孤不欲有征伐之心，國人請戰者三年矣，吾不得不從民人之欲。今聞大夫種諫難。」

越父兄又諫曰：「吳可伐，勝則滅其國，不勝則困其兵。吳國有成，王與之盟。功名聞於諸侯。」

王曰：「善。」於是乃大會群臣而令之曰：「有敢諫伐吳者，罪不赦。」

蠡種相謂曰：「吾諫已不合矣，然猶聽君王之令。」

10.1. In the fifteenth year of King Goujian (482 BCE), the king planned to launch a military expedition against Wu.[1] He spoke to Grand Minister Wen Zhong, saying, "I, the orphan, adopted your strategies, sir; I avoided the punishment sent down by heaven and returned to my homeland.[2] I have indeed persuaded the people to attack Wu with me. The people are all delighted by this. However, you, sir, in the past have said that once there is an opportunity granted by heaven you will come and tell me immediately.[3] Is there any sign of it?"

Wen Zhong said, "The reason Wu is powerful is because of Wu Zixu, but he is already dead for admonishing his ruler as a loyal official. This is evidence of the fated demise of Wu as foretold by heaven. I wish Your Majesty would wholeheartedly convince the people of this."

The king of Yue said, "Please listen to the words I, the orphan, spoke to the people:[4] 'I, a man of little virtue, did not know that my power was not sufficient to seek revenge against a strong state,[5] consequently I caused the bones of my people to be exposed in the wild. This was the fault of mine, a man of little virtue. I will sincerely change my strategy.' I thereupon buried the dead and soothed the injured. I consoled those who had lost their relatives and congratulated those who have joyful matters. I saw off people

---

1. The "Yue yu xia" 越語下 chapter in *Guoyu* reports more discussions between Goujian and Fan Li on getting revenge against Wu. Goujian was so eager to exact revenge on Wu that he repeatedly sought advice from Fan Li on the right time for attacking Wu in the fifth, sixth, and seventh years after he returned to Yue. Each time, Fan Li advised Goujian that the opportunity had not yet arrived. See Xu Yuangao, 579–83.

2. In *WYCQ*, 5.27, Wen Zhong wrote to King Fuchai saying, "Previously heaven gave Yue to Wu but Wu refused to accept it, this disobeyed heaven. Goujian respected heaven and pacified his people, thereupon he was able to return to his state. Now heaven has rewarded the king of Yue's merit, he must respectfully accept this and dare not ignore it." This view of heavenly punishment is repeated in 7.2 in which Wen Zhong and Fan Li both confirm that King Goujian's slavery in Wu was predetermined by heaven.

3. 天氣 (*Tianqi*) refers to signs indicating the Mandate of Heaven.

4. The following speech by Goujian is basically adopted from *Guoyu*, "Yue yu shang" 越語上. See Xu Yuangao, 569–71.

5. 以 (*yi*) should be 與 (*yu*), "with, to be against," as seen in *Guoyu*. See Xu Yuangao, 569.

traveling away and welcomed those coming to Yue. I eliminated dangers for the people. Afterward, I humbly served Fuchai and three hundred Yue men went with me to Wu as servants. Wu enfeoffed me, the orphan, with land of several hundred *li*; I thereby invited my people,[6] their fathers, mothers, older and younger brothers and made an oath with them, saying, 'I, a man of little virtue, have heard that the sagely rulers of antiquity had people rendered to them from all over the world, as water flows downhill.[7] I, a man of little virtue, am incapable of governing, I wish to lead all of you to pair off, flourish, and multiply.'"[8]

"I also ordered that men in their prime cannot take older women as their wives, and that old men cannot marry women in their prime. If a girl has not yet been married at the age of seventeen, her parents are guilty; if a man has not taken a wife at the age of twenty, his parents are guilty.[9] If women who were about to go into labor reported this to me, the orphan, I would send a physician to attend to them. If a woman gave birth to two boys, I would bestow upon her a bottle of wine and a dog; if she mothered two daughters, I would award her a bottle of wine and a piglet.[10] If she mothered triplets, I, the orphan, would arrange a wet nurse for her. If she gave birth to twins, I would provide a cook for her.[11] If the oldest son died, the family would be free from governance services for three years. If the second son died, the family would be free from governance services for three months. I would certainly cry and bury the sons as if they were my own sons. I allowed widowers,[12] widows, the ill, and the poor to give their children to the state. For those who wanted to serve in the government, I measured

6. The "Yue yu shang" chapter in *Guoyu* has 致 (*zhi*), "to arrive," instead of 約 (*yue*), "to invite." Here 吳國 (*Wuguo*), "State of Wu," is probably a mistake for 越國 (*Yueguo*), "State of Yue." See Xu Yuangao, 570.

7. The "Yue yu shang" chapter in *Guoyu* has 寡人聞古之賢君，四方之民歸之，若水之歸下也 (I, a man of little virtue, have heard that, in the past, people from all over the world coming to sagely rulers resembled water flowing downward), which is a much clearer metaphor than this *WYCQ* sentence. See Xu Yuangao, 570.

8. 藩輔 (*fanfu*) means "vassal state." According to *Guoyu*, it should be 蕃 (*fan*), "to reproduce, to flourish, to multiply." See Xu Yuangao, 570.

9. The *Guoyu* commentary to this sentence explains: "According to the rites, a man takes a wife at the age of thirty and a woman marries out at the age of twenty. Here, Goujian's reason for disobeying ritual is to focus on the reproduction of the people." (禮，三十而娶，二十而嫁。今不待禮者，務育民也。) See Xu Yuangao, 570.

10. The *Guoyu* commentary explains that a dog is considered *yang* while a pig is *yin*. See Xu Yuangao, 570–71.

11. Zhang Jue cites a *Zuozhuan* passage and interprets 餋 (*yang*) as a "cook." See Zhang Jue, 289n19.

12. Based upon the sentence, 孤子 (*guzi*) here does not refer to orphans, it means widowers instead, so it is paired with widows in the narrative.

their capabilities and gave them homes, made sure their clothes were fine, fed them well, and selected the finest among them.[13] If worthy men came from all over the world, I would certainly receive them at court and treat them with courtesy. I loaded my boat with food and dishes when I toured the state.[14] When I, the orphan, met children who were playing,[15] I, the orphan, fed them food and let them eat, gave them affection, and asked their names. I would not eat if the food was not made of the grain I grew; I would not wear clothes if they were not sewn by my wife. For seven years the state has not levied taxes.[16] In the state, each household of the people has a three-year supply of grain. When men are together they are happy and sing; when women are together they laugh with joy. Now the fathers and older brothers in the state ask me daily, saying, 'Previously Fuchai humiliated our king in front of the many lords; for a long time you have been ridiculed by the world. Now Yue is rich and prosperous and Your Majesty lives in austerity. Please allow us to get revenge for your humiliation.' I, the orphan, have declined this, saying, 'It was I who was humiliated in the past, and it was not the fault of you gentlemen. How dare a man like me, a man of little virtue, trouble the people of my state to seek vengeance for me against my old foe?' The fathers and older brothers continued their requests, saying, 'Within the enfeoffed land of Yue,[17] everyone is the son of our lord. A son takes revenge on his father's enemy, a minister seeks retaliation against those his ruler hates, how dare they not make their best effort? We, your subjects, appeal again to be allowed to fight in order to get rid of Your Majesty's old foe.' I was delighted by this and approved their request."

Grand Minister Wen Zhong said, "When I, your subject, saw the king of Wu achieve his goals in Qi and Jin,[18] I thought that he would then advance to our land and approach the border with troops. Now he has dismissed his troops and let his soldiers rest.[19] A year has passed, yet he did not attempt to attack us; he has already forgotten us. But we cannot relax. I, your subject,

---

13. The *Guoyu* sentence reads: 而摩厲之於義 (*er moli zhi yuyi*), "and trained them with righteousness." See Xu Yuangao, 571.

14. *Guoyu* writes that Goujian loaded his boat with rice and meat. See Xu Yuangao, 571.

15. *Guoyu* contains 游 (*you*), "wandering," instead of 戲 (*xi*), "playing."

16. *Guoyu* reads "ten years" instead of "seven years." In early writings seven, 七 (*qi*), and ten, 十 (*shi*), looked similar to each other.

17. *Guoyu* has 越四封之内 (*Yue sifeng zhinei*), "in the enfeoffed land of Yue." 誠 (*cheng*), "if, instead," is probably a mistake for 越, "Yue." See Xu Yuangao, 571.

18. This refers to Wu's defeat of Qi in Ailing, where Wu won the upper hand in a covenant with Qi and Jin in Huangchi, see *WYCQ*, 5.23.

19. 疲 (*pi*), "exhausted," is the same as 罷 (*ba*), "to dismiss," here. See *Guoyu*, the "Wu yu" chapter, Xu Yuangao, 554.

have made a divination regarding him to heaven.[20] The people of Wu have already been exhausted by serving the troops, and have been afflicted by warfare. The markets have no accumulation of rough rice; state granaries are empty. The people certainly have the intention of moving away; when winter comes they travel to the coast of the Eastern Sea to collect calamus and clams for food. I have made a divination of worldly matters by oracle bones, and this prediction is also found by making use of yarrow sticks.[21] If Your Majesty raises your troops, believing that you can gain profit from going against Wu and thus invade its borders, this should not be done. Although the king of Wu does not have any intention of attacking us, we cannot ignite his anger. We should rather approach him when he is unsuspecting in order to learn his intentions."[22]

The king of Yue said, "I, the orphan, do not want to harbor any intention of attacking Wu, but the people of my state have been requesting the war for three years. I have to follow the wish of the people. Now I have heard you, Grand Minister Wen Zhong, suggest that it is infeasible."

The fathers and older brothers of Yue again admonished, saying, "Wu can be attacked. If we win, we can then destroy their state; if not, we can exhaust their troops. If Wu urges a truce and Your Majesty makes a covenant with them, your achievement and fame will be known among the lords."

The king of Yue said, "Excellent!" He thereupon gathered all the ministers and issued an order, saying, "Anyone who dares to remonstrate against attacking Wu will not be pardoned."

Fan Li and Wen Zhong spoke among themselves, saying, "Our admonishment is not appropriate now. We should still follow the orders of the king."

10.2. 越王會軍列士而大誡眾，而誓之曰：「寡人聞古之賢君，不患其眾不足，而患其志行之少恥也。今夫差衣水犀甲者十有三萬人，不患其志行之少恥也，而患其眾之不足。今寡人將助天威，吾不欲匹夫之小勇也，吾欲士卒進則思賞，退則避刑。」於是越民父勉其子，兄勸其弟，曰：「吳可伐也。」

20. According to *Guoyu*, 當 (*dang*), "should," is a mistake for 嘗 (*chang*), "an indicator of perfect tense." See Xu Yuangao, 554.

21. Oracle bone divination and prognostication by using yarrow sticks are two different divination systems used by the Shang people and Zhou people, respectively.

22. In *Guoyu*, Wen Zhong encourages Goujian to attack Wu immediately, which is very different from the *WYCQ* narrative account. See Xu Yuangao, 554–56.

10.2. The king of Yue assembled his troops, lined up his soldiers and exhorted them.[23] He made an oath, saying, "I, a man of little virtue, have heard that sagely rulers from the past did not worry that the number of their troops was not sufficient, they worried that their troops lacked a sense of shame in their will and conduct. Now Fuchai has one hundred and thirty thousand men wearing armor made of rhinoceros skin,[24] yet he is not concerned with the absence of shame in the will and behavior of his men; he worries instead that the number of his troops is not adequate. Now I, a man of little virtue, will assist in carrying out heaven's punishment.[25] I do not appreciate the petty courage of an unthinking person.[26] I want the soldiers to think of awards when advancing, and think of avoiding punishment when in retreat." Thereupon, among the people of Yue, fathers encouraged their sons, older brothers encouraged their younger brothers, and they all said, "Wu can be attacked."

10.3. 越王復召范蠡謂曰：「吳已殺子胥，道諛者眾。吾國之民，又勸孤伐吳。其可伐乎？」范蠡曰：「未可，須明年之春，然後可耳。」王曰：「何也？」范蠡曰：「臣觀吳王北會諸侯於黃池，精兵從王，國中空虛，老弱在後，太子留守。兵始出境未遠，聞越掩其空虛，兵還不難也。不如來春。」

10.3. The king of Yue summoned Fan Li again and told him,[27] "Wu has already killed Wu Zixu; it also has many flattering ministers. The people of my state again urge me, the orphan, to attack Wu. Can Wu be attacked?" Fan Li said, "Not yet. This has to be delayed until the spring of next year, and then it can be done." The king asked, "Why is that?" Fan Li said, "I, your subject, have noticed that when the king of Wu met the lords in the north at Huangchi, his elite troops followed him and the defense in his state was weak. The old and the frail were left behind and his heir apparent stayed as the regent. His troops have just begun to cross the border and are not far away. If he hears that Yue is taking advantage of his weakness, it will not be difficult for him to return the troops. We had better wait until the spring comes."

---

23. The following speech by Goujian is also adopted from the "Yue yu shang" chapter in *Guoyu*, see Xu Yuangao, 571–72.

24. Sizes of armies were usually exaggerated in early history. For example, the *Guoyu* passage writes that the number of Fuchai's soldiers wearing armor made of rhinoceros skin were "one hundred million and three thousand 億有三千." See Xu Yuangao, 571.

25. 威 (*wei*) means "punishment" or "to punish" here. The *Guoyu* passage states: "Now I, a man of little virtue, will assist heaven and destroy Wu" 今寡人將助天滅之. See Xu Yuangao, 572.

26. Goujian is saying that he does not appreciate courage without discipline.

27. The following conversation between Goujian and Fan Li is adopted from the "Hereditary Household of Yue King Goujian" chapter in *Shiji*. *WYCQ* revised the narrative into Fan Li's speech. See *Shiji*, 41:1744.

10.4. 其夏六月丙子，勾踐復問，范蠡曰：「可伐矣。」乃發習流二千人，俊士四萬，君子六千，諸御千人。以乙酉與吳戰。丙戌，遂虜殺太子，丁亥入吳，焚姑胥臺。吳告急於夫差，夫差方會諸侯於黃池，恐天下聞之，即密不令洩。已盟黃池，乃使人請成於越。勾踐自度未能滅，乃與吳平。

10.4. In the summer of that year, the *bingzi* day of the sixth month,[28] Goujian again asked Fan Li about attacking Wu. Fan Li said, "Now we can attack Wu." Goujian then dispatched two thousand exiles trained with fighting skills, forty thousand outstanding soldiers, six thousand men under his personal command, and one thousand orderlies to fight against Wu on the *yiyou* day of the month.[29] On the *bingwu* day, Yue then captured and killed the heir apparent of Wu. On the *dinghai* day, they entered Wu's capital and burned down the Guxu Terrace. Wu reported the urgent situation to Fuchai. At that time Fuchai was meeting the lords at Huangchi. Being afraid to have this known by the people of the world, Fuchai then kept this a secret and did not allow it to be revealed. After he had made a covenant at Huangchi, he then sent someone to Yue to appeal for a truce. As Goujian himself thought that he was unable to destroy Wu, he then negotiated peace with Wu.[30]

10.5. 二十一年七月，越王復悉國中士卒伐吳，會楚使申包胥聘於越。越王乃問包胥曰：「吳可伐耶？」申包胥曰：「臣鄙於策謀，未足以卜。」越王曰：「吳為不道，殘我社稷，夷吾宗廟以為平原，使不得血食。吾欲與之徼天之中，惟是輿馬、兵革、卒伍既具，無以行之。誠聞於戰，何以為可？」申包胥曰：「臣愚不能知。」越王固問，包胥乃曰：「夫吳，良國也，傳賢於諸侯。敢問君王之所戰者何？」越王曰：「在孤之側者，飲酒食肉未嘗不分，孤之飲食不致其味，聽樂不盡其聲，求以報吳。願以此戰。」包胥曰：「善則善矣，未可以戰。」越王曰：「越國之中，吾慱愛以子之，忠惠以養之，吾今修寬刑，欲民所欲，去民所惡，稱其善，掩其惡，求以報吳。願以此戰。」包胥曰：「善則善矣，未可以戰。」王曰：「越國之中，富者吾安之，貧者吾予之，救其不足，損其有餘，使貧富不失其利，求以報吳。願以此戰。」包胥曰：「善則善矣，未可以戰。」王曰：「邦國南則距楚，西則薄晉，北則望齊，春秋奉幣、玉、帛、子女以貢獻焉，未嘗敢絕，求以報吳。願以此戰。」包胥曰：「善哉，無以加斯矣，猶未可戰。夫戰之道，

28. The *bingzi* day was the eleventh day of the month.

29. This is the twentieth day of the month. The following *bingwu* is the twenty-first day, *dinghai* is the twenty-second day of the month.

30. This paragraph is adopted from *Shiji* as well. The *WYCQ* narrative added dates to the events, which not only makes the report sounds real but also presents a strong sense of tension as the dates of the events are close together. See *Shiji*, 41:1744.

知為之始，以仁次之，以勇斷之。君將不知，即無權變之謀，以別眾寡之數；不仁，則不得與三軍同飢寒之節，齊苦樂之喜；不勇，則不能斷去就之疑，決可否之議。」於是越王曰：「敬從命矣。」

10.5. In the twenty-first year of King Goujian (476 BCE), in the seventh month, the king of Yue again mobilized all the soldiers of his state to attack Wu. It happened at that time that Chu sent Shen Baoxu to Yue on an official visit.[31] The king of Yue thereupon asked Shen Baoxu, "Can Wu be attacked?" Shen Baoxu answered, "I, your subject, am poor at giving advice. I am not capable of predicting for Yue." The king said, "Wu behaves against the Way. Wu destroyed our altars of earth and grain, ruined our ancestral temples and razed them to the ground, causing our ancestors to be unable to enjoy the sacrifices.[32] I want to pray for heaven's justice for this matter;[33] however, now that the chariots, horses, weapons, armor, and troops are ready, yet I do not know how to use them to achieve victory. I sincerely ask you about the matter of warfare. What are the right things to do?" Shen Baoxu said, "I, your subject, am too unintelligent to know the answers." The king of Yue insisted on asking. Shen Baoxu then answered, "Wu is a strong state.[34] Its merit has been talked about among the lords.[35] I dare to ask, what is Your Majesty's reason for battling against Wu?" The king of Yue said, "For those who are beside me, I, the orphan, have never failed to share with them when I drink and eat. I, the orphan, do not eat food with all five flavors,[36] and I do not listen to music consisting of all five tones. I wish to use this to get revenge against Wu, and I hope to use this to fight." Shen Baoxu said, "These are good; however, they cannot be relied upon to secure a victory."

The king of Yue said, "As for the people of Yue, I love them indiscriminately, treat them as my own children and nourish them with a loyal and humane heart. I revised the law and lessened the punishments.[37] I desire what the

---

31. When Wu Zixu invaded Chu, Shen Baoxu was the Chu minister who went and cried at the Qin court in order to appeal for Qin to rescue Chu. See *WYCQ*, 3.6, 4:25. The following conversation between Goujian and Shen Baoxu is adopted from the "Wu yu" chapter in *Guoyu*, see Xu Yuangao, 556–57.

32. In ancient times when animals were slaughtered as sacrifices, their blood was also drained as a part of the offering. This is called 血食 (*xueshi*).

33. Zhang Jue reads this as: "I want to pray for heaven's blessing for my ancestors." See Zhang Jue, 296n5.

34. 良國 (*liangguo*) can have different interpretations. The *Guoyu* commentaries read it as a big or strong state. Zhang Jue, however, translates it as a "generous state." See Xu Yuangao, 556; Zhang Jue, 297.

35. The *Guoyu* sentence is: "Wu can broadly demand attribution from the lords" 能博取於諸侯. See Xu Yuangao, 556.

36. The *Guoyu* commentaries interpret 致 (*zhi*) as 極 (*ji*), "extreme," or "to exhaust." See Xu Yuangao, 556. Here Goujian is saying that he only eats simple food with plain flavors.

37. The *Guoyu* sentence reads 吾修令寬刑 (*wu xiuling kuanxing*), "I revised the law and lessened the punishments." The *WYCQ* sentence 吾今修寬刑 (*wu jin xiu kuanxing*), "I now revised and lessened the punishments," is a mistake for the *Guoyu* sentence. See Xu Yuangao, 557.

people desire and eliminate what the people dislike.[38] I praise their kind deeds and conceal their wrongdoings. I wish to use these to get revenge against Wu and hope to use these to fight." Shen Baoxu said, "These are good; still, they cannot be relied upon to secure a victory." The king said, "For the people of Yue, the rich ones—I give them protection; the poor ones—I attend to their needs. I give alms to those in need and levy those with abundance, making sure both the poor and the rich do not lose their benefits. I wish to use these reasons to effect revenge against Wu and hope to use them to fight." Shen Baoxu said, "These are good, but they cannot be relied upon to secure a victory." The king said, "To the south of my state there is Chu, the west my state is close to Jin, and to the north, Qi is not far. Each year I present these states with money, jade, silk, and girls as tributes; I have never dared to suspend my offerings. I wish to use this to get revenge against Wu and hope to use this to fight."

Shen Baoxu said, "Excellent! There is nothing more that can be added. Still, they cannot be relied upon to secure a victory. For in the way of battle, wisdom is the first priority; next, it relies upon humaneness; and then, it is determined by courage. If the ruler and the generals are not wise, then they do not have the adaptability in tactics to discern if the numbers of the troops are sufficient or not. If the ruler and the generals are not humane, they lack the moral principle to endure hanger and coldness with soldiers, as well as sharing joy and sufferings with them. If the ruler and the generals are not brave, they are not then able to resolve the debate of retreat or stay, nor decide what is feasible and what is not." The king of Yue thereupon said, "I respectfully receive your advice."[39]

---

38. Instead of 施民所欲 (*shimin suoyu*), "do what the people desire," the *Guoyu* reads 欲民所欲 (*yumin suoyu*), "desire what the people desire." My translation is based upon *Guoyu*. See Xu Yuangao, 557.

39. The determining quality a ruler must have in order to win a battle with another state is a favorite topic in *Zuozhuan*; the most famous example of this is Cao Gui's 曹劌 discussion with Lord Zhuang of Lu 魯莊公 as recorded in Lord Zhuang 10: "In the tenth year, in spring, the Qi army attacked us. Our lord was going to fight. Cao Gui asked for an audience. . . . Gao Gui then went in to see our lord in audience and asked what he would use to fight. Our lord said, 'Of the things I take comfort in wearing and eating, I do not venture to keep all for myself but am sure to share with others.' Gui responded, 'Such small kindnesses do not yet reach all. The people will not follow you for this.' Our lord said, 'In regard to sacrificial animals and ceremonial jades and silks, I do not venture to exaggerate and am sure to rely upon good faith.' Gui responded, 'Such small good faith does not yet cover all and the spirits will not bless you for this.' Our lord said, 'In both small and large legal cases, even when I am unable to investigate thoroughly, I am sure to rely on the actual circumstances.' Gui responded, 'This counts as a kind of integrity—with it you may indeed engage in battle. If you do battle, then I request to follow you.'" Translation is from Durrant, Li, and Schaberg, 161. See also Yang Bojun, 182–83. While Cao Gui emphasizes that fairness in legal cases will help Lu in order to win the battle, Shen Baoxu presents a military school view that pays particular attention to adaptability to changing circumstances, care for the soldiers, and resolute decision making.

10.6. 冬，十月，越王乃請八大夫曰：「昔吳為不道，殘我宗廟，夷我社稷以為平原，使不血食。吾欲徼天之中，兵革既具，無所以行之。吾問於申包胥，即已命孤矣，敢告諸大夫如何？」

大夫曳庸曰：「審賞則可戰也。審其賞，明其信，無功不及，有功必加，則士卒不怠。」王曰：「聖哉！」

大夫苦成曰：「審罰則可戰。審罰，則士卒望而畏之，不敢違命。」王曰：「勇哉！」

大夫文種曰：「審物則可戰。審物，則別是非，是非明察，人莫能惑。」王曰：「辨哉！」

大夫范蠡曰：「審備則可戰。審備慎守，以待不虞，備設守固，必可應難。」王曰：「慎哉！」

大夫皋如曰：「審聲則可戰。審於聲音，以別清濁。清濁者，謂吾國君名聞於周室，令諸侯不怨於外。」王曰：「得哉！」

大夫扶同曰：「廣恩知分則可戰。廣恩以博施，知分而不外。」王曰：「神哉！」

大夫計研曰：「候天察地，參應其變則可戰。天變地應，人道便利，三者前見則可。」王曰：「明哉！」

10.6. During the winter of that year, in the tenth month, the king of Yue invited eight grand ministers and spoke to them,[40] saying, "Previously Wu acted against the Way. It destroyed our ancestral temple, ruined our altars of earth and grain and leveled them, causing our ancestors to be unable to enjoy the sacrifices. I want to pray for heaven's justice on this matter. Now the weapons and armors are prepared, but I do not know how to apply them. I consulted Shen Baoxu about this, and he has already advised me, the orphan. I dare to ask you this, Grand Ministers, what is your advice?"[41]

Grand Minister Yeyong said, "Be prudent in awarding and then we can fight. In calculating awards, manifest your seriousness, giving no awards to those lacking in merit, and definitely granting awards to those with achievements. The soldiers therefore will not be remiss in their duties." The king said, "How clever is your view!"

Grand Minister Kucheng said, "Be prudent in punishments and then we can fight. In calculating the punishments, the soldiers then will be afraid of you and dare not disobey you." The king said, "How brave is your view!"

Grand Minister Wen Zhong said, "Be prudent in the banners and flags and then we can fight.[42] Clarifying the banners and flags, we can then

40. There are in fact only seven ministers involved in the discussion.

41. The following responses from the ministers are adopted from *Guoyu*, the "Wu yu" chapter. See Xu Yuangao, 557–58.

42. Wei Zhao's commentary to *Guoyu* interprets 物 (*wu*) as banners, flags, and other military signs. See Xu Yuangao, 558.

distinguish right from wrong. When right and wrong are clear, no one will be confused." The king said, "How discerning is your view!"

Grand Minister Fan Li said, "Be prudent in defense and then we can fight. Thoroughly prepare the defense and be careful in guarding, and use this approach to prepare for the unexpected. If the defense is established and security is enhanced, we can definitely deal with catastrophe." The king said, "How watchful is your view!"

Grand Minister Gaoru said, "Be prudent with your reputation, then we can fight.[43] Carefully maintain your reputation and distinguish the unsullied from the tarnished—the unsullied and tarnished imply that the name of our lord is known by the Zhou court, and beyond the border the lords will not hold resentment toward us." The king said, "How virtuous is your view!"[44]

Grand Minister Futong said, "Extend your favor and understand your duties, then we can fight. Extend your favor and apply it broadly; understand your duties and you will not violate the rule." The king said, "How wonderful is your view!"

Grand Minister Ji Yan said, "Observe heavenly phenomena, investigate earthly patterns, take reference and correspond to their changes, then we can fight. If there are signs of changes in heavenly phenomena, note their correspondence in earthly patterns and benefits in the human world; with these three conditions met, we can fight and win." The king said, "How wise is your view!"[45]

10.7. 於是勾踐乃退齋而命國人曰：「吾將有不虞之議，自近及遠，無不聞者。」乃復命有司與國人曰：「承命有賞，皆造國門，之期有不從命者，吾將有顯戮。」勾踐恐民不信，使以征不義聞於周室，令諸侯不怨於外。令國中曰：「五日之內，則吾良人矣，過五日之外，則非吾之民也，又將加之以誅。」

10.7. Goujian thereupon retreated from the court and purified himself.[46] He then issued a decree to the people in the state, saying, "I will announce an

43. In the *Guoyu* passage 聲 (*sheng*) should refer to the beating of drums and gongs in order to command the soldiers to advance and retreat. However, in the *WYCQ* conversation, Gaoru explains 聲, which means both "sounds" and "reputation," as the reputation Goujian should build for himself in the view of the Zhou court as well as in the eyes of the lords. This is different from the *Guoyu*. For the *Guoyu* passage, see Xu Yuangao, 558.

44. Zhang Jue reads 得 (*de*) as a loan word of 德 (*de*), "virtue"; Huang Rensheng translates it as 得體 (*deti*), "appropriate." See Zhang Jue, 299n9; Huang Rensheng, 333.

45. Ji Yan's advice is not found in the *Guoyu* passage. See Xu Yuangao, 558.

46. This refers to abstaining from meat and wine before offering sacrifice. Goujian was probably making a sacrifice to his ancestors in order to receive their blessing before battling against Wu.

unexpected decision. People from near to far should all listen to it." He then ordered the officials and people in the state, saying, "All who respond to my command will be rewarded; they should assemble at the gate of the capital on schedule. If there is anyone who does not follow my command, that person will be publicly executed." Goujian was afraid that the people would not believe him, so he sent an envoy to report to the Zhou household that he would only attack the unworthy, thus causing the lords in other states to not hold grudges against him. He commanded the people in his state, saying, "Those who come to the assembly within five days are my obedient people; after five days they are not my people. I will see them punished."

10.8. 教令既行，乃入命於夫人。王背屏，夫人向屏而立。王曰：「自今日之後，內政無出，外政無入，各守其職，以盡其信。內中辱者，則是子，境外千里辱者，則是子也。吾見子於是，以為明誡矣。」王出宮，夫人送王，不過屏，王因反闔其門，填之以土。夫人去笄，側席而坐，安心無容，三月不掃。

王出，則復背垣而立，大夫向垣而敬，王乃令大夫曰：「食士不均，地壤不修，使孤有辱於國，是子之罪；臨敵不戰，軍士不死，有辱於諸侯，功隳於天下，是孤之責。自今以往，內政無出，外政無入，吾固誡子。」大夫曰：「敬受命矣。」王乃出，大夫送出垣，反闔外宮之門，填之以土。大夫側席而坐，不御五味，不答所勸。

勾踐有命於夫人、大夫曰：「國有守禦。」

10.8. After his commands had been carried out, Goujian entered the palace and issued an order to his wife. The king of Yue stood against the screen and his wife faced the screen.[47] The king said, "Starting from today, matters of the inner palace do not involve anyone outside of it; issues of the court are not to be brought up in the inner palace. Each one attends to their own duties, thus to show their trustworthiness. If any shameful things occur inside the palace, it is then your responsibility; if any humiliation occurs ten thousand *li* beyond the border, it is then my fault.[48] I meet you here in order to issue you clear instructions." The king walked out of the palace; the wife saw the king off but did not go beyond the screen. The king then turned back

47. This conversation between Goujian and his wife is adapted from *Guoyu* as well. According to Wei Zhao, this is the screen in the king's bedroom. The king is facing north and his wife is facing south. At the court the king should be facing south and all his subjects, including his wife, should face north. Here the position is subverted as Goujian is entrusting her to handle all the matters inside the palace. See Xu Yuangao, 558.

48. Here 子 (*zi*) is probably a mistake for 予 (*yu*), "I" or "me." *Guoyu* clearly reads 我 (*wo*), "I." See Xu Yuangao, 558.

and closed the gate; he blocked the gate with earth.[49] The wife took off her hairpin and sat alone on the mat.[50] She quieted her heart and did not put on makeup. For three months she did not clean her room.[51]

After the king exited the palace, he again stood against the low palace wall while the grand ministers faced the wall respectfully.[52] The king then ordered the grand ministers, saying, "If the officers are not provided with equal supplies, the fields are not cultivated, and this causes me, the orphan, to be ashamed of the state; these are your faults. If the troops fail to fight when facing the enemy, if soldiers refuse to fight to the death, causing the humiliation of our state in front of the lords, and ruin our achievement in the eyes of the world—these are my, the orphan's, fault. From now on, affairs of the state should be settled within the state, affairs out of the state should not involve domestic consultation. I warn you about this in particular."[53] The grand ministers replied, "We respectfully receive your command." The king then exited the court; the grand ministers saw him off but did not walk beyond the wall of the court. The king turned back and closed the gate of the court and blocked it with earth.[54] The grand ministers reclined on their own mats, did not enjoy delicacies, and did not respond to the persuasion of others.

Goujian once more gave the command to his wife and grand ministers, saying, "The defense of Yue depends on you!"

10.9. 乃坐露壇之上，列鼓而鳴之。軍行成陣，即斬有罪者三人以徇於軍，令曰：「不從吾令者，如斯矣！」

明日徙軍於郊，斬有罪者三人徇之於軍，令曰：「不從吾令者，如斯矣！」

王乃令國中不行者，與之訣而告之曰：「爾安土守職，吾方往征討我宗廟之讎，以謝於二三子。」令國人各送其子弟於郊境之上，軍士各與父兄昆弟取訣。國人悲哀，皆作離別相去之詞，曰：

「躒躁摧長恧兮，擢戟馭殳，所離不降兮，以泄我王氣蘇。三軍一飛降兮，所向皆殂。一士判死兮，而當百夫。道祐有德兮，吳卒

49. The *Guoyu* writes that only the left half of the gate was blocked, and this, according to Wei Zhao, suggests closing the *yang* entrance will leave the *yin* entrance intact, which is a symbolic action of detainment. See Xu Yuangao, 558.

50. 側 (*ce*) should be interpreted as 特 (*te*), "alone." According to Wei Zhao, by custom, who have worries should sit alone. See Xu Yuangao, 558.

51. This is a gesture of being deeply worried.

52. 垣 (*yuan*) is the low wall surrounding the court in the palace. *Guoyu* states that Goujian met his ministers right outside and under the roof of the palace building. See Xu Yuangao, 558.

53. 固 (*gu*), "indeed," is used to emphasize the tone here.

54. Again, in *Guoyu* only the *yang* part of the gate, the left half, is blocked, suggesting detainment. See Xu Yuangao, 559.

自屠。雪我王宿恥兮，威振八都。軍伍難更兮，勢如貔貙。行行各努力兮，於乎，於乎！」於是，觀者莫不悽惻。

明日，復徙軍於境上，斬有罪者三人徇之於軍，曰：「有不從令者，如此！」

後三日，復徙軍於檇李，斬有罪者三人以徇於軍，曰：「其搖心匿行，不當敵者，如斯矣！」

10.9. The king then sat on an altar in the open; he had the drums arranged in a line and sounded them. After the troops were in formation, he had three criminals executed and displayed their corpses to the troops, commanding, "Anyone who fails to follow my orders will end up like this."

The next day, he relocated the troops to the suburb and executed three criminals and displayed their bodies to the troops, commanding, "Anyone who fails to follow my orders will end up like this."

The king then summoned people in the state who were not going on the campaign, he bid farewell to them and announced to them, "You should stay in the homeland at ease and mind your own duties. I am about to attack and punish the enemy responsible for ruining our ancestral temple. Thus, I bid farewell to you." He allowed people of the state to see off their sons and brothers at the suburb of the capital. All the soldiers bid farewell to their fathers and brothers. The people of Yue were saddened by this and all chanted the song of parting, which reads:

Hurried, hurried, we advance to remove the lasting shame,[55]
Halberds are pulled out, spears are in hands.
Even if a catastrophe occurs, we will not surrender,
We will not fail to ease our king's anger.
The three armies soar up high and descend from the sky,
No one is spared in our path.
One warrior fights to the death,
Yet one hundred men cannot stop him.
The Way protects the virtuous,
The soldiers of Wu will turn their weapons round.
Washing off the old shame of our king,
Our might awes the cities of the world.[56]
Nothing can change the determination of our march,
We are as furious as *pi* and *chu*.[57]
March! March! Each takes care of himself,

---

55. 躒 (*li*), "to leap," 躁 (*zao*), "hurriedly," 摧 (*cui*), "to push back," 恧 (*nǜ*), "shame, humiliation."
56. 八都 (*badu*), "eight capitals," refers to all cities in the world.
57. These are two legendary tiger-like wild beasts.

Alas! Alas![58]
At that time, all the bystanders felt sorrowful.

The next day, Goujian moved the troops further to the border area. He executed three criminals and displayed their bodies to the troops, saying, "Anyone who fails to follow my orders will end up like this."

After three days, he again moved the troops to Zuili. He executed three criminals and displayed their bodies to the troops, saying, "Those who are of evil minds, who have bad behavior, and who fail to stand against the enemy will end up like this."

10.10. 勾踐乃命有司大徇軍，曰：「其有父母無昆弟者，來告我。我有大事，子離父母之養，親老之愛，赴國家之急。子在軍寇之中，父母昆弟有在疾病之地，吾視之如吾父母昆弟之疾病也；其有死亡者，吾葬埋殯送之，如吾父母昆弟之有死亡葬埋之矣。」

明日，又徇於軍，曰：「士有疾病不能隨軍從兵者，吾予其醫藥，給其麋粥，與之同食。」

明日，又徇於軍，曰：「筋力不足以勝甲兵，志行不足以聽王命者，吾輕其重，和其任。」

明日，旋軍於江南，更陳嚴法，復誅有罪者五人徇曰：「吾愛士也，雖吾子不能過也；及其犯誅，自吾子亦不能脫也。」

恐軍士畏法不使，自謂未能得士之死力，道見蛙張腹而怒，將有戰爭之氣，即為之軾。其士卒有問於王曰：「君何為敬蛙蟲而為之軾？」勾踐曰：「吾思士卒之怒久矣，而未有稱吾意者。今蛙蟲無知之物，見敵而有怒氣，故為之軾。」於是軍士聞之，莫不懷心樂死，人致其命。

有司、將軍，大徇軍中曰：「隊各自令其部，部各自令其士：『歸而不歸，處而不處，進而不進，退而不退，左而不左，右而不右，不如令者，斬！』」

58. The last line is the soldiers singing to their families, telling them that they all should take care of themselves so they will not worry about each other. It is very typical in Han poems of departing that the final lines end with the sentence 努力加餐飯 (*nuli jia canfan*), which literarily means "please work hard and eat more." However, the word 努力 (*nuli*) in this type of poem from Han to Tang in fact means "to take care" instead of "to work hard." The most famous Han departing poem is titled "Xingxing chong xingxing" 行行重行行 (Marching on and on) found in the Nineteen Old Songs (*gushi shijiu shou* 古詩十九首). The poem describes a couple's separation by distance and the final lines say: "Thinking of you makes me old, months and years have suddenly passed. Forget it, I won't speak of it anymore, take care and eat a good meal." Translation from Daniel Hsieh, "The Origin and Nature of the 'Nineteen Old Poems,'" *Sino-Platonic Papers*, no. 77 (January 1998): 7. For more on the Nineteen Old Poems, see, for example, Anne Birrell, *Popular Songs and Ballads of Han China* (Honolulu: University of Hawai'i Press, 1993). See also Guo Zaiyi 郭在貽, "Shi 'Nuli'" 釋努力, in *Guo Zaiyi wenji* 郭在貽文集 (Beijing: Zhonghua shuju, 2002), Vol. 1, 258–63.

10.10. Goujian then ordered the officers on duty to thoroughly inspect the troops and told the soldiers,[59] "For those who have parents but no brother, please come and report to me. I have this serious matter of attacking Wu. You gentlemen have left the care of your parents and the love of your elders and have brought yourselves to the dire straits facing the state. You are fighting the enemy as my troops; if your parents or brothers are ill, I will treat them as if it is my parents and brothers who are sick. If any of them dies, I will set up a funeral and bury them as if it were my parents and brothers who had died."

The next day Goujian again inspected the troops, saying, "For the soldiers who are ill and are unable to follow the troops to the battle, I will provide them with doctors and medicine, and I will offer them congee and eat with them."

The next day he inspected the troops again, saying, "Anyone whose strength is not great enough to bear the weight of armor and weapons, whose morals and conduct are not good enough to follow the commands of the king, I will alleviate their burdens and lighten their duties."

The following day, he moved the troops to the southern bend of the river. He once more announced the stringent rule and executed five men who had violated the law. He inspected the troops, saying, "I care so much for my soldiers; even my love for my son cannot surpass it. However, if anyone commits a crime deserving the death penalty, even if he is my son he cannot be pardoned."

The king of Yue was concerned that the soldiers were afraid of the law but were not sincerely following his commands. He thought that he had not yet earned the soldiers' willingness to fight to the death for him. On the road he saw a frog enlarge its belly to show anger, which demonstrated its fighting attitude; Goujian then lowered his head to the front bar of his carriage to show respect to the frog.[60] Some of his soldiers asked the king, "Why did Your Majesty respect a small animal like a frog and lower your head to the bar?" Goujian said, "I have long been waiting for the soldiers' rage, yet no one has satisfied me. Now the frog is a creature without intelligence, yet it demonstrated anger when seeing its enemy, for this reason I lowered my head to show my respect." At that time when soldiers heard this, all of them bore the will to die happily for him, everyone wanted to devote their life to him.[61]

---

59. The following speech by Goujian is adopted from *Guoyu*, see Xu Yuangao, 559.

60. 軾 (*shi*) is the bar at the front of a chariot. Lowering one's head while holding the front bar was a way of showing respect in the Spring and Autumn period.

61. This episode is not found in *Guoyu*. This is a detail added by the *WYCQ* narrator.

The officers on duty and the generals thoroughly inspected the troops and said, "Each unit commands its division. Each division commands its soldiers: if the order is to return to the camp but you do not, is to stop but you do not, to advance but you do not, to retreat but you do not, to turn left but you do not, to turn right but you do not—those who fail to follow orders like these will be beheaded."

10.11. 於是吳悉兵屯於江北，越軍於江南。越王中分其師以為左右軍，皆被兕甲；又令安廣之人，佩石碣之矢，張盧生之弩。躬率君子之軍六千人，以為中陣。

明日，將戰於江。乃以黃昏令於左軍，銜枚溯江而上五里，以須吳兵。復令於右軍，銜枚踰江十里，復須吳兵。於夜半，使左軍涉江，鳴鼓，中水以待吳發。吳師聞之，中大駭，相謂曰：「今越軍分為二師，將以使攻我眾。」亦即以夜暗中分其師以圍越。越王陰使左右軍與吳望戰，以大鼓相聞；潛伏其私卒六千人，銜枚不鼓攻吳。吳師大敗。越之左右軍乃遂伐之，大敗之於囿，又敗之於郊，又敗之於津，如是三戰三北，徑至吳，圍吳於西城。

吳王大懼，夜遁。越王追奔，攻吳，兵入於江陽松陵，欲入胥門，來至六七里，望吳南城，見伍子胥頭巨若車輪，目若耀電，鬚髮四張，射於十里。越軍大懼，留兵假道。即日夜半，暴風疾雨，雷奔電激，飛石揚砂，疾於弓弩。越軍壞敗，松陵卻退，兵士僵斃，人眾分解，莫能救止。范蠡、文種乃稽顙肉袒，拜謝子胥，願乞假道。子胥乃與種、蠡夢，曰：「吾知越之必入吳矣，故求置吾頭於南門，以觀汝之破吳也。惟欲以窮夫差。定汝入我之國，吾心又不忍，故為風雨以還汝軍。然越之伐吳，自是天也，吾安能止哉？越如欲入，更從東門，我當為汝開道，貫城以通汝路。」於是越軍明日更從江出，入海陽，於三道之翟水，乃穿東南隅以達，越軍遂圍吳。

10.11. At that time, Wu stationed all its troops on the northern bank of the river and the Yue army was on the southern bank.[62] The king of Yue

62. According to Wei Zhao, this is the Song River 松江 that passes through Suzhou and Shanghai and finally flows into Lake Tai 太湖. See Xu Yuangao, 560. *Zuozhuan*, Lord Ai 17 also records this: "In the third month, the Master of Yue attacked Wu. The Master of Wu came out to confront him at the Li Marsh. They formed their lines on either side of the water. The Master of Yue formed detachments for the left and right and sent these out at night, one to the left and one to the right, drumming and shouting as they advanced. The Wu army then split up to fight them. The Master of Yue stole across with a third army and drummed them forward until they were directly in front of the Wu central army. The Wu army was thrown into utter confusion, and as a result Yue defeated it." Translation from Durrant, Li, and Schaberg, 1955. See also Yang Bojun, 1707. *Guoyu* has a similar account of the battle but with more details. The following *WYCQ* story is clearly developed from the *Zuozhuan* and, especially, *Guoyu*. See Xu Yuangao, 560–61.

divided his troops into left and right armies. All his soldiers were wearing armor made of rhinoceros skin. He also ordered staunch and stalwart soldiers to be equipped with stone-headed arrows,[63] and to pull crossbows that were made in Lu.[64] The king of Yue personally led his own guards of six thousand men as the central contingent of the army.

The battle was about to unfold the next day along the river. At dusk the king of Yue then ordered the left-army soldiers to hold sticks in their mouths and march five *li* upstream to await the Wu troops there.[65] He also commanded the right-army soldiers, keeping sticks in their mouths, to cross the river and await the Wu army. At midnight, the king of Yue ordered the left army to cross the river and beat the drums,[66] waiting for the maneuver of the Wu troops at the middle of the river. When the Wu troops heard the drums they were greatly frightened and talked among themselves, saying, "Now the Yue troops have divided into two and they are about to attack us from both sides."[67] They also, at night, while it was dark, divided their troops to besiege Yue. The king of Yue secretly ordered the left and right armies to pretend to fight, beating drums loudly so that Wu would hear. Covertly, the king of Yue smuggled six thousand of his own guards across the river. They also kept sticks in their mouths and attacked Wu without beating their drums. The Wu troops were soundly defeated. The left and right armies of Yue thereby took the chance and attacked Wu, further crushing the Wu soldiers at Yu.[68] Yue further defeated Wu troops in the suburbs of the Wu capital, and defeated Wu again at the ford outside of the capital. Wu was thus defeated three times in these three battles. The Yue armies then approached the Wu capital directly and surrounded the Wu troops at the western side of the city wall.

The king of Wu was greatly frightened and fled the capital at night. The king of Yue chased after the routed troops and attacked the Wu army. He

---

63. Huang Rensheng reads 安廣 (*anguang*) as the name of a county. However, as Zhang Jue points out, the Anguang county was established in Western Han and it is located in modern-day Guangxi 廣西, which is very far away from the Yue land. Here I follow Zhang Jue's interpretation. See Huang Rensheng, 342n4; Zhang Jue, 307n4.

64. Huang Rensheng believes 盧生之弩 (*Lusheng zhinu*) means "the crossbows invented by Scholar Lu." Zhang Jue argues 盧 (*Lu*) was the name of a small state near the Chu border. Because Chu was famous for using crossbows, and there is no other reference in early texts concerning Scholar Lu's crossbow, Zhang Jue's interpretation sounds better. See Huang Rensheng, 343. Zhang Jue, 307n5.

65. Soldiers holding sticks in their mouths was a way to ensure silent marching.

66. According to *Guoyu*, Goujian ordered both the left and right armies to cross the river and beat the drums. See Xu Yuangao, 560.

67. 使攻 (*shigong*) is probably a mistake for 夾攻 (*jiagong*), "attacking from both sides." See *Guoyu*, Xu Yuangao, 560.

68. According to Wei Zhao, this is the Li Marsh along the Song River. See Xu Yuangao, 561.

advanced to Songling on the north side of the river and wanted to enter Xu Gate.[69] When he was about six or seven *li* away from the gate, he looked at the southern wall of the Wu capital, and he saw Wu Zixu, whose head was as big as the wheel of a carriage, his eyes were as bright as lightening, and his beard and hair stood up.[70] The image could be seen from more than ten *li* away. The Yue troops were greatly afraid, they stopped and prepared to pass around the gate. During the middle of the night, strong wind and violent rain struck, thunder roared, lightening flashed, rocks hurtled through the air and sand flew about, faster than arrows loosed from a crossbow. The Yue troops suffered a disastrous setback because of this and the water of the Songling River flowed backward. Yue soldiers fell and died, men fled and no one could stop them. Fan Li and Wen Zhong therefore lowered their heads to the ground, bared their chests and arms, and prayed to Wu Zixu,[71] beseeching his approval to pass through the gate.

Wu Zixu then appeared in Wen Zhong's and Fan Li's dreams, saying, "I have already known that Yue would inevitably enter the Wu capital, for this reason I asked the Wu king to place my head on the southern gate of the city so I can witness your destroying the Wu capital. However, this was only intended to embarrass Fuchai. When it happened that you really were about to enter our capital, in my heart I could not bear to see this, therefore I stirred up wind and storm to cause you to retreat. However, Yue's attacking Wu is destined by heaven, how can I interrupt this? If Yue wants to enter the city, change your plans and enter from the eastern gate.[72] I will clear the roads, open the wall, and ensure your path is unobstructed." The next day the Yue troops thereby marched from the river and entered Haiyang. They crossed Sanjiangkou and arrived at Zhaishui.[73] Passing through the southeastern corner of the city wall they reached the inner city. The Yue troops thus besieged the king of Wu.

---

69. Songling is located in modern-day Wujiang 吳江 County, Jiangsu Province.

70. Beard and hair standing up is a popular description of anger in early Chinese texts. Taking *Shiji* for example, at the famous Hongmen Banquet 鴻門宴 during which Xiang Yu 項羽 planned to assassinate his rival Liu Bang 劉邦, the future Emperor Gaozu of Han, Sima Qian describes how Liu Bang's general Fan Kuai 樊噲 entered the tent at this critical moment with his "hair standing up" (遂入，披帷西向立，瞋目視項王，頭髮上指，目眥盡裂). Xiang Yu was awed by Fan Kuai's bravery and the assassination was not carried out. See *Shiji*, 7:313.

71. Lowering the forehead to the ground and pausing for a few seconds was originally a filial son's gesture for thanking people for attending his parents' funeral. It was later used to express apology. Baring one's chest is also a demonstration of guilt, an expression of apology, or an appeal for pardon.

72. *Shiji* records that Wu Zixu's final request before he was executed by Fuchai was for Fuchai to dig out his eyes and hang them at the eastern gate of the Wu capital so he could witness Yue's invasion and destruction of Wu. See *Shiji*, 66:2180.

73. 三道 (*sandao*) refers to Sanjiangkou where three rivers meet. See Zhang Jue, 156n23.

10.12. 守一年，吳師累敗。遂棲吳王於姑胥之山。吳使王孫駱肉袒膝行而前，請成於越王，曰：「孤臣夫差，敢布腹心：『異日得罪於會稽，夫差不敢逆命，得與君王結成以歸。今君王舉兵而誅孤臣，孤臣惟命是聽，意者猶以今日之姑胥，曩日之會稽也。若徼天之中，得赦其大辟，則吳願長為臣妾。』」

勾踐不忍其言，將許之成。范蠡曰：「會稽之事，天以越賜吳，吳不取；今天以吳賜越，越可逆命乎？且君王早朝晏罷，切齒銘骨，謀之二十餘年，豈不緣一朝之事耶？今日得而棄之，其計可乎？天與不取，還受其咎。君何忘會稽之厄乎？」勾踐曰：「吾欲聽子言，不忍對其使者。」

范蠡遂鳴鼓而進兵曰：「王已屬政於執事，使者急去，不時得罪。」吳使涕泣而去。勾踐憐之，使令入謂吳王曰：「吾置君於甬東，給君夫婦三百餘家，以沒王世，可乎？」吳王辭曰：「天降禍於吳國，不在前後，正孤之身，失滅宗廟社稷者。吳之土地、民臣，越既有之，孤老矣，不能臣王。」遂伏劍自殺。

10.12. After a year of stalemate,[74] the Wu army had been defeated repeatedly and the king of Wu was forced to hide on Mount Guxu. The king of Wu sent Wangsun Luo,[75] who stripped off his upper garment and went on his knees to beg for a truce in front of the king of Yue, saying, "Your estranged subject, Fuchai, dares to present my heart to you: previously I offended you in Kuaiji.[76] I, Fuchai, dared not to disobey your order and was able to conclude a peace with Your Majesty and return home. Now Your Majesty mobilizes your troops to punish me, your estranged subject, and I, your estranged subject, will be compliant with any of your orders. I wish Your Majesty could compare today's Mount Guxu to yesterday's Kuaiji. If I prayed for heaven's justice and was pardoned from the punishment of death by you, then Wu will forever be willing to serve as your servant." Goujian could not bear to listen to his words and was about to agree to the truce.

Fan Li said, "What happened in Kuaiji was heaven bestowing Yue to Wu, but Wu did not accept it. Now heaven is giving Wu to Yue, how can Yue refuse the mandate? Moreover, Your Majesty attends court in early morning and retires late; you grind your teeth because of your hatred, which is engraved in your bones. You have planned for over twenty years, wasn't it for today's situation? Now you have this opportunity but are giving up the proper plan? 'If heaven bestows it to you but you fail to accept, you will receive punishment.'

74. Xu Tianhu cites *Zuozhuan*, *Guoyu* and *Shiji* and argues that, in fact, Goujian besieged King Fuchai of Wu for three years. See Zhang Jue, 310n1; Huang Rensheng, 347n1.

75. In *Shiji* the Wu minister's name is Gongsun Xiong 公孫雄. See *Shiji*, 41:1745.

76. Referring to Fuchai's defeat of Goujian in 494 BCE. See *WYCQ*, 5.1.

Why does Your Majesty forget the distress in Kuaiji?" Goujian said, "I would like to follow your advice, however, I cannot bear to face his messenger."

Fan Li then beat the drums and moved the troops forward, saying, "The king of Yue has entrusted the command to me, his officer in duty; the messenger should leave immediately, any delay will be punished." The Wu messenger cried and left. Goujian pitied the king of Wu and sent an envoy to inform the king of Wu, "I will settle you on the eastern bank of the Yong River and provide you and your wife with a household of three hundred servants. This will sustain Your Majesty for the rest of your life, is it acceptable?" The king of Wu declined, saying, "Heaven descended catastrophe upon Wu. This did not occur before or after me. It is indeed me, the orphan, who lost the ancestral temple and the altars of earth and grain. Yue has already acquired Wu's land, ministers, and people. I, the orphan, am old and incapable of serving Your Majesty." He then killed himself with a sword.[77]

10.13. 勾踐已滅吳，乃以兵北渡江淮，與齊、晉諸侯會于徐州，致貢於周。周元王使人賜勾踐，已受命號去，還江南，以淮上地與楚，歸吳所侵宋地，與魯泗東方百里。當是之時，越兵橫行於江淮之上，諸侯畢賀，號稱霸王。

10.13. After Goujian had already destroyed Wu,[78] he then led the troops north and crossed the Yangzi and the Huai Rivers. He met the lords of Qi and Jin in Xuzhou and presented tribute to the Zhou court. King Yuan of Zhou sent emissaries to bestow gifts on Goujian.[79] After Goujian had accepted the title granted by Zhou,[80] he departed Xuzhou and returned south of the Yangzi River. He gave the land in the Huai River region to Chu, and returned to Song the lands that had been occupied by Wu. He also gave to Lu one hundred *li* of land east of the Si River. At that time, the Yue troops

---

77. We see a clear textual connection between *Guoyu* and *Shiji* in this episode. The *WYCQ* narrative is again adopted from *Shiji*. See Xu Yuangao, 561; *Shiji*, 41:1745. What is interesting is that in this chapter the Wu king Fuchai makes a resolute decision to kill himself. In chapter 5 of *WYCQ*, the "Inner Tradition of Fuchai," the Wu king is portrayed as too cowardly to commit suicide. The discrepancies might result from the different focuses of these two chapters, one of which concerns Fuchai and the other of which concerns Goujian. See *WYCQ*, 5.27.

78. This passage is adopted from *Shiji*. See *Shiji*, 41:1746.

79. The gift, according to *Shiji*, was the sacrificial meat from the Zhou court. Sharing the Zhou ancestral sacrificial meat with Goujian, who descended from Yu rather than from the same ancestor of the Zhou royal family, was a demonstration of respect by the Zhou king. See *Shiji*, 41:1746.

80. According to *Shiji*, the title the Zhou king granted to Goujian was 伯 (*bo*), Liege. See *Shiji*, 41:1746.

swept through the region between the Yangzi and the Huai Rivers. The many lords all congratulated Goujian.[81]

10.14. 越王還於吳，當歸而問於范蠡曰：「何子言之其合於天？」范蠡曰：「此素女之道，一言即合。大王之事，王問為實，《金匱》之要在於上下。」越王曰：「善哉！吾不稱王其可悉乎？」蠡曰：「不可。昔吳之稱王，僭天子之號，天變於上，日為陰蝕。今君遂僭號不歸，恐天變復見。」

越王不聽，還於吳，置酒文臺，群臣為樂，乃命樂作伐吳之曲。樂師曰：「臣聞即事作操，功成作樂。君王崇德，誨化有道之國，誅無義之人，復讎還恥，威加諸侯，受霸王之功。功可象於圖畫，德可刻於金石，聲可託於絃管，名可留於竹帛。臣請引琴而鼓之。」遂作《章暢》，辭曰：「屯乎！今欲伐吳可未耶？」大夫種、蠡曰：「吳殺忠臣伍子胥，今不伐吳人何須？」

大夫種進祝酒，其辭曰：「皇天祐助，我王受福。良臣集謀，我王之德。宗廟輔政，鬼神承翼。君不忘臣，臣盡其力。上天蒼蒼，不可掩塞。觴酒二升，萬福無極！」於是越王默然無言。

大夫種曰：「我王賢仁，懷道抱德。滅讎破吳，不忘返國。賞無所吝，群邪杜塞。君臣同和，福祐千億。觴酒二升，萬歲難極！」臺上群臣大悅而笑，越王面無喜色。

范蠡知勾踐愛壤土，不惜群臣之死，以其謀成國定，必復不須功而返國也。故面有憂色而不悅也。

10.14. The king of Yue returned to Wu. When he was about to return he asked Fan Li, "Why are your words so in accordance with the will of heaven?" Fan Li said, "It is the way of the Plain Girl[82] that any of my words are in accordance with the will of heaven. Your Majesty's affairs can find reference in the *Jade Gate*.[83] The essentials of the *Golden Basket* are to measure the advantages and disadvantages." The king of Yue said, "Excellent! Can

81. *Shiji* also writes that the lords called Goujian a hegemon 號稱霸王 (*haocheng bawang*). *Shiji*, 41:1746.

82. 素女 (*Sunü*), Plain Girl, was a legendary figure in Chinese religion and mythology. It is said that she was a contemporary of the Yellow Emperor and was knowledgeable about *yinyang*, music, and sexual practices for gaining longevity. A classic on sexual practice, *Sunü jing* 素女經, was attributed to her. She is probably a figure created by a Daoist school that emphasizes gaining longevity through sexual intercourse. The Han poet Zhang Heng 張衡 (78–139) describes the White Lady teaching sexual skills to a newlywed couple in a poem titled "Tongsheng ge" 同聲歌.

83. The sentence is ambiguous here. Both Zhang Jue and Huang Rensheng cite Sun Yirang who argues that 王問 (*Wangwen*) should be a mistake for 玉門 (*Yumen*, *Jade Gate*), a divination text both Fan Li and Wu Zixu mention several times in *WYCQ*. Both *Jade Gate* and *Golden Basket* are texts of divination. See Zhang Jue, 314n4; Huang Rensheng, 349n6.

the consequences of me calling myself a king be completely known?"[84] Fan Li said, "You cannot know them. In the past the ruler of Wu called himself a king, which usurped the title of the son of heaven.[85] Omens appeared in the sky, the sun was shadowed by the moon. If Your Majesty arrogated yourself with the title and did not abdicate, I am afraid that heavenly signs would appear again."

The king of Yue did not listen to Fan Li. He returned to Wu and prepared a banquet at Wen Terrace, where he entertained all his ministers. He then ordered the musician to compose a song commemorating his attack of Wu. The musician said, "I, your subject, have heard that a lute song is composed before the project starts;[86] a dance is created when it is accomplished.[87] Your Majesty values virtue, and teaches and transforms states obeying the Way. You punish men lacking righteousness, take revenge on your enemy and wash off your shame. Your authority awes the lords and you have achieved the merit of a hegemon. Your achievement should be inscribed on paintings and your virtue engraved on bronze and bones. Your fame should be written in music and your name imprinted on history.[88] I, your subject, request to use my lute to play for you." He then composed a song titled "Illustrating Merits";[89] its words read, "How difficult! Can Wu be attacked now?" Grand Ministers Wen Zhong and Fan Li continued, "Wu has murdered its loyal minister Wu Zixu; if we do not attack Wu then, when is a good time?"

Grand Minister Wen Zhong advanced and presented wine to the king, his words of celebration were:

Blessed by magnificent heaven,
Our king received good fortune.
Loyal ministers together made plans for him,
This is indeed because of the virtue of our king.
His ancestors assisted his rule,
Ghosts and spirits offered to help him.
Our king never forgets his ministers,
His ministers devoted themselves to him.

---

84. 不 (*bu*) is an auxiliary word here and does not mean "no" or "not." In the following sentence Fan Li answers that Goujian should not call himself a king.

85. Only the ruler of the Zhou court could be called a king; all other rulers of the states received other titles, for example, lord or marquise, from the Zhou king.

86. 操 (*cao*) is a type of song performed by playing the lute, and it usually expresses sorrow and frustration.

87. 樂 (*yue*) here specifically refers to music and dance.

88. 竹 (*zhu*), "bamboo," and 帛 (*bo*), "silk," for writing materials. Here they refer to history.

89. 章 (*zhang*) is used as a verb here: "to illustrate."

Blue is the sky above,
Nothing can be hidden; nothing can be concealed.
Twice I lift my wine,
Wishing my king endless fortune.
At this time, the king of Yue remained silent. Grand Minister Wen Zhong then said,
Our king is worthy and humane,
He cherishes the Way and embraces virtue.
He destroyed the enemy and defeated Wu,
And he kept in his heart returning to his homeland.
He is prodigal in presenting rewards,
And all evils are rooted out.
The king and his ministers are of the same heart,
Tens of thousands of folks have been blessed by good fortune.
Twice I raise up my wine,
wishing my king ten thousand years of boundless longevity.

All ministers on the terrace laughed with great joy, yet the king of Yue showed no happiness on his face. Fan Li knew that Goujian was parsimonious where the land of Wu was concerned and did not care about the deaths of his ministers. Because the king's plan had been accomplished and the states pacified, he consequently wanted to seek greater achievement and was therefore reluctant to return to Yue; thus, he wore a sad expression and was not happy.

10.15. 范蠡從吳欲去，恐勾踐未返，失人臣之義，乃從入越。行，謂文種曰：「子來去矣！越王必將誅子。」種不然言。蠡復為書遺種曰：「吾聞天有四時，春生冬伐；人有盛衰，泰終必否。知進退存亡而不失其正，惟賢人乎！蠡雖不才，明知進退。高鳥已散，良弓將藏；狡兔已盡，良犬就烹。夫越王為人，長頸鳥啄，鷹視狼步。可與共患難，而不可共處樂；可與履危，不可與安。子若不去，將害於子，明矣。」文種不信其言。越王陰謀，范蠡議欲去徼倖。

10.15. Fan Li wanted to leave the Wu capital. He was concerned that Goujian had not yet returned to Yue, so he would betray the duty of a minister if he left at that time. He eventually followed Goujian back to Yue. On the way, he addressed Wen Zhong, saying, "You sir, should leave.[90] The king

90. 來 (*lai*) is an auxiliary word here to stress the tone.

of Yue will definitely kill you." Wen Zhong did not believe Fan Li's words. Fan Li also wrote a letter to Wen Zhong,[91] saying, "I have heard that there are four seasons in nature. Spring is the time for growth and winter is for pruning. Men flourish and decline. Ultimate prosperity inevitably leads to distress. Probably only the worthy ones can know the right time for advancing and retreating, and are able to predict survival and demise without losing their principles. Although I, Fan Li, am not talented, I understand the importance of advancing and retreating at the right time. When the soaring birds scatter, the fine bow will be stored. After sly hares are gone, good dogs are cooked. As a person, the king of Yue has a long neck and a beak-like mouth. He stares like a hawk and walks like a wolf. He can share adversity with us but cannot enjoy happiness together with us.[92] He can endure danger with but cannot dwell in safety together with us. If you, sir, do not leave him, he will bring harm to you, this is clear." Wen Zhong did not believe Fan Li's words. The king of Yue schemed in secret; Fan Li proposed to leave the king and find his fortune elsewhere.[93]

10.16. 二十四年九月丁未，范蠡辭於王，曰：「臣聞主憂臣勞，主辱臣死，義一也。今臣事大王，前則無滅未萌之端，後則無救已傾之禍。雖然，臣終欲成君霸國，故不辭一死一生。臣竊自惟乃使於吳王之慚辱。蠡所以不死者，誠恐讒於太宰嚭，成伍子胥之事，故不敢前死，且須臾而生。夫恥辱之心，不可以大，流汗之愧，不可以忍。幸賴宗廟之神靈，大王之威德，以敗為成，斯湯武克夏商而成王業者。定功雪恥，臣所以當席日久。臣請從斯辭矣。」越王惻然泣下霑衣。言曰：「國之士大夫是子，國之人民是子，使孤寄身託號以俟命矣。今子云去，欲將逝矣，是天之棄越而喪孤也，亦無所恃者矣。孤竊有言，公位乎，分國共之，去乎，妻子受戮。」范蠡曰：「臣聞：『君子俟時，計不數謀，死不被疑，內不自欺。』臣既逝矣，妻子何法乎？王其勉之，臣從此辭。」乃乘扁舟，出三江，入五湖，人莫知其所適。

91. *Shiji* records that the letter was written after Fan Li had already left Yue. See *Shiji*, 41:1746.

92. This physiognomistic reading of Goujian's character is also found in *Shiji* as well as in the "Guxiang" (Bone physiognomy) in *Lunheng*. See *Shiji*, 41:1746; Huang Hui, *Lunheng jiaoshi*, 120–21.

93. The sentence is ambiguous. Huang Rensheng reads it as: "The king of Yue is used to secret plans; Fan Li wanted to discuss with Wen Zhong regarding leaving the king but Wen Zhong still lingered on his luck." Zhang Jue believes that the text is corrupted here and what should follow the sentence is missing. I follow Zhang Jue's reading of the sentence. See Huang Rensheng, 356; Zhang Jue, 316n5.

10.16. In the twenty-fourth year of King Goujian (473 BCE), day six of the ninth month,[94] Fan Li bid farewell to the king,[95] saying, "I, your subject, have heard that 'the ministers should work hard for him if the ruler is worried; the ministers should die for him if the ruler is humiliated. The principles are the same.' Now as for my, your subject's, service to Your Majesty, in the past I have not been able to root out disaster before it bourgeoned, after that I failed to save you from the calamity that had already fallen upon you. It's been said, I, your subject, have always been willing to assist you to become a hegemon, therefore I did not hesitate to face death and life.[96] I, your subject, privately thought that, in the past when I traveled to Wu and when Your Majesty had suffered humiliation, the reason I did not choose to die was because I was sincerely afraid Fuchai would listen to the slanderous words of Chief Chancellor Bo Pi and bring to pass Wu Zixu's suggestion. For this reason I dared not die in the past, and have been lingering on in my life. However, the thought of having been humiliated should not be allowed to grow; the shame of sweating as a servant should not be tolerated. Fortunately, blessed by the spirit of the ancestors and the awe-inspiring virtue of Your Majesty, we turned defeat into victory. This is equal to Tang and King Wu of Zhou conquering Xia and Shang and accomplishing the kingly way. Assisting Your Majesty to build your achievement and wash off your humiliation, these are the reasons I have been serving in power for a long time; but I, your subject, wish to depart now."

This caused the king of Yue to despair; his tears soaked his clothes. He spoke to Fan Li, saying, "All of the officials in the state believe in you; all the people of the state trust you—this is the reason I, the orphan, trust myself to you and accept the title of a king and wait for the Mandate of Heaven. Now, you, sir, mention that you want to leave and want to depart immediately. This is heaven abandoning Yue and leaving me, the orphan, to die. I have no one to rely on. I have words to tell you in private: 'If you, sir, remain at your post, I will share the state with you; if you depart, your wife and children will be executed.'"

Fan Li said, "I, your subject, have heard that 'the gentleman waits for the proper time. He never conceives a plan twice, never doubts himself even if he has to die and never deceives himself in his heart.' Since it is I, your

94. The date is wrong here. According to *WYCQ*, chap. 5, Goujian destroyed Wu in the tenth month in 473 BCE. Both *Zuozhuan* and *Shiji* record that Goujian destroyed Wu in the 11th month of 473 BCE. Fan Li's departure should be after Wu is conquered. See Zhang Jue, 317n1; Huang Rensheng, 355n4.

95. The following conservation between Fan Li and Goujian is developed from *Guoyu*, see Xu Yuangao, 588.

96. Fan Li is implying that he took the risk and went to serve in Wu with Goujian, and, while Goujian was humiliated by his defeat to Wu and by serving in Wu as a slave, Fan Li did not simply commit suicide as a loyal minister is expected to do.

subject, who wants to leave, what laws have my wife and children violated? Your Majesty should please yourself.[97] I, your subject, bid you farewell now." Fan Li then rode in a small boat, departed from Sanjiang, and entered Taihu. No one knew where he went.[98]

10.17. 范蠡既去，越王愀然變色，召大夫種曰：「蠡可追乎？」種曰：「不及也。」王曰：「柰何？」種曰：「蠡去時，陰畫六，陽畫三，日前之神，莫能制者。玄武天空威行，孰敢止者？度天關，涉天梁，後入天一。前翳神光，言之者死，視之者狂。臣願大王勿復追也。蠡終不還矣。」越王乃收其妻子，封百里之地：「有敢侵之者，上天所殃。」於是越王乃使良工鑄金象范蠡之形，置之坐側，朝夕論政。

10.17. After Fan Li had left, the king of Yue changed his expression out of fear. He summoned Grand Minister Wen Zhong and asked, "Can Fan Li be chased back?" Wen Zhong said, "It is too late." The king asked, "Why is that?" Wen Zhong said, "At the time when Fan Li left, the diagrams showed six divided lines and three single lines.[99] He was protected by the deities moving in front of the Sun and no one can control him.[100] When the gods of Xuanwu and Tiankong travel,[101] with their might who dares to stop them? They pass the Heavenly Gate,[102] cross the Heavenly Bridge,[103] enter the Tianyi Constellation from the back, and block the divine light in the front.[104] Anyone discussing them will die, anyone staring at them will go insane. I wish Your Majesty would stop chasing after him. After all, Fan Li will not return." The king of Yue then received Fan Li's wife and children and granted them one hundred *li* of land, swearing that "anyone who dares to bring harm to them will be punished by heaven." The king of Yue

---

97. Wei Zhao explains that Fan Li is suggesting Goujian should work on his virtue. See Xu Yuangao, 588.

98. This is adopted from *Guoyu*. *Shiji*, however, reports on Fan Li's life after he had retired from the Yue court. According to *Shiji*, Fan Li was very successful in trading and became a very rich merchant. He was then called Lord Taozhu 陶朱公. See *Shiji*, 41:1752–55.

99. In the *Book of Changes*, if the hexagrams are draw in divided lines they are *yin*, if they are in solid lines they are *yang*. Six divided lines is the *kun* ☷, three solid lines is the *qian* ☰; putting them together, *kun* above *qian*, then it is the hexagram *tai* 泰, which suggests pervading.

100. Zhang Jue interprets this as the *riyou shen* 日游神, a vicious god that harms people. See Zhang Jue, 319n3.

101. Huang Rensheng argues these are two vicious deities as well. Zhang Jue believes that *Xuanwu* is the god of ultimate *yin* who resides in the north and is in charge of the river. Because Fan Li left by boat, Wen Zhong is suggesting that Fan Li is protected by the god of water. See Huang Rensheng, 355n13; Zhang Jue, 319n4.

102. Referring to the *jiao* constellation.

103. These are the stars in the *dou* constellation.

104. Another interpretation of 神光 (*shenguang*) is that it is the name of a god. See Huang Rensheng, 355n18.

then ordered master craftsman to use metal and cast a statue of Fan Li; he put it on his left side and discussed government affairs with it morning and night.[105]

10.18. 自是之後，計研佯狂，大夫、曳庸、扶同、皋如之徒，日益疏遠，不親於朝。大夫種內憂不朝，人或讒之於王曰：「文種棄宰相之位，而令君王霸於諸侯。今官不加增，位不益封，乃懷怨望之心，憤發於內，色變於外，故不朝耳。」異日，種諫曰：「臣所以在朝而晏罷，若身疾作者，但為吳耳。今已滅之，王何憂乎？」越王默然。時魯哀公患三桓，欲因諸侯以伐之；三桓亦患哀公之怒，以故君臣作難。哀公奔陘，三桓攻哀公，公奔衛，又奔越。魯國空虛，國人悲之，來迎哀公，與之俱歸。勾踐憂文種之不圖，故不為哀公伐三桓也。

10.18. After that, Ji Yan pretended to be insane; grand ministers such as Yeyong, Futong, and Gaoru became more alienated day after day. They were not trusted in court. Grand Minister Wen Zhong was worried in his heart and did not go to court. Some slandered Wen Zhong to the king, saying, "Wen Zhong gave up the prime minister position and helped Your Majesty to become a hegemon among the lords. Now that his post is not promoted and rank not advanced, he thereby holds resentment in his heart. His anger rises up inside and it changes his facial expression outside, he thereupon does not come to court." On another day, Wen Zhong admonished the king, saying, "The reason in the past that I, your subject, attended court early in the morning and retired late in the afternoon[106] and exhausted myself working very hard was simply to plan for Wu.[107] Now we have destroyed Wu, what worries should Your Majesty have?" The king of Yue did not respond. At that time, Lord Ai of Lu was worried about the three Huan families and wanted to rely upon the lords to attack the Huans.[108] The three Huans were also concerned about Lord

---

105. This episode of Goujian commemorating Fan Li is adopted from *Guoyu*, see Xu Yuangao, 588–89.

106. According to Xu Tianhu, 在 (*zai*) is a mistake for 蚤 (*zao*), "early morning." See Zhang Jue, 321n3; Huang Rensheng, 358n1.

107. Zhang Jue cites a *Zhuangzi* passage and argues that 若 (*ruo*) should be a mistake for 苦 (*ku*). The sentence 苦身疾作 (*kushen jizuo*) therefore means "exhausts one's body and works very hard." 若身疾作 (*ruoshen jizuo*) means "as if one's body is struck by illness," which does not make sense here. I follow Zhang Jue's reading. See Zhang Jue, 321n3.

108. The Lu ministers Mengsun 孟孫, Shusun 叔孫, and Jisun 季孫 in Lord Ai of Lu's time were descendants of Lord Huan of Lu, thereupon they were called the three Huans. After the death of Lord Wen, the three Huans seized the power of the state. Lord Ai wanted to rely upon the lords of neighboring states to regain power from the Three Huans but was attacked by them, and Lord Ai was forced to flee to Yue for protection. See *Shiji*, 33:1545. See also *Zuozhuan*, Lord Ai 27.4; Yang Bojun, 1735; Durrant, Li, and Schaberg, 1991.

Ai's anger toward them, and for this reason, fights broke out between the ruler and the subjects and Lord Ai ran to Jing. The three Huans attacked Lord Ai of Lu, the lord fled to Wei and then to Yue. There was no ruler in Lu. The people of Lu were aggrieved by this; they came to Yue to receive Lord Ai and returned to Lu with him. Goujian was concerned that Wen Zhong might have bad intentions and therefore had not attacked the three Huans for Lord Ai.

10.19. 二十五年，丙午平旦，越王召相國大夫種而問之：「吾聞知人易，自知難。其知相國何如人也？」種曰：「哀哉！大王知臣勇也，不知臣仁也；知臣忠也，不知臣信也。臣誠數以損聲色，滅淫樂、奇說怪論，盡言竭忠，以犯大王，逆心咈耳，必以獲罪。臣非敢愛死不言，言而後死。昔子胥於吳矣，夫差之誅也，謂臣曰：『狡兔死，良犬烹，敵國滅，謀臣亡。』范蠡亦有斯言。何大王問犯《玉門》之第八，臣見王志也。」越王默然不應。大夫亦罷。

10.19. In the twenty-fifth year of King Goujian (472 BCE), on the morning of the *bingwu* day (seventh day) of the first month, the king of Yue summoned Prime Minister Wen Zhong and asked him, "I have heard that it is easy to know others but difficult to know oneself. How do I know what kind of man you, Prime Minister, are?" Wen Zhong said, "How pitiful! Your Majesty knows I am brave but does not know that I am humane. You know I am loyal but do not know I am trustworthy. I indeed have several times used strange theories and awkward sayings, reducing the performance of music and women and getting rid of dissolution and pleasure to admonish you and to express my loyalty; I have offended Your Majesty because of these acts. My words went against your will and were unpleasant to hear, I certainly will be punished because of this. It is not that I, your subject, dare to cherish my life and thus do not admonish; however, I will meet with death after I speak. Previously when Wu Zixu was in Wu and was about be killed by Fuchai, he told me, your subject, 'When sly hares are dead, good dogs are cooked; after the rival state is destroyed, advising ministers will die.' Fan Li has also mentioned this. Why did Your Majesty violate the eighth principle of the *Jade Gate* when asking me?[109] I understand Your Majesty's intention." The king of Yue remained silent and did not answer; the grand minister also did not continue.

10.20. 哺其耳以成人惡。其妻曰：「君賤一國之相，少王祿乎？臨食不亨，哺以惡　何？妻子在側，匹夫之能自致，相國尚何望哉！無乃為貪乎？何其志忽忽若斯？」種曰：「悲哉！子不知也。吾王

109. It is not clear what the eighth principle is.

既免於患難，雪恥於吳。我悉徙宅自投死亡之地，盡九術之謀，於彼為佞，在君為忠，王不察也，乃曰：『知人易，自知難。』吾答之，又無他語，是凶妖之證也。吾將復入，恐不再還，與子長訣，相求於玄冥之下。」妻曰：「何以知之？」種曰：「吾見王時，正犯《玉門》之第八也，辰剋其日，上賊於下，是為亂醜，必害其良。今日剋其辰，上賊下止。吾命須臾之間耳。」

10.21. After returning home, Wen Zhong chewed amaranth and it turned into the shape of excrement.[110] His wife said, "Do you, sir, despise the position of the prime minister of a state and disdain the salary your king offers you? Why do you refuse to eat dinner, but chew excrement-like food? What is the reason? You have a wife and children on your side. You achieved the position of the prime minister, rising from a commoner, what else should you expect? Perhaps you are greedy? Why is your mind as confused as this?"

Wen Zhong said, "How sad that you do not understand this! Since our king has already escaped from disaster and has already washed off the humiliation he suffered in Wu, I have completely changed my dwelling to the place where I will have myself killed. I presented the entire nine schemes. To Wu this is cunning but to the king this is loyal. The king failed to understand this; instead, he said, 'it is easy to know others but difficult to know oneself.' I explained to him but he did not respond. This is proof of misfortune and evil. I will go to the palace again but I am afraid that I will never return. I part from you forever; I will meet you in the afterworld."

His wife said, "How do you know about this?" Wen Zhong said, "The time I received the audience from the king happened to violate the eighth principle of the *Jade Gate*. If the heavenly stem of the hour overcomes the heavenly stem of the date, a minister will assassinate his ruler, and this means chaos and ugliness.[111] It will certainly bring harm to good people. Now, the time when I saw the king the heavenly stem of the date overcame that of the hour, this means the ruler will murder his minister.[112] My life will end in a flash."

---

110. The sentence is not clear here. Lu Wenchao believes there are missing words before it. Zhang Jue translates it as: "Wen Zhong filled the cauldron with the excrement of adults." Huang Rensheng reads 耳 (*er*) as 餌 (*si*), a type of cake-like food, and translates the sentence as "Wen Zhong chewed a piece of cake and the food was chewed like the shape of excrement." Zhou Shengchun also reads 耳 as 餌 but argues it is a type of amaranth. See Huang Rensheng, 361n7; Zhang Jue, 323n1; Zhou Shengchun, 180n4.

111. Hours symbolize subjects while dates symbolize the ruler.

112. According to *WYCQ*, 10.19, Wen Zhong received an audience from Goujian on the early morning of the *bingwu* day. Here the date is *bingwu* and the hour is *mao*. *Bingwu* is associated with fire, *mao* is associated with wood. In the overcoming theory of the Five Phases, fire overcomes wood, therefore Wen Zhong said the date overcomes the hour. See Zhang Jue, 324n9.

10.21. 越王復召相國，謂曰：「子有陰謀兵法，傾敵取國九術之策，今用三已破彊吳，其六尚在子，所願幸以餘術，為孤前王於地下謀吳之前人。」於是種仰天歎曰：「嗟乎！吾聞大恩不報，大功不還，其謂斯乎？吾悔不隨范蠡之謀，乃為越王所戮。吾不食善言，故哺以人惡。」越王遂賜文種屬盧之劍，種得劍又歎曰：「南陽之宰而為越王之擒！」自笑曰：「後百世之末，忠臣必以吾為喻矣。」遂伏劍而死。

越王葬種於國之西山，樓船之卒三千餘人，造鼎足之羨，或入三峰之下。葬一年，伍子胥從海上穿山脅而持種去，與之俱浮於海。故前潮水潘候者，伍子胥也，後重水者，大夫種也。

10.21. The king of Yue once more summoned the prime minister and spoke to him, saying, "You, sir, have secret schemes and military strategies to overturn enemies and conquer other states. We only adopted three of the nine schemes and we have already destroyed the mighty Wu. The remaining six schemes are still in your possession. I wish you would grant me the fortune of using the remaining schemes to make plans against the ancestors of Wu on behalf of my former kings." Wen Zhong thereupon looked at the sky and sighed, saying, "Alas! I have heard that 'if the kindness is too big it is not requited; if the achievement is too great it is not awarded.' It perhaps refers to this! My regret is that I did not listen to Fan Li's suggestion and therefore I am to be killed by the king of Yue. I refused to be fed by faithful words so I have to swallow excrement." The king of Yue then gave Wen Zhong the sword of Zhulou.[113] Holding the sword, Wen Zhong again lamented, saying, "The Prefect of Nanyang was captured by the king of Yue."[114] He ridiculed himself, saying, "From now to a hundred generations later, loyal ministers will use me as their reference." He then killed himself with the sword.

The king of Yue buried Wen Zhong on the mountain west of the capital. He dispatched over three thousand soldiers to ride towered boats to attend the funeral and constructed a tomb with an entrance shaped like a cauldron foot.[115] Some said Wen Zhong was buried under Sanfeng Mountain. A year after Wen Zhong was buried, Wu Zixu came from the sea; he opened the mountain and took Wen Zhong with him. He floated in the sea with Wen Zhong. Thereafter, the frontal waves that come, greet, and encircle are Wu Zixu. The following sequences of waves are Grand Minister Wen Zhong.

---

113. This is the same sword Fuchai gave to Wu Zixu when ordering him to commit suicide. See *WYCQ*, 5.19.

114. Wen Zhong was a native of Chu and once served as the Prefect of Nanyang in Chu.

115. 樓船 (*louchuan*) is a tall boat with towers on it. 羨 (*xian*) here refers to the entrance to a tomb. Cauldron foot is a common metaphor for important ministers.

10.22. 越王既已誅忠臣，霸於關東，從瑯邪，起觀臺，周七里，以望東海。死士八千人，戈船三百艘。居無幾，射求賢士，孔子聞之，從弟子奉先王雅琴禮樂奏於越。越王乃被唐夷之甲，帶步光之劍，杖屈盧之矛，出死士，以三百人為陣關下。孔子有頃到，越王曰：「唯，唯，夫子何以教之？」孔子曰：「丘能述五帝三王之道，故奏雅琴以獻之大王。」越王喟然歎曰：「越性脆而愚，水行山處，以船為車，以楫為馬，往若飄然，去則難從，悅兵敢死，越之常也。夫子何說而欲教之？」孔子不答，因辭而去。

10.22. After the king of Yue killed the loyal minister, he dominated the areas east of the Hangu Pass. He relocated his capital to Langye, where he built a viewing terrace that was seven *li* in circumference in order to overlook the Eastern Sea.[116] He had eight thousand warriors willing to die for him and three hundred boats with spears sticking out. After a while, he sought worthy men. Upon hearing this, Confucius led his disciples, holding an elegant lute from the former king's era, and brought music appropriate to the rites and played them in Yue.[117] The king of Yue put on Tangyi armor, carried the Buguang sword, held the Qulu lance, and went with three hundred death-defying soldiers to wait in formation outside of the pass.[118] Soon Confucius arrived.

The king of Yue said, "Yes, yes. What do you, Master, have to teach me?" Confucius said, "I, Qiu, can explain the way of the Five Emperors and Three Sovereigns. I will present this to Your Majesty through playing the elegant lute." The king of Yue sighed deeply, saying, "The Yue people are frail and unintelligent by nature. They travel on the rivers and dwell in the mountains. Boats replace carriages and oars are their horses. They are swift as the wind when advancing and impossible to catch when retreating. They are fond of battle and dare to die.[119] This is the nature of the Yue people. Do you, Master, have any teachings with which you would like to instruct us?" Confucius did not respond; he bid the king farewell and departed.

---

116. See Xin Deyong 辛德勇, "Yuewang Goujian xidu Langye shi xiyi" 越王勾踐徙都琅邪事析義, *Wenshi* 文史90 (2010): 5–61.

117. Confucius had already died in 479 BCE; it would have been impossible for Confucius to have heard this, and there is no other literary reference to Confucius's visit to Yue.

118. These are all famous weapons. *Yue jue shu* names the sword *Ciyi* 賜夷 and the lance *Lulu* 路盧. The Buguang sword and the Qulu lance were once gifts from Goujian to the Wu king. See *Shiji*, 67:2199–2200. See also Milburn, 226n20, 226n22.

119. *Yue jue shu* has 銳兵任死 (*ruibing rensi*), "sharpen their weapons and are willing to die." See Li Bujia, 222; Milburn, 226.

10.23. 越王使人如木客山取元常之喪，欲徙葬琅邪。三穿元常之墓，墓中生熛風，飛砂石以射人，人莫能入。勾踐曰：「吾前君其不徙乎？」遂置而去。

10.23. The king of Yue sent men to Mount Muke to retrieve Yuanchang's body, planning to move his tomb to Langye. The men dug three times before they reached Yuanchang's tomb.[120] However, a whirlwind occurred in the chamber, and blowing rocks and sand hit people. No one could enter the chamber. Goujian said, "Perhaps my former king does not want to move?" He then put aside this pursuit and left.

10.24. 勾踐乃使使號令齊、楚、秦、晉皆輔周室，血盟而去。秦桓公不如越王之命，勾踐乃選吳越將士西渡河以攻秦。軍士苦之，會秦怖懼，逆自引咎，越乃還軍。軍人悅樂，遂作『河梁之詩』，曰：「渡河梁兮渡河梁，舉兵所伐攻秦王。孟冬十月多雪霜，隆寒道路誠難當。陣兵未濟秦師降，諸侯怖懼皆恐惶。聲傳海內威遠邦，稱霸穆桓齊楚莊，天下安寧壽考長。悲去歸兮何無梁。」自越滅吳，中國皆畏之。

10.24. Goujian then sent envoys to Qi, Chu, Qin, and Jin and ordered all of them to assist the Zhou household. They had to swear an oath and make a blood covenant before their departure. Lord Gong of Qin disobeyed the order of the king of Yue,[121] so Goujian then selected generals and soldiers from Wu and Yue and marched west to cross the Yellow River and attack Qin. His soldiers felt miserable about this. It happened that Qin feared Yue's attack and admitted their fault first, and Yue thereupon withdrew its army. The soldiers were delighted and then composed "Song of the River Bridge," which was:

Cross the river bridge, cross the river bridge,
Mobilize the troops to attack the king of Qin.
In the tenth month, start of winter, often are the snows and frosts,
Brutally cold, the road is indeed hard to travel.
Before our troops crossed the river, the Qin army yielded,
The many lords are scared and have panicked.
Our fame has spread to the world and awes distant states,

---

120. Another reading is that "they dug into Yuanchang's tomb three times." See Huang Rensheng, 367.

121. The twenty-fifth year of King Goujian is the sixth year of Lord Ligong of Qin 秦厲共公, which is 160 years after the rule of Lord Huan of Qin.

Our king has become a hegemon, like Qin's Lord Mu and Lord Huan of Qi,
He is equal to King Zhuang of Chu.
The world is at peace, our lives can be long,
Our sorrows gone, there's no need for a river bridge to bring us home.
Since Yue destroyed Wu, states in the central plain have feared Yue.

10.25. 二十六年，越王以邾子無道而執以歸，立其太子何。冬，魯哀公以三桓之逼來奔，越王欲為伐三桓，以諸侯大夫不用命，故不果耳。

10.25. In the twenty-sixth year of King Goujian (471 BCE), the king of Yue captured and took the lord of Zhu back to Yue because of the latter's violations of the Way. He established the lord of Zhu's son, He, as the new ruler.[122] In the winter, Lord Ai of Lu came to seek refuge because of the aggression from the three Huans. The king of Yue wanted to attack the three Huans on his behalf, but did not do so because the many grand ministers would not follow his orders.

10.26. 二十七年冬，勾踐寢疾，將卒，謂太子興夷曰：「吾自禹之後，承元常之德，蒙天靈之祐，神祇之福，從窮越之地，籍楚之前鋒，以摧吳王之干戈。跨江涉淮，從晉齊之地，功德巍巍。自致於斯，其可不誡乎？夫霸者之後，難以久立，其慎之哉！」遂卒。

10.26. In the winter of the twenty-seventh year of King Goujian (470 BCE), Goujian was confined to bed because of illness. When he was about to die, he spoke to the heir apparent, Xingyi,[123] saying, "I, a descendant of Yu, inherited Yuanchang's virtue, was protected by heavenly spirits, and blessed by gods. Although from the land of poor Yue, I relied upon the force of Chu and therefore destroyed the army of the king of Wu. I crossed the Yangzi and the Huai Rivers, and roamed about in the land of Jin and Qi. Great was my merit and achievement. Coming to this status, how could I not be cautious? It is difficult for the descendant of a hegemon to sustain his success, so you must be careful." He then died.

---

122. According to *Zuozhuan*, in the eighth year of Lord Ai of Lu (487 BCE), Wu captured Lord Yin of Zhu and established his son Ge as the new ruler. Two years later Lord Yin of Zhu fled from Wu to Lu and then to Qi. In 473 BCE, Lord Yin of Zhu came to Yue and asked for help from Goujian. Yue then sent Lord Yin of Zhu back to Zhu, his son Ge had to flee to Yue. In 471 BCE, Yue arrested Lord Yin of Zhu on account of violating the Way. See Zhang Jue, 330n1.

123. In *Yue jue shu*, the name of the heir apparent was Yuyi 于夷; *Shiji* reports the name was Shiyu 鼫与. See Li Bujia, 222, *Shiji*, 41:1747.

10.27. 興夷即位一年卒，子翁；翁卒，子不揚；不揚卒，子無彊；無彊卒，子玉；玉卒，子尊；尊卒，子親。自勾踐至于親，其歷八主，皆稱霸，積年二百二十四年，親眾皆失，而去琅邪，徙於吳矣。

10.27. Xingyi died a year after he was enthroned. His son Weng succeeded him. After Weng died, his son Buyang succeeded. After Buyang died, his son Wujiang succeeded. When Wujiang died, his son Yu succeeded. When Yu died, his son Zun succeeded. When Zun died, his son Qin succeeded. From Goujian down to Qin, there were eight rulers and all of them were hegemons, spanning in total two hundred and twenty-four years. Qin lost his people, so he left Langye and moved to Wu.[124]

10.28. 自黃帝至少康十世，自禹受禪至少康即位六世，為一百四十四年，少康去顓頊即位，四百二十四年。

黃帝→昌意→顓頊→鯀→禹→啟→太康→仲廬→相→少康→無余→無壬（去無余十世）→無擇→夫譚→元常→勾踐→興夷→不壽→不揚→無彊→魯穆柳有幽公為名，王侯自稱為君→尊→親，失瑯邪，為楚所滅。

勾踐至王親，歷八主，格霸二百二十四年。從無余越國始封，至餘善返越國空滅，凡一千九百二十二年。

10.28. From the time of the Yellow Emperor to Shaokang, there were ten generations. From Yu's receiving Shun's abdication, to Shaokang's ascending the throne, there were one hundred and forty-four years. From Shaokang to Zhuanxu's ascendance, there were four hundred and twenty-four years.

The Yellow Emperor—Changyi—Zhuanxu—Gun—Yu—Qi—Taikang—Zhonglu—Xiang—Shaokang—Wuyu—Wuren, who was ten generations down from Wuyu—Wuze—Futan—Yuanchang—Goujian—Xingyi—Bushou—Buyang—Wujiang—Muliu of Lu adopted Lord You as his title,[125] King Zhihou called himself a lord—Zun—Qin who lost Langye and was destroyed by Chu.[126]

---

124. The *WYCQ* list of Yue kings is the same as that in the *Yue jue shu*. However, both *Shiji* and the excavated bamboo documents *Zhushu jinian* 竹書紀年 have a different succession line from the one in the *WYCQ* and *Yue jue shu*. It seems that *Shiji* and *Zhushu jinian* are more accurate than the two Eastern Han texts. See Zhang Jue, 331n2 for a summary of the king list in *Shiji*, *Zhushu jinian*, and *Yue jue shu*. See also Milburn's note on this, in Milburn, 227.

125. The meaning of this sentence is not clear. The text might be corrupted.

126. *Shiji* reports that King Wei of Chu 楚威王 destroyed Yue in 333 BCE. However, there are different theories about when Yue ended. Meng Wentong argues that after 333 BCE Yue was still active in historical writings; even before the First Emperor of Qin 秦始皇 (r. 247–220 BCE) unified

From Goujian down to King Qin of Yue, there had been eight rulers, and Yue had dominated for two hundred and twenty-four years. From the time Wuyu was enfeoffed until Yushan returned to Yue and was destroyed, there were in total one thousand nine hundred and twenty-two years.

---

China, Yue was among the states fighting against Qin conquest. See Meng Wentong, *Guzu zhenwei*, 327–37. See also, Li Jiahao 李家浩, "Chuwang Yanzhang ge yu Chu mie Yue de niandai" 楚王酓璋戈與楚滅越的年代, *Wenshi* 24 (1985): 15–21.

# Bibliography

## Frequently Cited Primary Sources

| | |
|---|---|
| *Guoyu* | see Xu Yuangao |
| *Hanfeizi* | see Chen Qiyou |
| *Hanshu* | see Ban Gu |
| *Hou Hanshu* | see Fan Ye |
| *Huainanzi* | see He Ning |
| *Jinshu* | see Fang Xuanling |
| *Liji* | see Sun Xidan |
| *Lunheng* | see Huang Hui |
| *Lüshi chunqiu* | see Xu Weiyu |
| *Shiji* | see Sima Qian |
| *Wu Yue Chunqiu* | see Zhang Jue and Huang Rensheng |
| *Yue jue shu* | see Li Bujia |
| *Zuo Tradition* | see Durrant, Li, and Schaberg |
| *Zuozhuan* | see Yang Bojun |

## Secondary Sources


Allan, Sarah. "The Identities of Taigong Wang in Zhou and Han Literature." *Monumenta Serica* 30 (1972–1973): 57–99.

Ban Gu 班固. *Hanshu* 漢書. Beijing: Zhonghua shuju, 1962.

Birrell, Anne. *Chinese Mythology: An Introduction*. Baltimore: Johns Hopkins University Press, 1993.

——. ed. *The Classic of Mountains and Seas*. London: Penguin Books, 1999.

——. *Popular Songs and Ballads of Han China*. Honolulu: University of Hawai'i Press, 1993.

Brindley, Erica Fox. *Ancient China and the Yue: Perceptions and Identities on the Southern Frontier, c.400 BCE–50 CE*. Cambridge: Cambridge University Press, 2015.

Cahill, Suzanne E. *Transcendence and Divine Passion: The Queen Mother of the West in Medieval China*. Stanford, CA: Stanford University Press, 1993.

Cai Zhemao 蔡哲茂. "Yin buci 'Yi Yin jiushi' kao—jian lun tuo- shi" 殷卜辭伊尹啓事考—兼論它事. *Zhongyang yanjiuyuan Lishi yuyuan yanjiusuo jikan* 中央研究院歷史語言研究所集刊 58, no. 4 (1987): 755–808.

Cang Xiuliang 倉修良. "*Wu Yue Chunqiu jijiao huikao xu*" 吳越春秋輯校匯考序. In *Wu Yue Chunqiu jijiao huikao* 吳越春秋輯校匯考, Zhou Shengchun 周生春, 1–14. Shanghai: Shanghai guji chubanshe, 1997.

Cao Jinyan 曹錦炎. "Lun Zhangjiashan Hanjian Gailu" 論張家山漢簡蓋廬. *Dongnan wenhua* 東南文化, no. 9 (2002): 62–69.

——. "Wu jizi jianming kaoshi" 吳季子劍銘考釋. *Dongnan wenhua* 東南文化, no. 4 (1990): 109–110.

——. "Wuwang Guang tongdaigou xiaokao" 吳王光銅帶鈎小考. *Dongnan wenhua* 東南文化, no 2. (2013): 90–93.

Cao Lindi 曹林娣. "Guanyu *Wu Yue Chunqiu* de zuozhe ji chengshu niandai" 關於吳越春秋的作者及成書年代. *Xibei daxue xuebao* 西北大學學報, no 4 (1982): 68–73, 89.

Chen Li 陳立. *Baihutong shuzheng* 白虎通疏證. Beijing: Zhonghua shuju, 2015.

Chen Qiaoyi 陳橋驛. *Wu Yue wenhua luncong* 吳越文化論叢. Beijing: Zhonghua shuju, 1999.

Chen Qiyou 陳奇猷. *Hanfeizi jishi* 韓非子集釋. Shanghai: Shanghai renmin chubanshe, 1974.

Chen Shou 陳壽. *Sanguo zhi* 三國志. Beijing: Zhonghua shuju, 1965.

Cheng Junying 程俊英. *Shijing yizhu* 詩經譯註. Shanghai: Shanghai guji chubanshe, 1995.

Confucius. *Analects*. Translated by Edward Slingerland. Indianapolis, IN: Hackett Publishing Company, 2003.

Csikszentmihalyi, Mark. *Material Virtue: Ethics and the Body in Early China*. Leiden: Brill, 2004.

Dong Chuping 董楚平. *Wu Yue wenhua xintan* 吳越文化新探. Hangzhou: Zhejiang renmin chubanshe, 1988.

Dong Shan 董珊. *Wu Yue timing yanjiu* 吳越題名研究. Beijing: Kexue chubanshe, 2014.

Du Yunhong 杜雲虹. *Suishu Jingji zhi yanjiu* 隋書經籍志研究. Beijing: Wenwu chubanshe, 2016.

Duan Yucai 段玉裁. *Shuowen jiezi zhu* 說文解字註. Shanghai: Shanghai guji chubanshe, 1998.

Durrant, Stephen, Li Wai-yee, and David Schaberg, trans. *Zuo Tradition/Zuozhuan: Commentary on the "Spring and Autumn Annals."* Seattle: University of Washington Press, 2016.

Fan Ye 范曄. *Hou Hanshu* 後漢書. Beijing: Zhonghua shuju, 1962.

Fang Xuanling 房玄齡. *Jinshu* 晉書. Beijing: Zhonghua shuju, 1974.

Feng Puren 馮普仁. *Wu Yue wenhua* 吳越文化. Beijing: Wenwu chubanshe, 2007.

Gu Jianxiang 谷建祥 and Wei Yihui 魏宜輝. "Pizhou Jiunüdun suochu bianbo mingwen kaobian" 邳州九女墩所出編鎛銘文考辨. *Kaogu* 考古, no 11 (1999): 71–73.

Guo Qingfan 郭慶藩. *Zhuangzi jishi* 莊子集釋. Beijing: Zhonghua shuju, 2015.

Guo Zaiyi 郭在貽. "Shi 'Nuli'" 釋努力. In *Guo Zaiyi wenji* 郭在貽文集, 233–236. Beijing: Zhonghua shuju, 2002.

He Ning 何寧. *Huainanzi jishi* 淮南子集釋. Beijing: Zhonghua shuju, 2015.

Hsieh, Daniel. "The Origin and Nature of the 'Nineteen Old Poems.'" *Sino-Platonic Papers*, no. 77 (January 1998): 1–52.

Hu Houxuan 胡厚宣, ed. *Jiaguwen heji* 甲骨文合集. Beijing: Zhongguo shehui kexue chubanshe, 1999.

Huang Dekuan 黃德寬. "Qinghua jian 'Chihu zhi ji Tang zhi wu' yu xian Qian xiaoshuo" 清華簡赤鵠之集湯之屋與先秦小說. *Fudan xuebao* 復旦學報, no. 4 (2013): 81–86.

Huang Huaixin 黃懷信, Zhang Maorong 張懋鎔, and Tian Xudong 田旭東. *Yi Zhoushu huijiao jizhu* 逸周書匯校集注. Shanghai: Shanghai guji chubanshe, 2007.

Huang Hui, ed. 黃暉. *Lunheng jiaoshi* 論衡校釋. Beijing: Zhonghua shuju, 2015.

Huang Rensheng 黃仁生. *Xinyi Wu Yue Chunqiu* 新譯吳越春秋. Taipei: Sanmin shuju, 1996.

Hubei sheng jingzhou shi zhouliang yuqiao yizhi bowuguan 湖北省荆州市周梁玉橋遺址博物館 ed. *Guanju QianHan mu jiandu* 关沮秦汉墓简牍. Beijing: Zhonghua shuju, 2001.

Jiang Lihong 蔣禮鴻. *Shangjun shu zhuizhi* 商君書錐指. Beijing: Zhonghua shuju, 2015.

Jin Qizhen 金其楨. "*Wu Yue Chunqiu* neiwu waiyue tanbian" 吳越春秋內吳外越探辯. *Gannan shifan xueyuan xuebao* 贛南師範學院學報, no. 1 (1993): 60–65.

Jin Yongping 金永平. "*Wu Yue Chunqiu* Xu Tianhu zhu qianyi" 吳越春秋徐天祜註淺議. *Hangzhou shifan daxue xuebao* 杭州師範大學學報, no 4 (1991): 101–105.

Johnson, David. "Epic and History in Early China: The Matter of Wu Tzu-hsu." *Journal of Asian Studies* 40, no. 2 (1981): 255–271.

——. "The Wu Tzu-hsu *pien-wen* and Its Sources." Pts. 1 and 2. *Harvard Journal of Asiatic Studies* 40, no. 1 (1980): 93–156; 40, no. 2 (1980): 465–505.

Knoblock, John and Jeffrey Riegel. *The Annals of Lü Buwei*. Stanford, CA: Stanford University Press, 2001.

Kong Yingda 孔穎達. *Zhouyi Zhengyi* 周易正義. Beijing: Zhonghua shuju, 1982.

Lao Tzu. *Tao Teh Ching*. Translated by John C. H. Wu. Boston: Shambhala, 2005.

Legge, James. *The Chinese Classics: The She King*. 2 vols. Hong Kong: Hong Kong University Press, 1960.

——. *The Yî King*. In *Sacred Books of the East*. Vol. 16, *The Sacred Books of China*, vol. 2 of 6, Part II of *The Texts of Confucianism*. Oxford: Clarendon Press, 1882.

Li Bujia 李步嘉. *Yue jue shu jiaoshi* 越絕書校釋. Beijing: Zhonghua shuju, 2016.

Li Jiahao 李家浩. "Chuwang Yanzhang ge yu Chu mie Yue de niandai" 楚王酓璋戈與楚滅越的年代. *Wenshi* 24 (1985): 15–21.

Li Ling 李零. *Zhongguo fangshu kao* 中國方術考. Beijing: Dongfang chubanshe, 2001.

Li Xueqin 李学勤. "Suigong Yin yu DaYu zhishui chuanshuo" 遂公盨与大禹治水传说. *Zhongguo shehui kexueyuan yuanbao* 中国社会科学院院报 (2003): 1–23.

Li Yanshou 李延壽. *Nanshi* 南史. 6 vols. Beijing: Zhonghua shuju, 1975.

Liang Zonghua 梁宗華. "Xianxing shijuanben *Wu Yue Chunqiu* kaozhi" 現行十卷本吳越春秋考識. *Dongyue luncong* 東岳論叢 1 (1988): 54–57.

Lin Xiaoyun 林小雲. "*Wu Yue Chunqiu* juanzhi kaobian" 吳越春秋卷帙考辨. *Minjiang xueyuan xuebao* 閩江學院學報 30, no. 4 (2009): 27–29, 33.

Liu An. *The Huainanzi: A Guide to the Theory and Practice of Government in Early Han China*. Translated and edited by John S. Major, Sarah A. Queen, Andrew Seth Meyer, and Harold D. Roth. New York: Columbia University Press, 2010.

Liu Chengqun 劉成群. "Qinghua jian 'Chihu zhi ji Tang zhi wu' wenti xingzhi zai tan" 清華簡赤鵠之集湯之屋文體性質再探. *Xueshu luntan* 學術論壇 39, no. 8 (2016): 100–105, 129.

Liu Guozhong. *Introduction to the Tsinghua Bamboo-Strip Manuscripts*. Edited by Christopher J. Foster and William N. French. Leiden, Brill, 2016.

Liu Xiang 劉向. *Gu Lienü zhuan* 古列女傳. Shanghai: Shanghai guji chubanshe, 1985.

——. *Zhanguo ce* 戰國策. Shanghai: Shanghai guji chubanshe, 1985.

Liu Xiaozhen 劉曉臻. "*Wu Yue Chunqiu yanjiu* 吳越春秋研究." MA thesis, Shangdong Normal University, 2005.

——. "*Wu Yue Chunqiu* zhong de zhanpu fangshi ji tedian" 吳越春秋中的占卜方式及特點. *Wenzhou daxue xuebao* (social science edition) 溫州大學學報（社會科學版）22, no. 1 (2009): 48–53.

Liu Yin 劉寅. *Weiliao zi jijie* 尉繚子直解. Yangzhou: Jiangsu guji chubanshe, 1998.

Long Jianchun 龙建春. "'Taigong' xingshi minghao kaolun" "太公"姓氏名号考论. *Taizhou xueyuan xuebao* 台州学院学报, no. 2 (2003): 24–28.

Long Yongfang 龍永芳. "Gudai guxu shu xiaoyi—jianlun Zhoujiatia Qinjian zhong de guxu fa" 古代孤虚术小议—兼论周家台秦简中的孤虚法. *Jingmen zhiye jishu xueyuan xuebao* 荊門職業技術學院學報 22, no. 2 (2007): 85–9.

Mair, Victor H. *Tun-Huang Popular Narratives.* Cambridge: Cambridge University Press, 1983.

Mao Ying 毛穎 and Zhang Min 張敏. *Changjiang xiayou de Xu Shu yu Wu Yue* 長江下游的徐舒與吳越. Wuhan: Hubei jiaoyu chubanshe, 2005.

Marubbio, Mayvis L. "Yi Yin, Pious Rebel. A Study of the Founding Minister of the Shang in Early Chinese Texts." PhD diss., University of Minnesota, 2000.

Mencius. *Mencius*. Translated and introduced by D. C. Lau. London: Penguin Books, 2004.

Meng Wentong 蒙文通. *Guzu zhenwei* 古族甄微. *Meng Wentong wenji* 蒙文通文集. Vol. 2. Chengdu: Bashu shushe, 1993.

——. *Yueshi congkao* 越史叢考. Beijing: Renmin chubanshe, 1983.

Miao Lu 苗麓. *Wu Yue Chunqiu jiaozhu* 吳越春秋校註. Nanjing: Jiangsu guji chubanshe, 1999.

Milburn, Olivia. *Cherishing Antiquity: The Cultural Construction of an Ancient Chinese Kingdom*. Cambridge: Harvard University Press, 2013.

——. *The Glory of Yue: An Annotated Translation of the Yuejue shu*. Brill: Sinica Leidensia, 2010.

Nanjing Museum 南京博物院. "Jiangsu Wuxian Caoxieshan yizhi" 江苏吴县草鞋山遗址. *Wenwu ziliao congkan* 文物资料丛刊, no. 3 (1980): 1–24.

Needham, Joseph. "Astronomy in Ancient and Medieval China." *Philosophical Transactions of the Royal Society of London, series A, Mathematical and Physical Sciences* 276, no. 1257 (1974): 67–82.

——. *Science and Civilisation in China*. Vol. 5, Part 6. Cambridge: Cambridge University Press, 2004.

Nienhauser, William, ed. *The Grand Scribe's Records*. 9 vols. Bloomington: Indiana University Press, 1994–.
Niu Hong'en 牛鴻恩. *Xinyi yi zhoushu* 新譯逸周書. Taipei: Sanmin shuju, 2015.
Ouyang Xiu 歐陽修. *Xin Tangshu* 新唐書. 20 vols. Beijing: Zhonghua shuju, 1975.
Peng Duo 彭鐸. *Qinfu lunjian jiaozheng* 潛夫論箋校正. Beijing: Zhonghua shuju, 2004.
Pi Xirui 皮錫瑞. "Hanbei yin wei kao" 漢碑引緯考. In *Hanbei yin jing kao* 漢碑引經考, 1–45b. Changsha: *Shifutang congshu* 師伏堂叢書, 1904.
Qian Zhongshu 錢鍾書. *Guanzhui bian* 管錐編. Beijing: Zhonghua shuju, 1979.
Ruan Yuan 阮元, ed. *Shisanjing zhushu* 十三經註疏. Beijing: Zhonghua shuju, 1982.
Sima Qian 司馬遷. *Shiji* 史記. Beijing: Zhonghua shuju, 1959.
Su Yu 蘇輿. *Chunqiu fanlu yizheng* 春秋繁露義證. Beijing: Zhonghua shuju, 2015.
Sukhu, Gopal. *The Shaman and the Heresiarch: A New Interpretation of the Li sao*. Albany: SUNY Press, 2012.
Sun, Xiaochun and Jacob Kistemaker. *The Chinese Sky During the Han: Constellating Stars and Society*. Sinica Leidensia 38. Leiden: Brill, 1997.
Sun Xidan 孫希旦. *Liji jijie* 禮記集解. Beijing: Zhonghua shuju, 1989.
Sun Xingyan 孫星衍. *Shangshu jinguwen zhushu* 尚書今古文註疏. Beijing: Zhonghua shuju, 1986.
Sun Yirang 孫詒讓. *Zhouli Zhengyi* 周禮正義. Beijing: Zhonghua shuju, 1987.
Wagner, Donald B. *Iron and Steel in Ancient China*. Leiden: Brill, 1996.
Wang Hui 王輝. "Guanyu 'Wuwang Gufa jian' shiwen de jige wenti" 關於吳王姑發劍釋文的幾個問題. *Wenwu*, no. 10 (1991): 89–90.
Wang Junlin 王鈞林 and Zhou Haisheng 周海生, trans. *Kongcongzi* 孔叢子. Beijing: Zhonghua shuju, 2012.
Wang Liqi 王利器. *Fengsu tongyi jiaozhu* 風俗通義校註. Beijing: Zhonghua shuju, 2015.
——. *Wenzi shuyi* 文子疏義. Beijing: Zhonghua shuju, 2015.
Wang Meizhi 汪梅枝. "*Wu Yue Chunqiu* Xu Tianhu yinzhu tanxi" 吳越春秋徐天祜音註探析. *Jiangxi jiaoyu xueyuan xuebao* 江西教育學院學報 25, no. 4 (2005):43–46.
Wang Peng 王鵬. "Dangdai *Wu Yue Chunqiu* yanjiu jianshu" 當代吳越春秋研究簡述, *Huangshan xueyuan xuebao* 7, no. 5 (2005): 64–66.
Wang Xianqian 王先謙. *Zhuangzi jijie* 莊子集解. Beijing: Zhonghua shuju, 2012.
——. *Xunzi jijie* 荀子集解. Beijing: Zhonghua shuju, 2015.
Wei Zheng 魏征. *Suishu* 隋書. Beijing: Zhonghua shuju, 1973.
Xiang Zonglu 向宗魯. *Shuoyuan jiaozheng* 說苑校證. Beijing: Zhonghua shuju, 1987.
Xie Chen 謝忱. *GouWu shi xinkao* 勾吳史新考. Beijing: Zhongguo wenlian chubanshe, 2000.
Xin Deyong 辛德勇. "Yuewang Goujian xidu Langye shi xiyi" 越王勾踐徙都琅邪事析義. *Wenshi* 文史 90 (2010): 5–61.
Xu Fuguan 徐復觀. *Liang Han sixiang shi* 兩漢思想史. Shanghai: Huadong shifan daxue chubanshe, 2002.
Xu Weiyu 許維遹. *Hanshi waizhuan jishi* 韓詩外傳集釋. Beijing: Zhonghua shuju, 1980.
——. *Lüshi chunqiu jishi* 呂氏春秋集釋. Beijing: Zhonghua shuju, 2015.

Xu Yuangao 徐元誥. *Guoyu jijie* 國語集解. Beijing: Zhonghua shuju, 2002.

Xu Zhen'e 徐震堮. *Shishuo xinyu jiaojian* 世說新語校箋. Beijing: Zhonghua shuju, 2001.

Xue Yaotian 薛燿天. *Wu Yue Chunqiu yizhu* 吳越春秋譯註. Tianjin: Tianjin guji chubanshe, 1992.

Xunzi. *Xunzi*. Translated and introduced by Eric L. Hutton. Princeton: Princeton University Press, 2014.

Yan Zhenyi 閻振益 and Zhong Xia 鍾夏. *Xinshu jiaozhu* 新書校註. Beijing: Zhonghua shuju, 2015.

Yang Bojun 楊伯峻. *Chunqiu Zuozhuan zhu* 春秋左傳註. Beijing: Zhonghua shuju, 1995.

——. *Liezi jishi* 列子集釋. Beijing: Zhonghua shuju, 2014.

Yao Zhenzong 姚振宗. *Hou Han yiwenzhi* 後漢藝文志. In *Shiyuan congshu* 適園叢書, edited by Zhang Junheng 張鈞衡. Shanghai: guoxue fulunshe, 1911.

——. *Suishu Jingji zhi kaozheng* 隋書經籍志考證. Shanghai: Shanghai guji chubanshe, 1995.

Zhang Han 張頷. "Shanxi Wanrong chutu cuojin niaochongshu ge mingwen kaoshi" 山西万榮出土錯金鳥蟲書戈銘文考釋. In *Zhang Han xueshu wenji* 張頷學術文集, 34–37. Beijing: Zhonghua shuju, 1995.

Zhang Jue 張覺. *Wu Yue Chunqiu jiaozheng zhushu* 吳越春秋校證注疏. Beijing: Zhishi chanquan chubanshe, 2014.

Zhangjiashan ersiqi hao hanmu zhujian zhengli xiaozu 張家山二四七號漢墓竹簡整理小組. *Zhangjiashan hanmu zhujian [247hao mu]* 張家山漢墓竹簡[二四七號墓]. Beijing: Wenwu chubanshe, 2001.

Zhou Shengchun 周生春. *Wu Yue Chunqiu jijiao huikao* 吳越春秋輯校匯考. Shanghai: Shanghai guji chubanshe, 1997.

Zhu Hongjie 祝鴻傑. *Bowu zhi quanyi* 博物志全譯. Guiyang: Guizhou renmin chubanshe, 1990.

Zhu Xiangrong 朱湘蓉. "Wenxueshi zhong Wu Zixu fuchou gushi qingjie de xingcheng—yi Hubei Yunmeng Shuihudi 77 hao Hanmu Wu Zixu gushi jian wei yiju" 文學史中伍子胥復仇故事情節的形成—以湖北云夢睡虎地 77 號漢墓伍子胥故事簡為依據. *Zhongyuan wenhuyanjiu* 中原文化研究, no. 2 (2015): 44–51.

# Index

www.ingramcontent.com/pod-product-compliance
Lightning Source LLC
Chambersburg PA
CBHW060807310726
48980CB00002B/271

* 9 7 8 1 5 0 1 7 5 4 3 4 0 *